CW00739834

RUSHING FOR GOLD

RUSHING FOR GOLD

LIFE AND COMMERCE ON THE GOLDFIELDS OF NEW ZEALAND AND AUSTRALIA

Edited by Lloyd Carpenter and Lyndon Fraser

OTAGO
UNIVERSITY PRESS

Published by Otago University Press
Level 1, 398 Cumberland Street
Dunedin, New Zealand
university.press@otago.ac.nz
www.otago.ac.nz/press

First published 2016
Copyright © the authors as named
The moral rights of the authors have been asserted.

ISBN 978-1-877578-54-0

A catalogue record for this book is available from the National Library
of New Zealand. This book is copyright. Except for the purpose of
fair review, no part may be stored or transmitted in any form or by
any means, electronic or mechanical, including recording or storage
in any information retrieval system, without permission in writing
from the publishers. No reproduction may be made, whether by
photocopying or by any other means, unless a licence has been
obtained from the publisher.

Editor: Paula Wagemaker
Page design and layout: Quentin Wilson & Associates
Index: Diane Lowther

Front cover photograph: Rob Suisted, Nature's Pic Images
www.naturespic.com

Printed in New Zealand by Printing.com, Wellington

Contents

Part Three: Gold-rush Women

Part Four: Goldfields Society

Part Five: Goldfields Heritage

1.

Introduction:
An Australasian Goldfield

Lloyd Carpenter and Lyndon Fraser

THIS BOOK AIMS to recast the extraordinary tale of the nineteenth-century gold rushes to New South Wales, Victoria, Otago and the South Island's West Coast as an episode in Australasian history. It builds on the solid pioneering work by scholars such as Geoffrey Serle, Philip Ross May, Geoffrey Blainey and Weston Bate, and on the more recent edited volumes *Gold: Forgotten histories and lost objects of Australia* and *Deeper Leads: New approaches to Victorian goldfields history*.[1] This volume also engages with the new goldfields scholarship that has opened our eyes to the cultural complexities of the mining frontier and provided fascinating glimpses into the everyday lives of Cantonese and indigenous miners, women, Irish-born migrants and 'casualties of colonisation'.[2]

We now know that the discoveries of gold not only led to a spectacular population explosion in the Australasian colonies but also ensured that mining regions as far apart as Castlemaine, Dunstan and Addisons Flat were closely bound through commerce, people and experience. Armies of restless diggers criss-crossed the sea highways joining Melbourne to Hokitika and Dunedin, moving on quickly at the news of fresh strikes. A colourful entourage of storekeepers and publicans, wardens, bank agents, domestic servants and musicians followed in their wake, seeking their fortunes in the bush or in ramshackle towns that emerged from crude encampments of canvas and calico.

The names of hotels and grog shanties commemorated this relentless advance: a succession of 'Old Bendigo' and 'Ballarat' hotels was established as New Zealand's Otago and West Coast goldfields expanded in the 1860s, while 'Otago', 'Maori Chief' and other distinctive New Zealand names adorned the businesses run by ex-miners who made their way back to Victoria with their gold earnings.[3] Yet this crucial trans-Tasman dimension of the gold rushes has too often been obscured in national histories of Australia and New Zealand. Rather than two separate narratives, however, the search for the latest El Dorado is best understood in an Australasian – and truly global – context. Business owners, Māori and Chinese diggers, Limerick barmaids, and migrants from

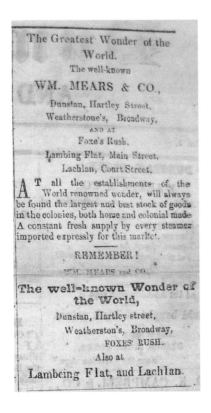

The Greatest Wonder of the
World.
The well-known
WM. MEARS & CO.,
Dunstan, Hartley Street,
Weatherstone's, Broadway,
AND AT
Foxe's Rush,
Lambing Flat, Main Street,
Lachlan, Court Street.

AT all the establishments of the
World renowned wonder, will always
be found the largest and best stock of goods
in the colonies, both home and colonial made
A constant fresh supply by every steamer
imported expressly for this market.

REMEMBER !

WM. MEARS and CO.

The well-known Wonder of
the World,
Dunstan, Hartley street,
Weatherston's, Broadway,
FOXES' RUSH.
Also at
Lambeing Flat, aud Lachlan.

'The Greatest Wonder of the World', an
advertisement for stores in the Dunstan (now
Clyde, Central Otago), Weatherstones (Gabriel's
Gully, Otago), Foxes (now Arrowtown), Lambing
Flat (now Young, New South Wales) and Lachlan
(New South Wales).

Source: *The Dunstan News and Wakatip Advertiser*,
30 December 1862, 2. Copy courtesy McNab New Zealand
collection, Dunedin Public Library

places such as Cork, California, Piedmont and Manchester risked everything to make
their pile on the Australasian goldfields, with or without tasting success.

The first part of this volume examines the trans-Tasman aspects in fine detail, but
the theme is revisited in each of the subsequent chapters. Chris McConville, Keir
Reeves and Andrew Reeves, a team of veteran Victorian academics with impressive
credentials in goldfields historiography, introduce this theme in Chapter 2. They
discuss the long-held, widespread and complex intercolonial personal, industrial,
governmental, legal, commercial and mining relationships that characterised the
trans-Tasman world of the mid-nineteenth century. Each subsequent chapter includes
some of this trans-Tasman idea, from the rush of Chinese, Māori and European peoples,
to the importing of goods, technology, entertainment, politics and leaders, and even
the exchange and development of ideas and national thinking.

In Chapter 3 American scholar Daniel Davy uses letters and journals to trace
the personal relationships and motivations of the miners who crossed and re-crossed
the Tasman in their restless search for gold. He finds a level of embedding of Otago
commerce in the Victorian economy that will surprise many, and his conclusion that
Otago's gold rush was actually a Victorian event will challenge the way we see these
events in both countries. His source letters change the rosy, idealistic or romantic ideas
that some hold of the rush era into the brutal, complex and lonely reality of miners
who died, lost all their earnings or were reduced to low-paid servitude, all while living

'Gabriel's Gully in 1862'.

Source: Vincent Pyke, *History of the Early Gold Discoveries in Otago* (Dunedin: Otago Daily Times and Witness Newspapers Company, 1887), 1

alongside neighbouring diggers who made so much money they could head back 'home' to the United Kingdom with enough gold to retire on.

In Chapter 4 Terry Hearn re-examines the geographical mobility of the trans-Tasman rushes and draws new conclusions about the experience of those who came to the Tuapeka following Gabriel Read's discovery of payable gold in Otago. Like the writers of Chapters 2 and 3, he finds not an Otago gold rush, but an Australasian one, where diggers chased their gold dreams in a headlong rush back and forth across the inconvenient Tasman Sea. However, unlike the conclusions cheerfully drawn in popular histories, he finds through his exploration of the economic and physical privations of those who made the trip that the rush was by no means a universal success; many individuals came to regret their impetuous decision to travel. His is a nuanced study that echoes some of the more private journeys detailed in Daniel Davy's previous chapter.

The late John Angus locates the political, legal and administrative basis for what developed in the New Zealand gold rushes in the ebullient, larger-than-life personality of Australian miner, merchant and booster Vincent Pyke. His examination of the local

'Vincent Pyke'.

Source: Vincent Pyke, *History of the Early Gold Discoveries in Otago* (Dunedin: Otago Daily Times and Witness Newspapers Company, 1887), facing 32

political landscape in Central Otago serves as a model for the evolution of mining law and society, and ultimately the development of personal enfranchisement on both sides of the Tasman. His timely re-examination of Pyke's place in the trans-Tasman world does not conclude the Australasian nature of this volume; each of the following chapters forces us to realise that what we, on each side of the Tasman, have held to be 'our' gold rush narrative is actually shared by our country neighbour.

In Part Two of the book attention turns to aspects of the ethnic mix of the trans-Tasman gold rushes. Lloyd Carpenter, himself a descendant of Cornish and Māori miners from Golden Bay in the Nelson region, explodes the myth that Māori were little more than bewildered observers of the rush for gold. Tracing a history which begins with participation in the Californian and Victorian gold rushes, Lloyd discusses the important contribution Māori made on the various Otago goldfields and, eventually, in the Yukon. In the twenty-first century, the full story of Māori engagement in trans-Tasman commerce and society is finally emerging, to reveal a surprising level of complexity and participation.

James Ng's survey in Chapter 7 of the Chinese mining experience in Otago details the society from which the miners who made such an impact on the trans-Tasman gold

Chinese Immigrant Act, Certificate of Exemption for Lie Muck dated 23 May 1882 and authorised by Ah Kew.

Cromwell Museum collection

story emerged. His examination of how and why the Chinese survived – and thrived – as sojourners in Otago covers an intriguing history lasting over half a century. His research reveals a previously under-examined complexity to the experience of Chinese miners in Otago, and also discusses comparisons with their Victorian counterparts. His consideration of European-Chinese commerce, converse and inter-marriage will intrigue many who have held to a dichotomised, prejudice-dominated narrative about the Chinese.

Joanna Boileau's examination (Chapter 8) of Chinese market gardening is another contribution that challenges prevalent myths of the experience of Chinese on the goldfields. Many authors have previously written of gardening as an activity that miners turned to when mining no longer paid, but this chapter reveals that for the Chinese in Otago gardening was a critically important commercial and lifestyle choice from the very beginning of the rush history. Drawing on Australian accounts as well as archaeological, historical and personal sources, Joanna narrates how the Chinese agricultural processes developed and honed in China were adapted and applied to the foreign environment that was Otago.

Lowe Kong Meng deserves greater recognition in both Australia and New Zealand's gold story. Paul Macgregor's examination in Chapter 9 of this Chinese merchant, community leader, immigration organiser and Anglophile provides a fresh impetus that will ensure Lowe Kong Meng gains the acknowledgement he deserves. The idea needs to be publicised that, far from being unwanted, the Chinese miners were invited and welcomed to Otago. Paul shows that many of New Zealand's Chinese population, especially the importers and retailers, were originally Australian settlers. He also discusses how these men worked to ensure that miners in the farthest reaches of Central Otago enjoyed the same foodstuffs as their countrymen in Daylesford, Bendigo and Guangdong province.

Part Three of the book throws new light on goldfields women, beginning with Sandra Quick's examination in Chapter 10 of female goldfields hoteliers. Focusing initially on the legal impediments, she reveals the battles some remarkable widows, single women and the occasional 'loose' individual fought to operate businesses in the predominantly male society of the goldfields. From her discussion of Australasian songster Charles Thatcher's 'Poll the Grogseller' to Queenstown's proprietress of the notorious Lady of the Lake Hotel, these cornerstones of remote mining communities emerge as significant contributors to social life on the goldfields – as well as extra fuel for myth-making and legends.

Julia Bradshaw's discussion in Chapter 11 of 'fallen women' may confirm some people's prejudice, but even with this topic, new, historiography-altering revelations provide a change from what is commonly believed. Again, the discussion is a trans-Tasman one, highlighting the behaviours of women and their (sometime) oppressors in the form of heavy-handed officialdom. By tracing the migrations and relationship dynamics of several representative women, Julia allows a truer picture of these colourful characters, their motives and their stories to emerge. Truer too, is the real story of how the legal process treated the crime of rape and other abuses of women in the nineteenth century.

APPLICATION FOR A PUBLICAN'S LICENSE.

I, REBECCA BOND, of Arrowtown, Hotel-keeper, do hereby give notice that I desire to obtain, and will at the next Licensing Meeting to be holden at Queenstown, on the 9th day of JUNE next, apply for a certificate authorising the issue of a PUBLICAN'S LICENSE for a house, situate at Queenstown, formerly licensed under the sign of "The Prince of Wales Hotel," and now known as the "Mountaineer Hotel," containing sixteen (16) rooms, exclusive of those required for the use of the family.

Dated this 18th day of May, 1885.

REBECCA BOND.

Advertisement: Rebecca Bond's 'Application for a Publican's License'. Source: *Lake Wakatip Mail*, 22 May 1885, 2

The migration, lifestyles and commerce of Irish women in Australasia in general and on the West Coast of New Zealand in particular is highlighted in Lyndon Fraser's study (Chapter 12). The various motivations for shifting from Ireland to the opposite side of the world reveal, just as this book has done for the trans-Tasman gold rushes and for the Chinese mining narrative, a more varied and substantially more complex story for this distinctive group in colonial Australasia than has been discussed previously. Of particular note is the examination of work by Irishwomen who sought, through public works, to relieve distress in their various communities. The same can be said of Lyndon's analyses of power within marital relationships and of wealth accumulation and disbursement by widows.

Commercial, sociological, political and legal relationships between and within trans-Tasman gold rushes are under-examined in the historiography of the gold rush era, yet each played a major part in the shaping of the societies of the time and therefore influenced the nature of the society of both countries today, as the chapters in Part Four of this book show. These relationships became ties that bound the rush economies of Australia and New Zealand together, facilitating the movement of money, people and goods with an ease and seamlessness that foreshadowed and pre-empted the Australia and New Zealand Closer Economic Relations Trade Agreement that came into force a century later.

Part Four begins with Tom Brooking's survey (Chapter 13) of the sociology of the gold rushes. Focusing primarily on Otago's gold history, he examines how, for each

Canvas-covered, wood-framed houses erected on the banks of the Manuherikia River (near present-day Alexandra), c. 1863.

Courtesy Lloyd Carpenter collection

Australasian rush locale, a field of tents, hastily erected to pursue a new field, morphed into a town and eventually a regional centre. He also shows how the mining itself led to changes in gold-rush society: the romanticised ideal of the miner working his own claim was very quickly replaced by mutual-benefit group collectives and then by corporate enterprise, both of which saw the emergence of large-scale sluicing schemes, quartz mine development and, eventually, the huge dredges of the 1890s. Tom's discussion of the miners' desire for order and of the rapid emergence of governmental structures and the trappings of society in the form of newspapers, schools and churches may disappoint some who enjoy notions of a 'wild west' rush era marked by violence, shootings and hedonism. However, as Tom makes clear, the settled society that residents and voters of today desire was just as important to the newest settlers to a gold-laden beach in an empty corner of Victoria or Otago.

Across Australasia, sparsely stocked runs worked by new colonial farmers experienced massive upheaval once others discovered that the creeks on their properties were laden with gold. Stock were slaughtered, watercourses muddied and fouled, trees cut down and woolsheds turned into temporary doss-houses. In Chapter 14 Rosemary Marryatt examines the impact of all of this on a typical sheep farmer, William Gilbert Rees of Queenstown. His story emerges as one of opportunities and losses, where dreams ended and new ones began, as the quest for gold wrought irrevocable changes to the landscape, society and commerce of the new settlements. Visitors to modern Queenstown struggle to see that the glass-fronted hotels, five-star restaurants and offices marketing jet-boat rides and bungy jumps are built on foundations first established by a young sheep farmer and his family, who sought nothing more than the chance to build an agricultural enterprise. Rees' story has a twin in Gibson and Fenton's Ravenswood run, where ironbark forests and meadows grazed by sheep became the famed Victorian town of Bendigo after rich gold deposits were found there in 1851. The difference between the two countries is revealed by their respective timelines: whereas Victoria had sheep runs in place for 15 or so years before gold was found, Otago had them in place for just 15 months!

The popular idea that the grog-merchants and shopkeepers made money at each of the goldfields, leaving their miner customers with little, is examined in Lloyd Carpenter's chapter (Chapter 15) on the merchants of the gold rushes. As well as being forced by isolation and ephemeral mining settlements to walk a precarious financial tightrope, these entrepreneurs and early society builders became the main source of venture capital for miners seeking to expand their operations with large capital projects involving hydraulic operations, dam construction and dredge-building. The risks, failures and successes make for an intriguing rewriting of another widely held belief.

Jeremy Finn writes in Chapter 16 of early trans-Tasman goldfield lawyers and, alarmingly, of those who *called* themselves lawyers without any of the requisite qualifications or genuine experience to do so. In a world of litigious miners, legislate-as-you-go governments and the potential for huge returns – and losses – the work of these lawyers was by necessity complex and fraught with potential for conflict. That so many lawyers functioned to maintain relatively orderly goldfields despite 'minor' complications such

The storekeepers of Cromwell, early 1860s.

Courtesy Alexandra Central Stories collection

as being struck off, sued or jailed seems, with the benefit of the hindsight afforded by this research, to be remarkable.

André Brett's examination in Chapter 17 of the enormous folly that was the Southland wooden railway and how this became the catalyst for ending New Zealand's provincial system provides an intriguing discussion of this little-known but vital aspect of the colonial narrative. Some Australians remain bemused that, unlike their system of states and federal government, New Zealand abandoned this for a central government and bicameral representation, then a single legislature. That one province's efforts to capitalise on the opportunities presented by the gold rush could provoke such a substantial governmental change is as surprising as it is amusing, yet this development is clearly revealed in the first examination of these processes since W.P. Morrell's 1964 *The Provincial System in New Zealand 1852–76.*

This volume covers much that is a narrative history, but as the chapters in Part Five of this volume remind us, it is possible (where modern urban, agricultural or industrial development allow) to visit the scene of many of the narratives in this book. The Chinese miners of Lambing Flat and Arrowtown left their distinctive huts behind, the sluicers and dredgers of each country carved their landscapes in patterns and stones, and old goldfields stores are now repurposed into cafes, houses and wine-tasting rooms. Heritage remains a visual key to unlocking interest in the past for each country, and the interpretation of this makes the unlocking possible.

The process of illuminating, interpreting and mediating heritage to the public is never an easy job, however, and in Chapter 16 Warwick Frost examines the many challenges faced by those who attempt to do so. Tracing interpretation efforts from Tombstone in America to Beechworth and Sovereign Hill in Australia and on to the hiking and cycling trails through Central Otago's gold-rush landscapes, Warwick examines the theories of Francis Tilden and discusses the constraints shaping the

This photo of the *Lady Barkly*, 'a folly on wooden rails' (replica built 2003, Invercargill) was taken in 2015.

Photograph by Anne Scott

reality that administrators and site owners must accommodate. Heritage and its meaning and importance to epistemologies such as national identity and national story, as well as the sense of belonging it brings to citizens, means that the mediating of heritage landscapes, structures and social processes is growing in importance, even if the budgets allocated by governments to do this task are shrinking.

Neville Ritchie had a dream job in Central Otago for an archaeologist: investigate, dig over, measure, record and collect data from every known archaeological site in the area due to be lost through the filling of a hydro-electric lake. As he recounts in Chapter 19, he and a team of colleagues and archaeology students spent 10 years examining a vast range of historic sites, sluiced areas, mines and landscapes. In so doing, Neville and his team rewrote the Māori history of the region prior to European contact and added important detail to the Chinese, miner-builder and commercial gold-rush narratives. In addition to detailing the processes followed during the project, Neville discusses and illustrates subsequent work by other archaeologists.

The final chapter of this volume (20) is a re-interpretation, in a play written by Fiona Farrell and Robert Hoskins, of the story of the iconic trans-Tasman goldfields entertainer Charles 'The Inimitable' Thatcher. Much has been written of this provoker, promoter and humourist, yet the cost in strained or lost relationships and the pressures

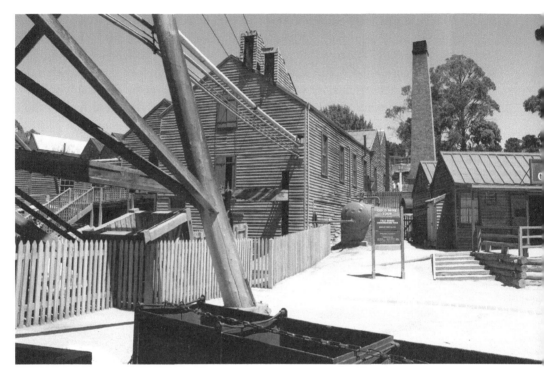

'The Fully Underground Gold Mining Tour', outdoor goldfields museum at Sovereign Hill, Ballarat, Victoria, 2012.

Photograph by Lloyd Carpenter

he experienced while dealing with a life lived on the edge of society, totally reliant on the goodwill of the paying public, has not been previously acknowledged. During the play, the cholera-stricken Thatcher remembers his goldfields days as a mixture of the good, the bad and the truly memorable.

Most of the essays published in *Rushing for Gold* were originally presented at '150 Years of Riches: The Central Otago gold rush, 1862–2012', a conference organised by Lloyd Carpenter, sponsored by the University of Canterbury and held in August 2012 in Cromwell, New Zealand. The conference was also supported by staff and academics from the Department of English at the University of Canterbury, most especially Professors Patrick Evans and Paul Millar and departmental secretary Jennifer Mildendorf.

The event brought together researchers, academics, family historians, heritage experts and goldfields enthusiasts from across Australasia, and sought to provide opportunity to reflect on Central Otago's rush story 150 years after the discovery of gold in the Clutha Gorge by Christopher Reilly and Horatio Hartley. The conference offered the first tantalising glimpses of what became a theme of this collection of essays: that the Central Otago gold rush was part of an intertwined Australasian phenomenon with a history reflected by and common to both countries.

That said, the conference also featured papers that reflected the vast differences between the two countries, pithily summed up by the anonymous Otago miner in an 1864 edition of Dickens' *Household Words*: 'Victoria wants fencing in; this island wants hammering flat.'[4] This academic conference also showed that people remain interested in goldfields history, with locals and folk from as far away as the West Coast and Dunedin attending to hear the various presentations. The breadth and calibre of the presentations prompted the logical step to pursue a high-quality publication based on some of these, together with invited contributions from other researchers.

We have accrued a number of debts in the making of this volume. First and foremost, we want to thank our families and friends. Lloyd's wife Bronwyn encouraged him to pursue his PhD examining Central Otago's gold rush, his son Jeremy joined him on several research and archaeological survey trips, and his ever-patient doctoral supervisors, Professor Paul Millar and Associate Professor Philip Armstrong, tolerated his endless diversions into sideshows and new ideas about the gold rushes in New Zealand and Australia. The fact that the PhD was completed despite earthquakes, conferences and other distractions is a reflection of their generosity of time and wisdom in guidance. Lloyd is also mindful of how much support Lincoln University (his employer since February 2014) has provided him by encouraging a Māori Studies lecturer to maintain and develop his goldfields interests through the completion of this book.

Lyndon would also like to express his gratitude to Anthony Wright, Sarah Murray and the staff at Canterbury Museum for his appointment as a research fellow in human history. That position gave him the time and space to be able to work on the book. He also wishes to thank Julia Bradshaw, Joanna Cobley, Chris Gallavin, Marguerite Hill, the late Ted Matthews, Katie Pickles, Judy Robertson, Greg Ryan and all the postgraduate students (and recent graduates) who remind him why history matters. They include Jennine Bailey, Rosemary Baird, Alice Bates, Diane Comer, Kathy Harrington-Watt, Hannah Herchenbach, Ruth Larsen, Zia Lilley, Geraldine Lummis, Ben McBride, Paulien Martens and Hannah Smith.

Many other people and institutions contributed to this volume, but special thanks are owed to the passionate, articulate and dedicated work of Central Otago's Ron Murray (1928–2010) who documented so much of the history of the region and who provided many of the pictures featured in this book. Ron was generous in his provision of images and advice and in his suggestions of areas of study to pursue. He was also kind enough to grant time to Lloyd, who at the time was just an emerging researcher from the University of Canterbury.

We would also like to give special thanks to the Cromwell Museum (which now holds copies of all of Ron Murray's pictures), Clyde Historical Museum, Central Stories Alexandra, Lakes District Museum, Hocken Library Uare Taoka o Hakena, France Pittoresque, Michael Gates Collection, New Zealand Department of Conservation, King's High School Dunedin, State Library of Victoria, Thomas Bradley Harris Collection, Chinese Museum Melbourne, Kevin Hayes, Anne Scott, Hokitika Museum, Alexander Turnbull Library, Toitū Otago Settlers Museum, Rosemary

Ron Murray in 1976 outside the Come in Time mine, Thompson's Gorge, Bendigo, Otago.

Courtesy R.W. Murray collection, Cromwell Museum

Marryatt, Southland Museum and Art Gallery, Warwick Frost, Jennifer Laing and Neville Ritchie. We furthermore thank, for their contributions to our publication, the many Central Otago residents who donated photographs to Lloyd Carpenter in aid of his research but wished to remain anonymous.

This book would not have been possible without the support of the contributors who shared our passion for goldfields history. We are also extremely grateful to each of our chapter contributors. They poured their heart and soul, as well as hours of their time spent in dusty archives, into writing their chapters. Keir Reeves, Chris McConville, Andrew Reeves, Daniel Davy, Terry Hearn, John Angus, James Ng, Joanna Boileau, Paul Macgregor, Sandra Quick, Julia Bradshaw, Tom Brooking, Rosemary Marryatt, Jeremy Finn, André Brett, Warwick Frost, Neville Ritchie, Robert Hoskins and Fiona Farrell: thank you for your part in creating this remarkable collection of essays.

We are deeply indebted to Wendy Harrex, the retired publisher of Otago University Press, who believed in the project from the beginning and offered us a contract. We have been very privileged to work with the current publisher, Rachel Scott, and her wonderful staff. Finally, we want to thank Paula Wagemaker for her incisive copy-editing of the manuscript.

I

Trans-Tasman Rushes

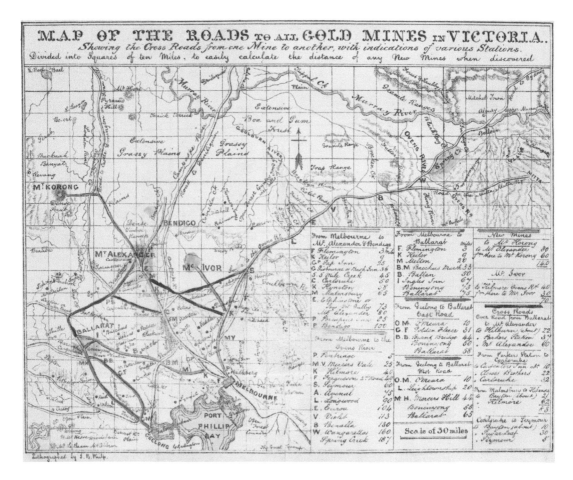

'Map of the roads to all gold mines in Victoria', lithographed by J.B. Philp in 1853. This map was a copy of Frederick Proeschel's 'Pocket map of the roads to all the mines in Victoria', issued earlier in 1853.

The Map Collection, State Library of Victoria

2.

'Tasman World': Investigating gold-rush-era historical links and subsequent regional development between Otago and Victoria

Chris McConville, Keir Reeves and Andrew Reeves

'Otago, by avoiding many of the rocks on which its neighbor [sic] Victoria, struck, has, if not so brilliant, a similar career before it', predicted Sigismund Wekey in his guide to gold-seekers'[1]

ASSERTIONS ABOUT COMMON characteristics across the Tasman Sea, together with hints at subtle differences, have coloured accounts of Australia and New Zealand through to the twenty-first century. In some more recent descriptive accounts, however, the differences have lost their subtlety and come to count for more than commonality, to the chagrin of at least one historian, James Belich. As the Wekey quote above suggests, lessons about similarity can be learned not only from trans-Tasman similarities but also from trans-Tasman differences. Seemingly mindful of this consideration, Belich queried the scale of historical analysis in New Zealand, wondering if a regional rather than a national focus might be more revealing of resemblances across the two countries. In looking back on the New Zealand and Australian colonies' 1901 division into two distinct nation-states, Belich thought about the loss of an 'old Tasman world', a world that was not simply Australasian but instead a 'great archipelago' in which there were four major islands – the North and South Islands of New Zealand, Australia and Tasmania.[2]

On the one hand, Belich applied the now commonplace 'imagined communities' to this place, noting that any number of identities could be simultaneously held by Anglophone settlers, from the regional through to the imperial.[3] On the other hand, in a more materialist reading of the landmasses and seas of the south-west Pacific, Belich correctly pointed out that to imagine the Tasman Sea as a barrier, as historians have too often done, missed a crucial point. The sea (and we might include Bass Strait in this discussion) was rather a 'bridge' in an era of sea travel, when a journey from Hobart to Perth involved endless changes of transport mode, and when shipping between Melbourne and Cairns in far north Queensland inevitably broke journeys at port after port.[4] Even the creation of railway links across the Australian continent (a critical stumbling block in any attempt to draw New Zealand into the Australian Federation) failed to resolve the dramas of inter-colonial travelling because the different railway gauges chosen by neighbouring colonies deliberately frustrated smooth travel.[5]

Far simpler than a rail trip from Melbourne to Brisbane in the years before World War I was a straightforward ship's passage from the port of Melbourne to Bluff (Southland) or to Port Chalmers (Otago). And when the Australasian colonies came together in the later part of the nineteenth century to fashion the all-important mail service from London to the South Seas, delegates from Otago, Southland, Victoria and Tasmania shared a vision of all mail shipping docked in the port of Melbourne.[6] The voices raised most vociferously against this trans-Tasman agreement were those of the New South Wales delegates.

Discussion about the common experiences of Otago and Victoria (or, more narrowly, the mining region of the Central Highlands of Victoria) could thus be extended to the circulation of ideas and cultural identity and overlapping industrial practices and governance structures; it was, after all, the Sandhurst, Victoria magistrate and gold warden Vincent Pyke who was charged with implementing the Victoria mining regulations on the Otago goldfields.[7] In other words, the structures of day-to-day life across Belich's great archipelago, its deep southern extremities of Victoria and Otago, in particular, shared a common political economy.

Some key organising themes are evident in the dynamic histories of this trans-Tasman world that we explore below. Almost all of these themes spring from the contiguity in the initial gold rushes of Central Victoria and Otago. The Melbourne *Argus* reflected this notion in its reporting of the Otago rushes: '[W]e shall be the first to offer our congratulations to the people of that settlement on this new acquisition to their means of prosperity. Whatever directly enriches one number of the Australian group of colonies must indirectly enrich all.'[8] The first reports of the Otago rushes spoke of Victorians and other foreigners arriving, suggesting that Otago and Victoria shared the same regional identity and a commonality of emergent trans-Tasman identity.

In this chapter we discuss and analyse the survival – and resilience – of a number of themes in the regional political economy of Victoria, Australia and Otago, New Zealand. Our particular concern is with the economic and social patterns that emerged in both places as returns from gold dwindled and industrial restructuring removed many of the autonomous digging collectives from the richest fields. And while the driving force of these themes remains located in the sites of the initial gold discoveries, the trans-Tasman world inevitably came to be centred on Melbourne and to draw in other localities, such as the north coast of Tasmania along with Southland and the West Coast of New Zealand's South Island. Our central contention is that throughout successive periods of economic transformation and restructuring, certain industries and their connected trans-Tasman social and cultural patterns endured and demonstrated unexpected resilience. The reason for this, we argue, was mainly due to economic factors such as raw staple industries and also social factors of communal identity and collaborative risk-taking behaviour that clearly linked into global economies.

The staple economic model is a compelling one for explaining the economic history of Australia and also the cyclical boom and bust that has underpinned economic activity based upon the exploitation of abundant natural resources in association with a small population base. Boom and bust has been the trend in Australia since the first European settlement of the continent in the late eighteenth century. James Belich also emphasises this pattern in his discussion of New Zealand's economic performance. Harold Innis and W.A. Macintosh, generally recognised as the two main academic proponents of the staple model, presented a similar argument in their claim that the emergence of regional Canadian economies was largely determined by their provision of raw staples to European markets. Innis's key argument rested upon his analysis of the fur trade and the Hudson's Bay Company that ultimately dominated economic life in central Canada and led to the business concentration profile that typifies much of Montreal and Toronto even today.[9]

John McCarty's staple theory of nineteenth-century economic history makes similar observations about raw factors of production in the Australian economy. McCarty's account complements Geoffrey Blainey's theory of the anti-clockwise movement of miners around Australia.[10] This movement not only explains the trajectory of mining but also the ancillary economic activities that we discuss in this chapter. Urban and regional histories, for example, were initially seen as complementary by those discussing the demography and economic history of Australia and New Zealand. H.J. Dyos and Asa Briggs inspired transnational views of urban history.[11] James Scobie's seminal book on Buenos Aires set out processes replicated in several New World cities, Melbourne and Dunedin included.[12] Eric Lampard identified Australasia as having one of the world's highest rates of urban concentration between 1850 and 1890, but saw both Dunedin and Melbourne as being past their golden zeniths by 1890 when neither appeared on his list of significant global cities. He further noted a New Zealand urban concentration level in the mid-twentieth century equivalent to that of the United States but less than that of either Australia or Canada.[13] Alan Mayne's earliest work presented comparisons of Sydney and Birmingham.[14] More recent trends in urban history have focused on major cities.

We consider that these economic and demographic trends have characterised urban history in Australia and New Zealand. The creation of Melbourne as an entrepôt city depended on gold, and Melbourne remained the lynchpin linking the gold centres of Central Victoria and Central Otago. Indeed, if Otago's nineteenth-century local newspapers are any guide, the regular contributions from Melbourne correspondents made the city appear even more significant to Otago and Southland than to much of regional Victoria (and certainly to New South Wales).

Our approach provides a longitudinal trans-Tasman regional study of some emergent staples driven by the initial gold finds. We propose that it is wrong to dismiss these activities as a regional aberration and that there is a need instead to identify them as linked into international economies long before their integration into national ones. Erik Olssen's historiographical observation that 'regional history really is international history' resonates throughout this chapter.[15] We also contend that the economic links

Ballarat (Victoria) appearing in Arrowtown, Otago. The first hotel to open in Arrowtown, then known as 'Foxes', in late 1862.

Courtesy Lakes District Museum, Arrowtown

between Victoria, Otago, Canterbury and London established during the gold-rush era were far greater than between, say, Victoria and Western Australia. Likewise, we assume that Otago's links with Canterbury, Victoria and Tasmania were stronger than they were with Auckland. In essence, these peripheral, staple-driven regional economies formed key parts of an international tapestry of trade and exchange which fed into key economic nodes such as the United Kingdom, China and the United States, from the second half of the nineteenth century up to and including the early twenty-first century. We also argue that the international dimension of staples in Victoria and Otago minerals are analogous to other notable examples of staple economies such as slavery, the spice trade and tea. In returning to the lost Tasman World, Belich's great archipelago, we have been able to identify a different chronology in the south-west Pacific as well as a political economy encompassing demographic and social links, industrial strategies and emerging political and cultural parallels.

The Trans-Tasman World: 1851–1901

In late 1851 the Victoria gold rushes began in earnest with the short-lived alluvial finds at Clunes, Buninyong and Ballarat in the western reaches of what were to become the Central Victoria goldfields. A decade later one of the men who joined this rush, Gabriel Read, discovered gold in the bed of the Tuapeka River in New Zealand's South Island, sparking another mass of diggers to set off for the rivers and ravines of the Otago gold rush. As the press of the day stated in July 1861: '... reports [have] reached the diggings of Victoria of a new El Dorado in New Zealand. For several weeks the news by the arrival of every steamer from Otago confirmed these reports, and convinced all that gold was actually being obtained there.'[16]

As news of the rich gold finds in Otago filtered through to the goldfields and towns of Central Victoria, it revived hope in the lucky strike and at the same time dismayed those intending to convert rough gold diggings into prosperous and settled townships. In 1862, as gold-seekers drifted off to dig around Otago's Clutha River, the local newspaper editor in the Victoria mining town of Talbot issued a warning. He said he would 'counsel the miners of Victoria to exercise caution before giving up their homes for what may yet prove in part a delusion'.[17] Thousands ignored this admonition and headed for Otago, many of them on a second-stage migration, having reached Victoria from California, Europe, Tasmania or China. In doing so, they initiated a long history of journeying between goldfields, townships and farms for which the Tasman Sea proved no barrier. Ballarat miner Alexander Don left an account of firstly mining in Central Victoria and then crossing the Tasman for Central Otago, after which he returned to Ballarat, tried his luck in New Zealand once more, this time along the Taieri River in Otago, and eventually settled back on a farm block in Warrenheip, near to where the first Ballarat rushes began.[18]

Subsequent anecdotal evidence pointed to a peak in Tasman crossings in the 1880s, with estimates of between 15 and 20 per cent of all immigrants into boom-time Melbourne coming from New Zealand and especially the South Island.[19] The crash of the Melbourne land boom and the economic depression of the 1890s then sent

The Old Bendigo Family Hotel and Bank of New South Wales in Clyde, Otago, c. April, 1863.

Courtesy Clyde Historical Museum collection

thousands back to Otago and Southland. Whereas not long before, authors of routine 'Our Australian (or Melbourne) Letters' to Otago newspapers had filled columns with dazzling images of the boomtown on Port Phillip Bay, by 1893 accounts presented the city as one near to collapse. 'Collins Street looks almost deserted, at any rate in comparison with its appearance any time from two to seven years ago,' lamented one correspondent.[20] The land boom crash may initially have thrown building workers out of a job and then forced civil service retrenchments on the Victorian Cabinet. By 1893 even the city's nouveau riche were suffering. Tailors complained that men were keeping their old suits for longer, observed one Dunedin correspondent. 'Collins Street is shabby genteel' sniffed another Otago newsbreaker. 'In the region of finance and commerce our Melbourne experiences continue depressing' reported yet another.[21] At the Melbourne Agricultural Show auctioneers were unable to secure sales, and implement makers had no customers. In New Zealand, journalists visiting the wharves of Port Chalmers and Bluff claimed that disillusioned labourers and carpenters were heading back to Dunedin as the Melbourne economy fell apart.

In explaining these movements, J.A. Dowie recalled the 'fundamental inversity' of the Australian and New Zealand economies.[22] Other scholars have identified the troughs and peaks in movement across the Tasman. G.A. Carmichael and others singled out four transitions, commencing with mass migration from Central Victoria during the early stages of the Otago gold rushes (1861–64) followed by a return migration during the 1880s' Melbourne building boom and the contraction of New Zealand mining. During the bleak 1890s, travellers again headed eastwards across the Tasman (see Table 2.1), with flows stabilising by the end of the decade. Then, after 1900, the destruction wrought by the 'Federation Drought' in Australia and the boom that refrigerated exports brought to New Zealand farming tilted the balance again in New

---

J. PATTERSON,

OLD BENDIGO FAMILY HOTEL

LOGAN TOWN,

BENDIGO REEFS.

—

Ample Accommodation for Travellers

Good Stabling.

Advertisement for Patterson's Old Bendigo Family Hotel at Logantown in Bendigo Gully, Otago, in the *Cromwell Argus* of 11 February 1872.

Table 2.1. Population Movements between Australia and New Zealand 1892

Colony	Arrivals	Departures	Excess of arrivals over departures
Queensland	14,646	13,564	1082
New South Wales	62,197	54,799	7398
Victoria	62,951	69,214	−6263
South Australia	17,433	14,474	2959
Western Australia	7440	2968	4472
Tasmania	23,744	24,407	−663
New Zealand	18,122	13,164	4958

Source: *Official Yearbook of New Zealand*, 1893

Zealand's favour. However, overall, as Carmichael noted, Victoria was the one 'great beneficiary' in this constant movement of people. Even in the depths of the Victoria Depression, more New Zealanders headed to Victoria than travelled back across the Tasman. And despite the greatly diminished prospects for work in Melbourne, Victoria still attracted more New Zealanders than New South Wales did.[23]

After federation, Australia as a whole remained by far the major source of New Zealand emigrants, with departures for Australia not outnumbering arrivals until 1909 (see Table 2.2).[24] In contrast to the nineteenth century, the increasing number of New Zealanders who emigrated to Australia throughout the twentieth century chose Sydney over Melbourne. In an important turning point, Queensland displaced Victoria as the second most popular destination in 1976.

The federation of Australia and subsequent rejection by New Zealand of inclusion in the new Commonwealth may not have been as directly consequential for such migration flows as Belich suggested. Until 1966 migration between Australia and New Zealand (and, it seems, more directly between Victoria and the South Island) seemed roughly balanced, a see-saw alternately weighted only marginally to one or the other end. But after 1966, with New Zealand's out-migration far exceeding any Australian departures for New Zealand, and with Sydney and eventually the Gold and Sunshine Coasts in Queensland, rather than Melbourne, becoming increasingly attractive, this long-standing connection for New Zealand emigrants may finally have broken.

By then, Otago, Victoria and parts of Tasmania were sharing a common cultural pattern. The men and women who moved between the two sides of the Tasman ensured that cultural practices as diverse as architecture, the theatre and literature (and, for a time, sport) developed in an integrated manner in both places. Smaller gold towns on either side of the Tasman exhibited similar formal lay-outs and some commonality in building form. The original mining towns of Clunes in Victoria and Lawrence in Otago, for example, shared a distinctive urban form, defining aspects of which were a creek, a commercial strip running more or less parallel to this water course, and public buildings commanding the higher points above the commercial strip and opposite to mined and much-altered hillsides.

Commercial structures may have been built to a smaller scale in Lawrence than in Clunes, and public buildings may have appeared later and carried a markedly less florid decoration, but the urban pattern of both vanguard mining settlements exhibited remarkably similar characteristics.[25] The ubiquitous double-fronted symmetrical single-storeyed 'miner's cottage' was replicated in New Zealand's and Victoria's mining towns. The urban set pieces of Dunedin's Octagon took on some of the built and planted character (and statuary) to be found in Ballarat's Sturt and Lydiard Streets.[26] Both of these grand focal points still include, for example, statues of the Scottish poet Robert Burns, completed and unveiled with enormous pomp in both cities in 1887.[27] Public buildings overlooking these memorials drew on similar revivalist inspiration for decoration and followed similar internal designs. Within this general structure there were of course localised idiosyncrasies, but the work of principal architects and the interest of common clients sometimes overshadowed these localised variations on a theme of ebullient, revivalist gold-town facades.

Both Australasian and British banking firms had raced one another for a share of gold receipts, concentrating on Central Victoria and Otago. Of every three pounds advanced by the Bank of Australasia in 1866, two went to either Victoria or New Zealand. By the 1870s the Union Bank was taking a third of all gold receipts through its expanding branch network in Victoria and Otago.[28] The firms that had the greatest success in the gold trade typically marked their pre-eminence by hiring a respected architect to design an imposing building in a mining town's principal street. Ballarat's Lydiard St North, for example, is fronted by the 1862/63 National Bank designed by

Table 2.2 New Zealand Arrivals and Departures 1905–09

	1905	**1906**	**1907**	**1908**	**1909**
Arrivals from					
United Kingdom	5553	8293	7449	11,348	11,184
Australia	25,132	28,699	26,916	31,769	25,548
Other British possessions	1028	1320	1216	1138	1141
Other countries	972	921	527	715	777
	32,685	39,233	36,108	44,970	38,650
Departures to					
United Kingdom	1854	2495	2440	2635	2676
Australia	19,367	21,722	25,848	26,468	28,995
Other British possessions	755	845	1244	1193	1326
Other countries	1407	1323	840	413	934
	23,383	26,385	30,378	30,709	33,931

Source: *Official Yearbook of New Zealand*, 1910

Leonard Terry. The 1860 Colonial Bank building in the same vicinity is again a Terry design, as is the Bank of New South Wales (1862).[29] The architects and builders of these structures often moved between colonies as civic commissions opened for tender and booms or busts in the building trade unfolded.

Perhaps the greatest influence on Dunedin's post-gold rush townscape was one of these architects, Robert Lawson. Lawson emigrated from Scotland to Victoria in 1854, working variously at mining in Ballarat, writing for newspapers in Geelong and designing buildings in that town as well as in Melbourne and small gold towns such as Steiglitz. From 1862 Lawson worked across the gold towns of Otago, with banks and churches his most lucrative contracts. Otago Peninsula's Larnach Castle and Dunedin's Otago Boys' High School are perhaps his most iconic designs, although Larnach Castle may have owed a great deal of its romantic Scottish decorations – and its futuristic waste-recycling systems – to the owner, William Larnach himself.[30] After the partial collapse of the Lawson-designed Seacliff Asylum (for a time New Zealand's largest building, situated on the coast north of Dunedin), Lawson fled back to Melbourne, where he built Earlesbrae Hall for the brewing magnate Collier McCracken. Ten years later he was again in Dunedin, and despite some sniping about his Seacliff Asylum disaster, was elected vice-president of the Otago Institute of Architects.[31]

The second trans-Tasman architect to shape both Otago and Melbourne (and smaller South Island towns) was William Armson, who arrived with his parents in New Zealand from London before leaving soon after for Melbourne. Armson completed his architectural training in Melbourne and designed at least one prominent bank building. He then crossed back over the Tasman to Dunedin in 1862, designing, among other buildings, St Luke's Church in Oamaru before sailing for Melbourne and then settling in New Zealand once again at Hokitika on the West Coast. Unlike Lawson's stone and brick structures in Dunedin, none of Armson's many timber buildings along the West Coast lasted into the twenty-first century. His most grandiose structure remains the Bank of New Zealand on Princes Street, Dunedin.[32]

The third significant Dunedin architect whose career began across the Tasman was William Clayton, born in Tasmania but trained in England. He returned to Tasmania where he is thought to have designed at least 300 buildings before leaving for the Otago rushes. Over six years in Dunedin, Clayton designed a string of prominent buildings, including Edinburgh House (on Bond Street) and the buildings (erected on the site of what is now Dunedin Hospital) for the New Zealand Exhibition held in 1865. He moved to Wellington following the decline of mining and won the post of New Zealand's first, and only, colonial architect.[33]

The lucrative commission of architects during the gold era caused a constantly mobile band of them to move back and forth across the Tasman. A hierarchy of fellow travellers joined them. At the top of this pyramid were churchmen. Leading figures in both the Catholic and Presbyterian churches in Otago and Victoria routinely crossed the Tasman in God's service.[34] Less exalted professionals followed. Musicians, performers and artists proved themselves frequent seafarers. Viennese-born Eugene von Guérard arrived in Victoria in 1852, perhaps after spending time in California.

He painted Victoria's central highlands and alpine regions with techniques perfected in presenting the 'sublime' character of the European Alps, and brought the same structure of representation to painting in the mountains of Fiordland and the New Zealand Alps.[35] Musicians, stage performers and even criminals followed the gold diggers from Ballarat and Bendigo to Otago. Charles Thatcher, whose lyrics captured the idiom of diggers in both Victoria and Otago, made a name for himself on both sides of the Tasman. His sympathy for the digger and ridiculing of elites (in Dunedin, the Old Identities, satirised in one of his most popular ballads) made him an iconic figure in mining towns on both sides of the Tasman.[36]

Beyond the irreverence of stage performers such as Thatcher, the Old Identities of Otago had every reason to reflect on Australia's export of its 'convict stain' to their province. Henry Garrett, transported to Tasmania with a 10-year sentence in 1845, had managed to disappear into the gold-digging throng in Ballarat by 1854. There he robbed the Bank of Victoria and fled to England. Discovered and returned to Melbourne, he was imprisoned on the notorious Williamstown hulks before being granted a ticket of leave and then setting out for Dunedin. Rather than being reformed by his time in the brutal hulks regime, 'Long Harry', as he was known, had perfected his skills and soon drew together his 'Garrett Gang' in Central Otago. After one daring highway robbery of 15 diggers on a track to Gabriel's Gully, Garrett again fled, this time to Sydney, before once more being recognised and sent back to Dunedin to serve another eight-year term. After a failed break-out, Garrett was released early and sent back to Melbourne, returning yet again to Dunedin and honest work as a cooper. But for Garrett, old habits died hard, and he was arrested for break-ins and possession of skeleton keys. Within six months of his release in 1882, he was caught trying to steal a bottle of wine and imprisoned in Wellington. He died there in 1885.[37]

Performers, thieves and others on the margins (it is extraordinary to reflect on the frequency with which single mothers gathered up children and sailed from one colony to another) may have crossed the Tasman more often than members of post-gold rush professions, depending critically as they did on the wealth of gold and the attractions of a mobile, often anonymous, population. The later phases of mining, however, brought with them a shared industrial experience, especially in the revival of mining in Otago through dredging. This time it was Otago miners who exported skills and workers to Victoria and Tasmania. Charles McQueen, who was born in Scotland, mined for a while in Victoria and then built up expertise and investments in gold dredging in Otago in the 1880s. He later sought to introduce dredging in Victoria and Tasmania. McQueen died in the solidly established Victoria gold town of Creswick in 1906 without having personally gained much from his Australian adventure but having successfully introduced dredging techniques into a number of Victoria's exhausted gold diggings.[38]

Dredging for gold (and tin) continued in Victoria into the 1930s. Some dredges worked over old goldfields in the Central Highlands while others tried watercourses in the north-east of the state.[39] All the while, the Victorian dredgers and investors looked across the Tasman to the progress of Otago dredging. But dredging remained a precarious business, with dredges springing leaks, occasionally capsizing and often standing idle for lack of water or because of broken machinery.

Problems with dredging apart, the wealth of mining and the thick web of voluntary association on the goldfields speedily produced one significant industry on both sides of the Tasman. Among the first organisations set up in gold towns were jockey clubs.[40] Other sporting links were speedily established in Australia. The distinctive Australian Rules football code created in Melbourne and played especially in Victoria's gold towns, made its way to Dunedin and beyond. Those South Island rugby union clubs that now lay claim to an exalted role as pioneers of their sport in New Zealand had characteristically begun life as promoters of the unique Victorian game.[41]

Along with the trainers and owners of thoroughbred horses taken from goldfield meetings in Ballarat or Bendigo to the tracks at Dunstan or Dunedin, other imaginative figures brought animals from eastern Australia to Otago. From the gold era onwards, acclimatisation societies were obsessed with diminishing the differences in flora and fauna between New Zealand, Victoria and Tasmania so as to manufacture a cosmopolitan natural world.[42] As part of the process of acclimatisation, Australian possums were sent to the South Island before 1850 and had made their appearance in Otago by the last years of the gold rush. At first prized for the Australian Aboriginal-made possum rugs, possums became a source of trade in skins in Otago, Tasmania and, for a time, in Victoria.[43] By the 1890s Victoria, Tasmania, Southland and Otago were vying with one another for direct access to London fur markets, in clear indication of regional awareness of transnational opportunities.

As a lucrative industry, possum trapping and shooting lasted well into the inter-war years until curtailed in New Zealand by fears of forest damage and in Australia probably because of the wholesale slaughter of other Australian marsupials during possum hunts.[44] Like the gold immigrants they accompanied (inertly as possum-skin cloaks), possums (or for much of the nineteenth century 'opossums') occupied a difficult position in Otago. On the one hand, acclimatisers saw the possum as a successful trans-Tasman voyager and demanded its protection, and hunters wanted it available for trapping and shooting. On the other hand, farmers demanded that the invader be exterminated. As one, who signed himself 'Late Catlins Resident', warned in 1911: 'If these animals are not checked we shall have a far worse pest in New Zealand than the rabbit, for it is utterly impossible to keep out of a property by means of rabbit-proof fences … I can say without fear of contradiction that the animal is far more plentiful in some parts of Catlins than the rabbit.'[45]

The other great animal import proved itself both lucrative and, as the Late Catlins Resident had warned, destructive. The rabbit sustained a local industry until the middle of the twentieth century, largely in defiance of central government policy and with Dunedin and Central Otago critical to the trade. By the last decades of the nineteenth century, North Island bureaucrats were demanding that land-owners take steps to destroy rabbits on their property. At the same time, local families facing declining returns from mining relied on rabbiting to survive. Some businesses in Otago developed a lucrative export trade in rabbit carcasses and fur, thereby earning

New Zealand a solid income stream in American dollars (by way of the hat trade in New York).[46] Victoria and Otago seemed capable of squeezing the larger New South Wales trade out of London markets as well. In 1902 the New South Wales agent in London reported that the demand in London made 'the rabbit industry well worth careful fostering'. However, 'Victorian and New Zealand rabbits bring 1s [one shilling] per case more than New South Wales rabbits, owing to the unsuitable packing and inferior quality of the latter.'[47] Otago rabbiters continued to take a leading role in the trade well into the twentieth century, with the New Zealand export trade concentrated in Dunedin into the 1950s.[48]

Parallel Journeys: 1901–61

Miners who turned to the fur trade, either in possum skins or rabbit skins, had made an imaginative leap into a global market. To survive, they had to manage, often in defiance of central government policy, a growing but threatened resource. Treading a fine line between allowing indiscriminate breeding and extermination, they succeeded remarkably well. While small-scale, under-capitalised miners and farmers turned to hunting possums and rabbits, others with an enterprising bent in the early twentieth century applied capital from mining and dredging to more structured businesses, especially the processing of raw staples. The last decades of the nineteenth century saw great enthusiasm for a local flax industry. In this, however, Otago faced the same difficulties as producers in other parts of the islands – failure in machine-based processing. The standard labour-intensive practices of washing and bleaching flax proved extremely 'tedious', and 'if some kind of machinery could be got that would take off the edges it would be of great benefit; doing so by hand comes to be very expensive'.[49] Hope was held out for a new machine produced by William Fairweather. By 1909, 19 flax mills were operating in Otago and Southland.[50]

The native flax industry seemed a productive response to the demands of a global market and the raw staples available in Otago and Southland. But as the industry expanded with intermittently strong government support, the first inklings of a division in the trans-Tasman world appeared. In 1906 flax-millers responded with a strange lack of enthusiasm to a plan wherein the New Zealand government would pay bonuses. As part of the scheme, flax plants would be exported to Victoria 'to encourage cultivation there', an activity which, one miller warned, seemed to be 'an unwise thing to do, and … the Government should reconsider its action'.[51] In fact, the trans-Tasman world seemed something of a threat to a range of Dunedin manufacturers and workmen interviewed by the *Otago Daily Times* as New Zealand prepared to respond to the federation of Australian colonies. Rather than a commonality in industry and cultural life ensuring Australasian integration, the closest of these ties seemed to hasten a twentieth-century distancing of the regions.

The generally accepted reasons for New Zealand's resistance to federation give prominence to Australia's record of violent treatment of Aboriginals, its convict inheritance, and the voting rights enjoyed in New Zealand by Māori. There is no doubt a degree of exaggeration in Pākehā historians' reflections on and turn-of-the-century parliamentary concerns over New Zealand's resistance to federation being a product, in part, of Māori rights. Fears about excluding Māori from voting rolls was as much about New Zealand's calculations of loss of numbers of votes and hence seats as it was about a concern for fair and equitable treatment of indigenous peoples. The driving fears of those in Dunedin and Otago were very rarely, if at all, connected to Māori rights, but instead reflected the same concern as the flax producers' – trade and commerce would suffer in any union that included a tariff-protected Victoria.

By the time of federation and New Zealanders' rejection and then revisiting of integration into an Australasia, the old trans-Tasman world, instead of ensuring an ongoing close connection, was doing the opposite. New Zealanders, and especially those in Dunedin and Otago, joined with the flax millers in maintaining that a federated Australasia, governed from a protectionist Victoria, would mean the obliteration of local industry; the free trade policies of the New South Wales government engendered no such fears.[52]

At a time when free trade opportunities seemed an attractive bonus of federation, New Zealand's royal commissioners noted that less than 10 per cent of New Zealand's exports and less than six per cent of its imports were being transacted with the new Commonwealth, a marked decline since the gold-rush days.[53] Some trades, though, remained especially vulnerable; most, as it turned out, were concentrated in Otago. Furniture makers, for example, stood to suffer because of the successful Chinese carpentry trades in Melbourne.[54] The absence of compulsory arbitration between employers and employees troubled the commissioners despite Victoria's factory legislation and wages boards having more progressive and equitable structures than their counterparts in other colonies had.[55]

In the main, though, the protectionist governance of Victorian industry was deemed the most troubling. Dunedin barrister F.R. Chapman noted in evidence that federation was really the product of 'the activity of Victorian politicians and Victorian interests in seeking to broaden their market – what I might call their protected area'.[56] Mr Slater, secretary of the Dunedin Trades and Labour Council, was convinced that federation would take New Zealand's labour laws backwards, in a 'levelling down' of working conditions rather than any 'levelling up'.[57] Henry Rodd of the Bootmakers Union of Dunedin worried that 'our trade might have to go to the dogs'[58] because of competition from bootmakers in Victoria. Presenting the viewpoint of manufacturers in general, Mr Burt of Dunedin asserted: 'If federation took place I am sure that, under existing arrangements, a good many of the manufactories going on in Dunedin would be stopped.'[59]

As these comments indicate, fears about federation showed in particular the strength of Victoria's protected trades, themselves a product of the gold-mining era. Historians have written extensively about this late-nineteenth century craft structure with its cooperative industrial relations, although, as Graeme Davison made clear, any employer–employee harmony had declined somewhat through the greater scale of the expanded Melbourne of the 1880s. Davison observed that 'the men who founded Melbourne's factories in the wake of the gold rush saw them not only as a source of present livelihoods but as a school of future craftsmen'.[60] Regardless of these ambitions, machinery had begun to oust craftsmen, apprenticeship systems were breaking down, and an impersonal machine-like structure reflected 'the passing of the first generation of pioneer manufacturers – which as much as anything else severed the old bonds of attachment between masters and men'.[61] Similar transitions struck Erik Olssen, who, in writing about Dunedin, remarked that 'like "Marvellous Melbourne", a city with which Dunedin had many links, these years [the 1880s] marked the first dramatic stage in transition from pre-industrial community to modern city'.[62]

This more professional–less paternalistic industrial scale to trans-Tasman enterprises, still shaped by compacts between workers and management in exchange for tariff protection, was centred on Otago, where New Zealand's industrial core still lay. As in Victoria, capital from gold and the skills of miners had combined to create a vital manufacturing base. The transition from craft-based personalised relationships to the more antagonistic class-driven suspicion apparent to Davison and Olssen was, until at least well into the twentieth century, masked by government support for industrialisation and a closed market for goods. Dunedin and Otago generally had exploited this framework to the full. Even some years after the peaks of gold production the industrial base of Otago remained strong, with more factories operating across the province than anywhere else in New Zealand (see Table 2.3).

As an advanced industrial centre, Otago relied on the same compact between workers and management as did Melbourne and the major provincial (gold-derived) centres of Victoria, Ballarat, Bendigo, Castlemaine and Geelong. Olssen's history of the Dunedin suburb of Caversham indicates the nature of transitional challenges in one Otago industrial concentration, the metal trades of Hillside.[63] Olssen pointed out that the dredging boom of 1899–1904 led to heavy investment in metal workshops in Dunedin, but that even if New Zealand had entered the Australian Commonwealth, 'firms in the new Australian Commonwealth displaced local ones'. Nonetheless,

Table 2.3. New Zealand Major Industries, 1906

	Number of Industries, excluding Mines and Quarries, 1906
Otago	889
Auckland	885
Wellington	846
Canterbury	696
Taranaki	247
Nelson	229
Hawke's Bay	214
Westland	112
Marlborough	68

Source: *The Official Yearbook of New Zealand*, 1908

the 'anchor' industry in the railway workshops prompted other firms to cluster at Hillside and employ Caversham men in a complex hierarchy of skill encompassing blacksmiths and semi-skilled turners through to patternmakers and moulders.[64] The carefully structured wage order implemented in workshops maintained some of the same agreement between workers and employers as that in Melbourne, Ballarat and Bendigo. Labour relations in the Phoenix Foundry workshops in Ballarat, for example, were occasionally marked by working-class resistance but more often by workers' agreements with employers that respected skill differentials and translated tariff margins into both profits and wages.[65] It was not until the 1920s that the liberal compromises between workers and employers broke down at Hillside and then, some years later, in Ballarat.

One Otago firm that made the most of trans-Tasman opportunities was Stevenson and Cook Engineering. Established at Port Chalmers, the company exported dredges to Victoria and eventually set up a branch factory at Bright in north-eastern Victoria. By 1908 the company had formed a partnership with Ruwolt engineering in Melbourne.[66] However, some of the fears of those who presented arguments to the Federation Royal Commission did seem justified by what ensued for Stevenson and Cook. Charles Ruwolt, a German immigrant, quickly set up his own factory in Victoria Street, Richmond, and floated his company in 1920. By 1938 it was one of Australia's largest engineering firms. With branches in Queensland and Western Australia, it dwarfed its former partner from Otago. When Ruwolt died (1946), the company searched for a buyer and was eventually absorbed into Vickers Limited, based in Great Britain.

Less obvious connections existed in retail trades. For a time New Zealand's largest retail chain, Hallenstein Brothers, operated with strong familial connections across the Tasman. Not until Emil Hallenstein (born in Melbourne in 1867) died in Dunedin in 1932 was this long-standing connection across the Tasman broken.[67] The New Zealand branch of this familial empire was created by Bendix Hallenstein, who had emigrated from Germany in 1835.[68] He reached Melbourne in 1857 and then went to the goldfields at Daylesford, Victoria, where his two older brothers had already established a drapery business. Within a decade, Bendix had opened stores in the New Zealand towns of Invercargill, Cromwell, Arrowtown and Lawrence. He founded his New Zealand Clothing Factory in Dunedin in 1873. In Victoria, Isaac Hallenstein and his uncle Moritz Michaelis also ran clothing businesses before shifting their attention from a declining Daylesford by branching into leather goods, with a tannery in Footscray and branches of the firm in New Zealand.[69]

Lost and Found Connections: 1950–2014

The manufacturers and workers who testified before the Federation Royal Commission in 1901 may have assumed that industrial success in New Zealand depended on remaining outside the Australian Commonwealth. Even so, the deregulation of the New Zealand and Australian economies in the 1980s had a profound impact on both Otago and Victoria. Erik Olssen noted the long-term decline of Otago's industries commencing in the 1950s, although he queried the definition of decline in relation

Hallenstein's Shop, Cromwell, Otago, c. 1872.

Courtesy Lloyd Carpenter collection

to Otago and addressed the same concern with respect to Victoria.[70] David Lange's Labour government in New Zealand accelerated tariff reduction at a meeting on 11 February 1985.[71] The Hawke/Keating Australian Labor Party was quick to follow; eventually, on both sides of the Tasman, the manufacturing concentration – built in the first instance from reinvesting the capital obtained from gold and the remoulding of goldminers' skills – ceased to exist. At Fisher and Paykel's whitegoods factory in Mosgiel, near Dunedin, 120 workers walked away for the last time in April 2009. 'It sucks, really, but what can you do?' remarked one of the whitegoods workers.[72]

Fisher and Paykel had commenced local production in 1934, taking advantage of the new tariff protections introduced by the Labour government. By 1955 the company had acquired the iconic iron-manufacturing and appliance business of Henry Shacklock, whose foundry once operated from Princes St, Dunedin, and went on to produce over one million dishwashers in the Mosgiel plant. Other local industries had also collapsed by the start of the twentieth century. The Mosgiel Woollen Mill operated from the 1870s to the end of the twentieth century. As exemplified by the closed production of dishwashers and woollen rugs, parallel manufacturing structures of the early to late-twentieth century collapsed speedily, but in both Otago and Victoria older industries were constructed afresh and a new range of activities added. In both regions, gold-mining has had recurrent rebirths.

One characteristic industry to emerge from mining was winemaking. Romeo Bragato, the Victorian government's viticulturalist so supportive of winemaking in old Victorian gold towns such as Great Western and Castlemaine, had toured late nineteenth-century Otago, pronouncing the virtues of a local winemaking industry. During the last decades of the twentieth century, wine production not only re-emerged in great force in Central Otago but also developed strong international connections.[73] In both Otago and Central Victoria, prescient planning for transnational tourism had emerged by the 1930s, but with an obviously stronger base in New Zealand than in Central Victoria.

The built form of gold towns and the relics of mining in the forests of Central Victoria and the ranges of Central Otago are now highly valued for their intrinsic aesthetic and for the contribution they can make to a lucrative tourist industry. Even the surviving racing clubs of Otago can draw in commissions from transnational and sometimes global wagering. We are not suggesting here that these resilient industries by themselves can make good the destruction of the welfare state in Victoria or New Zealand or counter the insecurities of neoliberalism, given that the harshness of economic restructuring since 1975 seems to have fallen most inhumanely on regions of once wealthy mines and manufacturing, on both sides of the Tasman. However, the revival of industries such as winemaking (or indeed gold-mining itself) suggests that any strategy in response to the inequities of neoliberalism ought to commence with a respect for local resilience and communal identity and, in so doing, draw on the strength of established regional knowledge and practices. The challenges of relatively small populations in a national context, restricted educational opportunity and the removal of an industrial base means that once-wealthy gold regions must constantly readjust to transnational opportunity and openness to markets. There are sufficient indications in their histories to suggest that they can respond creatively to an unstable, unforgiving global economy.

Conclusion

The significance of these economic and social connections driven by key industries and pastimes transcends perspectives in national historiographies of Australia and New Zealand. Perhaps it is only among labour historians that some of these connections have been most fully explored in their regional rather than their national contexts.[74] The regional perspective also underscores the need for greater collaboration in history and other fields of New Zealand and Australian scholarship in order to a develop a dynamic cross-regional, trans-Tasman perspective of the south-west Pacific during the second half of the nineteenth century. Peter Hempenstall, for example, has observed that 'writers on both sides of the Tasman have produced national histories that talk past one another, ignore shared pasts and neglect historical parallels, at least since Federation, which acts as a kind of "zero point", freezing each side's history into a "before" and "after" narrative'.[75] The implication of our chapter is that regional connections permit a better linkage of these histories than does a comparative, national one. In this respect, we have engaged with Donald Denoon, Philippa Mein-Smith and Marivic Wyndham's assertion that Australia, New Zealand and the Pacific Islands are not a 'self-evident region'.[76]

In response to this perspective, we have instead emphasised the regional and international characteristics of the gold-seeking societies of Victoria and Central Otago, and our discussion coincides with James Belich's observations about the historical significance of the 'old Tasman World'. Because of this confusion in national, regional and global historiographies, it can be difficult to distinguish the emergence of distinctly regional or national identities from the overtly British social and economic structures that defined so many facets of settler colonies society during the second half of the nineteenth century. The 150 years of mining for gold in Otago and Victoria is both a starting point for such a localised response and a symbol of enduring industrial and cultural patterns too often overlooked by national histories in settler societies.

3.

'A Great Many People I Know from Victoria': The Victorian dimension of the Otago gold rushes

Daniel Davy

IN 1852 AT THE AGE OF 13, John Henry Watmuff and his father, Steven Watmuff, left their home in Adelaide, Australia, to join the rush to the Bendigo goldfield. The two were moderately successful at gold digging and so were able to finance Steven's return to England in 1859 to protect the family's inheritance. Meanwhile, John Henry continued to support their family in Adelaide through gold seeking in Victoria. When news of the Otago gold rushes reached Melbourne in 1861, his younger brother Ned joined the throng of diggers leaving Victoria for the new field. John Henry soon received glowing accounts from his brother at Gabriel's Gully, and decided to follow Ned to Otago. He continued to prospect in Otago until 1864, when he gave up gold seeking and returned to Melbourne.

Shortly before sailing for Otago, John Henry Watmuff lamented in his diary that he was leaving 'so many pleasent [sic] friendships and am endeared to by so many associations … that I shall ever regret parting with'.[1] However, his diaries show that gold seeking in Otago never constituted a clear break from his connections in Bendigo. Stories of old friendships reawakened on the goldfields filled nearly every diary entry he wrote while in Otago. Within hours of arriving in Dunedin, Watmuff joined a party of former mates from Bendigo. When the party arrived at Weatherstones, near present-day Lawrence, he remarked that there were 'a great many people I know from Victoria'.[2] Another evening, a few months later, he wrote that his tent 'was crowded with neighbours. Spent [the evening] very jolly singing, card playing and reading with a little gambling'.[3] At the same time as Watmuff renewed old friendships in Otago, he maintained connections with diggers and family members in Victoria. He exchanged letters monthly with former mates still working at Bendigo, making him and his friends aware of conditions in both places.[4] Surrounded by acquaintances in Otago, exchanging letters with friends and relatives in Bendigo, and returning to Victoria after two years, Watmuff remained oriented to Victoria throughout his brief time in Otago. For Watmuff and other gold seekers like him, the Otago gold rushes were more a series of events in Victorian than New Zealand history: the Otago rushes flowed out from gold seeking in Victoria and remained firmly connected to Victoria throughout their course.

Narratives such as Watmuff's are at odds with the historical memory of the Otago gold rushes. In their respective studies of the West Coast rushes, Philip Ross May and Lyndon Fraser[5] both stress the flows of people and information between Victoria and New Zealand's West Coast, but the relative neglect of Otago by historians leaves the connections between Otago and Victoria largely unexplored. When the Otago rushes are discussed, scholars are very much concerned with the rushes' role in forming a national economy and society and thereby overlook these trans-Tasman connections.[6] Even William Morrell's and J.H.M. Salmon's magisterial studies of the nineteenth-century gold rushes are largely chronological histories, charting the movement from Victoria to Otago and on to the West Coast. They consequently neglect the two-way traffic of people, goods and knowledge across the Tasman Sea and the ways in which events on one side of the Tasman Sea influenced developments on the other during the 1860s.[7]

Links between Victoria and Otago are overlooked to an even greater degree in the literature on the Australian rushes, where the Otago rushes are discussed only as prospectors leave Victoria. The moment individuals left Australian shores, the Otago rushes are depicted as no longer relevant to this national narrative.[8] Implicit

James Lawson, formerly of Ballarat (Victoria), mining at Berwick, Otago, c. 1886.

Courtesy R.W. Murray collection, Cromwell Museum

in these separate historiographies is the assumption that gold seekers were Australians while in Victoria and New Zealanders while in Otago. Gold seekers, however, were neither here nor there; most migrated seasonally across the Tasman Sea and remained connected to mates and relatives on both sides. It is therefore most accurate to speak of a single trans-Tasman gold-seeking population that migrated between Melbourne and Dunedin.

This chapter counteracts these nationalising approaches by placing the Otago gold rushes within the regional Tasman world, which existed 'across bridges, or in the spaces between the ramparts of cultural formation on either side' of the Tasman Sea.[9] Its analysis shows the ways in which British and Irish transnational social networks and geographic mobility were extended to Australasia and manifested in frequent migrations between Victoria and Otago throughout the gold rushes. Here it connects to Frank Thistlethwaite's plea to analyse the ways in which mobility continued after an individual first travelled overseas.[10] These personal networks also problematise clear divisions between Otago and Victoria when individuals remained attached to two places. Some individuals in Otago dug alongside mates from the Victorian diggings while they remained connected to loved ones on the other side of the Tasman Sea.

This analysis of mobilities and networks links up with recent geographic approaches to the British Empire that map the flow of people, knowledge and commodities between colonial sites rather than exclusively from Britain and Ireland.[11] This networked perspective also reveals multiple regional centres across the British Empire. The chapter argues that throughout the early 1860s, Melbourne remained the financial hub of the Otago goldfields on the other side of the Tasman Sea. Moreover, Otago diggers relied overwhelmingly on products shipped by Melbourne merchants, and a steady two-way traffic of people and knowledge moved in both directions between Dunedin and Melbourne. The flow of diggers and commodities had a profound impact on both societies. With newspapers in both places competing for an itinerant population of trans-Tasman gold seekers, both colonial sites 'were constituted through their transactions with one another'.[12]

Motivations

The arrival of thousands of diggers in Dunedin often had as much to do with economic conditions on the Victorian goldfields as with the quantity of gold dug up on the other side of the Tasman Sea. Just as rushes in Victoria followed boom and bust cycles of the colonial economy, migration from Victoria to Queensland or Otago to the West Coast coincided with the contraction of the Victorian goldfield economy.[13] As David Emmons demonstrates in his study of Butte, Montana, gold seekers migrated to new fields when older diggings were worked out.[14]

In the early 1860s the Victorian economy was in the midst of a depression. In 1860 the collapse of the speculation-driven quartz mining industry in combination with a drought and the arrival of some 43,000 migrants from the United Kingdom crippled the colony's economy.[15] When the American prospector Charles Ferguson later recounted his journey from Melbourne to Port Chalmers, he recalled that many of the diggers he travelled with from Bendigo to Otago had lost everything during the collapse of quartz mining on the Victorian diggings.[16] Andrew French was almost destitute when he rushed from Victoria to Otago in 1862.[17] As the *Mount Alexander Mail* commented in 1861, many in Victoria would rather migrate to Otago than work for 'bare tucker' in Victoria.[18] The contrast between the expectations of prospectors and the conditions on the Victorian goldfields also influenced many to migrate to Otago.

Caution should be exercised, however, against equating migration entirely with economic necessity. As Geoffrey Serle and Susan Lawrence both show, absolute destitution was minimal on the goldfields.[19] Colonial legislation in Victoria allowed gold seekers the legal right to a block of 20 acres adjacent to their claims on which they could build a house and farm the land. The extension of the railroad into the goldfield districts also drove down the cost of living.[20] Many diggers enjoyed a varied diet of beef, pork, vegetables, eggs and dairy.[21] In addition, a sustained heavy rainfall early in 1863 increased gold yields throughout the goldfields at the same time that the Wakatipu rush swelled the numbers of those leaving for Otago. A writer for the *Bendigo Advertiser* cautioned that amidst abandoned claims and derelict equipment 'a waste is being made of what might have been a paradise'. The editorialist argued that gold seekers left because 'they wait with mouth wide open expecting the nuggets to drop into it like ripe plums'.[22]

As the author of this article argued, there were some gold-rush migrants who pursued riches rather than fled poverty. Trans-Tasman migration was often a calculated decision made possible because it was a relatively small and inexpensive jump to Otago when compared to travel from Britain and Ireland to Australasia. As was the case with Irish migration to Britain in the twentieth century, the Otago diggings' close proximity to Victoria meant they appealed to individuals' 'aspirations towards a higher standard of living, and not simply sheer economic necessity'.[23] Trans-Tasman migrants employed the same premeditation that earlier allowed them to choose Australasia after critically weighing information about potential destinations.[24] James Gascoigne left a claim on the Loddon that paid £3.0 a week when the Tuapeka rush rippled through Victoria.[25] When John Henry Watmuff received two letters from mates at Gabriel's Gully, he decided to migrate to Otago, stating that 'my sole object in taking this step will be in the hope of realising a lump sum of money that I may be enabled to enter into some other pursuit that I've been engaged in so unprofitably for such a number of years'.[26]

However, in contrast to Irish migrants in Britain, who pursued better wages and a higher standard of living across the Irish Sea, Victorian gold seekers migrated to a region with a more hostile terrain and climate, and fewer and more costly supplies.[27] They did this because the goldfields offered the possibility of wealth and a better livelihood in the future in exchange for Otago's harsher conditions in the present. As Watmuff observed shortly before sailing for Otago: 'My only regret is that I am leaving a certainty for an uncertainty.'[28] The smallness of the Tasman Sea in this regard and the volume of the flow also combined to maintain individuals' connections to acquaintances in Victoria and to map Victorian social networks onto the Otago diggings.

Commercial and Personal Networks

While economic conditions in Victoria encouraged migration, networks directed prospectors to Otago.[29] When the mining collapse of 1860 crippled the Victorian goldfields, the colony already possessed an extensive infrastructure catering to the needs and wants of gold seekers within its borders. Shipping lanes, railways and an army of merchants and tradesmen facilitated the shipment of commodities and consumables to Victoria from Britain, India and around Australasia.[30] The commercial webs extended across the Tasman during the Otago rushes pulled the province further into this Victorian network. Supplies arriving into Melbourne from across the globe that for the last 10 years had fed, clothed and entertained diggers in Victoria were now shipped from Melbourne to Dunedin by a merchant fleet.[31] In return, Otago gold went to Britain alongside Victorian gold.[32] Because all letters and newspapers from Britain and Ireland also travelled through Melbourne, connections between Otago residents and loved ones at home depended on this trans-Tasman link.[33] These findings echo Earl Pomeroy's and Daniel Marshall's respective arguments that San Francisco during the North American rushes became a nodal point for goldfields scattered west of the Rocky Mountains.[34]

Victorian capital and commerce flooded into the province with a rapidity that stunned Otago colonists. In 1861, shortly after Victorian gold seekers began arriving, Thomas Burns remarked that the arrival of shopkeepers, publicans and land speculators increased the price of real estate in Dunedin. 'Everyone,' Burns stated, 'is a shopkeeper or owns a gin palace.'[35] Shopkeepers also followed their customers out to the diggings in Central Otago, where they lined their shelves with flour from Tasmania, socks from Aberdeen, sugar from Mauritius and tea from India.[36] While on the way back to Dunedin from the Lakes District, one digger recognised many 'bakers, storekeepers, publicans and sinners' he had known at Bendigo.[37] One of these may have been Bendix Hallenstein, who left Bendigo to open a wholesale store at Queenstown in 1863. Several Victorian businesses established local branches in 1864 at Hamiltons, a gold-rush town on the eastern flank of Central Otago near modern Patearoa.[38] That same year, William Mears was operating his store, the ebulliently named 'Wonders of the World', on both the Wakatipu and Dunstan goldfields alongside branches in Melbourne, New South Wales and the Victorian diggings.[39]

In a 'sped-up' society, the desire for more diggers, more commodities and more immediate news pulled Otago closer to Melbourne during the rushes.[40] An editorialist for the *Otago Daily Times* commented in 1862: 'The saving of time is the object ever kept in view – the compressing into the narrowest duration that interchange of ideas from which springs knowledge … The railway, the steamer, and the telegraph ceaselessly toil on in their never-ending mission – the lessening the obstacles interposed by time and space. Rapidity has become the watchword of the age.'[41]

Enclosing the Otago rushes within New Zealand history neglects the ways in which commercial networks stretched back to Victoria. From the province's relationship to global commercial and financial networks down to the digger beside a campfire and reading a letter from home while drying his socks and cooking his dinner, the Otago gold rushes would be inconceivable without their links to Victoria. In a multitude of ways, the Otago goldfields existed more as a periphery of Melbourne than of Dunedin. As Phillip Ross May argues of New Zealand's West Coast later in the decade, the gold rushes made Otago a frontier of the Victorian colony during the early 1860s.[42]

While prospectors and products poured into Dunedin, letters and newspapers travelled in the opposite direction. Between 1862 and 1864, 391,780 letters and many newspapers were sent from Otago to Australia.[43] Although the Otago government did not distinguish between the Australian colonies, most letters and newspapers were likely sent to Victoria, given that most gold seekers came from that colony. Diaries from the Victorian diggings also sometimes recorded the steady flow of news from Otago. In 1861 the Ballarat prospector Frederic Ramsden briefly noted the arrival of letters from an acquaintance on the Otago diggings;[44] a year later, Charles Jarvis Coles also mentioned in his diary that he had received several letters from acquaintances in Otago.[45]

The flow of correspondence from Otago made trans-Tasman migration self-perpetuating, with successive waves of prospectors often deciding to migrate 'based on the guidance of pioneering migrants'.[46] James Gascoigne rushed from Castlemaine to Otago when he received a letter from his brother that was 'altogether favourable'.[47] Near the end of 1861 John Henry Watmuff travelled across the Tasman upon receipt of positive reports from his brother on the Tuapeka.[48] From Buckland Valley, Henry Morgan commented that 'the news of the gold mines in New Zealand is of the most flattering nature, both by the press and from private sources and there are a great number going there'.[49]

Framing the Otago rushes within the Tasman World also reveals a range of personal networks in Victoria that diggers abandoned or maintained while in Otago. Within the working lives of gold seekers, mining parties often formed in Victoria before migration or were composed of diggers who had previously worked together. Rather than emerging as a pragmatic and situational response to thin settlement, as Jock Phillips argues, gold-seeking party formation drew on these Victorian networks.[50] Martin Gardner and David Rattray dug alongside each other in Ballarat before rushing to the Tuapeka in July 1861, where they formed a gold-seeking party with two other acquaintances from Ballarat – Alexander Don and William Rattray.[51] Henry Hawkins and Frederick Carpenter, mates and friends for 28 years, prospected together at the Arrow; Robert Webb and Carl Sorrenson were mates for 10 years before they joined the Otago rush in 1863.[52]

Trans-Tasman connections extended beyond gold seeking. The binding of the gold rushes within national history often imagines the gold seeker as an itinerant loner or as part of an egalitarian masculine culture.[53] Yet by shifting our gaze back to Victoria, the gold seeker emerges as a husband or son, a brother or father. The geographically dispersed family was rooted in the experience of migration from Britain and Ireland; most gold seekers came from families in which overseas mobility was a fact of life.[54] For some diggers who either settled down or grew up in Victoria, 'home' had slowly shifted to this colonial periphery, and many families replicated this system of family dispersion in Victoria during the Otago gold rushes. However, transience did not necessarily break down kinship bonds, as Angela McCarthy demonstrates.[55]

Susan Lawrence shows that by the early 1860s strong kinship networks had materialised on the Victorian goldfields as earlier gold seekers encouraged subsequent waves of migrants composed of relatives and friends.[56] The Otago rushes directed these networks across the Tasman, and many gold seekers remained connected to loved ones through correspondence and seasonal returns from Otago. The McMillan brothers, Hamilton, James and John, and John's brother-in-law, rushed twice to Otago, yet remained connected to their stepfather, John McCance, of Chewton, Victoria, despite frequent mobility. For the McMillan brothers, McCance's home became the nodal point for a wide range of family migrations throughout Australasia.[57] All through his time in Otago, John Henry Watmuff exchanged letters with his mother, siblings and cousins at Bendigo. On one occasion, after receiving a letter detailing the 'most extreme poverty' of his mothers and sisters in Melbourne, Watmuff lived 'nearly … on dry bread' in order to send home £3.[58]

There were also instances of husbands and fathers on the Otago goldfields reneging on their responsibility to care for wives and children in Victoria. The Victorian government's lack of success in encouraging return migration from Otago undoubtedly contributed to this state of affairs. As an editorialist for the *Mount Alexander Mail* asserted: '[A]lmost every postmaster could tell of more than one pale and anxious woman, who trembling enquires for letters from New Zealand which never come, betray an unfathomed death of hopes deferred of and of silent sorrow … while she, perhaps, is struggling with poverty to maintain her offspring, their natural guardian is rejoicing in emancipation from irksome lives and sacred duties.'[59]

Whether through premeditation or the failed expectations of gold seekers, instances of abandoned wives requesting government aid were frequent.[60] In 1864 a Mrs Merrie of Collingwood, Victoria, left to care for her four children, was entirely dependent on government aid when her husband failed to send money for two years. The local mayor took up a collection to pay for the family's passage to Otago in order to track down the husband.[61] Wife desertion extended beyond the populace of the Victorian goldfields, however. Mrs Scott in Tasmania was forced to break stones for road-building in order to sustain herself and her six children when her husband, John Scott, did not send any money for a year. The governor's wife, Harriet Browne, paid for the family's passage to Otago. After Mrs Scott notified the Otago provincial government, a magistrate summoned Scott from the Dunstan to appear in court, where he saw his wife and children. The digger was ordered to take care of his family or pay them a weekly allowance of £1.0.[62] As one doctor in Hobart noted, the town's benevolent society was unable to care for the many families left destitute by breadwinners 'having gone to New Zealand'.[63] There were likely far more cases of abandonment that went unnoticed. For most prospectors, 'the only effective imperative to act upon their familial responsibilities was internalised'.[64]

The departure of kin also affected family members in emotional ways. Thomas Pierson, an aging American gold digger at Ballarat, was ill equipped to cope with the departure of his son Mason for Otago, alongside his wife's declining health and his ostracism by local residents because of the American Civil War. Although his son was away only six months, Thomas filled his diary with comments about absent letters, offering evidence that they were a poor emotional substitute when they did arrive. He remarked in his diary in January 1862: 'Frances and me alone in Australia, all of our relatives in America except Mason our son who is in N. Zealand about 1000 miles from here. It seems dreary – to be wandering as we wander here, so aimless dark and weary.'[65] On another occasion, he lamented: 'No bright spot to look upon nothing but sadness. Oh! That some oasis might come to our view in this our Desert life, some fragrant Savannah.'[66] Two weeks later, the situation was little improved: 'Several mails arrived from N. Zealand but they bring us no letters from Mason, which occasions us to feel very weary.'[67]

For those left behind in Victoria, the Otago exodus could be a moment of impoverishment and loneliness, revealing that there were two sides to what was a trans-Tasman event.[68] An account of the gold rushes in Otago needs to emphasise not only the societies, families and individuals left behind but also the societies and cultures formed within the political boundaries of Otago.[69] As I observe below, the impacts of the human tide that flowed to the Otago goldfields stretched beyond personal networks to upend the colony at the same time it transformed Otago. While Otago and Victorian colonists watched the flow of diggers alter their societies, the press in both places attempted to control the flow of knowledge about the goldfields.

Trans-Tasman Press Networks

The Otago gold rushes, like all of the rushes in the second half of the nineteenth century, only became possible during the age of steam power. The advent of the steamship and mechanised printing press constituted a 'conquest of distance' that quickened communication and pulled distant societies closer together.[70] These technologies also mediated the role of the Victorian press during the Otago rushes. When success often depended on being the first to arrive on a field, the gold rushes always magnified the importance of immediate and timely news. The volatility of the rushes also necessitated continuous coverage of a goldfield.

These factors combined to amplify the importance of the instantaneous and the regular because the gold seeker in Victoria could only hear from the diggings echoes a week old, the time it took for the Otago mail to arrive in Melbourne. News from the Otago goldfields in Victoria oscillated every week between feast and famine, with articles and commentary followed by a week of silence before the next steamship carrying the Otago mail arrived. Even after an individual decided to migrate to Otago, it could take him upwards of two weeks to collect supplies, travel to Melbourne, obtain a passage and more recent information, before finally travelling out to the diggings. Passage by sail extended the travel time to well over a month.[71] For many gold seekers arriving on the Otago diggings, the environment they found was generally very different from the one on which they had first based their decision to migrate. Many gold seekers booked a return passage to Victoria almost immediately after arriving at Port Chalmers.[72]

The Tasman Sea shaped the Otago rushes in another way. When the volatility of gold seeking gave preference to those procuring the timeliest knowledge, the Victorian newspapers were always at a disadvantage compared to the Otago press. Throughout the rushes, Victorian newspapers relied heavily on the Otago press for their coverage of the rushes but at the same time accused Otago papers of puffery. The Melbourne-based *Argus* and all of the goldfield newspapers regularly copied articles from Dunedin newspapers for the most current news from Otago.[73] Victoria was flooded with Otago newspapers: 349,715 issues arrived from Otago between 1862 and 1864.[74] Reading cultures in Victoria could also quickly swell a rush. For most gold seekers who depended on newspapers and correspondence, gaining knowledge about Otago was a social endeavour. As Alan Atkinson observes, colonial reading was done in homes, public houses and miners' institutes and on claims, with gold seekers often debating and discussing the merits of the Otago and Victorian diggings.[75] This is not to say that private information was not relevant; indeed, readers usually regarded it as more trustworthy. However, the need for rapid and regular news of gold discoveries when news was scarce gave the press a greater role in directing the flow of migrants than it did trans-oceanic migration, which relied to a marked extent on personal correspondence.[76]

The difficulty with newspaper accounts from gold-rush Otago was that they frequently did not present a single coherent message. In the first months of the Tuapeka rush, Julius Vogel's two papers, the *Otago Witness* and the *Otago Daily Times*, often gave contradictory messages to diggers when Vogel wanted to encourage a rush to Otago – only not too big and not too soon. Two months later, when some 7000 migrants had arrived in the province from Victoria, the Tuapeka diggings were filled beyond capacity; thousands of idle diggers rambled about Dunedin when no new diggings were discovered to rival Gabriel's Gully. Under these circumstances, the editors of the *Otago Daily Times* thought it necessary 'not to encourage such an invasion by any statement that may in the least degree give an erroneous or exaggerated impression of the extent and richness of our Gold Fields'. They then went on to state that the goldfields were much smaller than the richest Victorian diggings, and that 'it is decidedly unwise for miners who are doing well in Australia to leave for Otago'. The editors concluded by deflecting blame onto Australian merchants who were circulating 'an erroneous notion of our field'.[77] The opinion of the newspaper changed again in December 1861 when it stated that 'it is certain that Otago is now considerably under-populated'.[78]

Gold rushes always affected communities on both sides of a rush, and these inconsistent reports, and the exodus they caused, left their mark on the Victorian goldfields. Moreover, when the Victorian economy was entangled with the success of its own diggings, the impact of this Otago exodus reached far beyond the gold-seeking population. 'The fever has seized upon every one,' George Wakefield told his father in September 1861 from Ballarat. 'Publicans have left their Hotels, Storekeepers their shops and in fact all who are not fixed and can raise the money are off. 8,000 have already left and I believe 80,000 or more are prepared to swell the throng.'[79] That same month a correspondent in the *Mount Alexander Mail* warned that if the Otago diggings proved permanent, the Victorian goldfields 'will shrivel up with as rapid a decay as their growth was'.[80]

Amid the exodus for the Dunstan and Wakatipu goldfields the following year, an editorialist for the Melbourne *Age* again warned that Otago gold would unravel Victorian society: 'There is not a miner ... who will not be seized with an almost irresistible desire to migrate ... Bendigo, Ballarat, and the rest of the Victorian gold-fields will bewail the exodus of the stalwart industrious men who will have made them prosperous. In short, we are in for it ... The "diggers" ... will move by the thousands. The democratic element which has troubled Conservative politicians is clearing away ... it is vain attempting to control the torrent.'[81]

Local developments in Victoria, combined with the Dunstan and Lake District rushes, threatened to overwhelm the Victorian economy. By December 1862 virtually all goldfield shopkeepers and publicans were freezing orders in Melbourne, fearing a wholesale exodus to Otago.[82] At Bendigo the freeze had been immediately preceded by a drought that stagnated mining and plummeted prices; many stockholders decided to sell their livestock rather than continue to operate at a loss. When the Dunstan rush set in, prices for the scarce supply of food in Bendigo skyrocketed. Many diggers who remained on the field faced destitution as the cost of living mounted and employment evaporated.[83] 'The colony,' the *Bendigo Advertiser* lamented in 1863, 'is to let.'[84] When the Dunstan and Lake District rushes, drawing no more than 15,000 diggers from across Victoria, were able to cripple a goldfield with 30,000 inhabitants, they were clearly able to punch above Victoria's weight. The instability of the rushes constantly swung Victorian society between a surplus and a shortage of labour. In addition, the unpredictability of the rushes and the itinerancy of gold seekers seemed to amplify the impact on local communities of the smallest piece of information circulating about Otago. These factors magnified the role of the Victorian press in controlling and directing the flow of diggers to Otago.

In order to counteract what it deemed the 'hearsay gossip, of uncertain origin and conflicting character, which has found its way into Otago papers', about the Tuapeka rushes, the Melbourne *Argus* dispatched a correspondent to Dunedin in September 1861.[85] The picture of the Otago rushes the reporter presented was very different from the one filling the Otago newspapers. On the goldfields, prices were high, fuel was scarce and carriage difficult, which made gold 'hardly worth the trouble of a search'.[86] On another occasion the correspondent argued that the diggings were far more populated and parties' returns far smaller than the *Otago Daily Times* had assumed.[87] Dunedin was overflowing with diggers, who, unable to return to Victoria, were employed in government labour or simply doing nothing.[88] The *Argus* warned that the 'greed for intelligence' among gold seekers had caused the Otago press's 'injudicious publication [of material so false] to have emanated from the father of lies'.[89]

Alongside these press networks, the Victorian newspapers published private letters from Victorian prospectors in Otago, revealing an image of the province that contrasted strongly with the images in the Otago press. As elsewhere, newspapers in Victoria were profit-making enterprises, and their proprietors shared a vested interest in moulding knowledge about the rushes in a way that aligned with their own commercial interests.[90] In September 1861 William Mahay wrote from Dunedin that 'this is the worst place I ever was in. Everything on the diggings is very dear, and the road very bad. Tell anybody inquiring for news to stay where they are.'[91] The same day, the *Argus* wrote that two gold seekers had recently returned with news that hundreds of Victorian diggers were starving in Dunedin and unable to return to Victoria.[92] In February of the following year, the *Ballarat Star* carried a letter in which a digger warned that 'there is three times the amount of population on these diggings more than newspapers state'.[93] 'Dunedin,' one correspondent stated, 'is a very wretched place ... The streets are crowded with men looking the perfect pictures of misery.'[94] An even greater evil, a gold seeker argued, were its colonists: 'Maoris in open warfare would not matter, but to have to put up with religious Scotchmen is too much.'[95] Another group of diggers put it more bluntly: 'Those chaps are asses.'[96] The *Witness* fought back. In October 1861 it stated that it was the Victorian rather than the Otago press that manipulated gold seekers with misinformation:

> The extraordinary effect of our Gold Fields is to be found in the tone and style of the [Victorian] press, which has endeavoured to pooh-pooh the whole affair ... endeavouring to persuade its readers that the state of Otago is so frightful, that no one should venture to go there ... Now the fact is that we have avoided, as far as it is possible, giving any exaggerated reports. We have carefully weeded the information that has been given us ... and any stories of extraordinary finds which were not fully confirmed by the most satisfactory evidence we have invariably omitted.[97]

Six months later the situation was little improved. The editor of the *Otago Witness* argued that the *Argus* desired, above all, 'to depreciate Otago in the eyes of the world. Pretending to take a friendly interest in the progress of the new gold country ... the *Argus* yet lets no occasion slip that offers the le[a]st opportunity for disparaging its resources or throwing doubt upon the permanence of its prosperity.'[98] In 1863 the *Daily Telegraph* argued that all those who returned to Victoria were 'drunk and disorderly [and] hate a well-run police' and the Victorian press was willing to publish their accounts 'no matter how reliable'.[99] The paper stressed confidence, however, that 'the thousand and one letters from the scum of those who have visited these shores – the persistent exaggeration in editorials, and the "write to order" misrepresentations of "Our Own Correspondent", have failed to cover with disfavour the Gold Fields of this Province'.[100] On another occasion in 1861, the *Otago Daily Times* contended that 'the Victorian journals indulge in a lot of absurd attempts to run Otago down. According to them our goldfields are unproductive, of no extent, and not likely to be long-lived. The more gold there is found, the more vehemently they repeat their assertions.'[101]

The one thing that the Otago and Victorian newspapers could agree on was the power of the press to determine the movements of gold seekers. As Aled Jones and Mark Hampton argue, nineteenth-century newspaper editors shared a confidence

Veterans of Victorian quartz mines at the Day Dawn quartz crusher mill, Bannockburn, c. 1888.

Courtesy Cromwell Museum collection

in their ability to shape understanding of the world.[102] Time and again, editors in Victoria and Otago found that confidence deserved. An immediate rush to Otago often followed the publication in newspapers of new finds or higher yields. In 1862, upon publishing news that had arrived in the Otago mail about gold found on the Molyneux, the *Bendigo Advertiser* stated that 'the rush [to the Dunstan] is as certain to set in this day as the sun is to rise'.[103] In 1861 Charles Clifford rushed to Gabriel's Gully upon reading about the discovery in the *Otago Witness*.[104] William Wright and John Martin wrote in 1862 that the *Otago Daily Times* duped them into believing payable gold was widespread on the Dunstan. On at least one occasion, however, newspaper editors held back knowledge. In December 1861 a Dunedin colonist complained that the Victorian press refused to publish his favourable letter about Otago. He believed that 'had it comprised a series of disasters, deaths, starvations, &c., it would of course have been published with "comments", and a separate paragraph to draw attention to it'.[105]

In a way, this exchange was not simply an inter-colonial debate but a trans-Tasman one; editors and press correspondents in Otago often travelled from Victoria with prospectors rushing after gold. Julius Vogel, who previously had served as the editor of the *Maryborough and Dunolly Advertiser* and the *Inglewood and Sandy Creek Advertiser*, also recruited most of his staff from Victoria.[106] The paper constantly jockeyed with Victorian periodicals for the attention of the trans-Tasman group of gold seekers who migrated between Victoria and Otago. The manner in which the Victorian and Otago presses helped shape the flow of information about the goldfields meant that the Otago rushes always existed at any moment in the spaces between these two accounts.

Conclusion

The Otago rushes depended on public knowledge of them circulated in Victoria, which placed the events between the accounts contained in the Victorian and Otago newspapers. In his study of European migration, Dirk Hoerder observes that most images of emigrant destinations circulating in sending communities tended to be positive because those writing home were often the successful or those wanting to justify their decision to migrate.[107] In Victoria, however, the proximity of the Otago diggings and the continual flow of migrants across the Tasman flooded the colony with both negative and positive accounts from Otago, giving the prospective digger a multitude of contradictory images of the province's goldfields.

Gold seekers struggled to make sense of this cacophony of information as the rushes overwhelmed societies in both Otago and Victoria, and yet many 'wanted so much to believe that their normal scepticism dropped away'.[108] While there were many prospectors who criticised the Otago press for 'puffing up' its goldfields, thousands of diggers abandoned claims the moment favourable news of Otago arrived. The 'new, the exceptional, or the large [always captured] the imagination' of diggers and lent the province its 'magnetic qualities'.[109]

When the flow of knowledge from Otago to Victoria fuelled migration, these trans-Tasman networks became self-perpetuating. The migration of consumers extended Victorian commercial networks to Otago; a web of shipping firms, carters and shopkeepers transported goods from Melbourne and sold them to Victorians on river flats and in crevices across Central Otago. Meanwhile, the volume of the population flows allowed Victorian goldfield networks to be mapped onto Otago at the same time that the province's relative proximity to loved ones and acquaintances in Victoria allowed individuals to maintain relationships that were 'neither here nor there, but in both [localities] simultaneously'.[110] The Otago rushes were, in many ways, a series of events in the history of Victoria.

4.

'If I Was Not Here, I Would Not Come Here Now': The Tuapeka gold rush, 1861–62

Terry J. Hearn

MOST ACCOUNTS OF OTAGO's gold rushes assume that the influxes of 1861 to 1863 blended seamlessly one into the other and that waves of men infused with a sense of liberation, keen expectation, adventure and hope of instant wealth swept up the river valleys and gorges and across the hills of Central Otago. That an initial surge of enthusiasm and expectation often gave way to dismay and retreat rates barely a mention.[1] Alone, Vincent Pyke noted that after the influx of miners during September 1861, 'a feverish reactionary movement' had set in and that new arrivals being 'insufficiently provided for the purpose … [had] hurriedly returned [from the Tuapeka] to the familiar streets of Dunedin'.[2] Although data relating to population flows to and gold production from the Tuapeka goldfield are rudimentary, they do offer insights into the timing and scale of that 'reactionary movement'. Together with letters written by miners who participated in the rush to Gabriel's Gully and reports prepared by newspaper correspondents, they suggest a rather different picture from that usually presented.[3]

Discovery and Influx: June–September 1861

The available data suggest that the Tuapeka rush (defined here as June 1861 to July 1862) might usefully be subdivided into four sub-periods: discovery and influx, June to September 1861; crisis and efflux, October and November 1861; renewed inflow and consolidation, December to January 1862; and renewed efflux and contraction, February to July 1862.

The circumstances surrounding Gabriel Read's May 1861 discovery of gold, 'shining like the stars in Orion on a dark frosty night', have been well established.[4] By the end of the first week in July, some 400 persons were on the field.[5] A few days later around 1000 miners were present, and by the end of July 2000, 1300 of whom were in Gabriel's Gully and the balance in Munro's and Wetherston's gullies.[6] Already the

This depiction of Gabriel's Gully in 1861 appeared in the *Otago Witness*, 31 May 1921.

highly sought-after ground along the watercourse that flowed through Gabriel's Gully had been occupied: from the hills enclosing Gabriel's Gully an early visitor described 'the glittering watchfires streaming more than a mile in one continuous line, gracefully following its windings and glistening like glow-worms on the bank'.[7] T.B. Gillies, who arrived on the field early in July, noted that later arrivals had to select claims up the sides of the gully.[8] 'The best claims having water frontage are occupied,' noted another, 'and a hungry horde, still with good rich ground, is behind, clamorous for water advantages.'[9]

By the end of July 1861 it was apparent that not all miners were doing well: reports surfaced of a lack of suitable ground for mining, inexperienced and ill-equipped miners, widely varying returns, sickness, high living costs, frost, scarcity of fuel and 'indescribable mud'. A small return flow to Dunedin had begun, while the movement to Gabriel's Gully slowed until miners started arriving from elsewhere in New Zealand. Few details of coastwise arrivals are available. Returns prepared by Dunedin Customs indicate that for the quarter ended September 1861 there were 1596 arrivals, including 1519 adult males (Graph 4.1). Although the data probably understate the number of arrivals (while taking no account of those who made their way overland), they do suggest that the 'New Zealand' component of the influx was comparatively modest.

News of Gabriel Read's discovery reached Melbourne during July 1861, at first

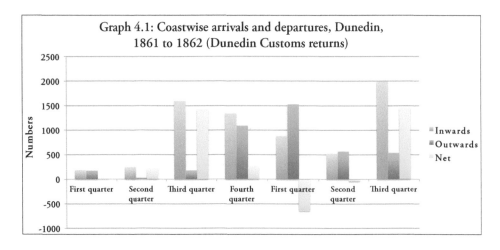

Graph 4.1: Coastwise arrivals and departures, Dunedin, 1861 to 1862 (Dunedin Customs returns)

through private letters and subsequently through press reports. The glowing accounts offered by the former were sufficient to encourage mining 'companies' to assess the prospects of the new field. The *Oscar*, which arrived in Dunedin on 27 August, carried many miners from Ballarat who had been deputed to test the ground, secure claims if warranted and possible, and report to their colleagues.[10] The Victorian press, however, invoked the spectre of the 'duffer rushes' of Canoona (1858) and Kiandra (1859), pointing to the field's limited extent, the allegedly shallow nature of the ground, ruinously high living costs, cold winters, scarcity of fuel and Otago's 'imperfect settlement', by which was meant the limited alternative employment prospects. Such strictures were in vain: 'rush-sickness' or 'Otagomania' set in, despite predictions that many would return from Otago duped, disappointed and disheartened.

Three sets of data offer some insights into the influx from the Australian colonies. The first are those published by the Victorian Government. Graph 4.2 sets out the data

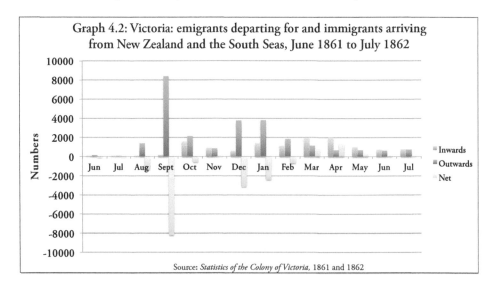

Graph 4.2: Victoria: emigrants departing for and immigrants arriving from New Zealand and the South Seas, June 1861 to July 1862

Source: *Statistics of the Colony of Victoria*, 1861 and 1862

for all departures for and arrivals from New Zealand (largely Otago) and the South Seas (largely adult males). The surge in the number of departures during August and especially September is clear: 1378 persons departed in the former and 8377 in the latter month, with adult males comprising 95.1 per cent of the August and 98.3 per cent of the September outflows. The sharp contraction during October and November was followed by a new surge in departures during December 1861 and January 1862. The numbers recorded in the statistical registers of the colony of Victoria accord closely with those given by the second source of data, with the exception of the peak month of September 1861, for which a difference of 439 persons appears between the two estimates.

The second set of data comes from the *Passenger Lists – Victoria Australia Outwards to New Zealand*.[11] Anecdotal evidence suggests there was considerable under-recording of departures, and the lists did not include stowaways, whose numbers were often considerable. Nevertheless, Graph 4.3 depicts gross arrivals for the period from January 1861 to July 1862. The peak inflow was in September 1861, after which the number of arrivals contracted sharply until a renewed inflow occurred during the summer months of December 1861 and January 1862. Thereafter, the number of arrivals declined steadily.

To establish the structure and composition of the inflow, I drew a random sample of 1742 persons. Males made up 90.5 per cent of the inflow, but the gender balance changed through the period as a whole: while females constituted 0.8 per cent of the

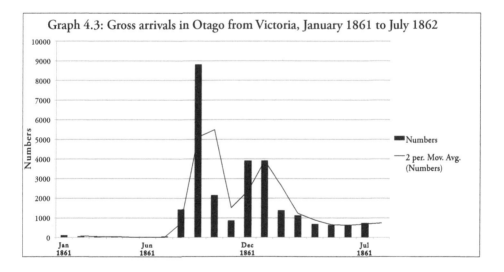

September inflow, they constituted 6.3 per cent of the October and 12.5 per cent of the November inflows. As the total inflow quickened again during December 1861, the proportion fell sharply to 3.8 per cent, only to rise as the total inflow slowed once more from February through to July, exceeding a quarter in each month between March and July 1862 inclusive, and reaching as high as 45.0 per cent in May 1862. In short, the peak monthly inflows were markedly male dominated, with females making up a significant proportion of the inflows in the following months.

With respect to age (Graph 4.4), 78.4 per cent of the males fell into the age range 20 to 34 years, there being a dearth of both young and adolescent boys and older males.[12] The Otago discoveries proved immensely attractive to this young, energetic and mobile segment of Victoria's population. Some 91 per cent of all male arrivals were single.

The evidence suggests that those who arrived in Otago were not, as a group, as experienced in mining or the likely attendant hazards as is often supposed. It also seems likely that many had not had opportunity to accumulate the financial resources

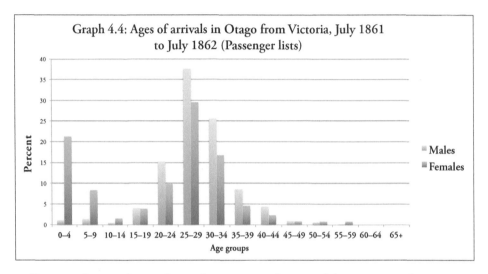

Graph 4.4: Ages of arrivals in Otago from Victoria, July 1861 to July 1862 (Passenger lists)

sufficient to finance the purchase of equipment, the cost of the voyage, and sustenance (especially during a period of high inflation) as they endeavoured to secure claims, open the ground, and extract gold. Indeed, it is clear that many miners borrowed or otherwise secured money from diverse sources to finance their 'Otago adventure'.

The third source of data was the returns of arrivals at and departures from the Port of Dunedin collected by Customs and published on a quarterly basis for 1861 and a monthly basis for 1862.[13] Graphs 4.5 and 4.6 set out all adult male arrivals and all arrivals from the Australian colonies by quarter. Of the 5595 who arrived in the third quarter of 1861, 5391 were adult males, as were 10,326 of the 10,738 who arrived in the fourth quarter. The total for the six months of 15,717 was smaller by 1448 than the 17,165 recorded by the Victorian outwards passenger lists as departing for Otago, that number representing the very much smaller inflows from Tasmania and New South Wales. Thus, Otago, with an estimated December 1860 population of fewer than 13,000 people, experienced a large and rapid increase, mostly of young single men intent upon finding a fortune in what was generally acknowledged to be a field of limited extent in a remote location largely bereft of timber, firewood, shelter and supplies.

Many explanations were advanced for the apparent propensity of Victorians to sell or abandon 'paying' claims and stake all on Gabriel's Gully. While love of adventure, credulity and the machinations of the shippers were cited, it is likely that declining claim yields, a shift to capital-intensive mining, falling real wages, unemployment,

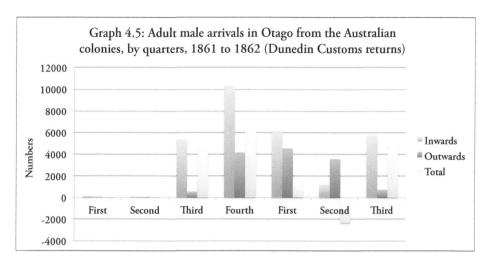

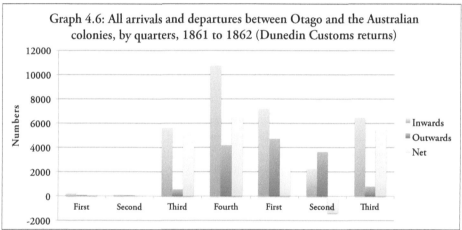

resistance to wage dependency, limited alternative employment opportunities for displaced miners and resistance to the arrival of Chinese miners all played their part.[14] For many, Read's discovery stirred memories of a simpler era: '[W]hen a decent competence could be obtained by much luck and a little labor in a month, and knocked down at the nearest public-house in a week by dint of much drinking and of more "shouting". Those were mad times, and the memory of them rankles in the mind of many a man who misused his opportunities then, and flatters himself that he would make a better use of them could they but come back again.'[15]

Few heeded warnings that most of the likely profitable ground would have long been secured. Men allowed themselves to be lured by the prospect of immediate returns; small claims which promised liberal access; low costs of entry in the form of simple (and easily transportable) equipment, elementary shelter, and a miner's right for £1.0 per person for 12 months; simple regulations that rewarded those with initiative and courage and willing to take risks; and the prospect of self-regulation in the form of elected mining boards.

In addition, no restrictions were imposed on the right to sell claims or shares in claims, and thus on the prospect of substantial capital gain or on the right (subject to a duty of 2s-6d per troy ounce) to export gold.[16] Essentially, the institutional arrangements familiar to Victoria's miners were replicated in Otago because of their emphasis on the law of capture, opportunities for small producers, ease of entry, clearly defined rules governing mining, procedures for dispute resolution, legal certainty and political stability. Moreover, there was no landed elite that might have obstructed prospecting or taxed miners: land held under pastoral licence was Crown land and therefore open for prospecting and mining.

Crisis and Efflux: October–November 1861

During the fourth quarter of 1861, 10,326 adult males arrived from the Australian colonies, but 4151 returned, a sharp increase over the 549 who had done so during the previous quarter. Although there was a net increase of 6175 adult males, a sharp reversal in the migratory tide clearly had occurred. In addition, the inflow of adult males from elsewhere in New Zealand slowed from 1519 during the third quarter to 1171 during the fourth quarter, while the number of departures rose from 154 to 862.

The return flow across the Tasman began in earnest during September, even as the inflow from the Australian colonies quickened. Some new arrivals were dismayed when greeted with shouts of 'Duffer' and 'Port Curtis' from departing miners lining the rails of the ships making their way down Otago Harbour to Taiaroa Head. Several of the miners who arrived on the diggings during August did procure good claims, but by early September it was clear that most of the best ground had been secured. On 7 September 1861 Commissioner Strode reported to the province's superintendent that the expected imminent influx from Victoria rendered the discovery of new ground 'indispensable'.[17] By the middle of the month, miners on the diggings were privately reporting that a 'crisis' was developing: it was plain that there was insufficient ground to support the thousands already congregated. Many miners offered their tools for sale, resorted to fossicking or begging for food, or returned to that 'most wretched place', Dunedin.

As the anticipated crisis developed on the diggings, a sense of trepidation emerged in Dunedin as the town, already anxious that 'the mob expected down from the diggings' would raid stores for food, awaited an influx from Victoria. Thousands of young men, those arriving infused with eager expectation and those returning from the diggings loud in bitter disappointment, were expected to prove difficult to manage. Even Gabriel Read expressed the hope that 'something could be done to keep back the Victorian hordes'.[18] When Charles Money arrived in Dunedin early in September, he recorded that the town was 'filled with some thousands of men and the most lugubrious of reports were in circulation … the scarcity of gold was loudly proclaimed by most of those who had returned from the diggings.'[19] Many wired home for their return fares.

From Mount Stuart ('Mount Hard Struggle' to the miners) on 16 September, Thomas Murray raised concern over 'a crisis which may be pending … I see hundreds toiling on to the diggings each day, while numbers are returning begging for bread, having, in the hope of success, remained at the diggings and spent their last farthing.'[20]

On 23 September a 'Victorian' delegation pressed upon the superintendent its view that Victorian miners collectively were 'decidedly disappointed': it urged the government to allow miners to pitch tents on Crown lands, to cut firewood from the Dunedin Town Belt and to provide large tents or 'slight buildings' for new arrivals.

The next day, placards were erected indicating where tents could be pitched. Subsequently, the government purchased 50 'military' tents, ordered the construction of a temporary building next to the immigration barracks, induced the captains of the *Lightning* and *Empress of the Sea* to remain in port so that as many diggers who wanted to do so could return to Australia, and made available a small sum to 'facilitate' the return of those without means.[21] The *Lightning* had arrived off Taiaroa Head on 24 September with 703 passengers on board. It departed a week later with 263.

On 28 September the provincial government decided to offer temporary employment on public works in an effort to meet what the superintendent later termed 'a pressing emergency', and issued a proclamation intended to slow the trans-Tasman influx.[22] By mid-October some 650 men were employed. The government also requested troops. A 110-strong contingent of the 70th Regiment arrived on 10 November. After parading through the streets, they set up camp adjacent to the miners' 'canvas town'.

On arriving in Dunedin towards the end of September, one miner recorded that 'we saw hundreds of people – the town seemed literally crammed with people loitering about with their swags, evidently not knowing what to do'.[23] Hundreds of miners, the Melbourne *Argus* reported, had congregated in the town, 'straining every nerve to get back to Victoria'.[24] Dunedin, claimed another miner, 'is a mass of people. A great number were coming down [from Gabriel's Gully] and a great number [were] afraid to stir. There are hundreds going up that do not know the consequences, and hundreds coming back that know the difference.' Another recorded, on 4 October, that Dunedin was 'densely thronged with hungry, anxious men and, from both the sea and the mines, their numbers are constantly and rapidly increasing to the alarm of the people and to the consternation of the storekeepers, and many fear – not without reason – that the town will be rushed.' Some made it clear that they would not starve even if it took 'some act that will give us gaol food'.[25] The *Lyttelton Times* correspondent was 'struck … by the hundreds of men who are tramping the streets' and reported that many residents feared riots.[26]

From 'The Camp outside Dunedin' on 14 October, J.L.S. Keen claimed that of the hundreds arriving each week, 'one half of them go back by the same ships, if they can possibly scrape money enough together; twenty out of each hundred of the other half having funds push on; and what do the rest do, those who have no funds? Why, they wander about the streets day after day, and are actually starving.'[27] Some did make their way to the diggings. 'Dear Brother,' wrote one miner, 'I am compelled to go up to the diggings for I have not the means of returning. I may as well suffer there as to remain in the town.' Even some of Dunedin's merchants began to advocate caution, advising their Melbourne counterparts that 'unless new ground is rapidly opened by the experienced hands arriving, there is no room for the numbers threatened'.[28]

In letters home, miners complained of soaring living costs, over-crowding, crude sanitation and sickness; a shortage of firewood and consequent lack of warmth and cooked food; the limited area of auriferous ground and its early 'monopolisation'; frequent and costly duffer rushes; and, in Dunedin, bigotry and intolerance on the part of residents.

The influx contracted sharply during October, and the decision of many to return to Victoria saw the tensions ease. Many men had arrived with minimal capital, equipment and supplies, and had come in the expectation of immediately finding gold or securing paid employment. A trickle of miners returning to Melbourne during September quickly swelled. The *Aldinga* returned on 24 September 1861 with 65 'disappointed wanderers';[29] some 100 arrived back on the *Oscar* a few days later. Widely regarded as the advance guard of the main body to follow, they offered 'not only a desponding but a despairing account of the state of affairs there'.[30] The *Argus* claimed that during October 2471 miners retuned to Victoria from Otago, among them many 'really practical miners who had tried and failed'.[31] As far as the Victorian press was concerned, 'The nine days' wonder' was over.[32] The rush to Otago, claimed the *Argus*, 'has passed into the limbo of exploded delusions'. The paper also noted that the Victorian government was being pressed to assist an estimated 5000 Victorian miners stranded in Otago to return, much as it had intervened in the Port Curtis rush to rescue men from the consequences of their 'infatuated folly'.[33]

Renewed inflow: December 1861 and January 1862

The panic of October and November was followed during December 1861 and January 1862 by a modest revival in the number of adult males arriving from the Australian colonies. The proximate reason lay in the opening of the Waipori goldfield, some 22 kilometres east of Lawrence. Graph 4.7 sets out the escort returns for the period from July 1861 to July 1862. The information in it suggests that the peak of production was reached in early November, that is, following the September influx and the opening of the Waitahuna field, south of Lawrence, in that same month. Part of the reason for the large jump in the mid-November return lay in the earlier inability of the newly opened Waitahuna field's storekeepers to purchase all the gold offered, and the absence of any banks in the district. It is also possible that miners who elected to participate in the duffer Blue Mountain rush disposed of their gold before departing in pursuit of Sam Perkins.[34]

After the mid-November peak, the quantity of gold brought down by escort declined more or less steadily through to July 1862: the decline apparent in January was attributed to 'the festive season' and to 'the extremely unpropitious state of the weather' and the resulting 'heavy and destructive floods' that afflicted the goldfields during the first week of the new year.[35] The exhaustion of the superficial deposits, the later short winter days, frozen ground, frozen watercourses and generally inclement weather were blamed for the continuing declines, together with the contraction in the number of people on the goldfields to about 7000 by July 1862. The returns from Tuapeka for the month of July 1862 were just 16.6 per cent of those recorded for January 1862, and for Waitahuna 20.9 per cent. The June 1862 return for Waipori was 12.7 per cent of that recorded six months earlier.

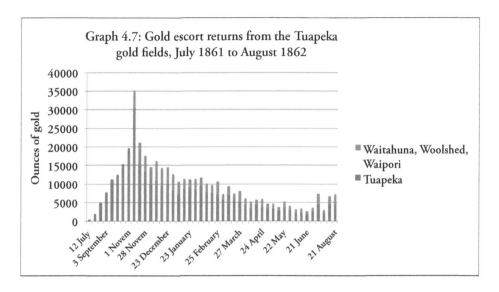

Graph 4.7: Gold escort returns from the Tuapeka gold fields, July 1861 to August 1862

Escort returns understate the true level of production because a good deal of gold was brought to Dunedin by private hand: the returns of gold exported offer a better indication, although it is not clear whether gold 'exported' to other centres in New Zealand was included. Graph 4.8 sets out the quantity of gold exported from Dunedin from August 1861 to July 1862. As gold escort returns reached their peak in November 1861, so did exports. Monthly exports then declined slowly until February 1862 when they contracted sharply through to July 1862. The sole exception was May, when exports rose, in all likelihood because of the substantial return flow of miners to Victoria during the preceding month. Gold exports in July 1862 were just 23.7 per cent of their November 1861 peak.

The inflow of 10,326 adult males from the Australian colonies during the last quarter of 1861 was offset by the departure of 4151, thus leaving a net gain of 6175. The 3284 who arrived during January 1862 resulted in a net gain of 1984. Although young single

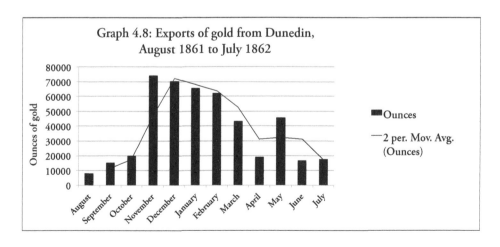

Graph 4.8: Exports of gold from Dunedin, August 1861 to July 1862

males still dominated the inflow from the Australian colonies, the character of the immigrant stream had changed. Table 4.1 sets out the number of adult female arrivals per 100 males: most notable are the very low ratios in the third and fourth quarters of 1861, the sharp increase in the second quarter of 1862 and the sharp contraction during the succeeding quarter. The third quarter of 1862 included September and thus reflected the sharp increase in arrivals that followed the Dunstan discovery. The number of children per 100 adult females did not exhibit the same variability: the low ratio suggests that the arrivals constituted families in the first stages of the family life cycle.

Table 4.1: Adult females per 100 males, and children per 100 adult females, arrivals from Australian colonies in Otago, by quarter, 1861 to 1862

Quarters	Adult females per 100 adult males	Children per 100 adult females
First 1861	37.32	41.51
Second 1861	15.66	84.62
Third 1861	2.13	77.39
Fourth 1861	2.37	68.16
First 1862	9.54	76.79
Second 1862	44.68	85.82
Third 1862	7.39	71.69

Source of data: *Otago Witness*, 4 January 1862, p.3; *Otago Daily Times*, 19 September 1862, p. 6, and 6 October 1862, p. 4.

Table 4.2 sets out the same information by month for 1862. The lift in the ratio began in February 1862 and continued through to June of that year before contracting: the influx of arrivals from the Australian colonies in December and January was followed by a pronounced change in the inflow's gender balance. The available evidence suggests that the women and children were largely the families of miners. The data drawn from the passenger lists confirm the change in the gender balance of the inflow and indicate that 56.1 per cent of female arrivals were 20–34 years of age and 55 per cent were married. Most of these women either arrived alone, that is, with neither husband nor children, or with children only, and most of the nuclear family units were those in which the wife was under 45 years of age and childless, or those in which all children in the family were under 10 years of age. In other words, many couples had only recently married and had yet to start a family or had not long embarked on family formation.

Given the close relationship between the number of miners and gold recovered in this labour-intensive phase of the industry, the fact that the modest influx during December and January did not result in an appreciable lift in escort returns is interesting. Indeed, there was a marked decline in March and April 1862, exactly when an increase might have been expected. The evidence is clear that a good many made their way to the Waipori diggings. By early January 1862 some 2000 miners were on the field, distributed along the banks of the Lammerlaw Creek and the Waipori River,

Table 4.2: Adult females per 100 adult males, and children per 100 adult females, arrivals from Australian colonies in Otago, January to August 1862

Months	Adult females per 100 adult males	Children per 100 adult females
January	4.72	67.74
February	11.61	80.30
March	20.50	79.82
April	44.37	81.74
May	44.26	93.83
June	45.79	83.82
July	24.44	68.18
August	20.32	74.07

Source of data: *Otago Witness*, 4 January 1862, p.3; *Otago Daily Times*, 19 September 1862, p. 6, and 6 October 1862, p. 4.

and some 3000 by the end of March.[36] The escort returns from that field showed a modest lift during the period from January to March 1862.

Others among the new arrivals joined mates who had secured good claims. From the outset there had been considerable 'churn' within the mining population as a keen trade in claims and shares attested. Many of the first arrivals, the Otagonians, having extracted the most accessible gold from gully-floor claims and in anticipation of the coming winter, sold out and invested their newly acquired wealth in land, farms and assorted business ventures.[37]

The decline in production also reflected major changes in the industry. As it became plain that much of the early mining had been haphazard and inefficient and that the ground warranted reworking, many miners became engaged in preparations for a greatly expanded scale of operation in the form of sluicing, deep sinking and cement crushing. In February and July 1862, the provincial government amended the mining regulations in an effort to foster investment. Improved mining appliances were introduced, with numerous applications being lodged during the early months of 1862 for permission to erect puddling machines.[38] Because these machines and hill sluicing of less remunerative ground required water, some miners invested in the construction of lengthy water races to tap into regular, reliable and sufficient but distant water supplies: applications for water rights rose accordingly. Such changes generated conflict between the 'hill sluicers' and the 'gully miners', culminating in threats, petitions and legal action during August 1862.

By early May 1862 the Gabriel's sluicing parties who had completed their races were about to commence operations, while in June 1862 the *Otago Daily Times* reported that a party of miners at Waipori was about to begin hydraulic sluicing as 'adopted in California with extraordinary success'.[39] Other parties formed specialised water-supply companies to supply miners. Friction developed between these suppliers and miners: the latter raised the spectre of monopolies and price gouging, while others claimed they were being deprived of water altogether. The preparatory work for sluicing on what was described as 'a gigantic scale' continued into the autumn and winter months.[40] Some of these races required very substantial investment and large numbers of men working for long distances over rugged country (using tunnels, viaducts and fluming) to deliver water at a height sufficient to command the supposedly auriferous ground.[41]

Renewed Efflux: February 1862 to July 1862

Neither the opening of the Waipori field, the purchase of existing claims nor employment in race construction was sufficient to hold the thousands of miners congregated on the Tuapeka goldfield. A net increase in the number of adult male arrivals from the Australian colonies of 1984 in January 1862 fell to just 56 in February and turned into a net loss of 2771 over the next four months. Graphs 4.9 and 4.10 set out the monthly gross and net flows between Dunedin and the Australian colonies for both adult males and for all arrivals. The outflow during March included small flows to the Coromandel, the Buller River, British Columbia (Canada) and the Lachlan diggings in New South Wales.

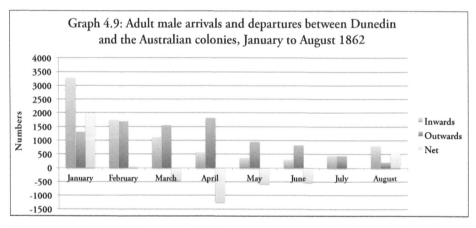

Graph 4.9: Adult male arrivals and departures between Dunedin and the Australian colonies, January to August 1862

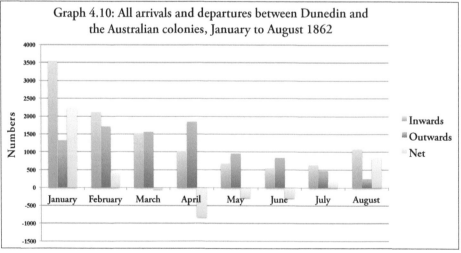

Graph 4.10: All arrivals and departures between Dunedin and the Australian colonies, January to August 1862

By the end of March Tuapeka's population had declined by about one third on its early January numbers. Some miners had given up hope of striking 'pile claims', while others had wearied of working claims that proved to be 'stringers', profitless fossicking and participating in fruitless rushes, or had abandoned efforts to buy into the relatively small numbers of existing and remunerative claims. The provincial government assisted local prospecting associations to mount prospecting expeditions or directly financed such ventures, all without dramatic result. Many more miners set out privately to prospect in 'far out of the way places'; run holders and station hands occasionally stumbled across them in lonely gullies or discovered traces of their recent presence.

In Dunedin, merchants and storekeepers began to struggle: overstocking on the expectation that the summer inflow would continue resulted in fierce competition, falling margins, wavering property values and rising debt defaults. Fears of a commercial collapse emerged; one miner predicted that Dunedin 'will soon fall into its natural lifeless state'. On the diggings, most miners remained 'cribbed, cabined, and confined' to the main gullies on the Tuapeka from where Charles Dillon conceded, in February 1862, that 'I have perpetrated a great folly … and paid the penalty in loss of time, money, and health.'

As winter approached, miners privately and publicly expressed anxiety over rising living and heating costs and unworkable ground. Typhus, typhoid fever and dysentery began to take their toll, together with deaths from suicide, exposure, drowning and claim collapses.[42] The Otagonians' departure during the autumn persuaded some Victorians to spend the winter in Dunedin. However, many more, believing that discretion was the better part of valour where Otago's winter was concerned, returned to Melbourne. Some, it was reported, took 'considerable earnings' and had in mind 'knock[ing] some of it down in Melbourne'.[43]

The Returns for Miners

Underlying all the movements of miners were the returns of gold won. Unfortunately, systematic data do not appear to be available, while calculations of average earnings based on estimates of the number of miners and of total gold yield are inherently unreliable.[44] It does seem reasonably clear that the prime rewards were secured by those first on the field – men whose initiative and enterprise were protected by the field's comparative isolation and who could thus prospect, select and mine ground for some months before the influx from Australia materialised. Early in October 1861 one of the original parties recovered 19 pound-weight of gold, each of the five partners having already 'cleared upwards' of £1500 from the same claim.[45]

One source *may* convey some insights, namely, the lists of miners departing for the Australian colonies that were published from time to time together with the quantity of gold each took. Details are available for 679 miners who departed between December 1861 and June 1862: they took 17,555 ounces, or an average 25.85 troy ounces, while the median was 18 troy ounces. The average declined after January 1862, reflecting possibly declining yields and/or difficult mining conditions as winter advanced. The miners were not a randomly selected sample, so whether their earnings were in any way representative is not clear: it is also assumed that the amounts taken represented each man's net earnings. Nevertheless, Table 4.3 suggests that most miners enjoyed only modest success for what is assumed to have been at least several weeks' work. Modest returns were almost certainly the single most important reason for the departure of so many during the months leading up to the outbreak of the rush to Central Otago, which began in August 1862.

Table 4.3: Average 'earnings' of miners leaving for the Australian colonies, December 1861 to June 1862

Period	Number of miners	Average gold taken: ounces	Range
December 1861	115	27.20	14dwt to 255.11oz
January 1862	132	33.78	10dwt to 384.00oz
March 1862	60	23.66	8dwt to 118.00oz
April 1862	199	23.46	4dwt to 196.00oz
May 1862	54	18.28	8dwt to 108.00oz
June 1862	119	24.30	4dwt to 266.00oz
Total	**679**	**25.85**	

Source: 'Exports', *Otago Daily Times* issues across the dates specified.

Conclusion

In his review of Philip May's *The West Coast Gold Rushes*, Patrick O'Farrell draws attention to 'the harsh other side of the goldrush coin. The rushes,' he notes, 'established a pattern of boom, exploitation, and decay, of drift, insecurity and misery.'[46] The short account in this present chapter of the Tuapeka rush, by drawing on various statistical series, miners' letters, and the accounts of a range of observers, lends weight to that assessment. Many nineteenth-century rushes, including Tuapeka, involved a measure of significant overreach, defying the old adage that where gold is concerned, predictions should extend no further than the end of a miner's pick. That many miners suffered loss, hardship and suffering is incontestable. That Dunedin came near to serious civil unrest during late September and October 1861 is clear. Romanticised accounts of the rushes scarcely do justice to the courage and enterprise displayed, to the dangers, privation and hardships to which miners were exposed, the disappointments that so many endured, and the meagre to modest returns that most were obliged to accept.

5.

Populism, Parochialism and Public Works: Politics on the Otago goldfields from the 1860s to the 1880s

John Angus

In 1877 Vincent Pyke, Member of the House of Representatives (MHR) for the Dunstan electorate, found himself in considerable political strife. Chairman of the new Vincent County Council, he was caught in a dispute between residents in the small settlements of Clyde and Cromwell over which town would be the county seat. The matter was one of some moment. Gaining the county seat would have advantages for the chosen town. There would be building work for the new offices, jobs on the county payroll, and money to be made in serving the councillors' needs. Best of all, there would be easy access to those giving out county works contracts.[1]

Pyke was heavily entangled in the dispute, despite his efforts to avoid it by presenting himself to both sides as if in their support. During his successful efforts to secure a seat on the council for a riding near Cromwell, Pyke had implied – if not explicitly promised – to the Cromwell business leaders who organised his campaign that he would vote for Cromwell as the county town. Clyde residents, however, assumed that his personal ties with their town, where he lived, would ensure its selection. Pyke did nothing to dissuade them from that view. Both towns lobbied hard. In Cromwell, a deputation saw Pyke and then declared that he had promised to support their town. Clyde leaders held a banquet for the councillors to mark their first meeting in the town. According to one report, the drinking and eating started at 4.00 pm and lasted until midnight, when 'the company broke up fully satisfied with themselves, and apparently with the world'.[2] But Pyke's strategy was about to unravel at the meeting the next day.

The council had eight members, four from southern ridings and four from northern ridings, with the latter including Pyke's. Pyke had earlier been elected council chairman. At the meeting, members proposed Clyde as the county town. Amendments in favour of Cromwell and Ophir were defeated, and an attempt to defer consideration ruled out of order. When the original motion for Clyde was put forward, the four southern members voted for it, and the four northern members, including Pyke, against. Then

Pyke, as chairman, gave his casting vote the opposite way. Clyde won the day – five votes to four.

Pyke's action was marked down as treachery in Cromwell. The residents were furious. The *Otago Daily Times* correspondent in the town reported:

> As soon as the news reached Cromwell and received the requisite confirmation, the utmost excitement prevailed. Business was suspended, and, as if an earthquake had occurred, everyone was in the street and many and deep were the imprecations upon the delinquent's head. Ultimately an effigy of Mr Pyke was suspended from the flagstaff of the Town Hall, with one of the gloved hands behind his back, palm upwards. The brass band played The Rogue's March and some willing hands finally cast this effigy into the River Clutha, when it was observed that on this occasion at least he would 'go straight'.[3]

Action continued for several months. Public meetings at Cromwell and Bannockburn called for Pyke's resignation as county chairman and MHR. Cromwell businessmen formed a 'separation committee', with the object of having the northern ridings of Vincent County and possibly part of the neighbouring Lake County combined to form a new county. To achieve this aim, the committee needed to present a petition to parliament calling for new boundaries, but the petition relied on securing the signatures of at least 60 per cent of the ratepayers in the Vincent and Lake ridings. The committee accordingly appointed a paid canvasser who set off to tour the district, supplied, the Clyde newspaper editor claimed, with a large 'whiskey fund' to reinforce his powers of persuasion. Some 300 signatures were gained, and the petition was presented to parliament.

Meanwhile, Pyke was also active. A counter memorial from his southern supporters urged him to stay in parliament. Conveniently, the county established a rates assessment tribunal to hear objections to valuations in Kawarau Riding, where Pyke was the councillor. The tribunal considerably reduced the rateable value of many properties and consequently the rates burden on many of Pyke's electors. This outcome was one Pyke may well have been confident of, given he was both the principal assessor for the county and the arbiter in any disputes. When the petition on separation was presented in Wellington, Pyke managed to cast sufficient doubt on its authenticity to have it investigated and eventually refused. Pyke weathered the storm. He remained ensconced as both county chair and local MHR.

This local imbroglio, 15 years after the rush for gold to the Dunstan, illustrates some common aspects of politics on the goldfields in the 1860s and early 1870s – the use of petitions and demonstrations and the part played by spontaneous crowds and public meetings. But it also demonstrates several features of the new politics that were emerging in the 1870s. These included the weight given to the interests of small towns, the importance of commercial sectional interests, and the leadership role played by businessmen in the small towns.

This chapter explores this change in political structures, issues and outcomes. It focuses on the years from 1862 to the end of the 1880s and covers politics in the Otago goldfields, with particular attention given to the Dunstan field and, to a lesser degree, Tuapeka – the region from Lawrence to Cromwell. My thesis is that the politics of the rushes, a populist politics focused on immediate issues and spontaneous actions, immediately gave way to the politics of localism, where local commercial interests dominated political organisation and representation, where political issues centred on local economic development, and where parochial interests drove much of political behaviour.

The Context: The Dunstan goldfields 1860s–1880s

Our period starts with the discovery of payable gold on the Clutha River and its tributaries in 1862 and the consequent rush of prospectors, along with those hoping to profit from them, to a succession of locations on and around the river. The rushes led to an influx of mostly men into the region and the establishment of camps, then settlements and then small townships near the mining sites and at important communication points such as river crossings. This new pattern of activity and settlement was imposed on a land previously the preserve of runholders, pastoral labourers and hundreds of thousands of sheep.

A census taken in 1878 found that Vincent County had a European population of just over 3000, with 424 people residing in Cromwell, 312 in Clyde and 200 in Alexandra. Some 70 per cent were male, and 50 per cent of the adult males were working in the mining sector. The other major occupational sector was pastoral farming. The census recorded a population of 519,000 sheep in the county.[4]

A Chinese population of 600 to 700 could also be found in the area in 1878; almost all of these people were adult males. In many ways, they inhabited a parallel world to that of the Europeans. They did not compete with Europeans for gold-mining claims, often working on previously worked land. They ran separate commercial enterprises and usually lived in separate settlements. Apart from a few spasmodic clashes and casually discriminatory actions by Europeans, the Chinese went their separate way. They had no political rights or power and were not a factor in goldfields politics during this period. The racist appeals to anti-Chinese prejudice for political purposes occurred later in the nineteenth century. Thus, in terms of demographics, the context for politics was small scale, European, male and, in terms of occupation, mining dominated.

Two other aspects of the social and economic context of politics are important. The first is the significance of small towns. Among them, Clyde and Cromwell were the commercial centres. Established in 1862, they remained essentially frontier towns throughout the period, as contemporary photos show. Ramshackle buildings, empty sections and a great number of hotels were features of the built environment. Sandstorms in the summer, floods in the spring and mud in the winter were features of the climate. And although prize fights, street brawls and dancing halls were less prevalent in the 1870s than in the 1860s, the towns remained boisterous social centres where speculation, gambling and heavy drinking were common pursuits.

But paradoxically the towns had another side. Remarkably quickly the goldfields towns had a smattering of solid stone buildings, churches, schools, hospitals at Clyde

Two gold-funded grand buildings of Clyde, Otago. Left, the Dunstan Lodge; right, the town hall.

Photograph by Lloyd Carpenter, Christchurch, 2013

and Cromwell, masonic halls, libraries, and political and social institutions such as borough councils, town improvement committees and newspapers. These signs of stability and sustainability existed side by side with the frontier-like aspects of the towns. Unlike the wooden frontages on the buildings that gave street fronts the illusion of solidity but masked the temporary mien of the corrugated iron cladding behind, these civic buildings were more than a façade. Stone structures, social institutions and local government reflected an aspiration for permanence and a faith in the future.

The paradoxes in the physical and cultural fabric of the small towns had its echo in public discourse. Newspaper editors, local politicians and commercial leaders voiced optimism about progress and future development, even as floods and dust storms came and went, mining and commercial ventures floated or sank, and populations fluctuated. While indications of impermanence were all around – and it was by no means certain that settlement in Dunstan would be established in the long term – a belief in progress was an article of faith for most of its leaders.

The engine of progress was economic development. In the context of the Dunstan goldfields during the period spanning the 1860s and the 1880s, such development meant better communication (in particular, in the form of roads and bridges), closer land settlement and greater investment in mining enterprises. Much of the focus of public life, be it at public meetings, in newspaper articles or in the debates and actions of local mayors and borough councillors, was on local economic development.[5]

The second significant aspect of the economic and social context of politics in the Dunstan was the impact of new methods of production on investment and ownership in the goldmining industry that began during the second half of the 1860s and continued on through the 1870s. Small-scale operations by individuals and informal partnerships that primarily involved shovels and hand-worked cradles or simple modes of extraction were soon replaced by larger operations involving sluicing and large-scale paddocking. At Bendigo and Carrick, mining for gold-bearing quartz began. The need for capital investment in water races, dams, flumes, sluicing gear, the driving of adits, sinking of shafts and erection of stamper batteries became crucial. This need changed the ownership structure: partnerships were formalised and investors from the commercial sector of the small towns became owners. It also changed employment relationships for many miners, with some becoming wage workers. In addition, a new group of mining agents and company promoters emerged. As we shall see, small-town mining investors, mining agents and promoters became important political actors in the 1870s.[6]

Goldfields Politics in the 1860s: Populism and containment

By 1862 colonial New Zealand already had an established, albeit new, form of federal government, consisting of a parliament in Wellington (a legislative-council upper chamber and a house of representatives with members from constituencies across the colony) and provincial governments in each region. Provincial governments consisted of a directly elected superintendent and a provincial council of elected constituent members. Landowners and merchants dominated the political establishment, and the franchise was restricted to adult male property-owning or leasing British subjects.

Political leaders, aware that exclusion of miners from representation had led to riots in Ballarat, Victoria, in 1853, were quick to react to the potential and then actual influx of miners. First, between 1860 and 1863, political leaders at both colonial and provincial levels took a series of measures to contain what they feared might be a miner-led democratic contagion. In 1860 parliament passed legislation entitling males who held miner rights (i.e. licence to mine) to vote in colony-wide and provincial elections.[7] In 1862, as a result of lobbying by Otago leaders led by the province's superintendent Major J.L. Richardson, the franchise was amended to remove the right to vote for the provincial superintendent and to increase the period of residency in the province from three to six months.[8] Changes in 1863 provided for holders of business licences on goldfields but further tightened electoral procedures.[9] The miners had the right to vote, but the potential impact of that right, at provincial level in particular, was limited.

Miners' electoral power was contained in two other ways. While new parliamentary electorates were created (the multimember Otago Goldfields electorate in 1862 and later the Goldfields Towns electorate), these contained many more electors than those in the established settlements. Similarly, at the provincial level, new seats were established, but there were still many more potential electors than extant seats. Miners thus had representation but not representation commensurate with their numbers. The other measure containing miners' potential electoral power came about through regulations requiring miners to register as electors, an activity that often meant a considerable journey to the place of registration and time away from productive work. Thus, the political establishments acted to maintain the power of existing property owners by containing the impact of the miners' right to vote.[10]

The Otago provincial government, which had responsibility for land management, acted quickly to set up administrative structures on the goldfields, thereby limiting the likelihood of lawlessness or self-determination filling any vacuum. News of finds at Dunstan near what is now Cromwell reached Dunedin in August 1862, and by 1 October Major Jackson Keddell was on site at Dunstan as commissioner (the predecessor to a warden) of this designated goldfields district.[11]

After an initial dalliance with locally controlled administration through an appointed board at Tuapeka, the provincial administration opted for a centralised approach.[12] In April 1862 it recruited Victorian goldfields administrator Vincent Pyke. He immediately set about developing a bureaucracy of inspectors and wardens. Appointed wardens exercised authority through wardens' courts, which had administrative and judicial functions. On the Dunstan goldfields, these institutions were

'The PYKE loveth to abide where RUSHES do most plentifully abound. It is a fierce fish, and a voracious; and riseth greedily if a good fat PLAICE be used as a bait. – Vide Waton (not Isaak).' Pyke caricatured by *Dunedin Punch*, 1 July 1865, p. 39.

Courtesy Hocken collections, Uare Taoka o Hakena, University of Otago, Dunedin

Vincent Pyke, c. 1877.

Courtesy Lloyd Carpenter collection

quickly put in place. Miners welcomed the exercise of some control over the many disputes relating to infringements of property rights, as well as the exercising of some control on behaviour.[13]

The miners who flooded into Central Otago were in no way apolitical. Many had experienced the politics of Victoria in Australia, including the storming of a government stockade at Ballarat and other direct actions to obtain voting rights.[14] Some had come from California. Each year throughout the mining centres of Australia and New Zealand, they celebrated July 4 as a democratic festival. Nor were they too busy working to be politically active. As the author of the most comprehensive study of administration on the Otago goldfields has noted: 'The assumption that gold miners were too preoccupied with industrial and casual pursuits to develop an active public life is a myth.'[15]

Miners had many reasons and numerous opportunities to comment on aspects of the administration of the goldfields and on the prioritising and management of public works, two aspects of politics directly related to miners' wellbeing. Miners also voiced concerns about the price of foodstuffs, grazing rights on the commonages near their settlements and the perennial problems of communication. The common issues in the early 1860s were roads (their absence or poor condition), mining regulations (such as the size of claims), and the quality of administration and administrators. Miners were often dissatisfied with mining administration and at various times sought a change in officialdom or more generally for the responsibility to go to the central government.

The political expression of these concerns was ad hoc, spontaneous, collective and male dominated. Public meetings of greater or lesser formality were common. These might occur in response to rises in the price of flour or allegations of price gouging by local suppliers (the runholders' meat monopoly was much criticised). They might be about goldfield boundaries or public works, such as extension of the telegraph or formation of a new road or access to land for housing and grazing. Sometimes there was an element of radicalism in the rhetoric. A public meeting in Queenstown, for example, passed by acclamation a motion 'opposing the grasping policy of the squatter and the capitalist'.[16]

The actions generated from these meetings were much more cautious than the rhetoric, and well within the political conventions of the day. They might include a memorial or memorandum from the meeting, a deputation to the warden or a petition to the government in Dunedin or Wellington. Petitions started over all manner of things, from the importation of cattle for cheaper meat, through to where roads might go and who would be a new official, and on to the need to register in order to vote. Activity was considerable, but no barricades were erected or manned and no ramparts stormed. Grievances were generally well managed by wardens and police.

The form of politics being practised was a populist one. Many of the miners' political concerns were about matters that were immediate and affected the population as a whole, such as the aforementioned price of meat or the state of the roads. Such concerns generated wide popular support, which was given effect through attendance at meetings or signing petitions. The leaders of the crowds gave expression to shared concerns and sought to express the will of the local people. From time to time that expression included an antagonism to the economic and political elites of the time, such as runholders, urban merchants and senior officials, and the power they wielded. Most of the activities were spontaneous, specific and short term. They neither constituted nor generated what might be called a miners' political movement; nor did they throw up a populist political leader.

Thus, politics on the goldfields in the 1860s did not generate a sustained democratic movement, let alone the democratic contagion the political establishment in Dunedin and Wellington feared. No democratic movement arose from what might be argued were the fertile grounds of considerable numbers of miners (many of them politically aware and active), enfranchisement, and a set of issues that generated widespread if disparate support.

Several reasons can be given for this situation. First, the barriers to political action, other than short-term local events, were high. They included work pressures, communication difficulties and the costs of registering and exercising a vote. Gerry-mandering of electorates limited the number of representatives, and no strong faction arose in parliament to provide leadership. Second, no single issue emerged for a political movement to coalesce behind, unlike the issue of non-representation in Victoria. Third, local issues were usually well managed by local officials without recourse to coercion. And, finally, many miners did not see the Dunstan as their final destination. It was a temporary worksite, open to being abandoned in the next rush, as indeed happened in the late 1860s. Many miners did not have the emotional or economic attachment to the region that might have impelled sustained political action.[17]

From Populism to Parochialism: Politics on the goldfields in the 1870s and 1880s

While political crowds, petitions and spontaneous actions continued to be aspects of politics on the goldfields in the 1870s, as Pyke found to his discomfort, political activity during that decade in Dunstan came to be dominated by a new group and new institutions. These people were not miners taking leadership at public meetings, but small businessmen in the goldfields towns operating through electoral committees and associations.

In the parliamentary elections of 1879, five of the seven candidates in the seats of Tuapeka, Dunstan, Wakatipu and Mount Ida were part of the local commercial sector – small-town businessmen we would call them today: two commission agents, two lawyers and a journalist. The two most successful Otago goldfields politicians in terms of holding office across the two decades were J.C. Brown in Tuapeka, who held the seat from 1870 to 1890, and Vincent Pyke, who held Dunstan from 1875 to 1890. Brown was an unsuccessful miner at Tuapeka who became a mining agent and promoter and turned to politics as a career.[18] Vincent Pyke, goldfields administrator, journalist, mining agent and promoter, was a man whose personal interests were in local economic development. His associates were archetypal nineteenth-century men of commerce, such as local investors and mine owners, traders, and the proprietor/editors of the local newspapers.

In 1876 provincial government came to an end, and a new system of local government was instigated based on boroughs, counties and locally elected councils. At the county level, small businessmen quickly came to dominate. Five of the eight councillors on the first Vincent County Council, elected at the end of 1876, had links with commerce: two were storekeepers, two investors in mining companies, and Pyke was the local MHR with, as noted above, close links with commerce. The parochial disputes described at the start of this chapter were led by small businessmen in Cromwell and their counterparts in Clyde, and fuelled by their confrères, the editors of the local newspapers.[19]

The predominance of small-town commercial leaders can be explained by two features of the economic and social context. First, it reflected the increased importance, brought about by the economic and technological changes described earlier, of the commercial sector and the power of those within it. As settlement progressed, the role of suppliers of goods and services, whether retailers, carriers or whatever, became more important. As mining techniques changed, requiring more capital investment, the role of resource developers (promoters of water-race ventures, for example) and mining company investors became more important. The owners and editors of local newspapers shared their interests and assiduously promoted their issues.

Second, politics reflected the strong motivation of those in the commercial sector to exercise political power and influence political decision-making. For local commercial leaders, the main driver of profits and capital gains was economic growth. These men therefore had a keen interest in such contributors to economic growth as investment in gold mining and water races, closer land settlement and better transport and communications. Government had an important role in each of these areas in terms of supporting extractive industries (by subsidies for water schemes, for example), facilitating land settlement on Crown land, and building the transport infrastructure. Public life came to be dominated by commercial interests, while political actions and institutions became the domain of men of commerce interested in profits, capital gains and public works.

Parochialism, Public Works and the Politics of Localism

The predominance of small-town men of commerce was just one important aspect of the new politics of the 1870s and 1880s in goldfield electorates. The second significant feature was the weight given to parochial interests. Local interest was the most important consideration among those making decisions about candidates and engaged in voting, and it was the driver behind advocacy for public works. Activities focused on general elections provide a good illustration of this second feature. As a general election approached, local newspapers editorialised about the need for a 'local man'. As campaigns progressed, parochial interest was the most common theme in political rhetoric and commentary, evident in newspaper editorials and in reports of speeches and other political activity.

Parochialism also influenced election results. Polling booth returns show a pattern of voting for the man most expected to benefit the local area. For example, J.C. Brown in Tuapeka could count on the Lawrence vote, but over several elections at Blue Spur, votes went to his opponents, reflecting Blue Spur residents' disillusionment with Brown and the attempts of Blue Spur-aligned candidates to profit from it. In neighbouring Wakatipu in 1879 and 1881, candidates with Arrowtown and Macetown affiliations took the vote in those centres, but the victor held sway in Queenstown. In 1890 both Pyke and Brown lost their seats. In each case, the main factors in defeat were boundary changes incorporating new areas that their opponents – men with local ties – used as the base for success.

A third feature of the new politics, carried over from the earlier decade, was the focus on public works. The building of roads, railways, bridges and public buildings along with government subsidies for capital development in mining continued as very much the stuff of public affairs. In the local economies of Dunstan and the goldfields more generally, public works played an important part in economic stimulation, both as an economic activity in their own right and, in the case of roads and bridges, through creating an infrastructure that could support further development. Local districts competed for access to government funding. From time to time, regional schemes were promoted. These included campaigns for land settlement in 1881 and for an Otago Central railway many times throughout the period. Pyke was a prominent crusader for both.

The focus on public works was both a product of and reinforced the parochialism that drove much political activity. Advocacy for public works was nearly always specific to some particular branch railway, road, bridge, water race or sludge channel associated with a particular small town or mining area. Local interests and local politicians competed very directly with their peers for funding, and the competition accentuated parochialism. Persistently advocating local interests in Wellington led to a reputation for advocacy in high places that had a local political payoff. J.C. Brown, for example, was known as 'the high priest of parish politicianists'.[20]

In understanding the power and persistence of this form of politics, it is important to remember how much of life in rural Otago in the 1870s and 1880s took place in very geographically constrained domains. Most people operated within physically restricted economic and social worlds. People lived in communities of a few hundred residents, worked in very small enterprises and traded in local markets. Travelling further afield was slow and laborious and other communication was difficult. How well the local economy fared, the extent of opportunities for security and wellbeing from the employment and profit-making opportunities of growth and economic development, bore very directly on residents. Politics on the goldfields in these two decades reflected this economic and social context. Local interests were the main influence on political behaviour.

The form of politics that predominated was not peculiar to goldfield electorates. Rather, it was a variant of what has been called the politics of localism, a form of politics that predominated in rural Otago in the 1870s and 1880s. In the politics of localism, local businessmen dominated in electorate organisations, candidacy and representation. Issues of interest to the commercial sector predominated in political discourse. The most influential political structures were not parties or factions (and their local apparatus), but groups of political agents for MHRs, usually acting for the commercial sector. The most influential figures were not colonial or provincial leaders, but local men. The goal of political activity was regional or local economic development, and the main issues were often about expenditure on specific local public works, closer land settlement and, on the goldfields, support for mining ventures. In short, the politics of localism prevailed, and politics was primarily the domain of parochial commercial interests.

Vincent Pyke

Let us end by returning to the story of Vincent Pyke, who survived his effigy being cast into the Clutha River and remained a significant political figure in goldfield politics for another 15 years. Pyke was a man with an unusually wide range of interests and talents. He was not only a prominent public administrator and successful central and local government politician, but also a journalist, publicist, historian, novelist, prominent freemason and Anglican Church leader. Pyke undoubtedly had a capacity for hard work and a facility for public speaking and writing that was out of the ordinary. However, our interest here is in what Pyke had in common with his political peers, for his social position, manner, political skills and actions were similar to those held by many of his contemporaries who were active in politics on the goldfields of the 1860s through to the 1880s.[21]

The main markers of Pyke's life can be quickly set out. Born in Somerset in England in 1827, he immigrated to South Australia in 1851. From there he went to the Victorian goldfields, where, as a young man, he engaged in that mixture of public administration, politics and journalism which characterised his career. He eventually became a goldfields administrator in Bendigo and a member of the Victorian parliament. Pyke and his family moved from Victoria to Otago in 1862 when he took up a position heading the Otago provincial government's administration of the goldfields. When the position ended in 1867, he became the goldfields warden at Clyde. In 1873 Pyke became MHR for Wakatipu, changing electorates in 1875 to Dunstan, which he represented for 15 years until defeated in 1890. Pyke died in Lawrence in 1894, having returned to politics in 1893 as the member for Tuapeka.

The Masonic Lodge at Clyde, c. 1873. Vincent Pyke is in the doorway.

Courtesy *Otago Daily Times* historical collection

Pyke's appearance, manner and behaviour were typical of his peers in late nineteenth-century public affairs. Bearded, waist-coated and upright, they appear in the photographs of the time as staunch, stout and, in Pyke's case, pugnacious. Pyke's manner was typical too: self-confident, loquacious, his views delivered at length with a mixture of bluster and good humour, using language redolent of the St James version of the Bible. Pyke's public behaviour was also similar to that of several of his peers. He had, contemporary references would suggest, a capacity for liquor and larrikinism befitting his goldfields experiences. As one biographer wrote, Pyke was 'a vigorous debater, lecturer and raconteur', possessing 'a formidable memory and an incisive wit'. He was also of 'uncertain temper, erratic and imperious', capable of 'sustained invective and stubborn stonewalling'.[22]

Pyke's main political preoccupation, apart from staying in office, was local economic development. In this he was again typical of his peers. He publically promoted several causes, including closer land settlement and the Otago Central railway line. Privately, he was involved in mining ventures of varying success. Pyke's domain was the commercial sector of small towns. He seldom spent long in Dunedin, and in the early 1870s his antagonism to the urban centre and the provincial government based there led him to strongly support the abolition of the provincial form of government. His links were not only with the small towns of the goldfields – Cromwell, Clyde and then Lawrence – but also with small-town men of commerce. Like most successful goldfield politicians of his era, Pyke played the politics of localism very skilfully at the colonial level. He fitted this mode of politics thoroughly and became well known in Wellington as one of those indefatigable advocates for the interests of his electorate. The politics of localism was Pyke's game, and he made a career of it.

The fourth and final aspect of Pyke's public career that makes him typical was his mingling of public and private interests. Pyke was not alone in this. A certain vagueness about the boundaries of what was public interest and what was self-interest was common in nineteenth-century public life. Pyke was not a wealthy man and was therefore dependent on income from public office. He sought and obtained a large payment as Vincent County Council's chairman and fought to retain that position even when absent on parliamentary duties. He switched between administrative civil service positions and elected offices with an ease that would be surprising in contemporary public life. At Vincent County Council, he managed to be both chairman and chief executive.

This mixing of roles reflects in part the small scale of public life in late nineteenth-century Otago. Few citizens had the motivation and talent to take on the administrative and executive leadership responsibilities of public body work. However, the mix also reflects a public life in which governance and management roles were often interchanged and sometimes intertwined, thus further blurring the boundaries between public and private interest.

ELECTORS !

VINCENT PYKE is in favor of:---

Opening up the Lands in Large Blocks
Free Selection and Deferred Payments
Due Restrictions to Exclude Monopolists
Free Grazing Rights to every Agriculturist
Reduction of the Gold Duty to Sixpence per ounce
Granting Subsidies to *bona fide* Prospectors
Manhood Suffrage, pure and simple
Roads and Railways to the Interior
Bridges over the Rivers and Creeks
Equal Educational Privileges to all the Community
Liberal Support to Hospitals and other Charitable Institutions

VINCENT PYKE believes in :---

Political Honesty and Principle
Measures *and* men
A Bold and Progressive Policy

VINCENT PYKE will oppose :---

All attempts to Sacrifice the Interests of the Goldfields
The Inequitable Expenditure of Public Money on the lower districts
The setting of Class against Class, to the injury of all

VINCENT PYKE confidently seeks :-

The Support of every Elector who concurs with these views.

THE PAST POLITICAL CAREER

OF

VINCENT PYKE

IS A

SUFFICIENT GUARANTEE

FOR HIS

FUTURE CONDUCT.

ELECTORS! VOTE EARLY & VOTE STRONG

Vincent Pyke's election advertisement on page 5 of the *Tuapeka Times*, 12 June 1873.

Conclusion

Were Pyke's effigy to be dragged up from the bottom of Lake Dunstan and somehow brought to life, the man represented by it would find a very different politics at play than those he successfully operated in during the period encompassing the 1860s to the 1880s. He would find a politics dominated by New Zealand-wide political parties, national leaders, nationwide issues, television and social media. And he would find women playing a substantial role in public affairs.

Politics on the goldfields in the 1860s through to the 1880s was a very different game to what it is now. In the 1860s it was characterised by short-term issues with a focus on local concerns, and specific – often spontaneous – actions, such as ad hoc public meetings, petitions and deputation. This ephemeral, populist form of politics was followed in the 1870s and 1880s by a politics dominated by small-town men of commerce. Political activists were most commonly drawn from the commercial sectors of these small urban centres. Their interests were in local development, and the politics they knew and operated was the politics of localism: small scale, personal, parochial and dominated by the interests of the commercial sector.

2

MĀORI AND CHINESE

6.

Finding 'Te Wherro in Otakou': Otago Māori and the gold rush

Lloyd Carpenter

NEARLY EVERY HISTORY OF OTAGO gold begins with Vincent Pyke's 'That the Maoris were aware of the occurrence of gold, before the arrival of European colonists, is a tolerably well established fact.'[1] However, the story of Otago Māori mining gold in the early 1860s has a history far more complex than one might suppose from Pyke's statement.

The Historical Record

During the heady days of the early 1860s when swarms of miners crossed and re-crossed Otago in a headlong scramble for gold, Māori were there. Analysing reports about them is problematic because, in the absence of personal journals, colonial newspapermen were the only recorders of Māori activities. Rather than providing objective reports of what they saw, these men wrote with an enduring frisson of excitement of the mysterious, mythological Māori culture.[2]

This approach, mixed with the otherness of deeply-etched facial tattoos and ritualised culture, made for instant mythopoeia, constructing Māori as noble savages at best or possessing a latent threat hidden beneath a thin veneer of European 'civilisation' at worst. The Otago press of the 1860s also characterised Māori fighting colonial and imperial troops to retain their lands in the north as an 'impudent', 'savage race'[3] waging a war of 'rebellion' with the Crown.[4] Australian newspapermen seized upon this portrayal. Dismayed at the loss of miners to Otago in 1861, they raised the spectre of hordes of Māori as an inducement to miners to stay in Victoria:

> [I]t is to be hoped that those disposed to try the new field will count the chances before they start … already provisions are at famine prices nearly on the new gold field, the weather is severe … [and] the chances of a rush of Maories have also to be considered, as though the natives are not in any strength in that part now, they have a keen appreciation of the value of gold, and will soon be on the spot.[5]

The Australian editor's comment that Māori 'have a keen appreciation of the value of gold' had a longer lineage than is widely understood. The first to write of this was a 24-year-old Frenchman.

Jules de Blosseville's Mines

Jules de Blosseville, a midshipman on the French expeditionary vessel *Coquille* under Louis-Isadore Duperrey[6] visited Australasia in 1824.[7] While in Sydney de Blosseville took an avid interest in New Zealand, reading and transcribing shipping accounts and journals, interviewing renowned 'Pākehā Māori' James Caddell and his wife Tokitoki[8] and talking to all the sealers, whalers, ship's crews and visiting Māori he found from New Zealand. That interest and pattern of greeting and meeting stayed with him when he visited the Hokianga shortly thereafter.[9]

Midshipman de Blosseville's report, *Essai sur les moeurs et les coutumes des habitants de la partie méridonale de Tavai-Poénammou*[10] was added to the encyclopaedic *Nouvelles annales des voyages de la géographie et de l'histoire* collection in Paris. A comment about the resources of the South Island raises an intriguing conundrum: 'Fine trees, useful for all maritime purposes, flax in abundance and numerous seals whose furs are very valuable – these are the resources that *Tavai-Poenammou* has to offer … If some day these lands are colonised by Europeans, the South Island will only be a branch of the North, unless some valuable mines concealed in its ranges and already talked of by the natives give the island an importance later on.'[11]

Is the reference to 'some valuable mines concealed in its ranges and already talked of by the natives' the first hint by South Island Māori that gold could be found in the mountainous interior? If so (and this reference pre-dates Te Pouho's 1836 Ngāti Tama

Jules Poret de Blosseville, 1802–1835. Image from carte de visite c. 1830, when de Blosseville was appointed to command *La Lilloise*.

Print by Francois Jacques Dequevauviller, courtesy La France pittoresque

war tauā from Wakapuaka to Tūtūrau, which killed nearly all Central Otago-resident Māori[12]), then clearly Māori recognised that the gold they had seen in the interior had value to Pākehā. Māori knew that gold was there in abundance, and they talked about it – talk that reached de Blosseville. Nothing came of de Blosseville's comment, but as time passed, more Ōtākou (Otago) Māori spoke of gold.

'Palmer, an Old Whaler'

The first historian to write of Māori and Otago gold was the goldfields commissioner Vincent Pyke. To write his history of Otago gold finds, Pyke sought contributions from both Otago Māori and the Pākehā settlers. Pyke's often-quoted comment forms the basis of much of the analysis of Māori attitudes towards gold:

> That the Maoris were aware of the occurrence of gold, before the arrival of European colonists, is a tolerably well established fact … in 1862, I was informed by Mr. Palmer, an old whaler, then resident at East Taieri, that, many years previous to the settlement of Otago, he was told by a native chief … that 'plenty *ferro*' or yellow stone, such as that of which the watch-seals of the white men were made, and which had attracted the old chief's attention, was to be found on the river beaches inland, and that the Matau or Molyneux River was the place where it principally occurred … Other Natives freely made similar statements when they observed the value that the new-comers seemed to place upon golden coins and ornaments.[13]

Despite his research, some history of Māori gold-finding escaped Pyke.

The *Amazon* at California

In 1848 whaling-ship captain and founder of Riverton on the Southland coast, John Howell, built the *Amazon*, a 130-ton schooner and, with the support of a crew of his Māori in-laws and a few Europeans, launched it. His first commercial voyage in early 1849 saw him engaged by the French government to take French immigrants unhappily resident at Akaroa to Tahiti. When he arrived there, he found the island buzzing with news of gold in California and vessels more than eager to take local hopefuls there.

With would-be gold-seekers as passengers funding the voyage, Howell and his crew were among the first foreign groups digging for gold on American Creek, California. Howell was dumbfounded when, after the party had found its first valuable strike of gold, his Māori relations said that it was a waste of time coming so far for such stuff given it was plentiful in New Zealand rivers. Howell and his companions continued to do well, but after an assault by one of the many groups of roving bandits on the field, they took their gold and returned home at the end of 1849.[14] However, once the party was back in New Zealand, the Māori miners said that the violence and corruption they had seen gold generate had convinced them to refuse to reveal where gold could be found locally. Howell spent years telling the joke against himself, saying he 'took a party of Maoris thousands of miles to find gold when the same stuff existed, and they knew existed, in the district from which he set out'.[15]

Māori Miners in Australia

But Māori were mining elsewhere too. Two hundred years before politicians voiced concerns about New Zealanders migrating to Australia, Māori moved there to take advantage of employment opportunities and to facilitate trade. Māori first settled, in 1835, to the south of the Yarra River, where they laid out their 'Ārepa' marae.[16] They worked on kauri that they and Pākehā brought in from Hokianga and Taranaki, and planted New Zealand flax to begin a local industry. Māori were on the Sydney docks,[17] and they crewed the whaler *Australian*,[18] the French survey schooner *Hydrographe*,[19] and the Sydney lifeboat on which Captain William Beechey was the only non-Māori,[20] among other vessels. In the annual Newcastle regattas, Māori were so competitive that their whaleboat entries were subject to handicap.[21]

As for their mining activities, Fred Cahir notes frequent mention of Māori miners in early accounts of the Australian rush: up to 150 Māori at Ballarat and a total of 300 on the Victorian fields.[22] Their presence was no secret. At Bendigo, there was a 'well-known payable locality called the Maori Hill',[23] which was 'a long worked area of profitable ground',[24] and in Napoleon Gully, one of the more consistent claims was known as the 'Maorie's puddling machine' syndicate.[25] Several areas at the Whipstick near Bendigo were famed for Māori mining success: '... the New Zealanders were among the very first to open up these gullies, and some of them will always be found both in Red and Blue Jacket, especially the latter, where more than one Maori has raised a pile'.[26] When a resurgence occurred at Red Jacket in mid-1858, the local correspondent reported that 'a 2 pounds nugget and some coarse gold ... [was] got there in shallow sinking, by a party of Maories during the week'.[27] The neighbouring Elysian Flat had 'a party of Maories, it is well known, got from 17 to 20 ounces from three loads of wash dirt'.[28] When that area quietened, the same Māori miners were noted for their persistence at 'old Scotchman's Gully, of monster nugget fame'[29] and Truck Gully.[30]

In 1863 a headline appeared in the *Bendigo Advertiser* that both congratulated a Māori miner and emphasised his exotic otherness:

> A RED JACKET NUGGET
> That den of nuggets, Red Jacket, yesterday yielded to the industry of John Williams, a New Zealander, one of those lumps of gold for which that locality is so famous. The nugget ... weighs 176 ozs, or 14 lbs 8 oz, and represents a money value of £600 ... the lucky tattooed individual has it all to himself, as he belongs to the genus "hatter," to whom fortune is usually generous, especially with regard to nuggets.[31]

Comments made about Māori indicate that they were sufficiently distinctive among the racial polyglot of the goldfields to stand out, and also that they were there in large enough numbers for newspapermen to make generalisations about them. The writer of an *Argus* (Melbourne) article emphasising the spectacle of newly arrived Chinese miners – 'numerous beings, with umbrella-shaped coverings on their heads, who seem to have just stepped out of the chinaware whose grotesque figures were wont to excite our youthful wonder' – passed this judgement: '... to their credit be it said, that on the goldfields they are characterised by general peaceableness and industry, and are seldom seen under the influence of intoxicating liquors ... in the latter respect, they furnish a contrast to the Maories and American blacks among us.'[32]

On the other hand, a Melbourne *Age* commentator, responding to news of Otago gold finds, referred to what he termed 'the probable influence of gold discoveries on the Maori':

> If he is a bold and skilful warrior he is also a steady and intelligent toiler. He tills and herds, he builds mills and navigates ships. Even so far back as the close of the last century, most of the whaling ships at this end of the world were manned by New Zealanders ... Numbers of the same race have worked at our diggings with a uniform repute among the European mates for steady industry and good conduct. In the agricultural way they not only supply their own wants, but bring in their produce largely to the food markets of the colonists.[33]

This depiction suggests a level of tolerance or acceptance in the Australian field that has not been previously explored, and suggests that Māori were far from a curiosity whether they were working at basic labouring levels of mining, or developing – and profitably working – larger technical claims. Once the Aorere (Nelson) field in late 1856 or the Otago fields in the early 1860s were declared it is not clear whether Māori miners returned from Australia to work the new gold regions of their homeland.

Expeditions to the Golden Interior

With news of the rush to California and gold finds in New South Wales and Victoria filling local newspapers, frequent comment by Otago Māori that local rivers had gold in them could not be ignored. Local leader Raki Raki of Waitaha, Ngāti Māmoe and Ngāi Tahu, who grew up at Lake Wakatipu, disclosed that 'he once picked up a piece of "simon" (gold) about the size of a small potato on the banks of the Molyneux, but did not know its value, and he threw it into the river'. Raki Raki reported that others had seen 'the small "simon" on the sides of the river, where their canoes had been lying ... in the sands of the Molyneux'.[34] In 1851 these accounts led to the first expedition to verify their accuracy.

James Crane was at Henley when Māori arrived from a trip up the Clutha River. Raki Raki told him and his friends that 'when towing his canoe up the Matau [Clutha], near Te Houka [Balclutha], he picked up a stone the colour of a Pakeha sovereign'.[35] Acting on this information, Crane, William Palmer, James Whybrow, John Bennett and two Māori men, Teraki and Tuera, rowed a boat as far as the Pomahaka Falls, but came back without doing anything apart from catching some eels. Palmer had set up and managed the Tautuku whaling station in 1839.[36] He is almost certainly the 'old whaler' who wrote to Pyke in 1862 and is quoted in Pyke's *Story of the Early Gold Discoveries in Otago*.[37] Teraki had guided Otago Company surveyor Frederick Tuckett in 1844,[38] while John Bennett achieved a small notoriety when he found one dwt (pennyweight) of gold in the Mataura River in 1857. Bennett was the first to write to the *Otago Colonist* to request that a reward be offered for finding a payable goldfield.[39]

In 1852, again on the recommendation of Raki Raki, another attempt was made. Thomas Archibald provided a boat and, with Crane and an escaped American whaler called Californian Sam and two Māori men, rowed as far as the mouth of the Tuapeka.[40] Contrary to his original intention, Archibald decided not to look for gold, seeking instead the 'burning plain' (a lignite area in the Pomahaka). Despite California Sam identifying the landscape as being similar to that of gold country in California, Archibald insisted that the party return and make no further attempt to find gold.[41]

Common to both narratives is the chief, Raki Raki. During their survey work, J.W. Barnicoat and Tuckett employed him as their 'native guide', and his sketch of the lakes of Central Otago appears in Barnicoat's journal of 1843–44.[42] His local knowledge was critical in convincing the settlers that gold was to be found.

Some Māori went mining in Otago. The first, hesitant 'rush' in Otago was to the Mataura, following surveyor Charles Ligar's 1857 disclosure that he 'found gold very generally distributed in the gravel and sand of the Mataura River at Tuturau'.[43] Māori mined there alongside scattered local farmers, shepherds and assorted amateurs who attempted to work Mataura gravels despite having neither experience nor expertise. Gold was found there, though, and through the efforts of Māori miners New Zealand's first gold export occurred in April 1857. Mr F.L. Mieville of Glenham Station passed through Tūtūrau on his way to Port Chalmers from where he intended to leave for England. He met a group of Māori who sold him a large wooden matchbox filled with a gold and sand mixture. He took this with him to England and had it made into jewellery for his wife.[44]

Central Otago Miners: Tuapeka

When the rush to Gabriel's Gully broke out in 1861, the editor of the *Otago Colonist* reported that 'a considerable number of Maories have already gone'.[45] An early arrival from Australia wrote to a friend in Bendigo that 'Maories have brought down several nuggets from the high ranges, where a good lot of them are dwelling',[46] a statement which shows that Māori miners knew richer ground lay in the interior of the province but concealed the source. The Otago correspondent to Melbourne's *Argus* wrote: '[T]here is a camp of [Māori] at Gabriels Gully … and [they] are uniformly well conducted … men and women together, there are about 50 of them. They are amenable to authority in a marked degree … to the questions of [Tuapeka Warden] Strode they only had one reply, "Kia koe te tikanga" (Do as you please). Not so tractable have been the European miners …[47]

The anonymous 'Yankee Gold-Digger', who later in 1861 wrote the tract *Otago, or a Rush to the New Gold-fields of New Zealand*, estimated that at least 100 of the locals at Gabriel's Gully were Māori.[48] Certainly, there were enough Māori miners at Tuapeka to warrant one of the richest gullies in Upper Waitahuna[49] being named Māori Gully,[50] although William Ayson, who mined at Gabriel's Gully in 1861, commented in his autobiography *Pioneering in Otago* that 'a good many Maoris came to the Gully, but did not stay long'.[51]

Māori Jack

The first Māori miner to achieve individual fame was initially renowned for his bravery rather than his gold prospecting. After working at John and Frank Hamilton's sheep station at Mavora Lakes as a shearer in 1859–60, 'Māori Jack' headed north.[52] In 1861 he and another Māori called Bill Leonard arrived at the western end of Lake Wakatipu. They had come up the lake on runholder William Rees' whaleboat, which was carrying supplies for Alfred Duncan and the other two shepherds tending a flock there.[53] According to Rees' journal, Jack and Bill came 'with the intention of making their way to the West Coast to look up some other Maoris said to be there',[54] the implication being that the two men were after gold.

Having tested the Dart and Routeburn Rivers and found nothing remarkable in or around them, Jack and Bill joined the six other Māori whom Rees had engaged as shearers, all working in a temporary shearing shed built of saplings and blankets. Shearing complete, Jack and the seven other Māori left Duncan and returned to Rees' homestead, where Jack was offered a permanent job.[55] However, he also continued prospecting for gold and at some point found it, possibly as early as May 1861.[56]

But it was Māori Jack's courage as a lifesaver that became the talk of New Zealand. Jack, along with William Rogers of Glenquoich Station and John Mitchell, a recently hired farm cadet on William Rees' station, set off for Rogers' farm in Rees' sailboat. With Māori Jack at the helm, they headed down the lake, and all went well until a squall sprang up and capsized the boat. Rogers drowned, and only the Herculean efforts of Jack, who supported the near-drowned Mitchell in the water and then ran all night back to the farmstead, saved the cadet from a similar fate.[57] A grateful Rees later worked with Otago Provincial Police Commissioner St John Branigan to organise a subscription to allow Māori Jack to purchase a dray and four oxen so Jack could go into business supplying miners on the nascent 'Wakatip' [sic] goldfield.[58] In response to Rees and Mitchell's application, the British Royal Humane Society awarded Māori Jack the society's medal.[59]

Māori Jack's real name is not certain. Pyke insisted that Māori Jack was Hatini Waiti, or Anthony White, of Ngāti Maru at Thames,[60] while Alfred Duncan, who knew and worked with Jack, insists that he was 'Jack Tewa' and proffers as proof the name Mitchell inscribed on the watch he awarded Jack in recognition of his bravery.[61] Philip Ross May called him Hai Monare Weti in his *West Coast* history.[62]

One of Māori Jack's workmates was Thomas Wilson; he and Jack visited the Shotover River one Sunday and found fine gold there. When Wilson wrote his recollections 50 years later, he recalled Rees' anger when they showed him the gold. Rees apparently told them 'that a gold diggings would ruin his partner and himself'.[63] In August 1862 Jack turned up at Rees' station door bearing a shovel of wash from the Arrow River, in which gold could be clearly seen.[64] Again, Rees was none too pleased. As he later wrote to Vincent Pyke: 'I then felt certain (for I had been at the Turon, N.S.W., in 1852) that it was only a question of a few months before I should be surrounded with diggers.'[65]

Māori Jack showed the gold he was finding to his workmates, one of whom wrote about this to the Taieri River ferry lessee, John MacGregor.[66] MacGregor, in turn, told his brother-in-law Thomas Low, who was living on Galloway Station in the Manuherikia Valley. MacGregor and Low accordingly bypassed the just-declared Dunstan rush to travel further inland, arriving at the Lake District via the Cardrona Valley and Kawarau Gorge, where they met and talked to Alfred Duncan. The party then split up, with MacGregor and Low heading to the Arrow and the others moving on to Rees' diggers' camp for food.[67]

When the enormously rich goldfield was announced, the Arrow was widely known as 'Fox's Rush', after larger-than-life veteran of rushes to California and Victoria, William Fox.[68] Fox, who earned the sobriquet 'the redoubtable' from early miners and newspapermen[69] for his incredible luck in finding gold,[70] was one of the giant personalities bestriding narratives of the early Otago rushes. Given his renown and his ebullience, the sobriquet 'discoverer' also seems to fit. However, Vincent Pyke, who had talked to Māori Jack at length when he provided guiding services to Pyke's provincial government-funded expedition over Haast Pass in late 1865,[71] was unequivocal about who first found gold at the Arrow: 'The association of Fox's name with this rush has caused him to be generally regarded as the discoverer of the Arrow Gold-field ... such was not the case ... McGregor [sic] ... commenced mining operations on the 4th October, and five days later Fox traced him to the spot. The real discoverer was the well known Maori Jack, who obtained a fine sample of gold from the same Stream in May, 1861.'[72]

William Grumitt, who had been district coroner in goldfields centres from Naseby to Oamaru[73] and had worked for the Bank of New Zealand,[74] published a letter written to him from 'the Redoubtable' William Fox in 1863.[75] Fox, like Low and MacGregor, met Alfred Duncan, who not only passed on the news of Māori Jack's gold finds but introduced Fox to Jack. Jack accompanied Fox to Rees' station for extra provisions and told him where and when he had found gold. Fox had no doubt that the credit for the first to discover gold in the Arrow and Lakes District area was Māori Jack,[76] but that did not stop Fox seeking a reward for its discovery later on, an attempt which was unsuccessful.[77]

Māori Jack, who after his award was identified as 'the well-known', fades out of the gold narrative at this point. He headed for Garston on a prospecting trip in January 1863[78] and was headlined for assisting Vincent Pyke on his epic journey to the West Coast via Haast Pass.[79] In 1865 he accepted a commission to guide 40 miners from the Dunstan field across Haast Pass to new West Coast goldfields,[80] a feat he completed several times. Later in 1865 Alfred Duncan met him in Queenstown, where Jack had just deposited £400 as his share from a claim in the Shotover. Jack told Duncan that now he had the means, he wished to travel to England to be introduced to 'Queen Wikitoria' and pleaded with his old friend to accompany him to make the necessary introductions at court. Duncan demurred and later said it was the last time he saw 'that good-hearted giant, Māori Jack'.[81]

After this, 'Māori Jack' disappears from the historic record. Other 'Māori Jacks' appeared, but none of these was Jack Tewa, and some were not Māori. On the West Coast in 1866 'John Reid, alias Maori Jack ... [was] a well-known most notorious

scoundrel, a native of America, aged 27 years, of low build and very dark complexion
… an old sailor … [who] was sentenced to two years' imprisonment, with hard labour,
for garrotting';[82] another was a horse thief, Mr B. Davis.[83] In Otago, an incorrigible
called James Anderson, who earned convictions as a sheep stealer[84] and for hotel
robbery,[85] was also known as Māori Jack. John Bright, the prospector who in 1880
found the Coronerville field, was 'better known as "Maori Jack"',[86] and an Australian
Māori Jack, who, unlike the West Coast men, *was* Māori, was among the early miners
at the Gympie diggings: 'The protection area on the south or Gympie side of the creek
was taken out … by Luca Muller, an Italian, and Emmanuel Thompson, better known
as Maori Jack, a nephew of the celebrated Wiremu Kingi.'[87]

Conflict on the Shotover

The original Māori Jack, Jack Tewa, was not the only Māori mining in the Lake
District. In 1863 Māori miners were at the Lake District goldfields in some numbers.
They became the team to beat in leisure pursuits. During weekends Queenstown
witnessed good-natured sports competition 'between Britons and Maories'.[88] These
involved Cumberland wrestling,[89] a six-mile rowing match in whaleboats (comfortably
won by the Māori crew, with upwards of £500 changing hands on the event), and a
200-yard foot-race between Byers 'the Māori' and Telford, a sprint specialist.[90] The
local correspondent for the *Otago Daily Times* commented: 'Enormous sums changed
hands on the different events … with a "champagne shout" into the bargain'.[91] But
for both Māori and Pākehā, these events were a side-line to mining activity.

During the early days on the Lake District goldfield, Māori made a significant find
in the Rees River. On 5 February 1863 a boatman returned from a supply trip and
breathlessly reported that the 'Maories were getting gold by the tin dishful'.[92] This
gasped message immediately sparked a rush, which was problematic and frustrating
for many wanting to get to the site because the only means of reaching it was by boat.
Subsequent reports said 'brilliant glowing accounts are coming in … the report of the
discovery of a pound and a-half weight nugget is spoken of. I can vouch for numerous
nuggets from one to ten ounces each.'[93]

Given the bonhomie of the social concourse of sports events the month before, it
came as a shock when the same *Otago Daily Times* correspondent reported a story of
conflict, writing with alarm that he had heard that at Rees River 'a conflict is said to
have taken place between the Europeans and Maories. It requires confirmation.'[94] What
happened, who the protagonists were and what resulted are not known because there is
nothing in the Warden's Court records and no subsequent reports in the newspapers.
One of the reasons this event was not elaborated on was because another conflict
happened contemporaneously, and it is the one that entered the realms of goldfield
legend. An account can be found in the summary report collated for transmission to
Melbourne in February 1863:

> Seven of the [Māori] men held an amalgamated claim some distance up the
> [Shotover] river, and it is an extremely valuable one. They were jumped by the

'professionals' upon the grounds that a 'white man' should be entitled to a claim before any other color. The jumpers proceeded to throw in their own tools into the claim, and to throw out those of Maories. After some altercation the latter withdrew and went up to their tents. The jumpers as may be supposed were in high glee at their easy victory and had already commenced trying the value of their newly obtained claim. In the height of their exhilaration and noisy congratulations, they saw the seven Maories returning in single file, each with a tomahawk in his belt. The Maories proceeded very deliberately to collect their tools, replace them in the claim, take out their tomahawks and prepare for work. The intruders did not relish this kind of work and upon second considerations thought discretion the better part of valor. They withdrew, stating that they should bring the Commissioner. It is needless to add that they did not upon further consideration, in this instance, consult that gentleman.[95]

Although this narrative is repeated in nearly every local history of the Otago gold rushes, and sometimes embroidered with depictions of added traditional weapons, a haka, actual violence and even death, contemporary newspapers never referred to it again. The incident is an example of restraint by Māori, at variance with their characterisation in the press's accounts of wars in the north.[96] There is also a degree of moralising in the tale, which suggests that the *Otago Daily Times* correspondent felt that (in his view) the 'simplistic' Māori had been wronged and did well in righting the situation without recourse to violence.

'The Maories' of Māori Point

Other Māori also attracted attention. In April 1863 an Otago-based correspondent for the *Taranaki Herald* disclosed that, as a sign of the increasingly favourable prospects of the Shotover goldfield, a party of three Welsh miners had bought a 20-foot by 40-foot area of streambed at Māori Point from its Māori owners for £800.[97] This report was the first of many extolling the wealth to be found in the upper reaches of the Shotover River, in Skippers Canyon and at Māori Point. One such account reported on six miners celebrating 60 pounds of gold per man in six weeks[98] and a second group that netted £20,000 out of a beach claim upstream from the point. Vincent Pyke first visited there 'to settle a complicated dispute … of imaginary boundaries in the flowing water. In the course of the hearing … a Māori waded into the river up to his armpits, and plunging a shovel into the rapid current, he succeeded after a few failures in bringing up a fine show of heavy gold on that implement.'[99]

In October, the country learned the origin of the name 'Māori Point' when Vincent Pyke's *Report on the Goldfields of Otago* for the parliamentary secretary of the goldfields, was published:

Higher up the Shotover numerous rich gullies were discovered, principally on the western watershed; and the beaches of the river itself were successfully prospected … One of these beaches is known by the appropriate name of "Maori Point", owing to its discovery by two natives of the North Island, Dan Ellison, a half-caste, and Zachariah [Hakaraia] Haeroa, a full Maori. As

these men were travelling along the eastern hank of the river they found some
Europeans working with great success in a secluded gorge. On the opposite shore
was a beach of unusually promising appearance, occupying a bend of the stream,
over which the rocky cliffs rose perpendicularly to the height of more than 500
feet. Tempting as this spot was to the practised eyes of the miners, none of them
would venture to breast the impetuous torrent. The Maoris, however, boldly
plunged into the river, and succeeded in reaching the western bank; but a dog
which followed them was carried away by the current, and drifted down to a
rocky point, where it remained. Dan went to its assistance and observing some
particles of gold in the crevices of the rocks, he commenced to search the sandy
beach beneath, from which, with the aid of Zachariah, he gathered twenty five
pounds weight (300 oz.) of the precious metal before night-fall.[100]

In 1886 Pyke revealed that his source was Hakaraia Haeroa himself, and 26 years
after that Ellison apparently wrote a letter to the organisers of the Dunstan Jubilee

Māori Point from the Pipeline Bridge, Skipper's Canyon (Māori Point is the flat-topped area
jutting into the river on the far bank).

Photograph by Lloyd Carpenter, 2011

celebrations of November 1912 stating that 'when he rescued the dog he saw gold clinging to its coat'.[101] When the partners sold out to the Welsh syndicate, Haeroa returned to the Otago Heads, which was where Pyke found him in September 1863: 'I had heard the story when on a visit to the district in the winter season of 1863 and on my return to Dunedin, I persuaded the Harbour Master Captain Thomson to take me in his boat to the Maori Kaik at the Heads, where we found Hakaria.'[102]

More is known about Haeroa's partners. Daniel (Rāniera) Ellison worked in whaling[103] and then crewed the pilot boat at Otago Heads. He left this job in 1862[104] to go prospecting with Hakaraia Haeroa and Hēnare Patukopa.[105] Like Haeroa, Ellison returned to the kaik after selling the claim to the Welshmen and went farming. He developed new farmland[106] and leased one of his properties as he expanded operations.[107] In 1882 he became converted to the cause of the exiled Parihaka leaders Te Whiti and Tohu when they visited the kaik at Ōtākou. He provided food for Parihaka followers imprisoned in Dunedin and made trips to Taranaki, where he contributed funds to rebuild the settlement.[108] Files in the testamentary archives reveal his work as executor to several Māori estates.[109] Ellison died in 1920, leaving a substantial land holding.

Pyke omitted Hēnare Patukopa from his story. At the time, Patukopa was either securing supplies for his mates (one report in early 1863 relating to the Lower Shotover commented that in any group of four miners, two would be mining, one improving his accommodation and washing and cooking for his partners, and one would be packing supplies from distant stores at Arthurs Point or even Queenstown or Arrowtown)[110] or engaged in the various tasks that miners in the harsh climate of the Shotover had to do to survive. Patukopa took his earnings, went to the Upper Clutha Valley and there purchased the Sandy Point store and ferry from George Hassing and William Ellacott.[111] The area of the Clutha River near Sandy Point carries a legacy of Patukopa's time there: like the rich ground in the Shotover River, this site too earned the name Māori Point, a name which remains today.

For Hēnare Patukopa, Hakaria Haeroa and Rāniera (Dan) Ellison, the decision to go mining in Central Otago in 1862 changed their lives and their fortunes. Stories of point-weight hauls from the area continued over the following three years, each referring to 'the celebrated Maori claim'[112] as its reference point.

Other Māori Miners in Central Otago

In early 1862 mounted constable Edward Garvey reported that eight Māori miners were one of the first groups on the new diggings on the Waipori River,[113] and at least two groups of Māori miners were in the Nokomai. One of these groups, comprising 10 men from Riverton, worked under Solomon, the kaumātua who had supplied Southland's district surveyor James McKerrow with knowledge of the lakes in the Hollyford and Waiau areas of the province.[114] This group worked the head of Victoria Gully and, according to the *Otago Witness*, had found small nuggets ranging in size from seven dwt to an ounce.[115] The second group fossicked with knives on their claim prior to working it in the usual manner. By this method, they recovered 12 ounces of 'shotty' gold and decided (significantly, given the numbers from Southland who returned home empty-handed) to stay and persist at the Nokomai.[116] This group developed a 'dry diggings' claim, which meant they had to sink their picks and shovels into the side of the hill to recover the relatively heavy gold from the soil there.[117]

Scurvy, a disease resulting from a diet lacking vitamin C, did not affect Māori because local knowledge provided them with the means to obtain the necessary nutrition, even in the sparse Central Otago landscape. It was therefore Māori miners travelling through the Upper Shotover that alerted authorities to a serious outbreak of scurvy among the miners there. The reports advised that the affliction was 'prevalent to a frightful extent, and already numbers its victims by hundreds'. In 'hut after hut they found none but sick men, some bedridden, others just able to crawl, none in any way capable of the exertion of travelling to the nearest point where fresh meat and vegetables the only chance of life, could be obtained'.[118] From inference made in the *Wakatip Mail* in August 1863, Māori advised where vitamin C-rich plants could be found, such as 'Māori Cabbage' (although one newspaperman wrote in March 1863 that this is 'a nauseous herb, having all the flavour, and more than all the toughness, of boiled hemp'),[119] sow thistle (pūhā) and speargrass root.[120] They also contributed to the fund set up to provide medicines to the ailing residents of the Sandhills.[121]

Other Māori, such as William Gilbert Mouat, were prominent later in the Otago rush. Trained as a surveyor, Mouat was a quartz mine shift manager at Bullendale and

Māori cottage at the Yukon, c. 1899.

Goetzman photo courtesy Michael Gates collection

Bendigo (Otago), owned a share in a rich sluicing claim in Bendigo's Rise and Shine Basin[122] and worked as an engineer on gold dredges.[123] Other Māori were mining, but ceased to be identified as separate to their mining brethren in the narratives in the records.

Māori were also present at the Klondike rush in the Yukon in 1898. Douglas Fetherling recorded the presence of Māori miners at Sheep Camp[124] near the Chilkoot Pass, and Michael Gates found a picture of a 'dwelling constructed near Dawson by two Maoris, using willow sticks, moss and mud to create a beehive-shaped affair with a small log porch entrance, fitted with a Maori figurehead over the entrance'.[125] Detailed correspondence from a Māori party at the Klondike (which records interaction with several other Māori miners there) is reproduced in Margaret Orbell's *He Reta Ki Te Maunga*.[126]

Recent scholarship by Keir Reeves and Fred Cahir reveals a significant level of Australian Aboriginal mining during that country's gold rush.[127] First Nation American mining at California has been an increasing field of study since the 1970s,[128] although it was mentioned in earlier seminal texts such as Caughey's 1948 *Gold Is the Cornerstone* and Holliday's *The World Rushed In*, amongst others.[129] Other scholars have examined the role of Māori miners at the Aorere rush in Nelson province and their significant role in opening the West Coast fields.[130]

Conclusion

As soon as Otago Māori comprehended the value their new Pākehā neighbours placed on gold, they were quick to realise that the heavy, shiny, yellow stones and dust scattered on the banks of their Mata-au (Clutha) River were exactly what the Europeans sailed around the world to find. It is surprising to discover how long it took for what was widespread knowledge to be adequately passed on to the new settlers. When the presence of this gold became general knowledge, Māori refused to be spectators, participating in and even starting rushes. Their indigenous knowledge helped them to avoid the perils of flooded river crossings and scurvy, and their collective power enabled those who would dispossess them of payable claims merely on the basis of colour to be fought off.

When I have talked of my research with other South Island Māori, many have expressed surprise that their ancestors might have been goldminers. Even more have been surprised to learn of the early migrations to Australia's mining areas. My research has revealed that Māori were not content to be passive observers, but sought – and won – a share of the riches the gold rushes afforded.

For Māori, the rush period can be seen as one of the first areas of New Zealand society where (despite instances of exotic otherness raising comment) there was a degree of colour-blindness and where the meritocracy of gold-finding established some Māori as pre-eminent. As such, these indigenous prospectors deserve to be regarded in the same light as the other legends of the early rush, such as Edward Peters, Gabriel Read, Horatio Hartley, Christopher Reilly and William Fox, among others, who occupy the pantheon of epoch-defining gold men in Australasia.

7.

The Otago Chinese Goldminers: Factors that helped them survive

James Ng

In December 1865 the first wave of Chinese goldminers came by invitation to Otago, New Zealand, to work its goldfields. Thus began the period (1865–1900) during which the majority of the Chinese population in New Zealand had gold mining as their chief occupation. Their numbers were never great, reaching a peak population of 4005 in 1871, when some migrated to the West Coast.[1] Most remained in Otago and did not spread to other New Zealand goldfields. The national population of Chinese residents in New Zealand was also small, numbering 5004 in the 1881 census. Of these individuals, 3858 were miners in Otago and on the West Coast. Only two Chinese women came to the Otago goldfields.[2]

The Chinese miners nearly all originated from a few subtropical rural counties in Guangdong province – and were of peasant and rural artisan stock.[3] They were predominantly Punti (early Han settlers in Guangdong) together with a few hundred Kejia (sometimes 'Hakkas', Han late-comers to Guangdong). The contemporary peasant economy in Guangdong was rife with disorder and offered little opportunity to acquire wealth.

In general, the Chinese immigrants had a high sense of the superiority of their culture but few material resources, no mining tradition in China, and poor education (if any), which meant few were able to speak and write English.[4] Given the considerable physical and social disadvantages arrayed against them, they might appear unlikely to have succeeded or even survived, but they were part of a stream of intrepid Cantonese migrants who followed gold rushes to California in 1850, to Victoria in 1852, British Columbia in 1858 and Otago from 1865. They called the countries that were home to these goldfields *Gim Shan* or 'Gold Mountain' (*Jingshan* in pinyin) and sought to rework those fields. The aim of the gold seekers was to be sojourners rather than settlers; to obtain savings and return home to China with their capital.

This chapter traces the story of the Chinese gold miners in Otago and notes

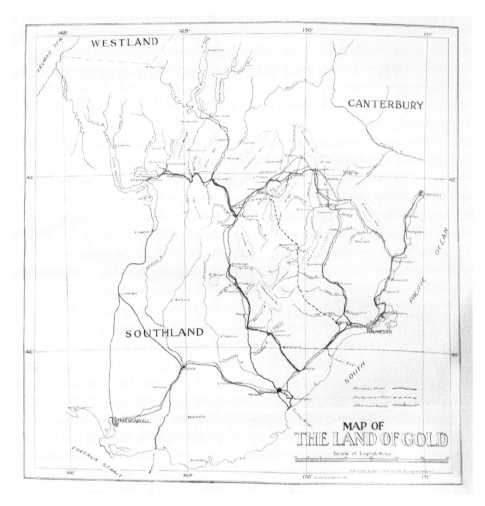

Map by Alexander Don, reproduced from *Memories of the Golden Road, A History of the Presbyterian Church in Central Otago* (A.H. & A.W. Reed, Wellington, 1936, inside front cover).

their persistent nature, capability and goals, degree of success and relationship with Europeans. It also considers the initial tolerance of the Chinese by Europeans followed by the growth of a sense of rivalry and competition between the two ethnicities, the plight of ageing Chinese miners, and the European and Chinese aid given to them.

The Otago goldfields were principally alluvial, offering shallow gold that was favourable for the small-claim mining of the Europeans and of the Chinese who followed them. The second phase of the Otago gold rush involved cleaning up this shallow gold, meaning gold earnings rarely equalled the £5 to £10 per week[5] of miners who struck it rich in the initial rush. Difficulties in mining included the relatively small size of the goldfields and their mostly fine, as opposed to nuggety, gold deposits, a tough climate and scarcity of water in the hot summers and harsh winters. Apart from mining hardships, the Chinese sojourners created difficulties for themselves by adhering to their culture, language, recreation and cuisine. They imported rice, preserved foods, condiments and Chinese liquor from Chinese merchants in Australia, Hong Kong and Guangzhou.

Crucial to the Chinese story were their survival factors, since Chinese were essentially a foreign intrusion into an early colony. These factors were both physical and social – the former to cope with the gold-mining work and environment, and the latter to help them gain the tolerance of Europeans. The emphasis in this chapter is on the latter, particularly because the Chinese did not bond firmly with the host people and were therefore vulnerable to negative shifts in how Europeans regarded them.

The social survival factors can be divided into external and internal origin. External factors included the law-and-order promise that the Otago Provincial Council set down in its invitation to Chinese to come to New Zealand. These factors also included the initially abundant gold-bearing land open to the Chinese miners, and the European use and appreciation of Chinese business, labour and services. Internal factors arose from within the Chinese themselves and so were primarily the characteristics of behaviour that they considered created a good public reputation. Their central factor was social organisation, which offered mutual support; in this, the Cantonese Chinese miners had a triple-level social grouping – kin, clan and county – that was largely informal yet gave a strong collectivism of camaraderie and aid.

Footholds

In Victoria in 1861 the Chinese numbered 24,724 men.[6] When the Otago gold rush began, these Victorian Chinese were naturally interested to hear of the discoveries, but threats from embarking Australian European miners meant only two Chinese men joined the Otago rush.[7]

That rush reached its peak gold production in 1863 with an estimated 18,800 miners in April 1864. This number fell to 6000 at the end of 1865[8] as miners returned to Australia or joined rushes to the West Coast and Wakamarina. To replace the precipitous loss, businessmen and the Dunedin Chamber of Commerce twice invited, through the Provincial Council, Chinese miners in Victoria to Otago in 1865.[9] These invitations meant that the political and commercial elites in Otago were amenable to their arrival, and the council promised the Chinese they would be treated equally before the law.[10]

The goodwill inherent in the invitations and the associated promise was a powerful survival factor for the Otago Chinese miners. Among the first Chinese men to respond to the invitations were bilingual men of substance, and included merchants.[11] They were Forsigh Wong Tape, a merchant who represented Siyi Cantonese interests and who is said to have led the first group of Chinese to Dunedin,[12] Lee Mow Tai, on behalf of Sanyi Cantonese interests, including those of eminent Chinese merchant Lowe Kong Meng in Melbourne,[13] Joseph Lo Keong, a Siyi fancy-goods shopkeeper,[14] and Ho A. Mee, a young entrepreneur and interpreter who also represented Sanyi.[15]

In December 1865 these men met Otago Goldfields Commissioner Vincent Pyke to discuss preparations to receive the Chinese. As a result of this meeting, Wong Tape and Lee Mow Tai established their store sites in Princes Street in Dunedin, close to the

'Arrival of Chinese immigrants to Little Bourke St, Melbourne', engraving by Frederick Grosse, published in *The Australian News for Home Readers*, 20 September 1866.

Rattray Street wharf where the Chinese would disembark. The first resident Chinese merchants in Dunedin were at the apex of an important supply chain to smaller Chinese merchants and storekeepers inland. Other Chinese premises were established in lower Stafford Street, closer to the wharf.

The Siyi Cantonese, the most numerous Chinese group in Victoria, went inland via Waikouaiti, Palmerston and Shag Valley and developed a stopover at Macraes Flat, one of the busiest fields in Otago. The Sanyi, the second most numerous Cantonese grouping in Victoria, went inland by way of Milton and the Manuka Gorge, with a stopover in Lawrence, centre for the Tuapeka goldfield.[16] There, mining agent Duncan Campbell was named 'Chinese agent' or 'protector'. Whether a European was similarly designated at Macraes Flat is unknown. It is probable that the first two Siyi and two Sanyi mining parties apiece went to gold claims pre-selected for them;[17] no miner's right was required of the Chinese till 1868.[18]

The Law

In 1868 Vincent Pyke, acting on the authority of the Otago Provincial Council, appointed two bilingual special constables: John Alloo, whose wages would be paid by the council, and Augustus Blewitt, who would be placed on the central government payroll.[19] These two men were called 'Chinese interpreters'. Their wages and the abeyance of the miner's right were the chief expenses incurred in inviting the Chinese to Otago, but these sums were partly offset by import duties on rice and opium. The special constables helped to implement the promise of equal justice for the Chinese and were involved in court interpretation, especially with respect to mining disputes as they arose.

In 1868 the Otago Provincial Council issued a proclamation stating that it would uphold the law towards Chinese.[20] This edict prevented further violence directed against the Chinese, such as the two or three incidents that had come to the authorities' attention. One such saw a police inspector dismissed for his lack of action in Naseby when a Chinese man was rolled down the main street in a barrel.

Overall, the Chinese made a good impression at the time, perhaps because they were mostly mining veterans familiar with Western ways. The veterans had knowledge not only of mining techniques and regulations but also of the social adaptations necessary to survive among a European population in Gim Shan. This knowledge was another survival factor because veterans passed on their experience to novices. In addition, the Chinese had affinity for the settled population of Scots in Otago, and they with them. Both ethnicities had a clan structure with strong family ties, good morality, self-discipline, industriousness, frugality and respect for learning. But nearly all European settlers regarded the Chinese as hardworking, peaceable and law-abiding;

Chinese miners at Bendigo, Otago.

Courtesy Hocken collections, Uare Taoka o Hakena, University of Otago, Dunedin, File S11-o61h

they minded their own business, seldom fraternised with women and were not intrusive in religion and politics. Their vices of opium smoking and Chinese gambling practices only occasionally spread to Europeans in Otago.

In 1868 and 1869 the Synod of the Presbyterian Church of Otago and Southland established a Chinese Mission with the aim of converting the Chinese gold seekers to Christianity and in the hope of bridging a fundamental gap between Chinese and European. The first missioner was Paul Ah Chin (1871–73 and 1876–77), a catechist from Victoria; the second was Alexander Don (1879–1913), a young school teacher, also from Victoria. This endeavour influenced the numerous Presbyterian communicant members in Otago and Southland to look kindly on the Chinese.

In inland Otago, the Chinese used a wide range of European traders and services. They quickly established stores stocking their particular foods and medicines, and providing their countrymen with mail facilities and other services, including grubstaking, which European stores rarely offered Chinese. However, Chinese miners patronised European stores too. This was especially so in the first years of the Chinese coming to Otago, when mining parties progressed to new goldfields and the establishment of Chinese stores lagged behind each rush. Indeed, European storekeepers were 'jubilant' with their Chinese customers, and the feeling was that the Chinese had saved their businesses, while 'they had nowhere lessened European [gold] gains'.[21] The Europeans would have found it difficult to stock some Chinese goods, but demand for rice and opium was relatively simple to anticipate and to procure from European firms in Dunedin.[22] Once Chinese stores were established, the price of tea and sugar fell.[23] Small farmers sold pigs and poultry to the Chinese,[24] and these were welcome cash transactions. Chinese staples were rice and pork, in contrast to European miners' bread and sheep meat.

The Chinese established market gardens; the first are mentioned in 1867. These lowered the price of vegetables[25] and eliminated scurvy.[26] In their main work of gold mining, the Chinese were soon contributing 30 per cent of gold exports from Otago,[27] and through the gold export tax and expenditure on mining and living costs, they contributed to the commercial life of the province. Chinese miners generally worked poorer-quality gold-bearing land and added to vital gold exports by doing harder, less profitable work in claims deemed to be second-rate.[28]

Until the late 1870s Chinese also filled general and mining labour roles for Europeans in inland Otago, including farm work such as harvesting, shearing and fencing.[29] They took up roading and railway contracts,[30] while the onset of railway construction – both north and south of Dunedin and inland – saw a noteworthy Chinese contribution, with 100 on the Milton to Clutha line and 300 on the Milton to Lawrence line.[31] Chinese cooks became a common sight in hotel and farm kitchens,[32] and when rabbits became a pest in the late 1870s, they took up rabbiting. Chinese doctors and herbalists accompanied their compatriots and served the European community by advising on and providing treatments for lesser medical conditions.[33]

The Chinese were therefore seen as useful and safe people who created value in colonial society, and these perceived attributes enhanced the goodwill towards them in the Otago goldfields. This broadly satisfactory relationship with Europeans was another survival factor. However, as the numbers of Chinese increased in 1870 and 1871, a localised outcry occurred, particularly in the Wakatipu goldfield, where C.E. Haughton, editor of the *Lake Wakatip Mail*, was notably anti-Chinese. But the *Otago Witness* and *Dunstan Times* still regarded the Chinese favourably, writing fair editorials on Chinese immigration,[34] while the Select Committee on Chinese Immigration in 1871 concluded on a positive note.[35]

With Otago's prosperity in the 1870s, the outcry faded. The principal instigator for the 1871 committee had been Haughton, but even he had changed his negative opinions by 1876; as government under-secretary of the goldfields, he praised the Chinese.[36] Vincent Pyke later observed: 'He [Haughton] knew perfectly well that in many parts of the country Chinamen were not looked on with any great aversion. They did not interfere with Europeans, and were such good citizens that their sudden removal would be very much felt.'[37]

Mining Skill

When the Chinese miners arrived in Otago, European miners held the best claims and water rights, so newcomers got the rest, including worked-over and abandoned ground. In poor-yielding land, the work had to be methodical, and the Chinese miners excelled at this by working in cooperative parties. They readily took up poorer auriferous ground, which was apparently plentiful and mostly free when they first arrived, a practice which minimised competition and irritation between Europeans and Chinese.

During the early years of the rush, purchase of a good gold claim could cost £200 – or somewhat more than the average yearly income of a successful European miner, or about the price of a substantial house and gardens in Dunedin. A very productive gold claim at Moke Creek sold to Chinese for £600, although most purchases were for more modest amounts. Nevertheless, it is not surprising that the Chinese began by taking up free or low-cost ground and used hand labour and minimal water until they had better established themselves. Gradually, they improved their workings, by purchase if necessary, so that by 1874 over 40 per cent of the Chinese miners were using hydraulic mining, principally ground sluicing.[38] Notwithstanding this, the four archetypal types of Chinese mining claims remained: river claims, which could require wing dams and Chinese pumps or 'dead-level' tail races to drain water; pit and hummock claims on level ground; paddocking, which required digging down to paydirt across the surface of the claim; and ground sluicing, where flowing water loosened the ground, thus making digging down to paydirt easier.

If minimal water was available, the Chinese washed paydirt by cradling, but when ground-sluicing, they diverted the tail race through a sluice box for gold-saving. Ground-sluicing and more advanced forms of sluicing replaced hand labour. The Chinese pump was originally used in paddy fields, and both Chinese and European miners in Otago widely utilised it to raise water as much as five metres, depending on pump size.[39]

European observers praised the Chinese mining parties for their collective work, skill and determination.[40] A commentator in the *Dunstan Times* described them working in a 'plodding' manner or 'a slow and go-easy style', and usually for two hours longer each day than European miners.[41] Although European miners also worked collectively in order to share work and expenses, decrease costs, widen the resources of experience and knowledge and so be able to work larger claims, European writers noted this collaboration as a special Chinese feature.

The Chinese reached their zenith in small-claim mining when about 500 worked the last developed, southern-most and most difficult field in Otago/Southland, the Round Hill goldfield. The peak years of their work there was from 1880 to 1882.[42] That the Chinese were effective miners was another important survival factor for them.

Earnings

Gold wardens' figures indicate that the average wage of the Otago Chinese miners in the 1870s was about 30 to 40 shillings weekly; some of these miners did even better when they struck gold deposits overlooked during the rush. In the same period, the average weekly wage of European miners was £3.0 or 60 shillings. The Chinese from 1873 to 1885 comprised 39 per cent to 45 per cent of the total population of Otago

Chinese miners, Macetown, Otago, late 1890s.

Courtesy Hocken Collections, Uare Taoka o Hakena, University of Otago, Dunedin, File 1610 01 013A

miners and earned 28 to 36 per cent of the average total wage.[43] This difference points to their generally inferior economic position and proves that many Europeans held better claims and water rights, and perhaps utilised better technology than the Chinese. Yet Chinese appeared satisfied with what they got. Their typical goal seemed modest, when viewed through European eyes: to save £100 over five years and return to China.[44] The exchange rate of three to four yuan to £1.0 sterling[45] and much lower cost of living in China,[46] plus a premium on gold in the sovereigns or raw gold they took home, made their overseas savings very worthwhile.

As sojourners,[47] whom the Europeans hoped would return home once the gold ran out, the Chinese miners had as their primary purpose going to Gim Shan to acquire capital. This aim was one that further developed their way of life because they endeavoured to achieve it by taking on repeat sojourns that would hopefully enable them to change over time from gold mining to humble urban occupations. Whenever possible, they also aided male kin, especially sons, to join them through a process of chain migration. These younger men also become sojourners intent on continuing or starting an overseas conduit for acquiring capital. In New Zealand, a total of three generations of sojourners (including the goldminers) ensued before Chinese settlement eventuated after World War II.[48]

A successful sojourner could enhance his overseas survivability by increasing the male family and kinship circle around him. These kin provided the closest support in any exigency, so this too was a significant survival factor. That said, sojournism proved to be a negative for the Chinese because early colonial New Zealand preferred the ingress of people who intended to settle permanently in the country. As will be seen, the Chinese sojourners' lack of permanence in this country set the scene for their eventual discomfiture.

Overestimates

Chinese immigration from Victoria was slow, and in late 1868 the Chinese in Lawrence thought they and others in Otago could or should bring out more men from their counties in Guangdong province. By 1870 the Otago Chinese population had reached about 2000 to 2500 men, including the first newcomers direct from China.[49] However, the Chinese in 1870 may have been further influenced by a report to the Otago Provincial Council in late 1865, which estimated that the Otago goldfields could then support about 11,000 miners.[50] Given that the fields had been continuously worked, the Lawrence Chinese may have concluded that the goldfields could now support 9000 to 10,000 miners. Of these, some 5000 currently were Europeans; hence 2000 more Chinese could find sufficient mining prospects.[51] Accordingly, in 1870 the Chinese arranged for 2000 compatriots to come from Guangdong, most of whom did so in 1871 in specially chartered ships that arrived direct from Hong Kong.[52]

The majority of the new Chinese arrivals were from upper Panyu County, a place that had seen its countryside ravaged during the Hongjin (Red Turban) rebellion of 1854–56 against the Qing government in Guangdong. The new groups' shipping, reception and dispersal in inland Otago were well organised and included the dispatch of the young Choie Sew Hoy from Lawrence to Dunedin in 1869 to set up a Panyu merchant store where newcomers could be received.[53]

These arrivals took the Chinese mining population in Otago to its peak of 4005 men in late 1871.[54] The consequences of 2000 arrivals on gold production were serious in the long term, since the influx made for a quicker working-out of the shallow gold of the fields, and meant both Chinese and European miners earned less in the ensuing years. The gold exported from Otago was 165,152 ounces in 1870 and 187,416 ounces in 1873.[55] This small increase was in spite of the substantially increased mining population and signified that Otago's shallow gold deposits were at full exploitation: figures after 1873 showed a steady decline to 102,869 ounces in 1879 and 62,107 ounces in 1888. Because of this 'full-house' phenomenon, the Chinese began to move to the West Coast goldfields, although the majority remained in Otago.

European reaction and concern arose in the goldfields with the Chinese influx of six shiploads in 1871 and the next in early 1872. The perception was that Chinese arrivals would use up the spare auriferous land which, although regarded by Europeans as poor ground, could act as a reserve for future harder times. As if to press the point, the European mining population also increased in 1871 and 1872. An outcry against the Chinese centred on the Wakatipu broke out, but the positive report of the Select Committee on Chinese Immigration in late 1871 allayed fears in the general populace, if not among the European miners. The Chinese also made it better known that the concentrated influx had ended with the arrival of the 2000 new Chinese miners, whereas earlier in 1871 few seemed to know how many were coming.

Kum Goon Wah & Co.'s store, Cromwell, Otago 1885.

Courtesy Lloyd Carpenter collection

Presumably, the European storekeepers and other businesses welcomed their share in another wave of Chinese customers, since a novice Chinese miner required around £24 to outfit himself with clothing and simple gear.[56] Above all, prosperity marked most of the 1870s in Otago, which meant Chinese navvies and farm labourers proved very useful. The Chinese influx of 1871 was also welcomed in some European circles for providing potential railway construction labour. On the farm, the demographic was also changing: the number of European miners dropped by nearly 2000 between 1873 and 1874 as their flow into mining reversed in favour of them leaving for work in coastal Otago. This migration also applied to European farm workers. A shortage of farm labour therefore developed with little chance of alleviating it except through hiring Chinese. All of these considerations settled the concerns that initially surrounded the 1871 influx.

Growing Antagonism

European ill-feeling grew again against the Otago Chinese miners as the shallow gold deposits noticeably declined in the late 1870s and competition for non-mining work became overt in the Long Depression of 1879 to 1896. The loss of the buffer of spare auriferous ground was remembered and resented; 'the Chinese took out every speck of gold' became a typical cry, while others asserted that the Chinese had 'ransacked' the goldfields. The growing animosity towards Chinese became evident not only among the European small-claim miners but also among the larger mining associations.

In 1874 Governor Sir James Fergusson received a Chinese delegation in Dunedin. He gave its members the only known advice by a European in authority as to how the Chinese could smooth their pathway towards greater acceptance in New Zealand:

> I trust that the Chinese will continue to respect the Europeans with whom they are brought in contact even more than you have done already. It is deeply to be regretted that those whom [sic] come from different branches of the great human family entertain feelings of jealousy one towards another, though in these British possessions we have been free from similar jealousy towards the Asiatic race. You have the remedy in your own hands, and by giving signs of your good citizenship, you will contract such feelings generally as will serve to assure the Europeans that you are valuable additions to the Colony, and will be of great assistance in the development of the resources of the country. I am sure that the people of Otago and of New Zealand will look with satisfaction upon the expression of good feeling which you have shown, and I myself will retain grateful recollections of it.[57]

But as Chinese misfortune would have it, the key moderating factor between them and the Europeans, the Otago Provincial Council, was abolished in December 1876. Furthermore, there was now a European population of greater diversity in the goldfields, both miners and recent immigrant arrivals, and some held a negative view of Chinese. The ill-feeling passed into anti-Chinese agitation among ill-disposed people, especially in the economically poor counties of Mount Ida and Tuapeka. This negativity aligned with a rising anti-Chinese opinion nationwide as some Chinese began leaving the goldfields in the late 1870s for other work. Although the initial outflow was small and chiefly into market gardening, the newly legalised trade unions and the fledging Liberal Party were opposed to Chinese immigration, primarily because they saw Chinese as potential competition to European labour and small businesses.

At Round Hill the old roles were reversed: the Chinese held the best claims and 'hundreds' of unemployed European miners had to find poorer claims or were left out altogether. Agitation arose, and anti-Chinese prejudice spread among the wider Otago society, at the same time as it was spreading nationally. Pockets of particular prejudice emerged, most notably at Alexandra in 1895, where a near-riot occurred when a gang set out to clear the Chinese from the centre of town. A Chinese man was probably murdered and another set on fire.[58]

Nonetheless, many Otago Europeans quietly held and kept a reasonable opinion of the Chinese, who were able to remain and survive in this province under negatively changed but still liveable conditions. Extrapolating from my father's generation in New Zealand, the worse overt behaviour ranged from the frequent taunts of young children to the occasional larrikinism of older children and young unmarried men. However, the really serious level of prejudice was less obvious outwardly but bit deeply: the legal discrimination against Chinese by regulation, most particularly concerning immigration. Nevertheless, aside from a few outspoken individuals, the married adult population was usually restrained in how they regarded Chinese neighbours and businesses, which meant Otago Chinese could still make a living.

Chinese behaviour did not change, but that of the dominant European society did. If the Chinese had been settlers, their mining skills and social characteristics could have been praised instead of criticised. Several times it was said that the Chinese were persecuted 'because of their virtues'.[59] Fundamentally, what the new attitudes underscored was the superficiality of Chinese bonding with Europeans, largely due to the former being sojourners who did not put down roots.[60] As a persistently foreign ethnic minority the Chinese were vulnerable to fears of their threat to the European working man, racial fears in general, contempt for China, and so on. The ill-feeling led to barriers to Chinese immigration from 1881 on, with these effected through various regulations.

The Third Stage of Otago Gold Mining

This stage began in 1878/79 with the development of the more powerful hydraulic sluicing techniques – hydraulic elevation, especially – needed to mine deeper gold deposits on land. Paralleling this was the development of new dredge designs that made possible the mining of river beds, beaches and flats.

Only a few Chinese participated in these advances. Those who did founded at least six quartz mines[61] and took up mining that required more complex and expensive techniques than those involved in alluvial mining. They also worked eight hydraulic sluicing and elevating claims. One remarkable pioneer further developed the existing dredging techniques.[62] In 1888 Choie Sew Hoy became a world-class pioneer in gold dredging when he introduced the 'Sew Hoy Dredge', possibly the second or third gold dredge in the world able to dredge into river banks and the beaches and flats alongside the river bed. This development sparked off the main Otago dredging boom, but by now there was rare praise for Chinese enterprise, and Choie Sew Hoy's leading role in gold dredging actually underwent obfuscation by officials.[63] Choie Sew Hoy also founded the Nokomai sluicing and elevating project in 1894, which for several years assumed the foremost national position in gold production by a public sluicing company.[64]

Outside of mining, three pioneers in commercial tobacco-growing in inland Otago and, from 1886, in cigarette manufacturing in Dunedin, namely Hong (Hang) Long, Ah Chie and Chau Mong, attracted only cursory mention at the time and today as well.[65] Hong Long and Ah Chie were Queenstown storekeepers and Chau Mong was the chief Lawrence Chinese merchant. In Taranaki, Chew Chong's pioneering use in 1889 of refrigeration in butter manufacture did receive contemporary recognition, possibly in part because two mixed-heritage sons went to war in World War I and one was decorated with the Military Medal.[66]

Notwithstanding Choie Sew Hoy's success, a majority of Otago Chinese remained small-claim miners to the last. At the turn of the twentieth century their gold returns were about 10 shillings weekly[67] if they were lucky, and the Chinese miners as a group had become an ageing, increasingly indigent population. A stream of the more fortunate retired to China, and younger miners moved in to take up different occupations elsewhere in New Zealand. These Chinese looked to urban New Zealand to make a living. Most remaining older Chinese endeavoured to return to China, but a significant number, perhaps a few hundred, were at risk of being left in the Otago goldfields as elderly human flotsam. The Chinese had not diversified much from mining in inland Otago because of the sparse population. They struggled, until the late 1890s, to establish businesses outside the goldfields because of the small general New Zealand population. At the end of the gold-seeker era (1865–1900), 46 per cent of the total 1901 population of 2857 New Zealand Chinese were still mining.[68]

The Select Committee on Chinese Immigration recorded that only one in five Chinese emigrants ever returned home,[69] but that was an earlier time in Gim Shan history. It is impossible to derive a credible conclusion from the available New Zealand departure statistics for the number of Chinese gold seekers who did return permanently, having acquired the desirable amount of capital. For example, the yearly departure figures from 1870–81 were 3315, from 1882–96, 2767 and from 1897–1900, 581, for an overall total of 6663.[70] But some were triumphantly bearing capital 'home', while others were making a second or third trip back. A few were returning for reasons such as a family emergency. The departure figures, though impressive in themselves,[71] are insufficient to allow the development of conclusions about the overall success of the Chinese miners.

Towards the end of the gold-seekers' era, the less successful Chinese became more visible because they were left behind in the goldfields. In 1896 Alexander Don met 1080 men on his annual tour in inland Otago. He recorded 917 of them in his *Roll*, noting whether they had ever returned to China.[72] He found that 832 had not. In addition, there had been a significant mortality rate; possibly 1000 Chinese died in Otago and on the West Coast between 1866 and 1901.[73] There was a higher morbidity rate; the very sick, disabled and indigent frail elderly were often sent home to China through Chinese charity (as were the dead), but these men are not included in the 'going-back' success category.

Charity

In the 1901 nationwide census, Chinese goldminers in Otago and on the West Coast numbered 1313 out of a total Chinese population of 2857 in New Zealand. By the time of the next census (1906), there were only 612, of whom 497 were 45 years of age or older. The reduced number was due to departure for China, taking up shelter with kin or friends in urban New Zealand, or death. In the goldfields, a miner was considered past his physical best at 40 years of age and an old man at 50. The average age of death for males in New Zealand in the 1896, 1901 and 1906 censuses was 36.80, 41.64 and 44.39 years respectively, so increasing numbers of deaths among the Chinese miners were more common as they aged. The Chinese miners steadily decreased in number to 59 in 1921. Of these individuals, around a dozen were employed, along with European co-workers, by Choie Kum Poy, son of Choie Sew Hoy, at his three successive Nokomai sluicing claims. Nationally, immigration restrictions also contributed to the falling Chinese population.

Inevitably, more Chinese died on the goldfields, either because they were unable to get back to China or because they did not want to. In the latter situation, one consideration was that they had outlived their generation in China, whose life-span averaged in the thirties. Another factor was the low esteem they may have felt if they had failed to financially uplift their families. Some had a reputation for being wastrels. Theirs was an unenviable old age; they had few or no relations in urban New Zealand, and their plight became even more serious when the Chinese stores and lodging houses that traditionally gave free shelter to indigent, elderly compatriots closed because of the decline in the Chinese population.

Some needy, elderly Chinese in Otago received two and sixpence to four shillings a week from the local Charitable Aid Board, and when they could no longer cope at all, they could be admitted for a free temporary or permanent stay in the Benevolent Institutes' Old Men's Homes in Dunedin and Invercargill. The late Dunedin leader, Chin Bing Foon, MBE, recalled that impecunious, frail Chinese gained eligibility for these benevolent institute homes as quid pro quo for the Chinese community's favourable consideration and help in recruiting Chinese navvies back in the early 1870s. This aid was also applicable to the Chinese on the West Coast.

Census figures show few Chinese on such European aid, however. The figures for 1896 and 1901 were three and 14 inmates in benevolent asylums respectively, while the 1906 census recorded seven 'recipients of charitable aid', 15 inmates in a 'benevolent asylum' and 22 'lunatics', who presumably got free temporary or permanent mental hospital care. But the Otago Chinese recipients of Charitable Aid Board help were higher, particularly in the 1900s. For example, in 1905 and 1907, Otago had 61 and 74 Chinese respectively on outdoor relief and 14 and 15 respectively in the Dunedin Home[74] because both the outdoor and indoor aid were periodic or because the recipient had died.

Indications are that apart from the aid boards and benevolent institutes, a number of ordinary European neighbours cared about the destitute Chinese and helped them with used clothing; three shillings could be spent on food supplemented with wild food, but this left nothing over for clothes. In contrast, European beneficiaries of the Old Age Pensions Act 1898 could get seven shillings weekly, but Chinese were not eligible, whether naturalised or not. Other Chinese residents were approached for donations to the Benevolent Institutes' Homes or to pay half the fare of 'worn-out' Chinese inmates of the homes who had recovered enough to travel back to China.[75] This was a kindness, but it also made financial sense, since it was cheaper to have these men return home than to keep them as inmates.

The Chinese donations could provide each of the returning old men with a little extra, say, £10.0, to take with them. The Bruce County Council, which encompassed the Adams Flat and Glenore goldfields, was notably kind to these elderly men, giving them four shillings weekly until their beneficence was over-ruled. The ending of that avenue of support was responsible for a Dunedin approach in 1905 to Premier Richard Seddon for increased help for indigent Chinese. The delegation suggested

Chinese miners, Nokomai, 1900s. These miners formed a small Christian congregation at the Nokomai River. Missionary to the Chinese, Reverend Alexander Don, is on right-hand end of the front row.

Courtesy Cromwell Museum collection

that the needed money could come from poll tax payments, but Seddon refused. An approach in 1907 to the Hon. George Fowlds, who was known to be somewhat kinder to Chinese, was similarly unsuccessful.[76]

By the turn of the twentieth century, central government and local authorities such as those for Mount Ida, Tuapeka and, in 1897, Wakatipu, had banned hiring Chinese employees, leaving private farmers and employers the only ones to hire them. Reverend Don subsequently recorded these men in a variety of labouring work to supplement gold earnings, such as flax milling and fellmongery work, although they were mainly employed in farming, often in work such as digging drainage trenches and 'fencing, shearing and turnip thinning'.[77]

Chinese Charity

The Cantonese gold seekers to Gim Shan countries, including New Zealand, organised themselves for comradeship and mutual support, such that most did not need to feel alone. Their organisation established informal yet very strong arrangements based on the family system and the local governance model in the Cantonese countryside. It became these men's principal survival factor, especially in bad times.

In China at the time, rural people lived not in scattered homesteads but gathered together in villages or suburbs of a single clan. In a village (or suburb), there were *doos* (village factions), each composed of immediate and extended families, descended from a particular clan forebear. All village *doos* contributed to common costs such as the upkeep of the ancestral hall, the village well, the commonage, the local primary school and policing, the cost of festivals and so on. Over time, the *doos* bought land together (called 'clan fields') and other investments that they could rent out, a practice that helped lighten the load of the common costs.

The *doos* of same clans in neighbouring villages were recognised not only as distant relations but also as descendants of a common clan ancestor within the wider geographical locality. Thus it was natural for nearby clan villages to form small clusters of villages known as *bos* (*paos* in Kuomintang government wording) for cooperative purposes. The clan villages were interspersed with those of other clans. For bigger projects, several *bos* of the same clan formed a *heung* (*hsiang* in Kuomintang wording), within the orbit of which was a market town and a secondary school for the clan. *Heung* varied in size but could number thousands of people.

The countryside was largely self-governing through the village *doos*, *bos* and *heung*. Membership was free. The heads and committees of the village, *bos* and *heung* were voluntary posts, with incumbents selected by consensus. These leaders lived an ethos of family and clan togetherness, and sought consensus, stability and cooperation rather than party politics. Self-sufficiency was the rule, except in large matters such as natural disasters and widespread disorder, at which point the government *yuan* centred in the county capital ('the *hsien* government') stepped in. Otherwise, the government exerted light control in the countryside; the *yuan* either did so directly or, in large counties, partly through the *kuoi* (the *chu*, districts), each of which encompassed a collection of *heung* of different clans. In the designated town of a *kuoi*, for instance, the government

Chinese Immigrant Act
Certificate of Exemption for
Lie Muck dated 23 January
1882.

Courtesy R.W. Murray collection,
Cromwell Museum

coordinated voluntary inputs when required, appointed a magistrate of lower rank to give judgments and assistance, stationed a squad of soldiers if necessary, undertook tax gathering and kept land records.[78]

In New Zealand, the Otago and West Coast adaptation of these combinations of family and clan ties and governance was very similar to that among Cantonese in other gold-rush countries. In the first instance, Chinese men usually migrated with village kin and others from neighbouring villages. They adhered to a kin and clan ethos with respect to helpfulness that led Reverend Don to observe 'they will go anywhere to help a clan member'.[79] However, given that the population of Chinese in nineteenth century New Zealand was small, some clans were barely represented. Therefore, as they had done in other Gim Shan countries, the Cantonese formed new, free, cooperative groupings based on a county or associated counties with a common history and dialect. These county groupings supplemented kin and clan affiliations and so were a wider source of camaraderie and support to members. The affiliations were the prime source of aid, but county members, despite originating in other clans, could be called upon for extra help. Consequently, county members mixed together on emigrant ships and worked together in mining parties almost as easily as kin and clansmen.

The social circles formed by kin, clan and county were also the main source of loans for their members because, as mentioned above, Europeans rarely lent money to Chinese. The loans were nearly always based merely on oral agreements. In other Gim Shan countries, clan associations that functioned as a type of benevolent society with lending facilities became established, but no such organisation existed in the small Chinese mining population in New Zealand.

Aid in the case of severe injury or sickness came first from a man's mining party, and if more help was needed, from family and clan. If help was still insufficient to complete a course of treatment or to send a man back to China, members of his county grouping locally or in the district were canvassed for donations; everybody was expected to give freely.[80] Such calls for help were common, given the high medical fees and prolonged treatments of the time. Other donations were solicited to send a body 'home', and this was regarded by Chinese as one of the highest charitable acts. Other

Elderly Chinese miner 'Tin Pan', Arrowtown region, early 1900s.

Courtesy Department of Conservation collection

donations were made to the local hospitals' yearly fundraising and to the benevolent institutions, and also to ameliorate the effects of natural disasters in New Zealand or China or to support community occasions such as Chinese festivals and feasts.

The miners' practice of giving was extended to help in sending frail old men to China. An extension of this was revealed in 2006, when the Historic Cemeteries Conservation Trust of New Zealand cleaned and repaired vandalised Chinese graves in Dunedin's Southern Cemetery.[81] There, one can still see two rows of graves with simple, small headstones. A high proportion of these were very likely the donated grave sites and markers of friendless inmates of the Dunedin Benevolent Institution's Home. In the absence of such support, burials could have been unmarked paupers' graves on the edge of the cemetery. This particular fate, or alternatively having one's unclaimed body routed to the Otago Medical School dissection room, were two fears in miners' old years, but these outcomes where generally averted by people sympathetic to the Chinese.

A solitary Chinese man or even an independent party had a high risk of not surviving in the goldfields given their limited English and resources. However, men within the social groupings of kin, clan and county, with their benefits of comradeship, support and greater repository of knowledge and resources, had a much better chance of success. As long as these groupings were extant either locally or even at a distance and assuming the ageing Chinese miner in the field still had contact with them, he would have felt less alone and vulnerable. For instance, the solitary Chinese miner Ah Quay (Chaak Hoi Yau, of Zengcheng county origin) appears to have been the only Chinese man left working at Skippers, but he kept in touch with Zengcheng people elsewhere in Otago. Upon his accidental death in 1904, someone or some grouping provided his burial in Skippers Cemetery with a bilingually inscribed marble gravestone and an iron railing around his grave.[82] In Cromwell, the cemetery burial book recorded several Chinese burials in the 1900s, with the same person coming from Dunedin to bury those of his clan or county.

The reality of Chinese charity was that donations did not help with ongoing living expenses; they were principally given for the completion of acute or semi-acute medical care, and if that care was unsuccessful, for return to China, dead or alive. This support ensured that the subject was not a continuing problem for the county donors. However, at the end of the gold era and the years after, there emerged the situation of lone Chinese men whose close comrades had mostly gone or died, and the remainder were too few, scattered or poor to help much. Such a person had probably lost contact or had little or no contact in the first place with other Chinese at a distance. In these cases, and there were not many, European charity was of considerable importance.

To the last, the remaining Chinese miners in Otago tried to maintain their independence. Only one Chinese man is known to have begged; a man on three shillings weekly probably had enough to eat with a trapped rabbit or eel, and if he cultivated potatoes and collected wild plants for extra food. However, as mentioned earlier he would not have had enough money for clothing, which accounts for old Chinese miners carrying their shoes. It is interesting to contemplate if men in this situation had actually reverted to their original financial state in China. Yet such was the apparent Chinese solidarity that previously when they were in fair numbers, they were known to be 'self-sufficient', an *imperio en imperium*. This togetherness was the main factor in their survivability.

Chinese Merchants

The key members of a county grouping were the merchants and their economically lesser colleagues, the storekeepers. Their importance explains the early arrival of these men to Otago. Usually they were better educated and better resourced financially than the rest of the Chinese. Their stores were essential for importing food and drink because the miners kept to Chinese cuisine. The proprietors also liaised with Europeans (thereby creating a certain degree of relationship), and they alerted their fellow Chinese to news, events and the latest regulations, and explained them.

From their premises, storekeepers grubstaked miners, invested in their projects, provided knowledge and advice on Chinese medicine, wrote letters for the miners, acted as a mail depot for letters from home and generally knew a miner's whereabouts; their stores were essentially social centres. Chinese storekeepers in New Zealand and other gold rush countries reversed the traditional Chinese social order. In old China, the trader (including the merchant) was ranked last after the mandarin, scholar, farmer and artisan. However, the successful trader in Gim Shan was first in social precedence.

The chief merchants in Otago were based in Dunedin, and they linked with their colleagues in the field. Those Chinese from small county groupings who had no merchant or storekeeper of their own would affiliate with a willing merchant of another grouping. Chinese miners patronised European stores as well, but they kept in touch with Chinese merchants because only Chinese stores could provide certain essential goods and services.

An important merchant service not yet mentioned in detail was the enabling of communication with China. There was no Chinese postal service in New Zealand until 1896, and once set up, it remained inadequate for years. Accordingly, the preferred way of getting letters and remittances of sovereigns home was to ask a relative returning to China to carry them back for a *li shee* (usually a 10 per cent commission). The relative may have seemed to be returning rich since he could be carrying sovereigns for several people.[83] Otherwise, miners used merchants and storekeepers, who charged fees for the service. Smaller storekeepers typically linked with their merchant supplier, who had counterparts in Hong Kong and Guangzhou.

The Cantonese called these storekeepers *Gim Shan jong* (*jinshanzhuang* in pinyin). They specialised in servicing the overseas needs, including communications, of the migrants and their merchants. Otago merchants sent them miners' letters but not miners' money, relaying instead only their instructions as to the amounts and how the remittances were to be disposed. The *jinshanzhuang* then complied with the instructions, typically using a private courier to send the letter and money into the countryside. Merchants in New Zealand periodically settled their accounts with their respective *jinshanzhuang* with consignments of sovereigns.[84] This conduit could also work in reverse, in getting a letter to a miner in the field. The earliest preserved letter to New Zealand is dated 1874.[85]

From a survival point of view, the county groupings brought forth Chinese merchants and storekeepers as leaders who provided their mining customers with essential items and services, and liaison with Europeans. These Chinese businesses did not tend to amalgamate because their essence was to serve particular groupings.

Conclusion

The invitation to Chinese to come to Otago was extended in anticipation that these newcomers would give the province an economic boost. The Chinese kept their side of the bargain. They were orderly and required little in the way of official or European charitable help with respect to mining or personal welfare. This scenario applied at the beginning of the Chinese men's time in New Zealand as gold seekers and could be said to be evident even at the end of those years. With respect to mining itself, Chinese reworked or opened up difficult auriferous ground (including Round Hill). Chinese leaders and workers were participants when the full potential of gold dredging was first developed, and they were when the Nokomai goldfield re-opened to sluicing.

The major missing survival factor for these Chinese men was diplomatic protection. Until 1876 the Otago Provincial Council acted as a diplomatic surrogate for the Chinese, but a diplomatic vacuum occurred when the council was dissolved. In 1892 Premier John Ballance refused the establishment of a Chinese consulate, prompting Governor the Rt. Hon. Earl of Onslow to comment 'they have no-one to defend them'.[86] A Chinese consulate was not accepted until 1908, and then the consul did not arrive until the following year. So the Chinese internal social survival factors, especially their collectivism, had to cope without diplomatic help as the external factors favourable to them waned.

When we recall the rise of antagonism against the Chinese goldminers, it is gratifying to consistently find in present-day inland Otago a generally positive memory and opinion of these men. Certainly, there is no residual hostility, only a vague guilt over past anti-Chinese attitudes. Today's goodwill is reflected in the wording of two bronze plaques, one at Clyde and the other at Waikaia, commemorating the 150th anniversaries of their goldfields in 2012. They celebrate the early Europeans and Chinese miners as pioneers together.

'Opening Wealth's Door': Chinese market gardening on the goldfields

Joanna Boileau

MOST RESEARCH ON THE CHINESE in Central Otago has focused on their involvement in gold mining. The significant role they played in providing food to the wider community has been neglected. In this chapter I discuss the development of Chinese market gardening in Central Otago, from the first arrivals of Chinese miners from the Victorian goldfields in 1866 through to the 1890s. I take a multidisciplinary approach, drawing on archaeological and documentary evidence and research in the fields of immigration, transnationalism and technology transfer. My starting point is the premise that the experience of technology transfer is influenced by an interrelated network of technical, economic, social, environmental and political factors that mediate the relationship between imported knowledge and the recipient society.[1]

The New Zealand goldfields were the southernmost goldfields in the world. Chinese immigrants adapted their traditional agricultural methods and technological skills to environmental, economic and social conditions that differed considerably from those of their homeland in subtropical southern China. As Warwick Frost has observed in the Australian context, the success of Chinese farmers was due not only to the simple transfer of agricultural skills from China, but also to their entrepreneurship and ability to adapt their techniques to the very different environments they encountered.[2]

The Physical Environment

The Chinese miners who travelled to southern New Zealand in the nineteenth century had to adjust to a climate very different to that of their homeland. A mountainous inland region, Central Otago has a climate that is more continental in nature than in any other area of the country. The region has some of New Zealand's highest and lowest temperatures, and lowest rainfall. For example, in Alexandra, mean temperatures range from an average maximum of 8ºC in July to over 37ºC in January.[3] This region would have presented a stark contrast to subtropical southern China. In 1897 the

Reverend Alexander Don, Presbyterian minister to the Chinese, spoke with a Chinese miner from Guangdong who was fossicking at Waipori. The miner compared the barrenness of Otago with the 'fatness' of his native district, where three crops were taken annually from the same ground.[4]

In choosing the locations of their gardens, Chinese gardeners considered key environmental factors – the availability of water, soil fertility, aspect and slope. Their market gardens were therefore generally located near watercourses, freshwater lakes or swamps, and on relatively flat areas of fertile alluvial soil. Water was a critical resource for both alluvial mining and market gardening. In 1911 Don recorded a couplet on the wall of a Chinese miner's hut in Nokomai, which highlights the crucial importance of water to the Chinese who settled in Central Otago. The Chinese term for water race is water dragon: 'When water runs gold is produced and all get profit/The dragon comes 1000 miles and opens wealth's door.'[5]

Discussing the insights that archaeological evidence can provide into the lives of the Chinese in southern New Zealand, Neville Ritchie highlights their adaptability and resourcefulness. They built shelters from whatever local materials were available in the remote, rugged gorges of Central Otago, by walling up rock overhangs or building huts of river cobbles, rock rubble, adobe or mud bricks. They also used flattened kerosene tins and rice sacks, for example at Lawrence. At Round Hill in Southland, where timber was plentiful, they built huts of timber and shingle. They also quickly adopted the practical European miners' work clothes and boots to combat the cold.[6]

Chinese miners in the Nevis Valley, c. 1902.

Courtesy Cromwell Museum collection

Chinese market gardeners adapted their horticultural practices and choice of crops to the hot summers, cold winters and steep terrain of Central Otago. Many gardens were established on terraces cut into the hillsides, or formed by widening naturally occurring river terraces, which had fertile alluvial soil.[7] The method of terracing slopes for agriculture is common throughout the world, particularly in densely populated areas such as Asia. Visiting Hong Kong in 1911, American agronomist Franklin Hiram King marvelled at the efficiency with which Chinese horticulturalists surface-fitted their gardens to the landscape, obtaining the maximum ground area for cultivation.[8] Terraced gardens constructed by immigrant Chinese communities have also been recorded in the remote Salmon River Mountains of Idaho in the United States. These commercial-scale gardens, the creation of Chinese miners attracted to Idaho by the gold rushes in 1869, were cultivated until the 1920s.[9]

The commercial crops that the Chinese gardeners in Central Otago grew were those suited to the temperate climate. They included potatoes, turnips, corn, cabbage, celery, onions, peas, gooseberries and strawberries, and they found a ready market among Europeans.[10] The Chinese also introduced new vegetables from their homeland, including Chinese cabbage, Chinese turnip, bean sprouts, Chinese celery, garlic, parsley and a variety of radish. However, there was little demand for these from European consumers, so they were generally grown for Chinese consumption only.[11] In 1865 the *Otago Witness* reported: 'The Chinese are the first market gardeners on the goldfields and they have already introduced several new vegetables previously not seen amongst us – one of them a species of beet known as "the Chinese cabbage".'[12]

The seeds of Chinese vegetables were imported from China, as evidenced by an incident that Reverend Alexander Don reported in 1883. He met a Chinese man travelling from Riverton to Round Hill carrying a sack of turnip seed. He told Don that he had imported the seed from China because he considered it better than the local variety.[13] According to James Ng, Chinese cabbage was the most common Chinese vegetable grown. This hardy plant grows readily throughout New Zealand, but acquires its best flavour in the colder south.[14] On his regular 'inland tours' through Central Otago, Reverend Don often stayed and ate with Chinese miners. During his 1905/06 tour, he climbed over a range a thousand feet high to reach Bannockburn, where three men had opened a claim in the river bed of the great gorge. Don reported: 'At 8.15pm we all riced together with an abundance of delicious white cabbage grown of seed from Canton.'[15] In 1901 he had written of a meal of rice, bacon, peas, eggs and 'Shantung cabbage' at Mareburn.[16] Earlier, in 1883, Don wrote that *wong nga paak*, a variety of Chinese cabbage, was being grown at Round Hill, and that three pounds of bean sprouts or *nga tsoi* could be bought there for one shilling.[17]

Market gardening was always a risky enterprise. Like all people on the land in Central Otago, Chinese gardeners had to cope with unpredictable weather and fluctuating prices for their produce. In October 1898 the *Dunstan Times* reported that one of the few remaining large-scale Chinese market gardens in Central Otago, run by Charlie Lock Chong (known to locals as Ah Lock) at Matakanui, at the foot of the Dunstan Mountains, had been destroyed by an unseasonal snow storm.

> The prevailing weather last week was rain, hail, snow and frost, accompanied by
> thunder and lightning. The storm did great damage to the gardens. Our local
> gardener, Ah Lock, told me that the crop of strawberries and plums in his garden
> will be a complete failure. This is a pity for Ah Lock goes to immense trouble
> with his garden and is not backward in giving employment to his countrymen.
> Last year his garden was a favourite resort of the townsfolk and visitors from a
> distance when his strawberries were ripe. His loss will be considerable.[18]

High winds were a danger for horticulturalists in many locations in New Zealand.
In 1874 the *Tuapeka Times* reported that a party of Chinese had started a garden by
Wetherstones' town boundary, notable for the fact that the men were using thistle
stalks to line the wires of their fences as protection from the wind.[19] This practice was
probably an adaptation to the more extreme climate of southern New Zealand. In
southern China, gardeners traditionally left their fields open to the elements, with no
enclosing walls or fences. One possible explanation for why gardeners did this was to
allow winds to blow freely through the growing crops and so discourage insect pests.[20]

Chinese gardeners in southern New Zealand continued the horticultural traditions
of their homeland, raising pigs and planting fruit trees as well as growing vegetables.
In Otago, they grew the stonefruit ideally suited to the continental climate, such as
peaches, plums and apricots, as well as apples and pears. Fruit could be a lucrative
supplement to vegetable growing, and some Chinese market gardeners became successful orchardists. One was Lye Bow. He originally came to Central Otago in search
of gold but quickly saw the demand for fresh food to feed the thousands of miners
flocking to the goldfields. He began a market garden in Butchers Gully, just outside
Alexandra, and branched out into what became a very successful orchard business.
By the 1890s he was regularly receiving prizes at horticultural shows for his apples,
pears and plums.[21] In April 1894 the *Otago Witness* reported that Lye Bow had 1200
apple trees, 500 trees of other varieties, and had produced 10 tons of apples for local
consumption that season.[22]

The Economic Environment

Chinese market gardening in New Zealand thus had its origins in the gold rushes.
Chinese immigrants took up gardening from an early stage: not all the men who
arrived from the Victorian diggings travelled directly to the goldfields; some remained
in Dunedin and leased land for market gardens. In August 1867 the *Otago Witness*,
reporting the arrival of 236 Chinese from Melbourne on the steamers *Rangitoto* and
Otago, stated:

> [G]radually they are being drafted off to different parts of the Gold-fields where
> those who preceded them have settled, and one or two drays daily are being
> dispatched with their goods and chattels. Not a few of their number seemed
> disposed to settle about the city, and in different places they have leased portions
> of ground, and are already at work, trenching, delving, and otherwise preparing
> their sections for the cultivation of garden produce.[23]

The evidence from the New Zealand goldfields supports the model of immigrant business development proposed by Jock Collins. Referencing international studies of 'ethnic' entrepreneurs, such as the study by Roger Waldinger and colleagues, Collins argues that market gardeners and other family farmers should be seen as 'small business people on the land'.[24] As Waldinger et al. point out, the initial market for immigrant businesses often arises within the migrant communities themselves because the business holders in those groups are the ones who best know and therefore can best serve the needs and cultural preferences of the people within them. Food is one of the major products involved. This commercial activity may then serve as a platform for expansion of the business into the open market.[25] Chinese miners probably initially grew vegetables to supplement their income from mining, and were involved in small-scale commercial activities, mainly supplying their own community. They moved into full-time market gardening once it became clear there was a wider market for their produce. Thus, ready access to customers beyond the Chinese community was an important factor in the growth of Chinese market gardening on the goldfields.

The discovery of gold in Central Otago in 1862 radically transformed the economic fortunes of Otago province and contributed to its political, social and cultural development. The population of Dunedin boomed, and the city became the largest and most prosperous in New Zealand.[26] However, as Charles Fahey has pointed out in regard to Australia, the heady days of alluvial prospecting when men could make their fortunes from the readily accessible river gravels were short lived; after only a few years, large amounts of capital and machinery were required to recover gold from underground leads. By the 1860s many miners were wage earners employed by mining companies.[27] Similarly, in New Zealand, the gold rushes were already experiencing a slump by 1865. The number of European miners in Otago fell from around 18,800 in early 1864 to around 6000 by the end of 1865, as the men either returned to Australia or followed the rush to newly discovered fields on the West Coast.[28] It was this economic downturn that prompted the Otago Provincial Council to invite experienced Chinese miners from Victoria to come to Central Otago in 1865. According to James Ng, it was anticipated that these miners would also benefit the general population of Otago as tillers of the soil.[29]

It is difficult to estimate the precise earnings of individual miners, as they were understandably reluctant to advertise the extent of their finds, but it is clear from contemporary accounts that mining was a risky enterprise. The gold rushes created a high demand for fresh food; often, a more reliable income could be made from supplying other miners with vegetables than from mining. A recent study of census and economic data from the Californian goldfields shows that, consistent with the historical literature, miners generally made small or negative gains while non-miners were much better off economically than if they had pursued similar occupations in their places of origin. This was true of both American-born and foreign-born miners. Thus, merchants and other service providers reaped most of the profits from mining.[30]

Given the uncertainty of returns from mining, the scarcity of fresh vegetables and the generally high cost of food, goods and services on the diggings, it is not surprising that miners in New Zealand diversified into other activities that generated a more reliable income. The high demand for fresh food on the goldfields made market gardening an attractive option. Chinese immigrants were quick to identify this niche market. Recalling the early days of the gold rush at Gabriel's Gully, a correspondent to the *Evening Post* (Wellington) wrote in 1899 that in the 1860s they had the Chinese to thank for supplying vegetables. Local runholders, the correspondent continued, had set up butchers' stalls along the route to the diggings and done a roaring trade.[31] Ng argues that because many Chinese on the goldfields were established in work that provided a more regular income than gold mining, they were better able to save, pay the poll tax and promote chain migration, thereby increasing their numbers.[32]

The archaeological evidence of the mining camps at Lawrence and Cromwell recorded by Neville Ritchie indicates that Chinese miners in Central Otago initially grew vegetables for their own consumption in small plots adjacent to their huts. One of the best preserved was the camp at Cromwell, which consisted of around 30 huts surrounded by small garden plots, complete with pig pens, hen coops and fruit trees. A spring provided water year round.[33] The miners thus recreated in the far south of New Zealand a form of subsistence similar to that which they had left behind in southern China. They established small self-sufficient farms where the raising of pigs and chickens provided both food and valuable manure for the vegetable plots.

Ritchie identifies two further categories of Chinese gardens in southern New Zealand, indicative of the development of commercial market gardening. The first encompasses the large garden areas established adjacent to Chinese settlements that were either communally owned or owned by a storekeeper or other affluent person. These gardens could be found in Arrowtown, Cromwell and Lawrence, settlements which, with their stores, gaming rooms and brothels, served as centres for the small groups of miners scattered throughout the surrounding districts. The second category – large market gardens – had become established in many towns by the 1880s. They operated on a full-time commercial basis.[34]

The documentary evidence supports this archaeological evidence. Drawing chiefly on Reverend Don's diaries, James Ng and Neville Ritchie record gardens in many scattered mining camps, including those of Weatherstones, Macetown, Conroys Gully and Bald Hill Flat in Central Otago and Round Hill in Southland, and suggest that Chinese gardeners began supplying the wider communities at these places with vegetables. By the 1870s there were gardens in townships such as Waitahuna, Tapanui, Lawrence, Roxburgh, Cromwell, Queenstown and Riverton. Large market gardens were recorded at Beaumont, Butchers Gully, Clyde, Ophir, Matakanui, Arrowtown and Palmerston.[35] Chinese gardeners and vegetable hawkers could be found wherever good business opportunities existed, including in larger towns away from the goldfields such as Milton, Gore, Oamaru, Invercargill and Dunedin.[36]

For some Chinese, successful market gardening became a springboard to other enterprises, such as storekeeping. For example, Ah Lum, a well-known Chinese storekeeper in Arrowtown, first came to New Zealand in 1870 as a goldminer, then moved into market gardening. In 1909 he became a storekeeper, purchasing a property

from Loo Lee. The property included market-garden land and a stone cottage used as a store, originally built in 1883 by the market gardener Wong Hop Lee. Ah Lum ran the store until his death in 1925, while continuing his market-gardening enterprise.[37] The store still stands in the Chinese village at Arrowtown.[38]

Technology

Chinese market gardeners on the goldfields employed the intensive agricultural methods of their homeland, developed over thousands of years. From the Qin to Yuan dynasties in China (221 BC to 1368 AD), intensive agricultural systems evolved that made maximum use of the available land and supported the ever growing population.[39] Given the large available labour force, the need to develop increasingly labour-intensive systems rather than increase productivity was essential.[40] In southern China, the agricultural system was characterised by sophisticated methods of water control and irrigation, continuous cropping of a variety of crops, thorough cultivation of the soil, intensive manuring to maintain soil fertility, and care and attention paid to individual plants, including regular weeding and hoeing to aerate the soil and hand removal of insect pests.[41] On the Otago goldfields, Chinese market gardeners had access to ready supplies of manure from the pigs and chickens they raised, and from local farms, stables and dairies. In 1874 the *Tuapeka Times* described a group of Chinese market gardeners at work in Lawrence:

> This party appear to work very systematically, having in their possession a horse and cart, which they employ in conveying manure to their garden from the various stables in Lawrence. Their mode of cultivating the soil is of the best description. They believe in having the earth worked very fine—in fact almost into a powder—and consequently expend a large amount of time in producing this result. The manure, which is scattered about somewhat lavishly, is also well worked into the ground.[42]

As Barry McGowan has noted with respect to Australia, the links between the technologies applied in gold mining and market gardening were close ones.[43] Chinese miners in Otago quickly adapted to local conditions. Their experience of irrigation in their homeland made many of them adept with mining technology such as waterwheels, water races and dams.[44] For example, Ng records wing dams built by Chinese in Otago and on the West Coast.[45] Similar technologies were applied to market gardening. In

---

Opposite page, top: View of Arrowtown Chinese camp overlooking the Bush Creek/Arrow River junction. Ah Lum's store (see also Chapter 19, page 295) is in the centre of the photograph. The Arrowtown Chinese Village, rebuilt in the 1980s, features several of the huts in the foreground.

Courtesy Lakes District Museum, Arrowtown, File EL1870

Opposite page, bottom: Chinese village at Arrowtown, c. 1901.

Courtesy Department of Conservation, Central Otago

Otago, before the introduction of more complex machinery, the water wheel and the so-called 'Californian pump' enabled waterlogged ground to be drained not only for mining but also for cultivating vegetable crops.

The Californian pump, named from its use on the Californian goldfields, derived from the traditional Chinese chain pump. It was a continuous belt, usually made of canvas, with buckets attached, and was commonly used on the Australian and New Zealand goldfields.[46] In 1877 a newspaper reporter described Chinese miners operating a Californian pump in Central Otago. When viewed from a distance, the miners appeared to be dancing: 'Passing along Gabriels Gully I observed about twenty-five Chinamen at work, in parties of three and four. They were engaged in dancing operations. What this means we fail to understand excepting they were pumping water out of their claims by foot – that is, driving California pumps with a wheel a la

Foot-powered waterwheel, South Dunedin, early 1900s.

Courtesy Kings High School, Dunedin

treadmill, a system very common with Chinese.'[47] In 1902 Reverend Don recorded the use of the chain pump on Chinese market gardens in Dunedin: 'The Chinese on the low-lying Forbury market-gardens are applying the machine that in China they use to raise the water from streams up to their rice fields, here to raise the water off their gardens into the street open drains to run off.'[48]

In his study of gold mining in the Alexandra district, John McCraw documents the battles over water rights that were fought out in the wardens' courts and the struggles of local authorities and residents to obtain adequate town water supplies when legislation gave priority to water for mining.[49] The orchardist Lye Bow used mining infrastructure such as dams, races and flumes to convey water to his gardens. He drew water from the same dam in Butchers Gully that his countrymen used when searching for gold in the bed of Butchers Creek. McCraw records the lengthy legal battles that Lye Bow and other Chinese fought in the local warden's court during the 1890s to maintain their water rights against the European mining companies operating large steam-driven and water-driven dredges upstream of their own operations.[50] At the same time, the Alexandra Borough Council approached Lye Bow to relinquish some of his water rights to serve the township's growing population. Eventually, in 1907, Lye Bow sold a portion of his water rights to the council.[51]

The Social Environment

Chinese miners in Central Otago, almost exclusively men, were sustained by social networks based on their ties to their family and home village in China. Many writers on the overseas Chinese in Australia and New Zealand have noted the fundamental importance of kinship, clan and district ties to the social and economic survival of these men.[52] Both miners and market gardeners worked in co-operative partnerships. In New Zealand, the records of Alexander Don in the early twentieth century show clusters of gardens operated by groups of men from the same district in China.[53] These flexible business arrangements enabled individual Chinese to draw on the economic and social resources provided by networks of kinship and friendship, and to share risks. The arrangements also accommodated the high mobility of the overseas Chinese community, as they could be easily terminated and investments liquidated. When one partner moved elsewhere, or returned to China, his place was taken by another.[54]

Initially, relations between Chinese and Europeans on the New Zealand goldfields were relatively good, with less physical violence than on the goldfields in Australia and California.[55] It appears that the initial favourable reception of the Chinese in New Zealand was due in part to their enterprise in supplying much needed fresh produce to the mining community, at reasonable prices, and the fact that they occupied an economic niche where they did not compete directly with Europeans. In May 1869 the *Dunstan Times* wrote of the 'immense value' of Chinese gold seekers. They had nowhere lessened European gains nor unduly competed on the labour market, they 'filled in gaps' by taking over abandoned ground and thereby kept up the value of mining property, they reduced the cost of vegetables with their gardens, and they generally acquitted themselves as 'respected members of society'.[56] The work of Chinese market gardeners in manuring and tilling also improved the quality of the soil for later European land users, a theme which recurs in later Chinese settlement in the North Island. In 1877 the *Tuapeka Times* commented on a survey of quarter-acre sections in the township of Roxburgh: 'The soil is of extra good quality, having been occupied by a Chinese gardener for the last three or four years, and the finest vegetables of all descriptions have been produced.'[57]

However, attitudes towards Chinese became less favourable as their numbers grew. In 1871 an enquiry was held into Chinese immigration after representations from the Otago Mining Commission expressing concerns about the Chinese influx. The Select Committee on Chinese Immigration concluded that there were no sufficient grounds for excluding Chinese, and that no legislative action should be taken to exclude them or impose special burdens upon them.[58] The contribution of Chinese in producing fresh produce on the goldfields was an important factor in the committee's conclusions. The evidence submitted to the enquiry commented particularly on the Chinese men's skill as gardeners, and made frequent reference to their industry, sobriety and honesty.[59]

Recent scholarship in New Zealand and Australia presents a more nuanced picture of relations between Chinese and Europeans, and highlights the complexities of cross-cultural encounters.[60] Rather than depicting Chinese as victims of institutional racism, these studies demonstrate the nuances of these contacts, which ranged from intermarriage and business partnerships at one end of the spectrum, to racist attacks and larrikinism at the other. Most commonly there was uneasy co-existence and limited interaction. So while Europeans recognised the horticultural skills of Chinese market gardeners and appreciated the fresh produce they provided, a complex set of attitudes and beliefs constrained their willingness to accept them socially. These notions included belief in the superiority of the European race and European technology, fear of miscegenation, a view of market gardening as a low-status occupation, fear of economic competition, and stereotyping of Chinese immigrants as diseased and vice ridden.

Conclusion

Adapting practices they brought with them from China, particularly their skills in water management and intensive cultivation, Chinese market gardeners successfully turned the impediments of life in the harsh climate of Otago to their advantage. They went on to make a significant contribution to the New Zealand economy. Following the movement of the general population from the South Island to the North Island in the wake of the gold rushes, they fuelled rural expansion and the rapid growth of country towns and enhanced diets with a wide variety of reasonably priced fruit and vegetables. By 1921, almost 44 per cent of Chinese in New Zealand were market gardeners.[61]

9.

A Trade in Chinese Men and Supplies: Lowe Kong Meng and the organisation of the Chinese gold rush in Otago

Paul Macgregor

THE USUAL UNDERSTANDING OF Chinese in nineteenth-century gold-rush historiography is that they were not welcome – and certainly not encouraged – on any goldfield in the white settler countries around the Pacific Rim. Yet in late 1864, influential Otago citizens forwarded an invitation to Lowe Kong Meng (劉光明 Liu Guangming)[1] and other Chinese merchants of the colony of Victoria to send Chinese miners to Otago. The white leaders of Otago saw the Chinese of Victoria as an attractive source of miners but were unsure of how to garner the attention of Chinese in Victoria, nearly all of whom were unable to speak or read English and who could not be attracted simply by the glowing accounts of Otago riches in the Victorian press. The Otago men accordingly decided that Chinese merchants could act as brokers to bring the miners to Otago, and Lowe Kong Meng's name was prominent when they issued their invitation.

Victoria had been, from the early 1850s, a major destination for Chinese men seeking gold outside China. Peaking at 46,000 in 1859 (nine per cent of the colony's population),[2] the number of Chinese miners in that colony exceeded the Chinese population of California, which had only 35,000 in 1860.[3] While declining yields in Victoria and the tightening of anti-Chinese mining taxes led many Chinese to leave Victoria for promising new fields in New South Wales from the end of 1859, there were, at the time of the Otago invitation, at least 20,000 Chinese miners in Victoria.[4] In contrast, James Ng relates that the numbers of European miners on the Otago goldfields had dropped from 18,800 in early 1864 to perhaps 6000 by the end of 1865.[5] The Chinese of Victoria also had a reputation for successful working of abandoned claims, and this type of ground was widespread in Otago.[6]

The usual paradigm for popular Australasian gold-rush migration history is a bilateral one, with miners leaving their country of origin for an overseas goldfield and then either staying there or returning. Yet there was considerable movement between the goldfields of the different Australasian colonies. Keir Reeves has also highlighted the significant movement of Chinese miners between goldfields on different shores of the southwest Pacific.[7] The passage of 10,000 Chinese to New South Wales from Victoria in the early 1860s[8] demonstrated the Chinese' willingness to change colonies in their search for gold, but New South Wales introduced its own anti-Chinese taxes in 1861,[9] leaving Otago as an attractive new alternative.

Lowe Kong Meng

Lowe Kong Meng, Chinese merchant of Melbourne, had a reputation throughout Australasia. He was no ordinary merchant. Within six years of his 1851 arrival in Melbourne at the age of 23, he was importing, in 2014 figures, £6 million worth of supplies per ship and had come to dominate the import trade from Hong Kong.[10]

Lowe Kong Meng, c. 1863.

Courtesy Thomas Bradley Harris album collection, 'Eastern Window': www.the-eastern-window.com/harris-introduction.html

By the early 1860s the Melbourne press was hailing him as a global trader on a gigantic scale, with few men in Melbourne wealthier than he.[11] Kong Meng was also a well-known charterer of ships, and his trade included the movement of Chinese by ship to and from Victoria. He was fluent and literate in English and thus was the ideal mediator between the deputation in Otago and Victoria's Chinese.

How did he come to achieve this reputation? The answer lies in his origins in the British port of Penang in Malaya. When Kong Meng was born in Penang in 1830/31,[12] the port had been British for 45 years. His father and progenitors, originally from Canton,[13] had been carrying on an extensive business for a century as merchants and contractors,[14] and his father, Lowe a Quee,[15] possessed considerable property on the island of Penang.[16]

Even before the establishment of British Penang in 1786, the port of Malacca, further south on the Malay Peninsula, was the destination of a Chinese-managed labour-import system that brought coolies from south China each year on junks when the northwest winds of the monsoon in January and February favoured the journey. Under British patronage and support, this system grew rapidly, allowing expansion of Chinese mining and plantations in the Malayan and Borneo hinterlands, especially after the advent of steamships in the Strait of Malacca in 1845.[17] By Kong Meng's time, Chinese merchants in Malaya had well-developed connections with Chinese merchants in south China, familiarity with British port and shipping systems, and well-established processes for recruiting labourers and their supplies from China.

But the British colonial agency in the East underwent major changes in this period, providing attractive opportunities for the Chinese to engage deeply in British commercial and cultural spheres. Roderick Matthews and Lakshmi Subramanian argue that the growth of liberalism in Britain led to the idea of a 'missionary' role for colonial government, with Britons educating locals in modern ways.[18] One manifestation of this development was the Penang Free School,[19] the first British school in the Far East, and it was there that Kong Meng received an education in English, French and Malay. He was taught modern subjects of the English schooling system and acquired characteristics of a British gentleman. He would have read the *Penang Gazette and Straits Chronicle*, one of the earliest modern newspapers in the Far East,[20] and in doing so, realised how a newspaper could facilitate commercial and shipping intelligence. Kong Meng also learned modern British forms of commerce and associated with British people in the settlement.

In 1847 when Kong Meng was 17, his father sent him to Mauritius,[21] then a major source of the world's sugar,[22] to perfect his English and French.[23] Although the British had captured Mauritius from the French in 1810, the island's plantation owners were still mainly French. There, Kong Meng established himself in trade as an importing merchant,[24] chiefly transacting Eastern produce[25] and connected to the firm of A. Goon(e) Frères.[26] His ventures were between Mauritius, Calcutta and Singapore during the years 1847 to 1853.[27] He generally travelled as supercargo,[28] plying a particularly intensive trade between India and Mauritius.[29]

British Ascendency

Though Chinese, Lowe a Quee and his son Lowe Kong Meng supported the British 1842 victory over China in the First Anglo-Chinese (Opium) War: Kong Meng's 'brother was killed in the Chinese war, in the service of the East India Company'.[30] They would also have been impressed by the establishment, subsequent to victory, of Hong Kong, the opening of the first five Chinese treaty ports to foreign trade,[31] the effective replacement of Chinese junks by European square-riggers[32] and steamers[33] in Asian waters, and the massive growth in British, European, Chinese and American trade between all ports on Asia's Indian and Pacific coasts.

Kong Meng and his father would furthermore have noted a parallel expansion of British ports and colonies throughout Asia and Australasia subsequent to Penang's founding. This Asian colonial enterprise created a web of ports tied by trade, mail, exchange of newspapers, personal and commercial networks, political developments and mutual interest, with Australasia a part of it all. During Kong Meng's early years in Melbourne, the city's leading newspaper, the *Argus*, regularly featured news from Asia and Indian Ocean ports; more if a war was in progress.

In Mauritius, Kong Meng heard of the Australian gold rush and came to Melbourne[34] in 1853 with cargo from that island.[35] He was the first Chinese merchant in the colony. After trying mining for three unprofitable months, Kong Meng sailed for India, resolving never to return to Australia. In Calcutta, his friends (presumably

Kong Meng and Co. premises, Little Bourke Street, Melbourne.

Source: 'Chinese Quarter, Little Bourke Street, Melbourne', *The Australian News for Home Readers*, 21 October 1863, courtesy State Library of Victoria picture collection, Acc No:IAN21/10/63/5

British, Indian and Chinese traders) induced him to change his mind.[36] He returned to Victoria with fresh merchandise from India[37] and in 1854 established the importing firm of Kong Meng and Company.[38]

Whether in Mauritius, Calcutta, Penang, Hong Kong, Singapore or Melbourne, Lowe Kong Meng would have seen himself as part of overlapping spheres of British and Chinese interests. He knew how to import men and goods from China and to source goods across the Indian Ocean. As well as fluency in English, Cantonese, French and Malay, he understood the European-Asian shipping system – the captains, routes, times and annual winds. He had commercial contacts with Chinese, French and British merchants across Asia, and he knew how to use the shipping and advertising columns of English-language newspapers to further his business.

By the time Lowe Kong Meng was living in Melbourne, hundreds of newspapers were being published in English across Asia and Australasia, and the main titles were systematically and frequently exchanged by ship, with articles copied verbatim from one to another, or summarised, on a regular basis.[39] Thus, with a time lag of only a few weeks at maximum, news and opinions circulated rapidly and widely, strongly enhancing a sense of international community across the region, at least among those literate in English. Kong Meng saw the benefit of this spread of information; between 1853 and 1880 over 2100 commercial advertisements and notices, placed by or mentioning him, appeared in the Melbourne and other Australasian presses, as did over 200 articles about his business and his civic and social activities.[40]

The Nature of the Imports

In 1866 the *Australian News for Home Readers* reported that 'Ever since his settlement in Melbourne [Lowe Kong Meng] has been carrying on an extensive business ... with his own countrymen and different Europeans.'[41] Calcutta had been Kong Meng's first choice (in 1854) for sourcing goods, which suggests an interest in supplying European tastes as well as Chinese. Fireworks, fancy goods, perfumery and silks from Hong Kong itemised in his 1859 import statistics were likely merchandise destined for affluent European consumers. In 1856 Kong Meng offered, through the *Argus*, 'Patna Rice, 60 tons of the best samples';[42] 'Opium – Three Chests Benares, also 300 Tins of Prepared';[43] and other goods: 'On sale, just landed, ex *Beatrice* and *Aurora*, White China sugar; brown ditto; Chinese oil, in jars; Ditto, in tins; Ditto matting; Preserved ginger'.[44]

The sources of Kong Meng's goods were widespread. One account stated that he was an importer of Chinese produce;[45] another said he had establishments in Mauritius, London and Hong Kong.[46] It was also maintained that he owned a fleet of half a dozen vessels, travelling regularly between Australia, India and China, some of which were involved in harvesting *bêche-de-mer* (sea slugs) from northern Australia and then exporting them to Hong Kong for the gourmet market.[47]

The principal categories of goods imported into Victoria in 1859 from the Asia/ Indian Ocean region were sugar, tea and rice; these comprised over two-thirds of all imports from the region. Mauritius supplied the great majority of sugar, with the rest from India, the Philippines and the Dutch East Indies. Virtually all tea was from China, and nearly all rice from India.[48]

A breakdown of Chinese products by port shows Foo Chow Fu (Fuzhou) and Macao provided mostly tea. However, Hong Kong provided the greatest diversity of cargo. The profile of these goods reveals that they closely matched the needs of a Chinese mining population: preserved foods, oils, opium, wine, spirits, medicines and clothing. Because most Chinese miners in Victoria were from Guangdong province, near Hong Kong, it made sense for the bulk of their supplies to come to them via this British colonial port.

A major anomaly is that most of the rice came from Calcutta. Although no ship from Calcutta had Kong Meng as agent, the volume of rice relative to the number of Chinese in Victoria indicates it was primarily for Chinese consumption. Given Kong Meng's Calcutta connections, it is possible Calcutta provided a cheaper source of rice than China did, and that Kong Meng had another agent handling the importing. This scenario is also likely to have been the case with other goods he was importing from places besides Hong Kong.

A Trade in Chinese Passengers

As well as making his fortune by dominating the supply of Chinese goods to Chinese miners, Kong Meng had a major role in the miners' movement as passengers. The majority of Chinese goldminers arrived as credit-ticket employees, bound in employment to the Chinese merchants and companies who had advanced them or their families the money to pay for the voyage. They were also bound to their employers until the debt was paid off (usually about three years) and often bound as well to live off the provisions supplied by those same employers.[49]

A report by James Dundas Crawford, a British consular official from Shanghai, identifies Lowe Kong Meng's company – all branches of which incorporated the term *kum* (金 *jin* gold) in their names – as central to the credit-ticket arrangements for Chinese miners in Australia. Crawford, who went to Australia in 1877 to investigate the Chinese population in the colonies, provides useful information about the nature of the relationships between Chinese merchants and miners at this time: 'In mining matters the merchant finds it more lucrative, rather than be himself the labour-master, to act as banker for mining-captains, as registrar of mining guilds, and charterer of immigrant ships, or camp purveyor through his agencies, leaving the arrangement of work to head-men of co-operative gangs and experienced mining captains, entrusted with bonded labourers and slaves, to work their claims.'[50]

A New Zealand account from 1871 shows how individual Chinese miners, once they had paid off their own debt and accumulated enough funds, could import a few employees of their own through the offices of a Chinese merchant. The report relates that a certain Kee Chang had just bought a gold claim at Orepuki on the south coast of the South Island for £168 and was going to bring down some of his countrymen to work it:

[T]hey not work on shares, me boss; pay so much a week and tucker. Me go to Dunedin to merchant man, say want twenty, fifty men – how much to pay? He say, so much for passage money, so much for keep since, so much for profit; you get 'em for twenty, thirty, fifty pounds a piece. Me pay the money; man belong to me till he pay me back what me pay for him. Me allow fifteen shillings the week, and feed him all the time; when he pay me back my money, he free Chinaman; can go work for self, and buy Chinaman like me when he gets money.[51]

An alternative option for Chinese free of their credit-ticket debt was to band together as equal 'shareholders' in a small- to medium-size 'company', called, in Chinese, *kongsi* or *gongsi* (公司). This collaboration is well documented in Barry McGowan's research on the Chinese goldfields of southeast New South Wales but was common in all colonies where Chinese had been for some years.[52] With all these methods of economic organisation, the Chinese merchant based at the main seaport of the colony stood to benefit in one way or another.

Reverend Alexander Don at the Chinese Shop, Nokomai, late 1890s. Shopkeeper Soo Yan was supplied by Choie Sew Hoy's imported goods.

Courtesy R.W. Murray collection, Cromwell Museum

Other Chinese Merchants

The *Sands & Kenny* and *Tanner* Melbourne directories for 1859 between them list only 13 Chinese merchants in Little Bourke Street, the city's Chinese quarter.[53] It is difficult to determine whether other Melbourne Chinese merchants were bringing in goods directly. Some may have used Kong Meng as agent while maintaining direct relations with Hong Kong businesses. Others may have used European-Melburnian shipping agents.

During a meeting on 31 May 1859 between a delegation of Chinese merchants and Victoria's chief secretary, John O'Shannassy, Mark Last King (lawyer and member of the Victorian Legislative Assembly), representing the Chinese merchants, claimed that he 'had acted as agent for Chinese merchants for a long period'.[54] R. Towns & Co., the firm of Robert Towns of Sydney, merchant and shipper, also commonly acted as agent for ships from Hong Kong into Melbourne.[55]

One other Chinese merchant who may have been a significant manager of the trade with China was Louis Ah Mouy (雷亞妹 Lei Yamo). Like Kong Meng, he spoke English, learned during a Singapore sojourn before he arrived in Victoria in 1851. He established a tea merchant's business in Swanston Street and sent large quantities of goods to Ballarat.[56] In September 1855 he and Kong Meng were joint agents for passengers travelling to China on the *Tremelga*.[57]

Interest in Otago

On 31 May 1861 the *Minerva* (829 tons) arrived in Melbourne from Lyttelton (New Zealand) with Kong Meng as agent,[58] his first recorded engagement with New Zealand. By 1861 gold production in Victoria was down by one third from its 1856 peak, and was continuing to fall. Many thousands of European miners had already moved to Lambing Flat and Kiandra in New South Wales in 1860, but in August 1861, when news of the Otago finds arrived, some 10,000 European diggers left within two months.[59] Kong Meng's Chinese-miner customer base halved, from 46,000 in May 1859 to 24,000 in 1861, so perhaps he saw Otago's rapidly increasing European population as a potential new market.[60]

On 4 January 1862, after the *Oithona* (766 tons, Captain Holmes) had arrived in Melbourne from London with emigrants and cargo, Kong Meng sent the vessel on to Otago, mainly with passengers. It returned on 23 February not only with 230 passengers but also 193 ounces of gold. Over a month later, on 28 March 1862, the ship left for Hong Kong, this time with 2260 ounces of gold and 38 sovereigns, as well as passengers.[61] A week later, on 1 April 1862, Kong Meng sent the Hamburg-registered *Jupiter* (499 tons, Captain Hoyrup) to Hong Kong, with 6289 ounces of gold and 12,150 sovereigns.[62] On 10 April 1862, he sent the *Joshua Bates* (620 tons, Captain Clark) to Otago.[63] The *Joshua Bates* had earlier arrived in Melbourne (on 22 February) from Hong Kong, the first time Kong Meng had chartered it, and was carrying tea, matting, ginger, silk, opium, soap, tobacco, handkerchiefs, rice, clothing, oil and sundry packages, as well as Captain Clark's wife and family and one unnamed Chinese passenger. The ship also had on board Hong Kong newspapers reporting on immediate trade and shipping prospects at the various ports of China. The information in the papers soon found its way into the New Zealand newspapers.[64]

When the *Joshua Bates* left for Otago, it carried 80 horses, sheep, drays, sundry general cargo and 12 passengers. The ship arrived in Port Chalmers (Dunedin's port) on 22 April with an extra 12 horses from Gippsland, which it had likely picked up at Port Albert harbour in Victoria en route to Otago.[65] After 20 days in Port Chalmers, the ship set sail again for Melbourne, this time with 98 passengers and an unspecified quantity of gold, arriving back in Melbourne, after a 14-day passage, on 29 May 1862.[66] It is not clear how much of the gold transported on these voyages was from New Zealand, but probably most was from Victoria.

Gold-rush historiography has paid little attention to the economic uses of Australasian-won gold. The general view is that most of it went to England, balancing both the import of goods from there, and capital investment from the London stockmarket.[67] It is also generally believed that most gold going back to China was the winnings of the Chinese diggers being taken or sent back to their respective villages. At the meeting with Chief Secretary O'Shannassy, Mark Last King said that 'shipments of gold to China were not to be regarded as profits' won from the diggings and thus leaving Victoria and the British imperial fold. Instead, he said, 'the greater portion of the money so transmitted was in payment for goods'.[68]

Kong Meng was a major gold exporter to Asia. As well as the shipments mentioned above, he shipped 7188 sovereigns and 121 ounces of gold on 27 October 1862 to Pointe de Galle (Ceylon) via the *Bombay*;[69] then, on 27 November 1862, he sent 9980 sovereigns by the *Madras*, again for Pointe de Galle.[70] He shipped 8000 sovereigns on the *Geelong* to Pointe de Galle on 22 May 1869, along with 2050 sovereigns on the *Joshua Bates* to Hong Kong on 4 June 1869.[71] During the 1860s, the steam route from Melbourne to Hong Kong was by way of Ceylon,[72] so it is unclear whether the gold Kong Meng sent to Ceylon was destined for India or China. It is probable that he also made many other shipments of gold. All of these represented a massive movement of currency, rivalling the shipments of the major banks in Victoria.

The Invitation

After Kong Meng completed his experiment with the shipments to Otago, it appears that he saw little future at that point in trading between Melbourne and Dunedin, as no further ships under his agency left Melbourne for Otago over the next few years. While his entry into the Otago market might have been tepid, articles about him started to appear in the Melbourne press from 1861 onwards. Some of these were reprinted in New Zealand newspapers, and it was this information which brought his reputation to New Zealand.[73] Intriguingly, Kong Meng's name is hardly mentioned in the accounts in the New Zealand newspapers of the invitation, sent via Chinese merchants in Victoria, asking Chinese miners in Victoria to come to Otago. Reference is usually made to Chinese 'gentlemen in Victoria' or 'a principal merchant in Melbourne',[74] but in the Wellington *Evening Post* on 27 December 1865, Kong Meng is confirmed by name as the principal merchant.[75]

Kong Meng did not leap at the opportunity the invitation from Otago offered. As an Anglophile Chinese who respected the British notion of fair play, he had been very disappointed by the legislative discrimination the governments of Victoria, South Australia and New South Wales had successfully brought in over the period 1855 to 1862. The discrimination took the form of poll taxes that Chinese passengers paid on entry to the colony. It also included higher mining taxes on Chinese.[76] A sequence of violent riots against Chinese miners in Victoria and New South Wales along with an incident where some Chinese were ordered off a ship in Melbourne bound for Dunedin would not have lessened his disappointment.[77] Kong Meng accordingly asked the Otago men who had issued the invitation that, as a condition of him and the other Chinese involved in the negotiations meeting the request, the provincial government would guarantee the following: no discriminatory taxes or regulations for Chinese if they were to settle in Otago, the protection of Chinese from attack and vilification on the goldfields, and equal rights before the law. This guarantee was granted, and held to by the Otago government for the rest of its existence (i.e. until the abolition of New Zealand's provincial governments in 1876).[78]

After this guarantee, Ho A Mee, another Anglophone Chinese, arrived in Dunedin in December 1865 on the *South Australian*, deputed by Kong Meng to inspect the mining districts and be reassured of a welcome for Chinese miners.[79] Pleased with his reception, Ho A Mee returned quickly to Victoria and advertised the Otago field through Chinese-text posters and letters sent around Victoria.[80] A small party of advance miners followed soon after on the *Otago*[81] to test the profitability of the mining. It is uncertain how much backing Kong Meng provided for this initial venture. In 1871 Ho A Mee wrote his own account of the 'expedition' of 1865/66, stating that he brought the party over at his own initiative and cost (£800) and so wanted recompense from the Otago Provincial Council.[82]

Perhaps Kong Meng had been uncertain of the potential for success in Otago and had either offered the speculation to Ho A Mee, or else Ho A Mee had offered to take the lead.[83] Certainly, the two men had an involvement with each other, because in June 1866 they were founding shareholders in the Pleiades Gold Mining Company, south of Woods Point in Victoria.[84] In addition, on 10 April 1867, the *Bruce Herald* stated that Tuapeka residents understood that 'Kong Meng will shortly make his appearance, and commence business on a large scale', so clearly he had a continuing interest in the Otago enterprise.[85]

The question of who really financed the first Chinese arrivals in January 1866 aside, Chinese gold prospects did not at first seem viable, and Ho A Mee eventually returned to Victoria. But the advance miners he left in Otago gained success after a few months, and from June 1866 onwards Chinese were arriving from Victoria in steady numbers. In August 1867 *The Mount Alexander Mail* (Castlemaine, Victoria) commented on the heavy traffic of Chinese catching the train to Melbourne en route to New Zealand.[86] By December 1867 the Chinese at work in Otago numbered 1185.[87]

In 1868 Ho A Mee returned to China, settling in Hong Kong as a government interpreter. Two years later, in October 1870, he was asked to arrange direct charter of passenger ships from Hong Kong to Dunedin, a venture which commenced with the *Whirlwind* in late 1870,[88] followed by several more shiploads in the 200- to 400-passenger range during 1871. James Ng estimates that by October 1871, 4200 Chinese were in Otago, the peak number for the province in the nineteenth century, and that the overall number of Chinese in New Zealand remained in the 4000 to 5000 range until the early 1890s.[89]

Lowe Kong Meng is not thought to have travelled to New Zealand, but his influence in New Zealand continued. By 1874 he was a partner in the Dunedin firm of Sun War On, probably acting as an offshore investor of money or goods.[90] James Dundas Crawford reported the presence of Kong Meng and Company branch offices in Dunedin and Wellington.[91]

Kong Meng also had an association with the prominent Chinese merchant of Dunedin, Choie Sew Hoy (徐肇開 Xu Zhaokai, also known as Charles Sew Hoy). Sew Hoy, originally from the Panyu district near Canton city, lived in Victoria in the 1860s before moving to Dunedin in about 1868.[92] While it is not known whether Sew Hoy worked initially for Kong Meng or whether Sew Hoy's emigration to Victoria was sponsored by Kong Meng, both Kong Meng's and Sew Hoy's family origins were in the same Num Pon Soon district near Canton. Common district of origin was a major way in which Chinese society and business in Australasia organised itself,[93] and the Num Pon Soon (南番順 Nanpanshun) district, otherwise called the Sam Yup (三邑 Sanyi) district, was notable for being the source of most of the Chinese merchants in Melbourne. An 1863 article states that the 'natives of the Sam Yup district … the number of whom in the colony is about 450, [are] nearly all … traders' and that Lowe Kong Meng's father was born in the city of Canton, which is within the Sam Yup area.[94]

The three counties that make up the Sam Yup district are Num-hoi (南海 Nanhai), Poon-yu (番禺 Panyu) and Soon-tak (順德 Shunde). When Choie Sew Hoy arrived in Melbourne on the *Lyttleton* on 2 April 1869 at the end of a voyage from Hong Kong, Kong Meng & Co. was the agent for the ship. Sew Hoy was also accompanied by Chun Yut, from the Nanhai district and another of Kong Meng's partners.[95] Kong Meng's example would have provided Sew Hoy with an impressive model of how to succeed in business in the colonies, and the later development of Sew Hoy's career in Otago has many similarities to Kong Meng's.

Technology and Progress

Lowe Kong Meng's interest in modern science and technology is demonstrated by his membership of the Royal Society of Victoria[96] and the Acclimatisation Society (also of Victoria). The latter's aim was to improve agricultural production and husbandry by importing useful plants and animals from around the world, often in exchange for Australian native fauna and flora.[97]

Kong Meng's trading success led to handsome profits. As well as purchasing his own ships, he put his capital to work in modern technology. From 1864 he engaged with the European business elite of Victoria in founding new enterprises, particularly

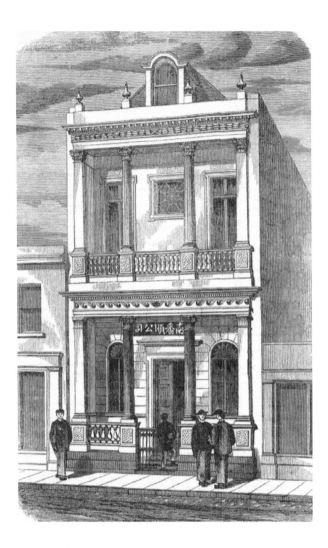

Num Pon Soon Society
Building 1863. Built by
Kong Meng for the society
1860/61.

Source: 'Chinese Exchange,
Little Bourke Street, Melbourne',
*Australian News for Home
Readers*, 21 October 1863, State
Library of Victoria, Melbourne,
picture collection, Acc. No.
IAN21/10/63/9

as an avid investor in Victorian joint-stock companies, an institution novel to Chinese society of the day.[98] He was often a founding shareholder and provisional director when the companies were floated, and was a principal player in at least five gold-mining and silver-mining companies, a coal-mining company, a deep-sea fishing company, a distillery and an insurance company. His name on prospectuses sits alongside those of prominent businessmen and politicians of the day, such as Thomas Bent, George Coppin and David Mitchell.[99]

Many of these enterprises were notable for their use of innovative machinery, and Kong Meng also acquired a reputation as being an expert in minerals.[100] It is a common belief that Chinese in Australasia did not involve themselves in capital-intensive or underground mining. This belief may have arisen simply because historians have not yet been alert to evidence of this participation. In 1865 a party of Chinese working a deep lead mine at Majorca in Central Victoria struck problems with underground flooding. They appealed to Kong Meng, who secured the ground under lease and provided a powerful pumping plant, engineered by the Melbourne firm of A.K. Smith & Co.[101]

Kong Meng's interest in technological progress may have influenced other Chinese capitalists in Australasia. Apparently the first Chinese in Australasia to invest capital in a mining company (the South Crinoline Amalgamated Quartz-Mining Company, December 1864),[102] Kong Meng was followed by Ho A Mee in 1865 (Guiding Star Quartz Gold Mining Company, March 1865),[103] who joined with Kong Meng in 1866 in the Pleiades venture above. Some years after his permanent return in 1868 to Hong Kong, Ho A Mee became a developer of modern mining endeavours in southern China, including silver mining on Lantau Island near Hong Kong.[104] Kong Meng's and A Mee's alacrity in mining investment may have influenced Choie Sew Hoy in Dunedin, who also involved himself in capitalist mining, both in hydraulicking and in financing the development of the self-channelling bucket dredge that contributed to a boom in Otago's economy during the 1890s.[105]

Cross-Cultural Enthusiasm

Kong Meng married an English-Australian from Tasmania, Annie Prussia, in 1860. They and their children lived as affluent upper bourgeois in grand homes in Melbourne's European suburbs.[106] It is remarkable how little the mixed-race nature of their marriage seemed to affect their reputation and their inclusion in many British Victorian social events. For instance, they attended the 1863 fancy dress ball held by the mayor of Melbourne along with fellow merchant Ping Kee. Kong Meng and Ping dressed as Zouaves and Annie as a Greek lady.[107]

Lowe Kong Meng was also invited to organise Chinese cultural and commercial displays for three of Melbourne's major exhibitions. Although he declined an invitation from Melbourne stalwart Sir Redmond Barry to curate a collection of Chinese works for the Melbourne Public Library Art Exhibition of 1869,[108] he was a commissioner for the Melbourne International Exhibition of 1880/81 and also of the Centennial International Exhibition of 1888.[109]

Kong Meng's cross-cultural enthusiasm did not extend to his children: all were Australian-born and adopted Western dress and values, and none appears to have learned to speak, read or write Chinese. Nor do any of his sons appear to have been involved in his business. When Lowe Kong Meng died of congestion of the kidneys, age 58, in 1888,[110] his business affairs were no longer thriving, and Kong Meng and Company was wound up.[111] Kong Meng had made his money off the trade in supplies for the Chinese miners, but this market shrank as the Chinese population decreased from 46,000 in 1859 to 13,000 by 1880.[112] His move into supplying tea to Europeans in Victoria was shattered when the British planters of Ceylon and India successfully muscled China tea into a marginal place in the Australian market.[113] His share portfolio at his death included scrip in only eight companies, with a total value of just £2578; he owned one property in Little Bourke Street, all his ships were gone, and he owed £3360 more than his assets.[114] Ironically, he had sold his investment in the Majorca

Annie Kong Meng (née Prussia), c. 1863, age 24.

Courtesy Thomas Bradley Harris album collection, 'Eastern Window': www.the-eastern-window.com/harris-introduction.html

mine, probably in the late 1860s, only to see it later become (after 1879) the suite of successful Kong Meng mines, still bearing his name but not his ownership.[115]

Perhaps in Kong Meng's case it was just bad business luck, for Choie Sew Hoy of Dunedin successfully elaborated on Kong Meng's business strategies, showing how they could work. Like Kong Meng, Sew Hoy committed his capital to the colony, invested his profits in mining activity, and achieved stellar success in the dredging and hydraulicking arenas. And akin to Kong Meng's *bêche-de-mer* venture, Sew Hoy harvested and exported Jew's ear fungus (*Auricularia polytricha*) from the North Island to China.[116] Sew Hoy was also fortunate that he married at a younger age than Kong Meng, and that his sons were able to partner their father in the business, taking over and expanding it after Sew Hoy died in 1901 at the age of 62.

For years, their Nokomai Hydraulic Sluicing Company was the top-registered sluicing concern in New Zealand. The Sew Hoy store moved from just being an importer and wholesaler of Chinese goods, to retail as well. Grandson Hugh took the business to a higher level again when he developed Sew Hoy and Sons in the 1950s, a major clothing manufacturing business with five factories in the Otago region and one in Christchurch that remained in operation until 1989.[117]

The Dunedin Chamber of Commerce in 1864 could hardly have imagined how much their invitation to Lowe Kong Meng would benefit Otago and New Zealand.

Acknowledgements

My thanks to James Ng for encouraging me to investigate the Victoria–Otago Chinese connections, and also for his very helpful advice and suggestions. His four-volume *Windows on a Chinese Past* (with the first volume published in 1993) is the magisterial work on Chinese history in New Zealand, for which my article is a useful footnote. I would also like to thank Pauline Rule for sharing a passion for the Victorian nineteenth-century entrepreneurial Chinese and their families, and for swapping citations, comments and research leads with me.

3

GOLD-RUSH WOMEN

10.

'A Magnificent Stamp of a Woman': Female sly grog sellers and hotelkeepers on the Central Otago goldfields 1861–1901

Sandra Quick

WHEN JANE MCBRIDE DIED in 1918, the *Lake County Press* described her as 'a magnificent stamp of a woman. She was particularly capable, wondrously bright and possessed of very singular charms. No more public-spirited citizen (as far as it lies in the power of a woman to qualify for that standing) has ever lived amongst us. In her day and generation her liberality and support of every worthy cause were proverbial.'[1]

This eulogy, simultaneously lavish and patronising, captures the life of one of many female hotelkeepers on the Central Otago goldfields: talented, hard-working, well respected and, by her very success and participation in public life, a challenger of gender boundaries. Jane McBride, née Crawford, arrived on the goldfields as a single Irishwoman in 1866 to join her sister. Within 10 years she had married, had a family and buried a husband and at least one child. She demonstrated considerable business acumen, which included extending her Queenstown facilities in 1880 and 1888 to cater to the emerging tourist market. McBride ran her Harp of Erin Hotel in her own right until 1908 and then leased it out until her death in 1918.[2] She developed her hospitality and business skills at the same time as New Zealand women won the vote via the support of a temperance movement that characterised the liquor industry as a dangerous place for women. McBride took advantage of new economic opportunities on the Central Otago goldfields and successfully negotiated a challenging climate for retailers of alcohol. Hotelkeeping offered opportunities for goldfields women that were substantively wider than the prescribed role of homemaking.

The idea that women's most powerful and, indeed, appropriate role should be in the private sphere – creating a home, instilling moral strength in children and providing the domestic labour that allowed men to pursue public roles – is well established in the discourse of colonial New Zealand. Clare Wright's exploration of the historiography of this notion of separate spheres for men and women persuasively shows why hotelkeeping was a respected and attractive option for women in business in Australia in the nineteenth and twentieth centuries. The role of the hotel and the hotelkeeper posed a challenge to the neat demarcations of public and private life so beloved of Victorian politicians and preachers. The traveller, typically male, required food, accommodation and a sense of warmth to abate the loneliness of travel. For the most part, Central Otago hotels were not large establishments, and travellers typically ate with the family of the proprietor. Domestic arrangements were seen as the preserve of women; in New South Wales, a single male licensee was legally required to prove that 'the domestic arrangements of the hotel will be in the hands of a respectable and capable housekeeper'.[3] In this respect, hotels blurred the space between a private domestic life typically seen as the preserve of women and the public life of commercial transactions and communal drinking typically seen as the preserve of men.[4]

Many women on the goldfields of Central Otago had spent time on the Australian goldfields. Mrs Martha J. Glendining, a veteran of the Ballarat goldfields in Australia, wrote about her decision to retire from storekeeping in the more settled post-gold-rush period, fearing that others would censure her husband for 'allowing' her to continue in business.[5] The wife of medical doctor George Glendining, Martha Glendining was a middle-class woman with financial security outside her own labour. Working-class women, particularly widows, may not have experienced the same pressures. During the gold rushes themselves, Irish miners encouraged Irish widows to set up (unlicensed) grog shops that they could then support, thus giving these women an income.[6] In Central Otago, the majority of women running hotels in their own right were widows, but married women also successfully ran hotels.

In Victoria, concern about drunkenness and disorder on the goldfields was such that the authorities banned alcohol. No wonder that goldfields balladeer Charles Thatcher had such good material about sly grog selling for his songs. New Zealand never took such an extreme approach, but historian Stevan Eldred-Grigg has suggested regional differences in women's access to hotelkeeping. Eldred-Grigg claims that because women were not granted hotel licences in gold-rush Central Otago if they were single, they had to style themselves as widows. However, on the West Coast, it was apparently easier to secure a hotel licence as a single woman.[7] How Eldred-Grigg came to this conclusion is unclear, especially given that Richard Seddon, one-time publican, later prime minister and, in 1880, the MP for Hokitika, proudly claimed that West Coast gold-rushes licensing officer Warden Matthew Price had refused to grant single women hotel licences.[8]

The Licensing Act of 1873 established new criteria for the granting or renewal of a hotel licence. In addition to ensuring that the previous requirements – for an applicant to be of good character and able to offer adequate accommodation facilities – were met, the licensing committee had to be satisfied that the licence was necessary for the district. Government reductions in licensed houses from 1873 onwards reflected attempts to eradicate the problem of disorderly drinking houses and also to address concerns about the detrimental effects of heavy drinking on family life. These restrictions mirrored changes in Australia. New legislation in 1881 set up substantively increased fees for the holding of a licence and established licensing committees elected by local ratepayers. Even more than before, local sentiment could influence the granting or declining of liquor licences.[9]

As in England and in the frontier societies of the western United States, widowed women in New Zealand enjoyed the best access to hotelkeeping in their own right.[10] From 1860 a deserted woman could apply for an order protecting her subsequent earnings from the grasp of her husband. Under this order, she became an independent legal entity in the same manner as if she were single.[11] The timing of the legislation suggests that the effects of gold fever on wife desertion rates prompted the law change. Until 1888 the law merely presumed that a married woman could not hold a hotel licence given that she was legally one entity with her husband.

In practice, though, some married women did hold the licence. In Dunedin in 1888, the Templars Union exploited an anomaly between the Licensing Act and the Married Women's Property Act in order to persuade the Supreme Court to rule that a married woman could not hold a publican's licence in her own right. An 1889 amendment to the 1881 Act stipulated that, except for those married women already holding a publican's licence at that time, no married woman was to be granted a publican's licence. Single women now had to give up their licences in favour of their husbands when they married, although transfer upon marriage or re-marriage was already common practice.[12] From 1893 single women were also barred from holding a publican's licence. This legislation was not repealed until 1952.[13]

Two schools of thought prevailed in the contemporary discourses relating to nineteenth-century women hotelkeepers. One regarded women as morally unfit for the occupation, while the other considered that the most respectable hotels were those kept by women. The evidence from the Central Otago goldfields suggests that local licensing committees looked to the skills and conduct of hotelkeepers rather than whether they were male or female.

Sly Grog Sellers (or Peppermint Tea Retailers)

This chapter looks at the sly grog sellers first – after all, everyone wants a story of the wild girl! In this, Thatcher obliged both the miners on the goldfields for whom he performed throughout Australasia, and those who listened to him elsewhere or read his songs in the newspapers. His song of Polly ('Poll the Grogseller') could be of a savvy young woman on any goldfield in Australasia.

> *Big Poll the Grogseller gets up every day*
> *And her small rowdy tent sweeps out;*
> *She's turning in plenty of tin people say*
> *For she knows what she's about.*
> *Polly's good-looking, and Polly is young,*
> *And Polly's possessed of a smooth oily tongue;*
> *She's an innocent face and a good head of hair,*
> *And a lot of young fellows will often go there;*
> *And they keep dropping in handsome Polly to court,*

And she smiles and supplies them with brandy and port
And the neighbours all say that the whole blessed day,
She is grog-selling late and early.
She is grog-selling late and early.

Two sly-grog detectives have come up from town,
And they both roam about in disguise;
And several retailers of grog are done brown,
And have reason to open their eyes.
And have reason to open their eyes.

Of her small rowdy crib they are soon on the scent;
But Polly's prepared when they enter her tent;
They call for some brandy – "We don't sell it here,
But", says Poll, "I can give you some nice ginger beer,"
And she adds, "do you see any green in my eye?
To your fine artful dodge and disguise I am fly;
For if Polly you'd nail, you'd have, without fail,
To get up in the morning early.[14]

Polly is young, pretty, making good money and savvy to who is genuine and who is not. We're encouraged to side with Polly as she outwits the bureaucrats. The reference to other illegal alcohol traders being 'done brown' develops the image of the new goldfields worker as 'green' or naïve of goldfield survival strategies. 'Do you see any green in my eye?' asks Polly, and here we know the obvious: women had to be savvy to survive on the goldfields, just like the men.

Thatcher's songs also reference two other aspects of the female sly grog seller's story. His song 'The Rowdy Mob' tells the story of a miner who becomes acquainted with a pretty young sly grog seller called Sal, an acquaintance that he greatly enjoys until he is beaten up one day in Sal's tent by a man who is part of an organised gang of thugs. In 'Changes on Bendigo', Thatcher pokes fun at the woman who starts out life as a party girl on the diggings in a sly grog shanty and then marries well and now prefers to hide her past life.[15]

Evidence in records from magistrates' courts and in contemporary Central Otago goldfields newspapers give us stories of actual women rather than Thatcher's legends. The newspaper reports regale the details of the court cases with relish, providing entertainment for the local population and creating local legends in the process. One such legend was Jessie McLeod, also known as Kate O'Reilly, who provided a range of goods and services to the goldfield communities in Dunstan and Queenstown.

McLeod first appeared in the extant court records late in 1862, when three men took her to the Dunstan court to reclaim debts.[16] On 3 February 1863 Daniel Labowithy took McLeod to court for 'making use of threatening language and putting [the] complainant in bodily fear'. Neither party appeared that day; the records note the case was settled out of court. But the next day, McLeod took Benjamin Delano to court for assault and robbery. The magistrate dismissed the charge, doubtless leaving the newspaper reporter as the person to gain the most from the experience.[17] The police later reported that they'd tried to run McLeod out of town, and for a while they were successful.[18]

In Queenstown, the surviving newspaper records demonstrate the entertainment service that McLeod provided for local newspaper readers as well as the range of goods and services she sold on her premises. Once in Queenstown, McLeod bought herself a hotel and set herself up as its proprietress. She ran the hotel, called the Lady of the Lake, with such vigour that the magistrate felt compelled to do something about her actions. He understood that Samuel Bell was the proprietor and licence holder and summonsed him to court for keeping his hotel open past 10 p.m. and for 'allowing a woman of immoral character to act as barmaid'. Bell explained he never had a licence for the bar. On the contrary, Jessie McLeod held the licence, a fact the constable could vouch for. McLeod was sent for. She explained to the magistrate that she had bought the licence herself, had a copy of the receipt, and didn't know Samuel Bell at all. The magistrate, finding the barmaid to be both licence-holder and partying prostitute, retained the licence.[19]

Undeterred, McLeod refashioned her premises as a restaurant. A few months later, the police took McLeod to court for selling sly grog. On this occasion, they had visited her restaurant to find her on the floor fighting with a man. The constable alleged that McLeod was a 'prostitute of the lowest class, and had been often before the court. She was well-known as a sly grog seller.' The Lady of the Lake, continued the constable, was 'a disgrace to the township'.[20] The following year, McLeod was twice taken to court for allowing disorderly and drunken conduct at her house.[21]

Jessie McLeod was no timid soul in need of protection. In August 1863 she assaulted an E. King, used abusive and obscene language towards the local constable and threw a bottle of ink at Henry Cohen when he abused her. The magistrate admonished McLeod that 'she must not take the law into her own hands, whatever the provocation', but his advice was futile.[22] In Cromwell in 1868, she was sentenced to seven days' imprisonment for vagrancy, despite giving her occupation as a dressmaker.[23] In nineteenth-century New Zealand, a person without lawful means of supporting him or herself could be charged with vagrancy. The appellation of vagrancy was frequently a code for a charge of prostitution. In February 1869 McLeod whacked William Petres on the head with a tomahawk. The magistrate noted that 'as great provocation in this instance had been proved, the utmost leniency would be exercised, and sentenced the prisoner to seven days, with hard labour'.[24] What was the great provocation? Given the circumspect nature of the recording of rape in nineteenth-century newspapers relative to crimes of a non-sexual nature, it seems very likely that Jessie whacked him over the head to prevent him raping her. Useful things, tomahawks.

Was Jessie McLeod representative of all female sly grog sellers on the Central Otago goldfields? The evidence suggests that she was not, or not over the longer period under discussion, even if she did provide the best entertainment for local readers and brave drinkers. Where exactly Jessie McLeod or other rowdy women went after the gold rushes is not clear. A Dunedin resident magistrate dealt with one troublesome prostitute called Barbara Weldon by giving her a one-way ticket to Hokitika in 1869, but there is no evidence of this 'remedy' happening in Central Otago.[25]

During the gold-rush period, licensing rules were neither as strict nor as tightly enforced as they were later on. Ann Box is recorded as selling liquor in 1864 in Bendigo.[26] In January 1868 she was fined £10 plus costs of 5s-6d for selling sly grog, and the liquor was confiscated. The police must have struggled to work out what to do with liquor seized in this way. Two months later, Box's application for a general licence was granted, although the licensing court's deliberations in December 1868 regarding her licence renewal and the charge against her for disorderly conduct in the hotel the following month, followed by charges of selling 'adulterated liquors' in 1870, suggest that her rowdy days were not over.[27] In an employment dispute before the Cromwell Magistrate's Court in 1874, police sergeant John Cassels declared that Mrs Box's hotel '[had] servants who were generally prostitutes … [and] was always called into by the loose characters who came to the town'.[28] Cassels grudgingly admitted that 'the house had been quieter lately. He believed it got a worse name than it deserved', but this did not stop him summarising his testimony with the statement 'Mrs Box was hot-tempered, and had a bad tongue.'[29]

Jane Wilson sold sly grog in the Cromwell area for nearly 25 years, defying the stereotype of the wild woman who kicked up in the gold-rush days and then left. Wilson was selling sly grog in Bendigo in 1864 and was before the courts in 1868 for both sly grog selling and vagrancy.[30] On the same day she appeared in court, her five daughters were sent to the Caversham Industrial School in Dunedin.[31] In January 1870, Inspector Dalgleish described Wilson's residence as the most disorderly shanty in the district. Wilson was fined £10 for sly grog selling on this occasion, and warned of a much heavier penalty if she appeared in court again.[32] The police attempted to get her convicted again in May of the same year, but failed: all the witnesses swore they were drinking peppermint tea.[33] Wilson was further convicted for sly grog selling in February 1871, August 1877, January 1883, June 1884 and April 1888.[34] Eventually, she sold her house on the Cromwell flat and from 1888 disappears from the historical record.[35]

Sly grog selling was a means of generating a cash income quickly with very little outlay. As a young girl, Irish-born Annie Patterson emigrated to Bendigo, Australia with her brother James. The siblings later moved to New Zealand and met up with their sister Mary. James and Annie started out at the diggings at Hog Burn and then moved to Clyde, where they bought the Old Bendigo Family Hotel. James Patterson kept the hotel for many years, and was joined by his parents soon after Annie moved to Alexandra to live with her sister. It was in Alexandra that Annie Patterson appeared in court for sly grog selling three times between May 1866 and July 1867. In October 1867 she married licensed storekeeper James Rivers, and the sly grog apprehensions ceased. James and Annie Rivers continued their storekeeping business for many years, and James later became a justice of the peace. When Annie died in 1909, local businesses closed as a mark of respect.[36] The case of Annie Patterson suggests that sly grog selling did not necessarily leave a lifelong stain on one's character.

Mary DeCarle was storekeeping at Waitahuna in 1871 when she was convicted for sly grog selling and fined £20 plus costs, or one month's imprisonment, a steep fine for the time. Later that year she married Danish miner Robert Kofoed, at which time her name too disappears from the records of sly-grog-selling prosecutions.[37]

As the number of licences issued was reduced from 1873 and more so after 1881, sly grog apprehensions from accommodation houses increased. Ann Byron Shade ran her business from Mount Pisa, a sparsely populated part of the Cromwell district. In 1877 her husband William applied for a new licence for the Mount Pisa Hotel, but the licensing committee refused to grant it because they considered there was no need for a licensed house in that locality. In August 1878 locals launched a petition calling for Mrs Shade to be granted a publican's licence for the house known as the Mount Pisa Hotel.[38] By 1881 Ann's son, Thomas Henry Byron, held the licence for the hotel. Mother and son were imprisoned for two months following a charge of maliciously wounding with intent to do grievous bodily harm (Thomas) and as an accessory to the same (Ann). In February 1882 Thomas Byron's licence was cancelled.[39] Ann Byron Shade was obviously undeterred by mere licence cancellations, for in November 1882 and January 1883 she was prosecuted for sly grog selling.[40]

Hessie Carson's court appearances for sly grog selling began after the hotel she and her husband John ran lost its licence. In April 1885 Hessie was fined £10, plus costs of 36s, for serving James Henderson a glass of ale with his lunch. Carson and her husband lived at Dunkeld in a house previously licensed as the Duke of Edinburgh Hotel. Constable Charles Daubney called at Hessie Carson's boarding house and observed her, her daughter and Henderson (visiting as the local rabbit inspector) in the dining-room. Daubney prosecuted Carson for charging sixpence for the beer Henderson had with his dinner. The *Tuapeka Times* noted that '[t]he fact of accused keeping a boarding-house did not relieve her from being prosecuted for selling liquor. There were a great many cases of this kind in existence, and the police invariably had great difficulty in securing a conviction owing to the reluctance of witnesses to give evidence.'[41] The following year, Mrs Carson was fined £15, plus costs of £2-14s, or two months' imprisonment. She spent one night in the cells and then decided to pay the fine after all. The editor of the *Tuapeka Times* was mystified as to why she had not received a harsher penalty for this second conviction.[42]

The prominence of boarding-house keepers in sly grog cases in the 1870s and 1880s was also due to the high cost of licences. At the Queenstown county licensing district meeting in 1888, Wesley Turton appeared for all county applicants wanting to protest the hardship that the £25 fee imposed on any such applicants who were within five miles of another licensed house.[43] 'Straight' claimed in his 1870 letter to the *Tuapeka Times* that 'The government, if they want to put an effectual end to sly grog selling, must reduce the licence to £10 or £15, and do away with bottle licences.'[44] Even as the pressure on licences intensified, there was no evidence in the sly grog records of women being targeted.

Hotelkeepers

Hotelkeepers were assessed primarily on their individual merits rather than on their gender. This was the case from the gold-rush period, which was characterised by high transience and frequent wife desertion. In 1866 Elizabeth Norrington sued her husband Thomas for desertion, but the case was dismissed. Elizabeth Norrington had previously been licensee of the Wakatipu Hotel in her own right and under her maiden name of Langford; yet, if her death certificate is to be believed, she married Thomas Norrington in England before emigrating. Elizabeth continued to run the Wakatipu Hotel, again in her own right, and when she died in 1876 was applauded as an active supporter of the Wakatipu Hospital and as someone known for 'warmly supporting every movement that had the good of the district at heart'.[45]

Married woman Maria Connolly ran the Hyde Hotel in her own right. Objections to Mrs Connolly's application for a licence renewal were filed at the June 1886 and 1887 meetings of the Kyeburn Licensing Committee, on the grounds that her husband, Phillip, was a bailiff of the resident magistrate's court at Naseby and must be interested in the house. By law, any person with a close interest in the law or a licensing committee was barred from holding a hotel licence. Mrs Connolly gave evidence at the 1886 hearing that she was the owner of the land on which the Hyde Hotel and store were situated, and that it was she who had dealt with the debts of the previous owner. All proceeds were deposited into her own Bank of New Zealand account. In support of the contention that Mrs Connolly was proprietress of the hotel and store at Hyde in 1887, an incident was recalled where a weight on the store premises had not been verified through stamping, and it was to Mrs Connolly that the inspector of weights and measures complained. In both instances, the objections were not upheld because they were found to be malicious.[46] By 1889, when the law was explicit that a married woman could not hold a liquor licence, Maria's daughter, Eleanor Jane Connolly, had taken on the licence of the Hyde Hotel. In 1897 and 1898, Maria's son Thomas Redmond Connolly held the licence.[47] When Maria died in 1913, she left an estate worth £2896.[48]

Mrs Catherine Lucas registered her hotel's licence in her son's name. Lucas had established the Albion Hotel (Roxburgh) in 1870, before which she was a storekeeper at Roxburgh for two years. She then built the Ballarat Hotel, part of which was moved across the river to form part of the Albion Hotel. Catherine Lucas's determination to remain independent of her third husband, Charles Lucas, is clear in her will, for in it she appointed her two sons as executors and directed that her husband must release all claims he might try to make on her Roxburgh section to her executors. She stipulated that her executors could give money to Charles Lucas as they saw fit, but that his entitlement should last only as long as he remained her widower.[49]

While parliament worried about the ability of women to independently keep hotels, local authorities were more concerned to *retain* a female presence in their local hotels. In 1888 W. Johnston applied for a new licence for the Alpine Club Hotel at Glenorchy, and was given until the next annual licensing meeting to get married, or else he would have to transfer his licence to a married person.[50] The police objection to renewing Edward Burrows' licence for the Maori Point Hotel in 1880 included that he was single and had no one to help him in the house.[51] The provision of good-quality accommodation facilities, often used as a benchmark of a reputable hotel, involved significant amounts of domestic labour, for which hotelkeepers' wives were considered eminently suitable. Indeed, some hotelkeepers specifically advertised the role of their wives in superintending accommodation and diningroom arrangements.[52]

Hotelkeeping was particularly suited to married couples on the goldfields because wives could perform the hotel work during the day while husbands worked elsewhere. Hotelkeeping in tandem with other occupations formed part of a larger diversification of economic activities in Central Otago after the gold-rush period. John Perriam pursued mining activities around Lowburn and Kawarau Gorge, while his wife Charlotte ran their Lowburn Ferry Welcome Home Hotel. Although John was a successful miner and storekeeper, the licensing board received complaints from the police about his 'intemperate habits'.[53] After John's death, Charlotte substantially increased the size, turnover, range of services and value of the Welcome Home Hotel complex, and it is her hotel shown in the illustration below.[54] Catherine Kerr (née Birmingham) ran the Terminus Hotel at Kingston, while her husband, John Black Kerr, ran a ferry business on Lake Wakatipu. In 1864, Catherine Brigit Birmingham gave her occupation as

The Welcome Home Hotel, Lowburn, c. late 1890s. Charlotte Perriam, proprietor, is seated in the centre of the picture. After John Perriam died in 1883, Charlotte built the enterprise into a substantial and profitable concern with a hotel, general store, bakery and farm.

Courtesy R.W. Murray collection, Cromwell Museum

'housekeeper' on the application to marry Kerr, but described herself as a hotelkeeper on their marriage certificate. Catherine ran the Terminus Hotel in her husband's name until his death in 1887, at which time she took over the licence. In 1878 she worked from temporary premises while the Terminus was rebuilt after being destroyed by fire. Although Catherine continued the hotel business as a widow, there is no evidence that she kept the ferry business.[55]

Kitty Holt maintained various hotels in Clyde, while her husband James ran a coal business. James Holt held the licence for the Sydney Hotel in 1873 and 1875/76, and then in 1883 for the Vincent County Hotel. After James' death in 1891 the coal business was bequeathed to the couple's children, but Kitty was left the stock and furniture of the hotel, plus a legacy of £50. In addition to her work hotelkeeping, Kitty also raised a large family, several members of which helped their father in his coal business. In 1892 the Vincent County Hotel, licensed to Kitty Holt, was a stone and iron building containing nine bedrooms and three sitting-rooms for commercial accommodation purposes. The police reported that the hotel was well conducted, and frequented by a good character of person.[56]

Despite Edward and Emma Barber keeping a hotel and a mail-delivery business, the couple's financial situation was precarious when Edward died in 1871; creditors of the estate received only nine shillings in the pound. Over the next 16 years Emma turned her fortunes around, obtaining a store, bakery, butchery, stables, slaughter yard and piggery. Her estate was worth £3190 at her death, and included property, the aforementioned businesses, shares in five companies and ownership of the Perseverance Mining Company. During Emma Barber's 25-year connection with the township of Hamiltons, she was 'held in universal respect by all classes' and made a substantial contribution to the local Union Church and Sunday School.[57]

Women hotelkeepers were prominent in the evolution of Queenstown from a gold-rush shantytown to a tourist destination. Jessie McLeod's Lady of the Lake Hotel was long gone by the late 1870s when a transition was evident between the lower standards of accommodation that sufficed in the gold-rush days and the new requirements of an emergent tourist town. Eliza Jenkins, an experienced hotelkeeper who held the licence for Queenstown's Edinburgh Castle Hotel in the 1860s, applied to renew the licence for her Melbourne Hotel in 1878, but withdrew it after police reported that 'there are very few persons who frequent this hotel of any class' and that it lacked stables.[58] Just five yards away from the declining Melbourne Hotel was Jane McBride's much more substantial Harp of Erin Hotel. By 1888, having added another extension to the building, McBride was reputed as offering excellent accommodation and hospitality and also 'first class' hacks and vehicles for those wishing to explore the countryside. The June 1888 Queenstown licensing meeting recorded that all four surviving Queenstown hotels were being run by widows – Jane McBride, Julia Eichardt, Jane O'Meara and Rebecca Bond.[59]

The Eichardt family was the most successful hotel-keeping family on the Central Otago goldfields. Julia Shanahan arrived in Queenstown from Melbourne as a single woman in 1863 and began her hotelkeeping career as the licensee of W.G. Rees' Queens

After her husband George drowned in 1876, Rebecca Bond bought the Ballarat Hotel in Arrowtown. The photograph was taken c. 1879.

Courtesy Lakes District Museum, Arrowtown, File EP0575

Arms Hotel. Albert Eichardt, whom Julia married in 1868, bought the hotel soon after. As a long-stayer on the Queenstown hotelkeeping scene, Julia maintained hotels that were deemed the most reputable in town. Preferring to cater to the accommodation needs of tourists and families rather than single miners, the Eichardts were advertising private apartments for families in 1866.[60]

Julia's mother, Jane O'Meara, arrived in Queenstown in 1869 and became the licensee of Eichardt's Supreme Court Hotel.[61] When Albert Eichardt died in 1882, he left his wife assets to the value of almost £2000.[62] By the time Julia died in 1892, she had turned this capital into assets worth almost £8000. These included the Supreme Court Hotel, which was managed on Julia's behalf by her mother.[63] As well as running a superior hotel, which boasted Sir George Grey among its patrons, Julia had considerable financial acumen, evident in her numerous real-estate investments. She was also the mortgagee of several properties, and in the year she died, these earned £57 in interest.[64]

The wealth developed through orcharding was reflected in substantial hotels run by women in Alexandra and Roxburgh. In 1901 Harriet Heron moved her business, the Commercial Hotel (Roxburgh), from its old wooden premises to a newly built brick house complete with special apartments set aside for ladies.[65] Catherine Lucas upgraded her Albion Hotel (also in Roxburgh) several times from the 1870s on. She owned property in Oamaru and nine sections in Roxburgh when she died in 1905.[66]

Eichardt's Hotel, Queenstown, c. 1889, photographed by William P. Hart.

Courtesy Lloyd Carpenter collection

The Rocky Point Hotel, Wakefield, Bendigo (Otago). After the business stood empty for a year, Elizabeth Reid successfully overcame police opposition to reopen and manage it from 1886 to 1891.

Courtesy Clyde Historical Museum

Mrs Elizabeth Reid. Local tradition has her as the midwife of Bendigo. She also owned shares in the Try Again Quartz Mining Company 1872–78, co-owned Bendigo's Solway Hotel with William 'Sydney Bill' Smith 1875–79, was the 'women's monthly nurse' in Cromwell 1879–86 and managed the Rocky Point Hotel 1886–91. She retired to the former Solway Hotel in Bendigo.

Courtesy Kevin Hayes, Ripponvale

By contrast, some other areas struggled to offset the loss of revenue as the goldfields declined. In June 1890 Violet McArthur applied for a reduction of her licence fee for the Phoenix Hotel at Skippers Reef from £10 to £5, as business was very quiet. The licensing committee initially declined her request but changed its mind when the police gave evidence that 'a house of the kind was very much required in the locality, as it kept down sly-grog selling'.[67]

In a rare example of gender being taken into account in granting a licence, the police objected to Elizabeth Reid's 1886 application for a publican's licence for the Rocky Point Hotel near Bendigo because they considered Reid was 'not a proper person to hold the licence, the house being a roadside one [and] nine miles from police protection'. One licensing committee member considered that 'no woman was capable of holding the licence of the Rocky Point Hotel', but the committee nevertheless voted to grant the licence, subject to the police presenting a report on the conduct of the house at the next quarterly meeting.[68]

Women hotelkeepers contributed to the wider good of their communities in public and private gestures. Sarah Dyson, one time hostess of the Macetown Hotel and later owner of the Ballarat and New Orleans hotels in Arrowtown, was 'of a very philanthropic nature [who] unobtrusively performed numerous acts of kindness and generosity'.[69] When Mary Kidd died of dropsy in 1876, the *Dunstan Times* admired her 'stirling qualities', including her generosity with hungry and distressed persons and the respect she commanded from 'all sections of the community'.[70] Celia Russell built a hall next to her Wanaka Hotel and general store in 1886, where a ball was held that Christmas. She was instrumental in a highly successful bazaar for the Pembroke

School in 1883. When Celia died in 1905, the *Cromwell Argus* noted that 'Mrs Russell has during a long, active and useful life been closely connected with the progress of the Wanaka district.'[71]

Afterword

The Central Otago goldfields offered many opportunities, both legal and illegal, for women hotelkeepers. Illegal sales of liquor were a particular feature of the gold-rush period. However, perhaps paradoxically, they rose again in the latter nineteenth century as the government enforced stricter measures to limit liquor licences. The most illustrious of female sly grog sellers entertained not merely their clients in the gold-rush period, but also the newspaper-reading public. These women's stories have entertained readers in various forms ever since, with the salacious sly grog seller one of our Kiwi goldfield legends.

Legal hotelkeeping on the goldfields followed the economic fortunes of the specific localities, and thus the success of individual hotelkeepers rose and fell. The legislation enacted at national level did limit the opportunities for female hotelkeepers, but many used the support of husbands, sons or daughters to formally hold their hotel licence and thus carried on. There is no evidence in the surviving records to indicate that before 1889 women were refused licences solely because they were women. Like many of the men they worked alongside, the women hotelkeepers made substantial and lasting contributions to the communities they lived in, proving that even in a society that promoted a woman's role as being private and home-based, they could indeed qualify as public-spirited citizens.

11.

'Forgetting Their Place': Women of abandoned character on the Otago goldfields

Julia Bradshaw

DISTINCTIONS AND BOUNDARIES WERE often blurred on the goldfields during the early phase of the rushes. This period sometimes offered women greater opportunities than those previously at hand, and a number of women took advantage of them. Anne Fitzgerald and Eleanor Metcalf, for example, worked together on a mining claim.[1] Unmarried women such as Julia Shanahan (later Eichardt) and Eliza Pocock ran hotels. And married women, amongst them Elizabeth Norrington and Eliza Jenkins of Queenstown, ran businesses independently of their husbands.[2]

Identity Reinvention and New Names
The early, tumultuous years on the goldfields, when people were moving from place to place, also made it easy for people to reinvent themselves. Both women and men left spouses or changed their names. Some women used a bewildering array of aliases, while others described themselves as married or widowed to suit the circumstance. When Mary Bailey was arrested in June 1864, her aliases included Mary Tripp, Mary Smith and Mary Doyle.[3] Similarly, when the judge presiding over a court case requested the defendant to give her name, she replied, 'Alice Stoker at present'. Asked by the judge to explain her statement, she said her maiden name was Alice Cummin; she'd been married to a Mr Caton but was now living with William Stoker. The judge again asked Alice to give her name, but she persisted with Alice Stoker. Exasperated, the judge told her that her name was Alice Caton.[4]

Women got away with living with men they were not married to and even marrying bigamously as long as they maintained a veneer of respectability and chasteness. The trick was to tell people nothing and to lie if asked questions. An example of the success of this kind of arrangement was Frederick Tyree and Annie Jane Rhodes who met on the Victorian goldfields, probably during the late 1850s. Frederick already had a wife, Mary Ann Williams, whom he had married in 1853, but undeterred Frederick and

Anne Jane Rhodes and Frederick Tyree, probably taken about the time of their marriage in 1871. Annie appears to be pregnant with the couple's sixth child.

Courtesy Lakes District Museum, Arrowtown, File EP1139

Annie lived together. Their first child was born near Ballarat in 1860. By the time of the birth of their third child, they had followed the gold rush to Otago.[5] The couple were always known as Mr and Mrs Tyree, and it was only after the birth of their fifth child that they were married in a secret ceremony conducted by Reverend Richard Coffey at the Queenstown parsonage. Annie was so used to signing herself as Anne Jane Tyree that she had to cross out Tyree and write Rhodes.[6]

Mary Bricheno broke some rules, but by the time she died, others probably would have said of her that she'd lived a respectable life. This, despite the fact she'd lived with a man she wasn't married to and then married another man bigamously. Mary's first marriage was to Thomas Rolls in England, and the couple, with their two-year-old daughter, went to Australia as assisted immigrants in 1849. A son was born on the voyage, and the couple had another five children at various New South Wales towns before the marriage broke down.[7]

In September 1861, Mary Rolls, living in a tent at Burrangong (Lambing Flat), began a relationship with Barney (Barnard or Bernard) Burns, one of the men charged with 'having riotously assembled with other evil-deposed persons' at Burrangong on 30 June 1861. He had also been part of the so-called Lambing Flat Riot.[8] Mary and Barney Burns then went to Otago, and were first at Dunstan and then at Hamiltons by February 1865. Around the time of the birth of the couple's third child in 1867,

Barney left the scene, at which point Mary, as Mary Rolls, applied for a licence to run the Liverpool Arms Hotel at Naseby.[9] Six years later, Mary married miner Daniel Robertson.[10]

Mary's first husband, Thomas, had married Janet Jessie Cumming in 1866, so Mary probably felt quite justified in marrying Robertson. On her marriage documents she claimed she was a widow, but she almost certainly must have known she wasn't.[11] Despite the bigamous marriages, the Rolls family kept in touch, and with most of her children settling in New South Wales, Mary was obliged to take at least one trip there. Explaining her connection to her children's in-laws must have been interesting, as Thomas's second wife and family would have been known to them.[12]

It seems that relationships such as these were ones where the details could be tidied up later, and they often needed to be once the goldfields settled down. Amalie Koch's husband, Charles Jessep, divorced her after she started living with her neighbour, storekeeper Charles Nicholson, at Millers Flat in July 1864. The couple finally married in 1874 after the birth of five children, but the marriage date was adjusted to 1864 in Nicholson's *Cyclopedia* entry of 1905.[13]

Reputations ...

People of the time set much store by their own and others' reputations, and given that damage to reputations was usually irreversible, preserving them was important. In 1864 Mrs Sarah King, the proprietress of the Morning Star Hotel in Arrowtown, was charged with assaulting Queenstown merchant Michael Cassius and breaking his arm. Cassius purportedly had been telling people he'd seen Sarah in bed with a man. When Cassius visited Sarah's hotel, she remonstrated with him for defaming her character, but instead of being repentant, Cassius called Sarah a notorious vagabond. Riled, Sarah grabbed a large stick and beat him with it, unfortunately guaranteeing that Cassius's story would be repeated in the local paper.[14]

The courts and public opinion were relatively unforgiving if women stepped out of the sphere of what was seen as acceptable behaviour for women at the time, as hotelkeeper Mary Butler found out. Mary was one of the Arrow goldfield's earliest female residents and seems to have had a hot temper. In March 1865 she was charged with assaulting her servant, Mary Anne Ayton, who she thought was 'trying to make mischief between her and her husband'. According to a witness, Butler jammed Ayton up against a wall and then beat and kicked her.[15]

In 1876 Mary was again in court, this time accused of hurling obscene language at William Plumb and assaulting him. Mary was said to have taken exception to Plumb not only because he was courting her 14-year-old niece but also because he had called Mary a larrikin and owed her 10 shillings for billiards. Mary supposedly had retaliated by calling Plumb a 'damned loafer, a bloody imposter and a Tasmanian pup'. When Plumb wouldn't leave the hotel, she grabbed him by the hair and attempted to drag him out.

The magistrate, H.A. Stratford, fined Mary 10 shillings for obscene language and commented that the language used 'was much worse coming from a woman's lips,

Mary Jane Butler (née Neylon), who was one of the first women at the Arrow River rush. Mary had married William Butler in Australia, and the couple's first two children were born at Ballarat. When the family followed the rush to the Arrow, Mary carried her younger child on her back through the Kawarau Gorge.

Courtesy Lakes District Museum, Arrowtown, File EP 0212

and that woman the mother of eight children'. Stratford then described the assault as unjustifiable and unprovoked: 'If anyone had a right to remove Plumb,' he said, 'it was Wm. Butler, and not his wife. She had no right to so far forget her place.' He also fined her one pound or seven days' imprisonment for assault.[16] The *Arrow Observer* tellingly commented that 'Mrs Butler … stepped out of a woman's sphere, and for this she deserved to be punished. Her husband can keep his billiard room and bar, and a wife has no business to act as she did.'[17]

… and Secrets

Women who had secrets usually managed to keep them well hidden, as many family historians have discovered. Due to these women's own particular misfortune, their addictions or simply because of their personality, some of these women didn't manage secrecy at all. Annie Quadri was a woman of 'impetuous temper'. Born in Newry, Northern Ireland, sometime around 1838, she was the daughter of J. Gologly or Golightly ('a poor overseer') and Christine McLean. Annie arrived in New Zealand in about 1863 and soon after married Daniel Quadri, a Swiss hotelkeeper, at Dunstan. She described herself at the time as 26-year-old widow Annie Young.[18] After their marriage the couple moved to the Kawarau Gorge, where they ran the Roaring Meg Hotel. In March 1865 Annie was charged with wounding with intent after attacking a man called John Hancock with a tomahawk. She was committed for trial at the Supreme

Revell Street, Hokitika, late 1860s. The Quadris' West Coast Hotel is the two-storey building in the centre of the photograph.

Hokitika Museum Collection, #1950.

Court in Dunedin but absconded from bail and was believed to have left the colony. In reality, the Quadris had moved to Hokitika and opened the West Coast Hotel.[19]

Here, Annie was again in the court pages of local newspapers, this time defending a charge that she and her husband had charged excessively for a wedding dinner organised by Raymond Bastick, who had married one of the Quadris' servants. In an interesting aside, Annie said she had warned her servant not to marry Bastick as he already had a wife in Melbourne.[20] Before moving on from Hokitika, Annie gave evidence against an accomplice of the Burgess and Kelly gang.[21] In addition, local miner Benjamin Jones charged both Annie and her husband with using abusive and insulting language. The couple were fined one pound each. The couple obviously knew how to make money, and later in the year travelled to Europe, returning in December 1868.[22]

By 1872 the couple were in the Inangahua District, where Daniel Quadri was licensee of the Blacks Point Hotel. Annie lived in a hut next door, as Daniel said he no longer wanted to live with his wife because she was 'a bad woman'. In September Quadri charged John Williams with assault after an altercation when Quadri and Annie's brother, Patrick Gologly, burst into Annie's hut and found her in bed with John Williams.[23] Despite the fact that she was no longer living with Daniel, Annie continued to use the name Quadri until about 1881. She also continued to find herself before the courts, variously charged with exposing spirits for sale without a licence, spitting in a woman's face (at the West Coast settlement of Lyell) and assaulting

Henry Harney by striking him on the arm with a butcher's cleaver. In the last of these cases, the jury (with mistaken kindness according to the editor of the *Westport Times*) was reluctant to convict on the more serious charge of wounding with intent and instead only found her guilty of common assault. Judge Weston said that women of 'impetuous temper … must be taught to control the violent passions which they too frequently gave loose reins to' and gave Annie a 12-month sentence, the maximum allowed for common assault.[24]

During the late 1870s and 1880s Annie was 'house-keeper' for Christian Mind-ermann of Inangahua Junction.[25] Mindermann had previously held a liquor licence but in 1878 was told he would not be granted a renewal unless he 'got rid of an objectionable inmate, a Mrs Quadri'. He must have liked Annie's company because she was still there in 1885 when she was sued by Wesport draughtsman H.W. Mason for the costs associated with commissioning drawing plans and specifications for a building she wanted to erect on Mindermann's land but which Mindermann claimed not to know about.[26] Annie 'Young' died at Westport in 1895 of heart disease and dropsy at the age of 57. She had no children, and the link with her husband (who died in 1907) had been completely severed. On both of their death certificates the details pertaining to spouse were given as 'unknown'.[27]

A 'Notorious Employer of Police Labour'

Barbara Weldon, who would come to be described as a 'notorious employer of police labour', was born in Limerick in about 1836.[28] Because she never married and didn't attempt to use aliases, her life is easier to track than are the lives of many of the other women who gained notoriety on the Australasian goldfields. Barbara first came to the attention of the police as a suspect in a theft at Sydney, New South Wales, in 1855, when she was 18 years of age.[29] She wasn't convicted of the crime, however, and at this stage of her life, she certainly wasn't poor. She had £78 in a bank account, and when she was robbed a year or so later she had a bank receipt for £100 and £30 cash.[30]

In 1856 Barbara travelled to Melbourne, where she gained her first conviction for drunkenness. Two years later she was at Ballarat, where she was charged with using obscene language and described as 'a woman of abandoned character'. Her prison record at this time describes her as a servant and her conduct as good. The record also notes that she was blind in her left eye.[31]

From 1860 to December 1862 Weldon was active in Melbourne, where she racked up at least 30 charges (mostly for drunkenness, obscene language and vagrancy), although again she wasn't poor. When she appeared at court in June 1862, the Melbourne *Argus* reported that 'although always looking dirty, she has a good balance at a bank and when fined offers to pay the fine rather than be locked up'.[32] Barbara's last court appearance in Melbourne was on 11 December 1862. Soon after serving her 24-hour sentence for drunkenness, she left for Dunedin.[33]

On 20 January 1863, only a few weeks after her arrival in Dunedin, Barbara 'Weldin' had her first New Zealand court appearance. At least 35 convictions and many more court appearances followed, with Barbara mostly fined for drunkenness, vagrancy or disorderly conduct.[34] In March 1864 she was charged with having no visible means of support. However, as Barbara told the magistrate, she had money 'as he well knew', as well as a house and a piece of land.[35] In September 1864 the *Otago Witness* commented that Barbara had been up before the court some 30 to 50 times during the last 12 months.[36]

Barbara's last court appearance in Dunedin was on 19 July 1869 when she was sentenced to 14 days for drunkenness. Immediately after her release, the authorities apparently paid for Barbara to travel to the West Coast on the *Tararua*. On her way there, she was charged with drunkenness in Wellington, but discharged in order to ensure that she continued her passage.[37]

It didn't take Barbara long to get in trouble on the West Coast. Her first entry in the Hokitika register of prisoners in November 1869 described her as being five foot and one inch tall with black hair, blue eyes (left eye blind), stout with a sickly complexion and the back of her head as being slightly bald.[38] Most of the charges and convictions that followed related to drunkenness and abusive language, but there were exceptions. One of them was in September 1870 when Barbara attempted to commit suicide by throwing herself in the surf on Hokitika Beach. Suicide was a criminal offence at the time, and in her defence Barbara said she didn't know what she was doing, as she'd been beaten by a woman that morning and also experienced one of the fits she was prone to that same day. The jury found her not guilty. After a lecture from the magistrate, Barbara was free to go.[39]

Barbara was not shy about speaking in court or commenting on a witness's testimony. In 1873, when on a charge of habitual drunkenness, she 'addressed the court in her usual eccentric style and averred that she had a bad leg, and had only just come from the doctor, who had put stuff on her leg which made her "roaring mad"'.[40] By now, Barbara's finances may not have been as healthy as they had been, as she was accepting prison sentences rather than paying fines as low as 10 shillings.[41]

In 1878 or thereabouts, Barbara began living at Kumara, although she still came to Hokitika to serve her prison sentences. There were times after her release that she was back in gaol before she'd had time to get home. Barbara died at Kumara in October 1882, when the cottage where she was living burned to the ground during the early hours of the morning. The *Grey River Argus* noted that she was said to have been intoxicated the previous evening and, in a wonderful understatement, informed readers that Barbara was 'somewhat addicted to liquor'.[42]

Janet Watson (née Bailey) also had a lifelong problem with alcohol. She was born in Scotland in 1838 and married fellow Scotsman John Watson at Emerald Hill, Victoria in 1859.[43] A tiny woman, no more than four foot, six inches tall (1.4 metres), Janet had a fresh complexion, dark brown hair and grey eyes.[44] She gave birth to four children on the Victorian goldfields, one of whom, John, died at the age of six months.[45] In 1866 John and Janet travelled to Otago, and by the time of the birth of their last child in 1868 were living at Naseby.

In July 1869 Janet charged her husband with knocking her down with a piece of wood and kicking her in the face. John admitted the assault but said that his wife 'misbehaved' in a 'gross manner'; she was constantly getting drunk and neglecting their four children.[46] Shortly afterwards, John left his wife. He returned to the district 10 months later, at which point he claimed that his children had not been well looked after and had them charged as 'neglected children within the meaning of the Neglected and Criminal Children's Act, 1867'. The courts agreed with John's assessment, and sent the four children (between two and 10 years of age) to the Industrial School in Dunedin. John paid their passage to Dunedin and agreed to contribute to their maintenance.[47]

Janet herself wasn't charged with any offence until April 1872, when she was arrested for being drunk and disorderly and then fined 10 shillings.[48] She appears to have supported herself by working as a prostitute and at times to have been supported by men with whom she cohabited. In March 1871 she had a son (James Higgins Watson) and in April 1873 a daughter – Johanna Jarvis Watson, who was later known as Jane Farmer.

In September 1873 Janet was charged with vagrancy 'for the sake of the children'. She, James and Joanna were living in a hut in Naseby made of 'sods and bags with holes in both the sides and roof'. A miner working nearby heard the children crying and found them on their own. Unable to find any food to give the baby, who had a 'most wretched appearance', he went to see the local constable, which led to Janet being sentenced to three months in Dunedin gaol. Her five-month-old daughter went into goal with her. James, now 26 months of age, was sent to the Industrial School.[49]

Once released from gaol Janet returned to Naseby, but further court appearances followed. Janet was evidently relatively comfortable in court. In April 1875, when defending herself against a charge of vagrancy, she cross-examined Constable Macnamarra, demanding to know if he had ever actually seen men at her house. She also stated that she received money 'in letters from Dunedin' (probably from her elder daughters, who were now working) and from using her washtub. Furthermore, she 'always kept her bills square' and she was 'almost as a wife' to John Farmer. Her arguments were to no avail. The *Mount Ida Chronicle* stated that Janet 'was very impertinent throughout the case, [and] was frequently cautioned that such conduct would only confirm the Court in its opinion that she was a bad woman'. The court sentenced her to another three months in Dunedin gaol.[50]

In February 1877 Janet was again charged with vagrancy and again sent to Dunedin gaol for three months. Her 'almost husband' John Farmer wrote a letter to the paper asking if someone could explain what vagrancy meant, as he employed Janet Watson as a housekeeper and paid her wages.[51] A few months later, Janet again demonstrated her ease in the courtroom when she conducted her own case against Mrs M.A. Smith for striking her with an iron pot. The *Mount Ida Chronicle* described Jane as conducting the cross-examination 'semi-professionally'.[52]

From about 1873, Janet lived with goldminer John Farmer 'on and off', and lived with Henry Jenkins when Farmer was 'down-country' for a few months. The latter period must have been in 1878 when Janet had a daughter (Mary Jenkins Watson) and unsuccessfully charged Henry Jenkins for support of the child. After Farmer's return, Janet lived permanently with him, and in early 1881 the couple had a child,

Janet's last.[53] Farmer seems to have been a stabilising influence, although Janet said she was afraid of him when he was 'in liquor' and that she slept in the coal-cellar on those nights.[54]

In May 1881 the police charged Robert Gollans with raping Janet Watson while she had her baby in her arms. They also charged Abraham Dilworth and George Bevan with aiding and abetting Gollans. Dilworth, furthermore, was charged with raping Mary Smith on the same night. On the night in question, Janet had gone home early, leaving Farmer at the pub. The three men came to the house, at which point Dilworth and Bevan pushed Gollans inside, who then raped Janet. When Gollans left, Janet went outside to look for her daughter, who had run off, but she was knocked down by Dilworth and Bevan and 'pulled along'. Her neighbour, Thomas Jackson, hearing her screams, opened his door. The two men, who were 'somewhere about her legs, in a stooping position', ran off.

The defence contended that the evidence was contradictory, that Janet was 'a woman of bad character' and that she admitted she wouldn't have brought the case herself having been 'astonished' when the sergeant, who was following up the assault on Mrs Smith, came to see her. 'Their Worships' agreed, saying that some of the witnesses (the only evidence heard was from Janet, John Farmer and the neighbour) 'were so completely untrustworthy' that they would dismiss the case. The other cases against the men, including the rape of Mary Smith, were also dismissed.[55]

When John Farmer (whose real name turned out to be Thomas Ford) died suddenly from a heart attack on 31 August 1881, Janet reverted to prostitution as a source of income.[56] Before long, the courts sent her son, John Farmer, to the Industrial School in Dunedin. This meant that all seven of Janet's children had been sent to this school, four of them before they had reached three years of age.[57] In November 1883 Janet was sentenced to 12 months in Dunedin gaol for being an 'incorrigible rogue'.[58]

One month on, Janet again experienced a severe physical assault, this time by Richard Ferguson, who attempted to rape her, but was foiled by two neighbours who came to her assistance. When Constable Willis arrived, Janet was crouching on the ground, injured and crying. Ferguson, who was being held by one of the neighbours, said that he thought Mrs Watson was common property. This time, the witnesses' evidence was incontrovertible. Ferguson received three months imprisonment with hard labour, demonstrating, it seems, that the law deemed raping a prostitute a lesser crime than that of vagrancy.[59] After this assault, Janet was not seen in court again until she was charged in 1893 with having no lawful means of support.[60]

In May 1894 the Naseby police took Janet to the Seacliff Lunatic Asylum near Dunedin after she'd shown symptoms of 'mental derangement' for some weeks. Janet was fearful and could hear voices but wasn't violent and talked 'pleasantly although somewhat incoherently'. When she was admitted, she was described as looking younger than her 65 years but very thin. Once at the asylum, Janet was well behaved and easy to manage. She was 'quick and smart in her speech and answers questions rapidly, sometimes sensibly'. She was visited by her eldest daughter, Isabella, who had married a chemist in Dunedin. Isabella had arranged for her brother David to work for one of her in-laws and for her brother James to work for her husband. In March 1900 Janet was transferred to Porirua Mental Hospital, where she died, probably in 1916.[61]

Janet Watson ended up living quietly in her old age despite her earlier criminal convictions. A similar pattern seems evident with regard to Nottingham-born Jane Shipston, who at the age of 16 married John W. Wilson, a sawyer, at the Wesleyan Church at Lyttelton in February 1856.[62] The couple moved around, probably seeking work, and had several children, whose births were consecutively registered at Kaiapoi, Dunedin and Timaru.

The couple first come to notice on the goldfields in late 1864 when they had a 'saloon' at Bendigo Gully.[63] Jane's husband, referred to as 'Jack the Drummer', is a shadowy figure, who appears to have been around until about 1866 when the last of the pair's children were born.[64] In 1868 Jane was convicted of vagrancy, so Jack presumably had departed the scene by then. By 1876, Jane was describing herself as a widow. When she was convicted of vagrancy in November 1868, the daughters living with her (ranging in age from two to nine years) were charged with being neglected children and sent to the Industrial School in Dunedin.[65] Her eldest child, George, presumably able to look after himself or having escaped detection, remained in the district.

After the conviction for vagrancy and the departure of her daughters, Jane's life spiralled further downwards. In January 1870 she was convicted of sly grog selling and fined £10.[66] Then, just before Christmas in the same year, her eldest child, George Shipston Wilson, who was working for a storekeeper at Lowburn, fell from a bolting horse and broke his neck near Quartz Reef Point. He was midway between his twelfth and thirteenth birthday at the time.[67]

In February 1871 Jane was in court again for selling liquor without a licence. This time, she was fined £50 or three months' imprisonment with hard labour. On this occasion, police described her as a prostitute, although usually her occupation was given as laundress. She could read and write and had an 'IOU' in her pocket book for £15. However, unable, to pay the fine, she was sent to Dunedin gaol.[68] In August 1874 she was sentenced to 14 days hard labour for assaulting Ann Box at Kawarau Gorge and was charged with assault yet again in 1876.[69] As Sandra Quick found in her research into Jane (Chapter 10 in this volume), Jane appeared in court several more times over the next decade, before finally disappearing from the court records in 1888.

In 1878 Jane's 16-year-old daughter, Eliza, gave birth to a daughter, Alice, at Cromwell but left the town soon after, leaving Jane to bring up her grandchild. This responsibility may have tempered Jane's behaviour somewhat given that her court appearances were not as frequent over the next decade as they had been. However, Jane appeared in the newspaper records in a different capacity in 1892, when she was required to identify the body of her granddaughter as part of an inquest in Dunedin into Alice's death from burns sustained when the 15-year-old tried to light a candle from a fire. Alice had been in the employ of a Mr Elmer at Waitati, near Dunedin, when the accident occurred, and Jane herself may have found more respectable employment, as she is described as 'laundress at the Coffee Palace' in Dunedin.[70] Jane lived a quiet life working as a laundress until her death in 1909, and was buried with her beloved granddaughter Alice.[71] She was survived by five daughters and, in what may seem an unlikely postscript to her life, they inserted a memorial notice in the *Otago Daily Times* on the anniversary of her death, 'in sad but loving memory of our mother, Jane Wilson'.[72]

Mixed Fortunes

Jane's story, like the stories of the other women in this chapter, is one of mixed fortunes, just as was so often the case for the many men who came to the goldfields. And like the men, terms such as adroitness, violence, sadness, resilience, addiction, and resourcefulness are indicative of their experiences. Yet contemporaries saw these women one-dimensionally – as prostitutes, women who drank, women who were violent. As such, they were simply bad and usually beyond redemption. However, the distance of time allows us to see that many of these women had very difficult lives and probably mental health problems as well. Today, they appear more as tragic survivors than incorrigible reprobates and, as their depictions in newspaper and other accounts of the period indicate, they were women possessed of a good measure of guts and often humour.

12.

'Prity Fare Trade at Present': Irish women, mobility and work on the West Coast goldfields

Lyndon Fraser

IN A RECENT STUDY published in *History Australia*, Catherine Bishop draws attention to the significance of gender, exchange and movement in the trans-Tasman world of the mid-nineteenth century.[1] She reminds us that women were mobile, connected and active, playing important commercial roles with spheres of influence beyond those of home and family. Mobility was therefore strategic and linked closely to work opportunities and money-making, as well as escape and kinship ties. Sandra Quick and Julia Bradshaw vividly illustrated these patterns on the goldfields in their chapters on hotelkeepers and 'wayward women'.

This chapter focuses on the working lives of Irish women who made their way to that other great southern El Dorado – the rugged West Coast – after spending time elsewhere. As Philip Ross May famously noted, the physical isolation of the region from the rest of the South Island helped turn it into 'an economic dependency of Victoria' during the rushes of the 1860s and made its capital, Hokitika, into 'a trans-Tasman suburb of Melbourne'.[2] Irish women, like women of other nationalities, were highly mobile within the region and travelled backwards and forwards across the Tasman at a time when land and not the sea presented the greater barrier.

Journeys and Connections

Irish-born women were strongly represented in the richly variegated communities that developed along the bush-lined rivers and alluvial terraces of the West Coast after the discovery of gold at Greenstone Creek in 1864. Census figures show that the Irish component of the foreign-born female population was almost one-third for the years 1867 to 1896, a proportion that fell dramatically thereafter in absolute terms and relative to other nationalities. Irish expatriates outnumbered their English-born counterparts until late in the century and retained a significant presence in the region until World War I.

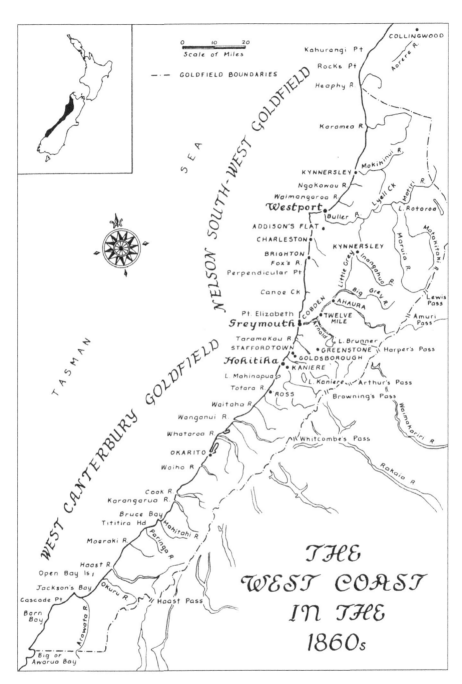

Map of the West Coast of New Zealand. Several hundred Irish-born women and their descendants lived in – or just passed through – the richly variegated communities that developed along the region's bush-lined rivers and alluvial terraces. Most made their way to the region directly from Victoria.

Source: Philip Ross May, *The West Coast Gold Rushes* (Christchurch: Pegasus, 1962)

This broad picture is complicated by the fact that a substantial number of Australian-born females recorded by the census enumerators were the second-generation children of Irish home backgrounds, some of whom had accompanied their parents across the Tasman Sea. We can also assume that the New Zealand-born contingent featured a sizeable minority with Irish parentage and that the published data for England and Scotland contained a small number who were descended from Irish migrants to Britain. The existence of these additional categories reminds us that the everyday lives of Irish women in goldfields communities were differentiated by generation, as well as by class, religion, age, marital status and parenthood. In total, then, Irish women comprised between one-quarter and one-third of the female population in Westland and southwestern Nelson over the years 1864 to 1922. We may surmise that they were highly visible in the region's ramshackle towns and mining camps from the beginnings of colonisation and played a powerful role in shaping the nature of local community life.

The movement of Irish women to the West Coast after 1864 was highly selective. An overwhelming majority were two- or three-stage migrants who sailed directly to the region from Melbourne after serving extensive colonial apprenticeships in Victoria. The regional origins of the inflow reflected this general trend and turned upon key centres of Australian emigration from Tipperary, Clare and Limerick in Munster, Galway in Connacht, and King's and Kilkenny in Leinster. Newcomers were most likely older than their compatriots venturing abroad between the Famine and World War I, and more than half had married before their arrival, three-fifths forming unions in the Australian colonies. As might be expected, the balance of Catholic/Protestant religious affiliations among the migrants (80/20) matched the patterns found in Victoria and diverged substantially from the Catholic/Protestant breakdown for New Zealand as a whole (55/45).[3]

Marist priest Nicholas Binfield's observation that miners came from the 'well-to-do classes at home' applies equally to the backgrounds of Irish women.[4] Despite its limitations, the surviving evidence suggests that many were drawn disproportionately from among the ranks of middling tenant farms and the families of an emerging post-Famine elite of prosperous farmers, shopkeepers, merchants and traders. For women such as these, the decision to leave Ireland was made within a familial rather than an individual context and represented a logical and practical option in a rural society where opportunities for undowered females were quite limited. Whatever these women's personal motivations, David Doyle's assertion that 'strong and medium farmers' daughters had, at worst, intelligent choices imposed on them' seems a more realistic characterisation of their migration than the fanciful depiction of an independent flight from patriarchal oppression.[5] The complex negotiations that preceded the departure of young women from the households of smallholders, labourers and urban artisans, however, remain inaccessible. Case studies of West Coast migrants from less affluent backgrounds, such as Catherine Bourke, Margaret McGirr and Maria Phelan, suggest that state funding was used as part of their families' economic strategies, but we may never know how many newcomers received subsidies or the extent to which private benefactors supplemented their fares.[6]

Regardless of their social origins or marital status, Irish women seldom travelled to the region as isolated individuals. Most newcomers were accompanied on their journey by kinsfolk or followed the paths of relatives and friends who had already settled on the West Coast. This was certainly the case for the so-called 'Limerick girls'. Ann Diamond (née Gleeson) from Adare in County Limerick spent three years in Dunedin with her husband Patrick and friend Mary Maloney before moving to Red Jacks, a remote Westland mining camp in which they established a substantial hotel and store. According to family tradition, the two women travelled to Victoria in the late 1850s with Ann's cousin, Johanna Shanahan (later Weir), on passages that had been paid by the Gleesons.[7]

Johanna stayed in Melbourne with two of her brothers until 1865, when she agreed to join the others at Diamond's Hotel, a 'carefully furnished' establishment that featured 'coloured prints of Wolfe Tone and Robert Emmet', and corner brackets 'decorated with green velvet plush and hearts and shamrocks'. She assumed responsibility for general management of the hotel and acted as the cook, producing 'excellent meals from an enormous stone fireplace equipped with iron hooks for hanging heavy iron pots and cauldrons, and a spit for roasting'.[8] Mossy headstones in the Notown cemetery give no clue to Ann's and Johanna's moneyed backgrounds.

The migration pathways of single women featured a similar reliance on kinship networks. Typical in this regard was Catherine Minehan of County Clare, who sailed to Sydney aboard the *Spitfire* in 1863. Accompanied by two brothers, Patrick and Sylvester, her departure was part of a much wider movement of family and friends from the parish of Kilcredan to New South Wales that began soon after the Famine and continued unabated until the 1870s. She was reunited in the colony with four elder siblings, Martin, Bridget, Jeremiah and Denis, and later joined by her younger brother, Michael, as well as numerous cousins and Old World neighbours. Catherine Minehan worked as a domestic servant in Sydney before venturing across the Tasman with four of her brothers in the late 1860s. It seems likely that she lived with Patrick and his Kilcredan-born wife, Honora White, during the years immediately before her marriage to Patrick Dunn at Ross in 1874. The couple later returned to Australia and eventually settled at Kyabram, Victoria, where they ran a hotel.[9] Such examples highlight the importance of family networks in structuring the migration of Irish women to the region and indicate that these connections often spanned the Tasman Sea in both directions.

Working Lives

As we have already seen, more than half of all migrant Irish women on the West Coast married before their arrival and most single females chose to marry and establish families soon afterwards. The main problem we face in trying to interpret their motivations, ambitions and strategies is the fragmented nature of the historical sources. Few personal letters have been discovered, and the exploits of these women were not as well documented as those of 'wayward women' such as Bessie O'Neil, who featured regularly in court records and newspaper reports.

Case studies taken from the West Coast death registers suggest that most of these Irish women were employed as domestic servants in colonial homes before they married in the Australian colonies and New Zealand. But single female domestics such as Honora White, Annie Dougan, Mirah Rooney and Margaret McKeogh were not simply 'prospective wives'. These women formed part of a mobile occupational group that made a substantial economic contribution to colonial societies during the nineteenth and early twentieth centuries. Once married, they continued to play a valuable economic role as full-time workers in the unwaged household sector, taking care of their families, preparing food, doing the laundry and managing resources. Housework, as Joanna Bourke argues, has significant economic value and constitutes production; without it, consumption could not take place, as it 'transform[s] income into disposable goods'.[10]

Philip Ross May plausibly argued that the same spirit of independence underpinning the attitudes of male diggers characterised the outlook of women migrants. In the 'upside-down society' of the Australian and New Zealand goldfields, 'everyone was somebody, servant-girls got the same wages as government clerks, and barmaids were even better off'.[11] The *Hokitika Evening Star*, in a revealing commentary from 1866, claimed that 'the colonial virtues flourished too mightily on the diggings':

> Were Thackerey [sic] living, and on the West Coast, he would certainly
> pronounce us to be a community of snobs … a slipshod, slatternly, stockingless,
> insolent servant woman demands and obtains from two to three pounds a
> week as wages besides her keep, while a thoroughly competent lady who opens
> a school for the education of girls, cannot get a sufficient number of pupils at
> four shillings a week to support her. Madame, the governess, the educated lady
> … cannot afford a mutton chop to her dinner. Mary, the maid of all work at
> an hotel has just thrown a dishful to the pigs, and when reprimanded for such
> waste, gave her mistress twenty-four hours' notice to leave.[12]

There was nothing unusual about these complaints in the wider Australasian colonial context. Both sides of the Tasman offered little in the way of significant employment openings for single females outside of paid domestic work, and servants were always in short supply. Some contemporaries lamented the quality of state-assisted domestics and the frequency with which they changed engagements in search of higher pay. Yet the attractions of domestic service for migrant women are easy to understand. Workers received full board and lodging, as well as wages, and may have been given clothing and furniture by their employers. Although they were under close supervision in local households or pubs, their position was relatively secure compared with the uncertainties of mining or male waged labour.

We do not know how Irish women viewed their experience of service on the West Coast or whether their working relationships involved an element of 'social oppression'. Some barmaids and 'dancing girls' were tied into unyielding contracts by 'greedy employers and unscrupulous agents'.[13] What does seem clear, however, is that the insatiable demand for domestic servants ensured dissatisfied workers such as

Catherine Flaherty of County Mayo could usually change jobs with little difficulty. Denied pay by an Orwell Creek publican in 1882, she simply walked out, moved away and found new work at the Star Hotel in Ahaura.[14]

Unlike Irish women in parts of the United States and Britain, Irish women on New Zealand's West Coast never dominated paid household labour, even though the majority of these women working for wages were engaged in domestic capacities. West Coast marriage records from the 1880s show that 78 of the 287 brides who listed domestic service as their occupation were Irish-born (27.2 per cent). Such was the case for Margaret McGirr, a labourer's daughter from Armagh, whose marriage to Patrick Bourke in Greymouth stemmed from a shipboard romance.[15] Mary Ann Lowry and Elizabeth Quirke, from farming households in the southern midlands, were both 34-year-old domestic servants at their respective weddings, while Mary Ann Scanlan of Cork was only 22 when she solemnised her union with Melbourne coach driver, Daniel Corboy, before a Presbyterian minister at a private residence in Hokitika.[16] English-born women in the region came from a wider range of occupational backgrounds and were less likely to be found in domestic positions.

The differences between Irish- and English-born women are partly explained by the unusually high number of widows among the latter (38.3 per cent): laundering and needlework, for example, could be done at home on a piecemeal basis, an important consideration when women were caring for small children. The extant listings also suggest that a disproportionate number of teachers and barmaids came from across the Tasman, English migrants were overrepresented in dressmaking, and Irish widows dominated the hotel trade. But the significance of these trends is impossible to assess given the defective nature of the sources. We are far better placed in relation to the general picture, which reveals that the occupational profile of Irish-born brides largely conformed to wider regional patterns, at least during the 1880s.

How did women's working lives change after they married? The chronic instability of everyday life in the region's goldfield communities made the paid and unpaid activities of women essential. Whether they lived in isolated mining camps or larger urban centres, the daily realities of female migrants were shaped by housework and the family-centred concerns of child-bearing and child-raising. Like Johanna Weir at Red Jacks, married women kept cows and poultry, cultivated vegetable gardens, made their own butter and jam, cared for the sick or those in trouble, nurtured children and carried out routine household tasks such as cleaning 'by strenuous scrubbing with wood ash on a damp brush'.[17]

These activities must have been especially onerous in the wretched living conditions of the mining townships. Bad weather damaged vegetables or saturated crude homes, and sudden floods ruined supplies and temporarily severed communications with other places. The harsh climate, the heavy burden of domestic labour and the constant battle with rats, mosquitoes and bush flies extracted an enormous physical toll on migrant women. And this workload increased dramatically when men were incapacitated or injured, leaving wives responsible for the economic welfare of their families. Ellen Cronin, for example, milked cows, made butter and worked a small Westland farm after her husband John became an invalid. She struggled to bring in an income of £1.0 per week on land that was slowly being eaten away by the Kokatahi River, a sum that provided their only support during the 10 years leading up to John's death in 1914.[18]

The high mortality rate among adult males on the goldfields ensured that many women spent a portion of their lives as widows, often scratching out marginal existences in remote locations. Catherine Wallace was left with 13 children, including a six-week-old infant, when her husband died in 1896. Coastal steamers arrived infrequently at Okarito with supplies of flour, tea, oatmeal, sugar, salt and syrup, which had to be purchased and then carried around three dangerous bluffs and across two rivers to the family homestead at Waiho Beach. Catherine grew potatoes and onions in a vegetable garden fertilised with seaweed, made bread and used 'an old muzzle-loader gun to good effect when the pigeon stew pot needed replenishing'. The family learned to live from the bush and seashore, catching fish and eels and dining on edible berries such as kiekie, fuchsia, miro and supplejack. One of Catherine's sons, Mark Wallace, recalled that his mother was '[o]ur house-keeper, our cook, our bread-maker, our seamstress, our nurse, our doctor, our spiritual guide, counsellor and friend … When the digestive processes became over-active, there was a flax-root brew to halt the trouble. When nature went into reverse, there was a brew from koromiko leaves. Mum's other names were initiative and resourcefulness.'[19]

Some grief-stricken widows fared badly. Martha Butler from King's County witnessed the tragic death of her husband Michael and seven-year-old daughter, both swept away when Michael pulled the reins so tightly while crossing the Arnold River that he drowned his horse. Michael's remains were never found, but his daughter's bloated body washed up on Cobden Beach several days later. Martha managed to identify the child from her prominent teeth: sea lice had eaten away all her hair. On

Born in Paulstown, County Kilkenny, Ellen Piezzi (née Walsh, later Maher) wrote to her brother, Patrick, in Ireland and sent letters to her husband's relatives in Swiss villages and in the United States. The surviving correspondence to her brother-in-law in California gives us rare glimpses into the experiences of a widow, mother and business-owner on the goldfields.

Courtesy Teresa O'Connor

Ellen Piezzi (1849–1922) was among the mobile, connected and active women who played important commercial roles with spheres of influence beyond those of home and family. She is pictured here in the doorway of the Helvetia Hotel in Goldsborough around 1895. The three children from Ellen's 1883 marriage to Dennis Maher are standing beside her. From left to right, they are Ellen, John and Veronica.

Courtesy Hokitika Museum, Ref. 1147

11 December 1871, three years after the accident, Martha married James Byrne at Totara Flat, a relationship that produced one daughter, Sarah, who died in infancy, and ended acrimoniously when the couple parted.[20]

Ellen Piezzi's husband Guiglio died from a hernia in 1876 when swollen rivers prevented a doctor from getting to Goldsborough. Pregnant at the time, Ellen struggled to care for two children and the couple's large hotel. After the birth of Julia later that year, Ellen endured periods of illness and expressed the fervent hope that God would 'spare me to my Dear littleones … [I] am very lonely after my poor Dear husband,' she confessed to her brother-in-law in California, 'and i soo yong. What hapend him to go from me i cant make it out that i am left like this atal [at all]'.[21] The vicissitudes of the local economy made matters much worse:

> I had a great many losses this year. Pepel gone true the cort turning onsolvent. I lost a fine cow £15 pounds wurt [worth] in a hole in the bush. I can not get any of my old acounts in. The pleas [place] is so poor. The business Was Never

quarter so bad before … The Weder is very dry A now and this is very bad for the diges canot doo Noting When they have Now Water.[22]

With 'not[h]ing dooing' in Waimea, Ellen moved on to establish the Swiss Mountain Hotel in Rimu, leaving her brothers to mind the old place. The new venture did a 'prity fair trade', but she returned each week to Goldsborough to 'setel up overthing' for th[e]m'.[23] It is ironic that Ellen apologised to her in-laws for being 'a bad riter' when she managed to maintain connections across the oceans and pen such moving accounts of widowhood and business life on the goldfields.[24]

Despite much onward mobility, close ties developed between local residents in goldfield settlements such as Rimu, Goldsborough, Addisons Flat and Red Jacks. These were undoubtedly a source of support for women in hard times and transcended religious boundaries. Mary Nolan of Queen's County, for instance, brought up 10 children on a property situated alongside the farming families of various nationalities in the South Westland wilderness clearing of Okuru.[25] At Waimea, Ellen Piezzi reported that one of her late husband's Swiss Italian 'countery men' took her son, Severini, 'to Hokitika and got his portret taken. I Will send one to you till see What [a] fien little fellow he is getting and tell me is like his papa. He wake like and his shape his very like him.'[26]

But the limits of frontier pluralism were also clear. Sarah Gillin discovered its outer edges when she nursed a 'Robber Chinaman' ill with pneumonia at Notown Creek and earned the opprobrium of locals alarmed at the actions of a 'Chow lover'.[27] Drunken prostitutes such as Barbara Weldon were barely tolerated beyond their dwindling clientele.[28] 'Respectable' widows, however, seem to have received generous community assistance, at least in the smaller towns and mining camps. When several of Catherine Wallace's children became chronically ill with typhoid and required expensive hospital treatment, Kokatahi residents rallied together to pay her debts, even though she had only recently begun leasing a dairy farm in the district.[29]

Clare-born Ann O'Donnell (née McNamara), who became the well-known proprietor of Waiuta's Empire Hotel, was left to support six children 'in very destitute circumstances' after her husband Edward died suddenly at their Kaniere home in 1894. According to the *West Coast Times*:

> On hearing the particulars Mrs Learmont at once sent down to the Womens' [sic] Benevolent Society and a large parcel of clothing etc., was got ready and taken up Saturday afternoon. Their immediate necessities in the way of food and clothing are thus being attended to and it is understood that residents on the locality are taking steps to get Mrs O'Donnell a better house, her present one being scarcely tenantable. It is to be hoped that a special effort will be made to assist them as they are a very deserving family. Perhaps the Hokitika Garrick Club or the Kaniere Dramatic Society will act on the suggestion.[30]

Local people also organised concert performances, dances and plays for the O'Donnell family. These events raised a substantial amount of money and helped

View over the West Coast mining settlement of Dillmanstown, set amid swathes of bush, smoke and fluming. Domestic labour must have been extremely onerous in these kinds of environments.

Courtesy Alexander Turnbull Library, Wellington, Ref. F-44217-1/2

Ann set up her first business, a grocery store at Woodstock. A decade later, Hokitika mayor and bank manager Joseph Mandl persuaded Ann to take over as licensee of the Rose and Thistle Hotel at Blackwater. Ann's decision to do this was an astute and timely one given the development of the Birthday Reef at Waiuta the following year. For Ann, the success of this venture (the hotel) and the ones that followed owed much to the capital accumulated earlier at Woodstock and the involvement of several of her children in the family business, as well as Ann's own fierce determination and shrewd financial management. It also illustrates the role of mobility as a key strategy for women in business.[31]

The working lives of Irish-born women who married differed little from those of women of other nationalities on the West Coast. Most were involved to varying degrees in housework and subsistence-related activities, including the collection of food from the bush, the henhouse and the vegetable garden. Many gave birth for the first time in rough mining townships and shared Isabella Graham's experience of nursing young children afflicted with nasty maladies such as diphtheria, watching and praying as they lingered for days between life and death.[32] Less serious afflictions required easier solutions, as Ellen Piezzi noted in a letter in 1881: 'I hope Lucy is getting strong.

Give her so[me] worms powders. The worms is at her. Severini past 4 large ones about 10 inses long. I gave him powders. He is all rite again.'[33] Travelling overland to seek medical attention or moving from one place to another was a daunting prospect, especially when children accompanied their parents. Ferry services eased the dangers of crossing the big rivers, but innumerable creeks and streams still had to be forded. The obstacles that confronted diggers' wives were well illustrated by Mary Magee's journey from Greymouth to the Ahaura with her three children in 1869:

> The first day took us to Langdon's Ferry, opposite the Arnold River junction –
> the second day to Camptown, near the mouth of Redjack's Creek. Next day we
> went to Nelson Creek on pack horses – I, a six months old baby on the knee of
> my mother who rode a horse side-saddle. My two sisters were put in gin cases
> and slung one on each side of a pack horse. The creek was forded about 10 times
> and in other places the mud was up to the horses girths.[34]

Despite the challenges of travel and communication, women in goldfield settlements were heavily involved in public work. Some of these activities, such as delivering cooked food to families in distress, or midwifery, remain hidden from the historian's gaze. But the role women played in community-building projects such as halls, churches, schools and charities is much more obvious in newspaper accounts and institutional records. Ann O'Donnell was among the few to receive public recognition for this kind of voluntary service when she became the first woman to be elected a Life Honorary Member of the Hibernian Australasian Catholic Benefit Society in 1927.

The survival of mining families on the goldfields depended on strong women and the close co-operation of husbands and wives. As a result, female migrants seem to have enjoyed far greater power within marital relationships than in Ireland: for example, they played a major part in the disposition of property in wills. This acknowledgment of Irish women's contribution to their husband's prosperity is evident in the bequests made to widows, among them Bridget Scanlon of Westport, who received the residuary interest in the estate of her husband, Michael, along with all his coal and goldmining shares and a hotel in Palmerston Street.[35]

For the most part, West Coast husbands entrusted their wives with the role of administering their estates and granted them absolute powers of disposal over property. Ellen McInroe, Ann Falvey and Honora Corbett were among those whose spouses left them full management rights, while Catherine Rogers and Ellen Healey shared this responsibility with others; even wives excluded from the roles of trustee or executor were likely to receive absolute shares in residuary property.[36] For these women, emigration was a source of empowerment rather than 'a passive experience to be born stoically'.[37]

Irish-born women were certainly not dispossessed proletarians; they easily matched other nationalities in terms of wealth holding. They accounted for 105 of the 400 estates handed down by women between the years 1876 and 1915 (26.3 per cent), including six of the 18 inventories valued at more than £2000 (33.3 per cent). The wealthiest, Bridget Scanlon, the Westport publican, was worth £8741 at her death in 1914.[38] Reefton storekeeper Ellen Harold (d. 1914, £5563) passed on the fourth largest fortune, while business-owners Mary Hannan (d. 1914, £2324), Sarah Taylor (d. 1912, £2270) and Mary Enright (d. 1915, £2225) held modest amounts of property.[39] Of the six, only Ellen Kennedy (d. 1902, £2125) of Addisons Flat had not been widowed.[40] She scattered bequests widely among her 11 children and named two married daughters, Mary Peters and Johanna Donohue, as trustees of her estate. Like women of other nationalities, all sought to preserve and transmit property to the next generation, sometimes equally among heirs, but often to give particular children a good start in life. In addition, all acquired modest fortunes through their commercial enterprise and a willingness to move at key moments in their lives.

Reflections

Women have not always been visible in Australasian goldfield histories, which have tended to emphasise men's working lives. The Irish-born women in my study arrived on the West Coast in large numbers and participated actively in the colonisation process and in building local community life. Many moved on in search of new opportunities; others stayed and established 'transnational lives'. Most had been 'thoroughly colonialised' by the time they arrived on the diggings and – like Ann Diamond, who served as a local midwife at Red Jacks – brought an array of skills and resources acquired in Victoria and Otago.

We are sometimes inclined to view colonial women such as these as quintessential Victorians, restricted by notions of domesticity that tied them to the private sphere of home and family. Yet, as Catherine Bishop has shown, this was not the way that the nineteenth-century worlds they inhabited actually worked.[41] Confronted by epic changes beyond their immediate control, Irish women from places such as Paulstown, Glendree and Rathcommane made the decision to travel abroad based on the advice of a wide range of kinsfolk and on the best available evidence.

For those who spent time on the West Coast goldfields, mobility within and across colonial spaces was already a central theme in their daily lives. Ellen Piezzi, for example, moved from town to town for work and business, travelling finally to Wellington; Sarah Gillin, who also spent time in Melbourne and Hokitika before marrying, was not unusual in crossing the Tasman to shop in the splendour of the Victorian capital. Whatever their motivations or occupations, Irish women such as these were highly mobile, active and connected to personal networks that transcended the local and spanned the oceans in many different directions.

This study and the two previous chapters in this section suggest two considerations for anyone exploring the lives and experiences of the women who inhabited the goldfields of mid-nineteenth century Australasia. First, we need to reassess our understandings of women's position in and contribution to goldfield economies. And, second, our analysis of women's lives on the goldfields must attend to their mobility and the dynamic movements, connections and interactions between Australia and New Zealand.

4

GOLDFIELDS SOCIETY

13.

Harsh Environment, Softer Sociology: The Dunstan gold rush 1862–2014 and the need for a fresh assessment

Tom Brooking

THIS SYNTHESIS ATTEMPTS TO reassess the Dunstan rushes by retracing the story of the main sub-rushes and treating them as a kind of snapshot. In telling these stories, I attempt to note how the four main phases of development involved in the transition from rush to mining played out in each location. I then round out the assessment of local variants by comparing them with other New Zealand rushes as well as some international rushes. With this information at hand, we should be better placed to understand what, if anything, was distinctive about the Dunstan rush. I conclude the chapter by calling for the writing of a new history of the Dunstan rush, hopefully as part of a wider Australasian reassessment.

Before proceeding any further, however, I want, with respect to this synthesis, to acknowledge my debts to a host of goldfield historians listed in the lengthy endnote. They range from Vincent Pyke through Frederick W.G. Miller and John Hall-Jones to Erik Olssen, Terry Hearn, James Ng, John McCraw and Grahame Sydney.[1] I would also like to express my appreciation of the contributions made by local historians, writers of theses in history, geography and archaeology at the University of Otago,[2] the numerous archaeological reports produced by the Department of Conservation (noted in other chapters in this volume) and the insights of international scholars, especially those relating to Victoria and California. Here, special mention must be made of David Goodman and Graeme Wynn.[3]

The area traversed is captured on Map 13.1, which includes the whole of Dunstan and Lake Counties. It excludes the Maniototo, however, on the grounds of space and, because (arguably) this rush was too far from the Dunstan to be counted as part of the Dunstan rush. Map 13.2 depicts the numbers of people living in the various Otago goldfield settlements between 1861 and 1870, the main period of goldmining activity in the region.

Map 13.1: Otago and Southland, c. 1865. This regional map shows the main rush-era urban centres. As well as the usual assortment of hotels and merchants, each tended to have a police station, post office and gold warden's office.

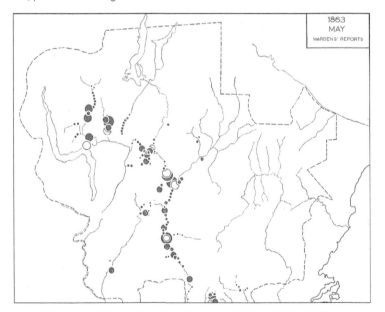

Map 13.2: Population and settlement on the Otago goldfields, 1861 to 1870.

Source: The map is a replication of James Forrest's map of the same title in the *New Zealand Geographer*, vol. 17, no. 1, 1961, p. 69.

Part 1: The Dunstan Story

The Big Rushes and Alluvial Mining

Hartley and Reilly: The alluvial phase up to the Arrow and Shotover rushes

In late July and early August 1862, the legendary American Horatio Hartley and 'American' Irishman Christopher Reilly extracted an extraordinary 1000 ounces, or 87 pounds, of gold (worth $NZ1,810,000 in 2015 terms) about one kilometre from the junction of the Kawarau and Molyneux (Clutha) Rivers. After a harrowing journey to Dunedin, they deposited their lucrative lode in a bank on 15 August and collected the £2000 reward the Otago Provincial Council had offered anyone who sparked a new rush. The council was keen to maintain momentum now that the declining Tuapeka rush centred on Gabriel's Gully was stagnating.

Hartley and Reilly had benefited from the water of the Molyneux River being at a very low level as a result of a particularly cold winter, a possible product of the mini-ice age occurring at the time, as exemplified by the River Thames in London freezing over. The low water level had made accessing the gold much easier than in previous winters. These 'easy pickings' enabled the iconic pair to move into a world of material comfort and a guaranteed place in the New Zealand hall of fame, but not before they showed the other miners who flocked to the area how to bench-mine rock, a process of gold extraction very different to that used on the Tuapeka and Victorian fields.[4]

When news of Hartley and Reilly's find became known, the contagion that was gold fever erupted once again. By September, some 2000 miners had rushed to the area from Dunedin in the east and the Tuapeka field to the south, leaving the latter deserted. The shanty town of Muttontown, situated on Watson Shennan's sheep run near what became Clyde, served as the centre of the new rush; by early September between 700 and 800 miners had set up camp there. Soon after, the spring flush pushed miners into the Nevis Valley, Bannockburn and even the Carrick Range.

At the end of 1862 some 24,000 hopefuls from Victoria were on the Dunstan, Victoria's accessible gold having been worked out. Despite widespread disappointment at the harshness of terrain in the 'dusty Dunstan' and the differences in mining practice from that previously experienced, miners had sent 70,000 ounces of gold to Dunedin on the well-guarded escort by year's end.[5] By the time the new year got underway, not only Muttontown but also the 'Kawarau Junction' (later Cromwell) were boasting some permanent buildings that housed and provided supplies to the miners still crowded into tents in these locations. All significant discoveries in the Dunstan area remained confined to the 'Molyneaux' until the autumn of 1863, when the Maniototo rush began. It continued on into 1864.[6]

During the summer of 1862/63 miners moved over the Pisa Range or up the valleys at the back of Lake Wanaka (known as 'Pembroke' at that time) through to Cardrona, yet another field with a name from the Scottish Borders. Returns from this area proved to be relatively modest, although the quartz rush to Carrick Town in 1871 would prove more lucrative.[7]

Cromwell, c. 1866. The 'lattice' bridge may be seen in the lower right corner.

Courtesy Cromwell Museum

Kawarau Junction, formally named Cromwell in 1866, when the town became a municipality, produced a solid 20,000 ounces by 1873. However, like 'Dunstan' (Clyde) and 'Lower Dunstan' (also known as 'Manuherikia Junction', then officially 'Alexandra' in 1865) further south,[8] Cromwell soon became more important as a service centre than a mining district, and fruit growing developed from the late 1860s. Mining remained more important at nearby Bannockburn and Bendigo. However, in the 1890s, dredges, especially those operating at Lowburn, revived the importance of mining in this district.[9] The advance of mining activity further west proved somewhat more chaotic.

Fox and the Arrow: Arthurs Point and Queenstown

William Fox, an Irishman noted for brawling, is reputed to have found a lucrative source of gold in the Arrow River in late October 1862. He, along with a few mates, managed to keep his luck a secret for six weeks.[10] About the same time, Thomas Arthur, a shepherd working for runholder William Rees, sifted out 200 ounces of gold at Arthurs Point in eight days and went on to make £4000.[11] Then three Māori gold seekers – Daniel or Dan (Rāniera Tāheke) Ellison, of Ati Āwa (Taranaki) and English parentage, who married Nani Weller (a granddaughter of Ōtākou chief Taiaroa Matenga), Hakaraia Haeroa and Hēnare Patukopa (related to Te Whiti o Rongomai of Parihaka) – extracted a further 300 ounces in another part of the Shotover River.[12]

In sum, these discoveries sparked the biggest rush in Otago's history to the Arrow-town and Queenstown areas. It was also easily the roughest, most chaotic and least law-abiding of all Otago's rushes. Violent claim-jumping became chronic, assisted by an absence of police and gaols. Petty theft, particularly of wood that was largely absent in the high and dry alpine environment, was commonplace. Sheep, stolen to supplement miners' meagre diet of flour and water, also disappeared from local runs at an alarming rate. Brothels proliferated along with questionable entertainment provided by the likes of the American whaler William Henry Hayes, better known as Bully Hayes. Drunkenness was rife and brawling commonplace.[13]

Even so, as Wayne Angus shows, by late 1864 the 500 or so miners left in the Queenstown area began to establish some kind of order. They built athenaeums as well as pubs, established cricket and jockey clubs, lodges, an Anglican church, a hospital, a permanent school and a fire brigade. They also championed the Chartist cause of universal suffrage, while an 'improvement committee' pushed for the establishment of municipal government in the district.[14]

Significant rushes also reached more remote Bendigo on the far (eastern) side of the Molyneux from Cromwell, and Macetown, further up the Arrow River, but both places soon turned to operating stamper batteries that involved the injection of a considerable amount of capital. 'Hard rock' mining of quartz also forced miners to work for wages and serve as employees of companies rather than operate as individuals. The big rushes to the Dunstan were now over. So began the second or 'associative' phase of gold mining in the Dunstan. Based on sluicing and water power, this stage was soon followed by the 'corporate' phase involving stamper batteries and underground mining of quartz seams in the hard rock.

The Associative and Corporate Phase in the Dunstan, 1864–1940s

Bendigo

Between 1867and 1869, a quartz stamping battery powered by a water wheel appeared on part of the McLean brothers' giant Morven Hills Station that ran down the Lindis Pass to Cromwell and back up to Lake Wanaka. Covering about a million acres, it was by far New Zealand's largest run on Crown leasehold land.[15] The battery had been erected by Logan and Co., also known as the Cromwell Company. Headed by Thomas (Tom) Logan, with initial backing from Cromwell investor and publican George Wellington Goodger, the company operated the most successful of the quartz mines in Otago. Between 1868 and 1872 the company was able to pay its four shareholders a dividend of £6000. By 1871 it was employing up to 40 miners, paying them the princely sum of £4.0 a week (more than double the average wage of about £1-10s and £1.0 more per week than other miners). All up, the company paid out £400,000 in shareholder dividends.[16]

By 1870 the settlement of Logantown, just northeast of Cromwell, hosted a butcher, a baker and seven hotels. A Good Templar's Lodge was added in 1875 and a school from 1881. Logantown and nearby Welshtown and Bendigo all held annual sports days in the mid-1870s.

Cromwell Company Mine, Bendigo, 1872.

Burton Bros. Photographers, courtesy Lloyd Carpenter collection

Macetown

When the Macetown field opened in 1863, it supported a stable population of about 120 that grew to 169 by 1870. The subsequent quartz 'boom' saw the population increase to 206 by 1896 before collapsing completely by 1921. In the 1870s and 1880s, groups rather than individuals applied for water rights. These groups were often constituted along kin lines – as Terry Hearn found from his research for his doctoral thesis and in subsequent research into the Nenthorn goldfield (east of Middlemarch), gold dredging and the key politicians of the area and era – and they included Italians, Swiss and Chinese as well as Scots, Irish, English and New Zealand-born miners and their families. These family-based groups were quite different from the individualistic 'hatters' celebrated by Stevan Eldred–Grigg.[17] Indeed, some families from Victoria settled in and around Macetown for 40 years.

In 1871 the area had 31 females for every 100 males, but relatively normal demographic patterns had emerged by 1896 when almost as many women as men were living in the environs. As Jennifer Dickson discovered for Otago as a whole, the majority of these women were married.[18] Macetown residents held regular dances and concerts. They also established a 'progress committee' in 1876 and revived it again in 1884 after it had been in abeyance for some time. When Macetown was connected by telephone to the Otago network in 1886, residents felt much less isolated. Throughout the time that Macetown remained occupied, the school struggled, but doctors' visits became more regular from 1881 once the town gained representation on the Wakatipu

Macetown, 1897.

Courtesy Lakes District Museum, Arrowtown

District Hospital Committee. The local store acted as a vitally important institution to the community by supplying goods as well as credit. Although Chinese miners worked on the Macetown field from the late 1860s, they always hovered on the edges of the community.

In time, declining gold yields, the poor road access and extreme isolation undermined Macetown's viability. However, the settlement was far from being dominated by disconnected, atomised individuals as Miles Fairburn would have us believe.[19] Community structures still operated in this difficult environment and isolated location so long as mining remained economically viable. In many ways, Macetown was not very different from many other small towns in nineteenth-century New Zealand.[20]

Skippers

Mining commenced from late 1862 on the Skippers field 1500 feet above the Shotover River. In 1863 some 700 miners were working there. Named after Malcolm ('Skipper') Duncan, a former sea captain from Northern Ireland, the field became famous for two large lodes of gold – Mount Aurum and Bullendale. John Aspinall, who had come to the area from England via Australia and then the Thames goldfield in the North Island, had initial success with tunnelling and underground mining, soon making around £8000 from his labours.[21] By the time of his marriage to Elizabeth Craigie in 1871, Aspinall is reputed to have had a bank balance of £10,000.[22]

In 1864 four men established the Scandinavian Prospectors Company with the aim of undertaking further hard-rock mining. The company took its name in honour of one of these men, Norwegian Alex Olsen, who was among the initial finders of the field's rich gold seams. This company, which later became the Great Scandinavian Quartz Mining Company, operated a large battery with 30 stampers, and was the first to use quartz mining as a way of extracting gold in the South Island.[23] Workers sledged the quartz-bearing rock for just over a mile to a tip before shooting it down an incline and trucking it to the battery.[24]

The Great Scandinavian evolved into the Phoenix Company in 1874 when George F. Bullen, a runholder from Kaikoura, and others bought it out. Soon, the area became known as Bullendale. Steam power gave way to electricity during 1885/86, with the transmission wires running over a 2000-foot-high ridge. This technological innovation constituted the first use of electricity in New Zealand's gold-mining history and, indeed, of the Southern Hemisphere.[25] As occurred elsewhere, hydraulic sluicing also commenced once the technology became available in 1872.

About 200 men made their living in this remote area as late as the 1890s. Despite continuing good returns, labour problems eroded profits, as did the high sulphide content in the lower levels of the lode and the difficulties of access. Mining came to a halt in 1907, except for some individual efforts on the edges of the field. By then, the population had fallen to 92. The field produced some 40,000 ounces of gold but lost its various promoters about £200,000. Small settlements at Charlestown and Skippers Point were short lived.

Despite being relatively sparse and itinerant, the local population instigated the establishment of schools at Skippers township (in 1876) and Bullendale (1890) and were willing to bring in teachers at their own expense, although they did receive assistance in this regard from the Otago and (later) Southland education boards. The Skippers school, initially known as Upper Shotover Public School and later Skippers Point School, opened in 1878 with 21 pupils and the Bullendale, known as Skippers Reef School, in 1891 with eight pupils.[26] The hardy settlers of this very cold place, despite being adversely affected by the huge floods of 1878, somehow managed to build a permanent bridge in 1901 and established a cemetery.

As with Macetown, the cooperative and corporate phases of gold mining coexisted at Skippers. Although the community never flourished, it exhibited many of the traits of other gold-mining hamlets with its emphasis on family life and improving education.[27] The ruined remnants of the once busy stamper batteries still stand as reminders of these earlier times and the extraordinary hard work involved in extracting gold from such a site.

Water and mining

Miners also continued sluicing around batteries and underground mines, as at Stewart Town above the man-made 'badlands' stretching beyond today's Mount Difficulty winery in the upper reaches of Bannockburn. As a result, both European and Chinese miners built nearly 500 miles of water races and laid down several hundred miles of

A Chinese miner's hut, Arrow Falls.

Courtesy Lakes District Museum, Arrowtown

piping, much of which is still visible.[28] It is a tribute to the engineering skill of the miners that many of the water races still flow effectively, helping the development of irrigation systems that assist in sustaining pastoral farming, horticulture and viticulture to this very day. In short, there was a coexistence of cooperative and corporate mining, and progress from one form to the next was neither stadial nor tidy. But either way, individual mining became much less important, and large concentrations of miners in any one place soon became a thing of a the past. The rushes were but a brief if transformative moment in time.

The Dredging Phase, 1890s to the 1950s

Research by former mining engineer Nic McArthur makes clear that the gold-mining dredge (basically, revolving buckets travelling up and down a ladder before depositing gravel on a screen set atop a steam-powered river punt resting on pontoons) was a New Zealand invention.[29] New Zealand engineers, mainly based in Dunedin, took technology developed overseas and converted it into something particularly helpful in the New Zealand context before re-exporting that invention overseas.

Small spoon dredges had been developed by European and Chinese miners and port authorities much earlier and used for deepening river and harbour channels in places such as the River Thames in London.[30] The New Zealand dredge was much larger than its predecessors. Consequently, Dunedin-based engineering firms such as

R.S. Sparrow's Victoria Ironworks, A.&T. Burt, and Kincaid and McQueen (along with Anderson and Co. in Christchurch) made much more money than most investors or gold-dredging companies because the enterprises proved to be highly speculative.[31] Various attempts were made throughout the 1880s, without producing much impact, as engineers fine-tuned designs and crews learned how to best exploit river-bed deposits.

From 1889, the Chinese merchant Choie (Charles) Sew Hoy and the Jewish Joel Brothers, who formed the Shotover Big Beach Gold Mining Company, fared better on the Shotover River near Queenstown.[32] The 1890 boom involved the formation of 28 companies with a nominal capital of over £390,000. Although short lived, this sudden rush of enthusiasm revitalised the Otago gold-mining industry throughout the 1890s and into the early twentieth century. Despite this renewed activity, Sew Hoy and many others soon lost money, although the introduction of new technology in the form of the 'tailings elevator' in 1894 enabled dredges to operate in deeper water and to take on larger banks of river stones, especially on the Clutha River.[33] The Electric Gold Dredging Company operated by the McGeorge Brothers won much gold in the late 1890s, especially through its large dredge named the Lady Ranfurly. The Hartley and Reilly Beach Gold Dredging Company and the Magnetic Company also did well on the Kawarau River, winning over £8000 worth of gold in 1899. Another boom ensued, followed by the seemingly inevitable bust.[34]

Despite many company collapses and much investor disappointment, some 155 dredges were operating on Otago's rivers at the height of gold-dredging activity in 1904. This activity occurred mainly on the Clutha, but dredging also took place on many other waterways, some of them in very remote places. Peak production was reached in 1902 at 105,000 ounces. Between 1899 and 1914, dredges extracted

Lady Ranfurly dredge at work, Kawarau River.

Courtesy Central Stories Museum, Alexandra

approximately 682,000 ounces of gold from Otago's rivers.[35] In the Dunstan, dredges concentrated around Cromwell. Significantly, only 93 of the 485 dredging companies registered during the peak period of activity between 1899 and 1905 ever paid out a dividend. The Electric, Cromwell and Alexandra Eureka Companies were very much the exception. They collectively paid out more than £100,000 in dividends.[36]

The static gold price during World War I brought the industry to its knees, but by war's end, bold plans had been hatched to drain both the Clutha and Kawarau Rivers. None of these fanciful schemes succeeded, even though rising gold prices in the 1930s stimulated one last effort at dredging. From the 1920s, dredges became ever more massive and began eating up orchard and pastoral farmland.[37] The new Labour government elected in 1935 tried to expand dredging around Roxburgh from 1936 on and then further up the river, but this operation staggered along until 1963, losing far more than it made. The last giant dredges operated at Lowburn by the Austral New Zealand Mining Company were truly monstrous; the biggest reached 94 feet in height and measured 348 feet to the end of the elevator. This giant extracted over 80,000 ounces of gold between 1940 and 1951, but ended up working Malaysian tin mines from 1953.[38]

These clanking machines extracted nearly a million ounces of gold, or about 28 per cent of Otago's total production of over 3.5 million ounces.[39] In doing so, they left the greatest mark upon Otago's environment and landscape. Special legislative exemptions allowed gold-bearing rivers to be reclassified as sludge channels (nine in Otago), which led to significant siltation of both large and small rivers. Some 457 million cubic yards of tailings were dumped along the Clutha River alone and can still be seen today.[40] (I discuss the significance of this careless approach at greater length in the second part of this chapter.)

The 1930s' Flurry

One final effort was made to revitalise land-based gold mining in Otago during the Great Depression of the early 1930s. In a desperate search for solutions to reduce escalating unemployment and in the hope of finding additional income streams, the coalition government pushed about 1000 miners into Central Otago in May 1932 to rework older claims. These men concentrated their efforts on the old Maniototo field, especially around Tinkers and Drybread at the back of Omakau, although some of the miners near Cromwell were successful, most notably the Bell-Hooper and Bell-Kilgour operations on the banks of the Kawarau opposite Bannockburn. The men on the government mining-work scheme had to put up with living in huts bereft of insulation, tents and even caves in the freezing central winters.[41] Small quartz claims were also developed, including the Rise and Shine Syndicate near Bendigo. Some Dunedin investors, led by Charles Todd (who was born at Bendigo), tried to revive Bendigo mining through an ambitious deep adit driven underneath the old mine workings. This endeavour failed miserably. Since then, there has been no revival of this type of large-scale mining other than that conducted by big Australian companies at, for example, Macraes Flat or south of Ettrick.

Bell-Kilgour Claim, Scotland Point, Cromwell Flats, July 1932. Percy Bell and William Kilgour are dumping spoil into Kawarau River.

Courtesy R.W. Murray collection, Cromwell Museum

Part 2: The Key Characteristics of the Gold Rushes and Gold Mining in the Dunstan

The stories related thus far in this chapter describe variations on a theme. Above all, they reinforce the point that, as was the case with most gold rushes, the initial influx of miners to the Dunstan constituted an anarchic moment of chaos and disassembling. For a year or so, there was a temporary return to a pre-industrial order. Individualistic fossickers escaped the trammels of rapidly developing industrial capitalism by scrambling over schist-covered mountains and treacherous river gorges into the remote wilderness of the Dunstan.

The situation was almost a counter-revolutionary one because time was compressed and trends reversed – but only momentarily. As other commentators in this volume suggest, the period had almost theological overtones, for it was both transformative and transcendental. It was also existential in much the same way as the Great Depression of the 1930s was, in that the rush seemed to involve the whole community and generated inclusive, long-lasting myths.[42]

The nature of the Dunstan rushes also aligns with James Belich's argument that booms such as the Dunstan's accelerated the economic growth of English-speaking settlements and colonies around the globe by attracting sudden waves of immigration, thereby peopling areas that had been previously unpopulated or very sparsely populated. Something British or European emerged from nothing, or at least very little, as seen through non-indigenous eyes.[43] The sudden, energising influx of white and Chinese miners also changed the older ethnic composition of the Otago settlement, with Central Otago becoming the least Scottish part of Otago/Southland.[44]

The Dunstan rushes seem little different in all these respects from those of the West Coast of the South Island, Victoria or California. Seven other aspects of the Dunstan rushes also seem rather typical of most gold-mining regions, although some distinctive elements can be discerned within the broader patterns.

First, the economic outcomes were typical of 'quarry'-type activity in terms of resources being extracted until they became exhausted.[45] The economic impact was therefore both sudden and transitory, but not before multiplier linkage effects stimulated the broader Otago and Dunedin economies. Some estimates suggest that each miner generated five jobs for others. The influx of miners and mining stimulated a wide range of economic activities that included farming; construction of infrastructure, housing, and transport systems; manufacturing of such necessities as bricks, soap and luxuries (e.g. beer); engineering; provision of law and order and related services; and the establishment of key financial institutions, especially stores, banks, stock and station agencies and insurance companies.[46]

The fact that modern-day Dunedin has only a modest population of 120,000 people in contrast to the three and a half million living in Melbourne and the six million living in San Francisco suggests that the Dunstan and other Otago rushes made for a relatively small overall rush. The Otago field produced only about four per cent of the world's gold at peak production compared with about a third from Victoria and a third from California.[47] Even so, it was still a much larger rush than later examples, such as the rush to the Fraser River in British Columbia.

Second, as Dan Davy's chapter in this volume makes clear, the Dunstan was a very Victorian place, much more so than either the West Coast or Thames/Coromandel. Up to 90 per cent of the Dunstan's miners came from Victoria, and although more returned than stayed, the influence remained. Links between Otago and Melbourne also persisted long after the rushes had ended. Even the University of Otago's Dental School, which opened in 1907, modelled itself on the Melbourne Dental School rather than on its British or American equivalents.[48] The importance of this influence must be acknowledged, and I can only support Davey's call to reassess the Otago rushes by viewing them through a trans-Tasman framework.[49]

Third, studies of individual mining sites show that 'instant civilisation' emerged during the Dunstan rushes despite the area's tough environment, isolation and under-developed character. Communities were built with remarkable speed, no matter what the prevailing 'rough and wild' mythology suggests, as Miles Fairburn, Stevan Eldred-Grigg and other historians have argued. The emphasis on self-improvement evident in the athenaeums, mechanics' institutes and literary societies was also echoed in the miners' demand for the vote, their fractious relationship with the Otago Provincial Council and their setting up of town councils and municipal boroughs. The establishment of volunteer fire brigades, horse-racing and cricket clubs, schools, churches, stores and newspapers, five of which are still available to the researcher (the *Lake Wakatip Mail, Cromwell Argus, Dunstan Times, Arrow Observer & Lakes District Chronicle* and *Lake County Press*) further attest to miners and their families' determination to build community, to help people help themselves, and to promulgate a more egalitarian view of how society should be ordered.[50] Yet this desire for self-government was tempered by the habit of turning to central government to sort out disputes with local elites and other groups, such as farmers, who pursued different development strategies.[51]

This emphasis on community building helps explain why the Dunstan rushes soon became law abiding and orderly after the few first anarchic months. Demographic shifts were also probably at work in that the Dunstan miners, compared with their Victorian and Californian predecessors, were often older and married with families.[52] A trawl through the rich repository of information in the online digital resource 'Papers Past'[53] makes clear that reports from the law courts continued to provide entertainment for the populace and that drunkenness, petty theft and small-scale prostitution remained ongoing problems. However, the Dunstan was largely free of bush rangers, armed robbery and gang conflict from 1864 on.[54]

Fourth, hostility to Chinese miners was typical of both the Otago and West Coast rushes within New Zealand, and of the Australian and Californian rushes. The same toxic mixture of raw racism and fear of losing hard-won gains regarding wages and conditions was evident in all these places in about equal measure. If prejudice expressed in the Dunstan was a little less severe than in other places, it was only because there were fewer Chinese and the fruit and vegetables they supplied were more appreciated

Naseby (formerly known as Hogburn), showing sludge channel in foreground, c. 1880s.

Courtesy Lloyd Carpenter collection

than in other, less hostile environments.[55] Moreover, as James Beattie makes clear, Chinese goldminers not only made a significant contribution to market gardening in New Zealand but also contributed to the more negative environmental impacts of the gold rushes via their efforts at sluicing and even dredging.[56]

Fifth, the fact that most miners who stayed moved on to become farmers, orchardists, storekeepers, small businessmen or small-town professionals dampened down the long-term political impact of the Dunstan rushes and explains the political swing from deep yellow (the colour of Liberalism) to true blue. This situation was quite different from the scenario on the West Coast, where the post-rush growth of coal mining and timber milling saw the emergence of the Labour Party. Essentially, the early establishment of a democratic goldfields' electorate did not shape Central Otago's long-term politics in the way that it did on the West Coast, where the charismatic Richard John Seddon provided a link and continuity between the Liberal and Labour parties.[57] The rapid growth of Melbourne into a large city helps explain the links between Liberalism and Labour in Victoria in contrast to the shift towards William Massey's moderate conservatism that occurred in rural and small-town New Zealand during the early twentieth century.[58]

Sixth, the Dunstan rushes, like most other major rushes, were technologically innovative, but arguably more so than many others because of the impact of the hydraulic elevator and the dredge.[59] Even so, the longest lasting impact has been environmental rather than technological. Dumping of tailings and declaration of rivers as 'sludge' channels through modification of English riparian law, as described earlier, meant that regulation of such activities was very permissive compared with the regulations in both Victoria and California.[60] Soft control of mining processes led to central government having to pay over £250,000 compensation in the 1920s to tidy up the Clutha and Taieri rivers.

Equally, the figures cited above on the scale of dumping ensured that gold mining brought about major landscape modification in the Dunstan. So, too, did the building of water races, some of which are still operational. The lack of heavy forest cover in the area compared with the West Coast and the Coromandel also ensured that the environmental and physical legacies of the Dunstan rushes, or what Simon Schama would call the 'sedimentation' of human activity upon the landscape, is much easier to see in the dry gullies and barren hills of the Dunstan over 150 years later.[61]

Finally, naming of mining sites and the attachment of legends to those sites is not all that different from these same processes in most other major gold-mining regions. The names initially imposed on the landscape tended to overwrite and bury those used by earlier indigenous peoples, as elsewhere. The names of Ophir and Aurum both suggest that the primary purpose of the area was the extraction of gold. Names such as Mount Difficulty accentuate the physical hardships involved, while mines with names like 'the Excelsior', found on the Carrick vineyard, are typically optimistic. The same can be said of the names of some dredges, such as the Enterprise and the Golden Gravel, while the Electric and the Magnetic company names indicate use of the very latest technologies and the most up-to-date fashions and trends. Others place names such as Pipe Clay Terrace or Target Gully were more prosaic, while yet others more distinctively remembered local characters such as Jackson Barry and Charcoal Joe. Surveyor John Turnbull Thomson laid peculiarly Northumbrian names such as Dunstan over the area, and less common Scottish names such as Saint Bathans and Mount Earnslaw, although he reserved his most notorious efforts for the Maniototo.[62]

So just how distinctive was the Dunstan gold-rush and gold-mining story? It seems that *the place* provided most of its distinctive features in that it possessed the harshest environment of all the locales that attracted miners during the Australasian gold rushes. The Dunstan was steeper, higher, colder in the winter and dustier in the summer than any other major field in New Zealand, Victoria or New South Wales. Later, Kalgoolie in Western Australia would be sandier than any other field, but even if cool at night, it never suffered from snow or frost, and seldom from flooding. The processes and stages of development and transition from rush to mining that unfolded, as well as the social structures and cultural mores that emerged in the Dunstan, were nevertheless not especially different from elsewhere. Judging by tourist promotions of this old gold-mining area, the popular mythology that goldminers were wild, rough individuals unattached to family, community, church, organisations or localities seems to have survived decades of quiet revisionism. Much the same can be said of most other New Zealand and Australian gold-mining areas.

Conclusion

The synthesis I have endeavoured to provide in this chapter suggests four main conclusions.

First, it is time for a new history of the Dunstan rushes and their immediate and longer-term impacts to be written, with these accounts based on primary rather than secondary sources and utilising, where possible, a comparative frame with other New Zealand and Australian rushes. This present publication represents a promising beginning, but the job needs to be completed by a solo author with a wide range of transdisciplinary skills, or a small team of historians and archaeologists.

Second, the new account must more systematically interrogate newspapers now that many are available electronically, as well as Warden's Court records (some of which are available electronically). Warden's Court records provide detailed accounts of individual effort and debt and, compared with many other archival sources, produce plenty of 'pay dirt'. Paintings, literary outputs, oral histories, diaries, letters and the rich photographic evidence held in collections such as those of the Hocken Library in Dunedin, smaller local museums, such as the Lakes District Museum in Arrowtown, and associations such as the Queenstown and District Historical Society[63] have much more to yield when assessed more systematically, and especially if researchers aim to seek out the perspectives of women and children more thoroughly.[64]

Third, we need more intensive local political studies (a task also made easier by the greater availability of newspapers and other primary-source documents online). Such studies will enable, for example, comparisons to be made between the Dunstan and the West Coast and Thames/Coromandel rushes in order to better understand the Dunstan's shift from deep yellow to true blue.

Fourth, and finally, in doing all these things, researchers cum authors must maintain at all times a balance between rigorous revision and an ability to discern those romantic elements that made gold rushes special and different. Realising this aim will mean paying particularly close attention to the Dunstan's distinctive environment.

14.

A Runholder's Dream Dashed
by the Discovery of Gold

Rosemary Marryatt

IN 1863 THE ONCE PRISTINE and peaceful Queenstown had become a place of busyness and noise. At nightfall, hundreds of miners swarmed into Harry Redfern's Theatre Royal in Beech Street, where Charles Thatcher, entertainer and *improvisitore*, sang ditties that satirised local personalities. No-one escaped the sharp eye of Thatcher – not even the pioneer settler, Mr Rees:

> *Oh! How it must knock off his perch Mr Rees,*
> *To see such a township and buildings like these,*
> *When a few months ago he was here all alone,*
> *And the fact of goldfields near the lake was unknown.*[1]

So who was the Mr Rees 'knocked off his perch' on seeing all the buildings springing up on his sheep run? Because Thatcher was right: William Gilbert Rees, the pioneer settler on the shores of Queenstown Bay, had to cope with problems created by thousands of miners pouring over his land. But notwithstanding the disruption the miners wrought, it soon became obvious that Rees was capable of accepting and adapting to the vast changes that the gold rush brought to the Wakatipu Basin. The physical and mental qualities he'd developed over the previous 35 years prepared him for his role as a leader in the rush town of Queenstown – a role that would eventually earn him the title 'King Wakatip'.[2]

Early Years

On 6 April 1827 Lieutenant William Lee Rees and his wife Mary, née Pocock, celebrated the birth of their first child, William Gilbert, at Derby Farm, Haverfordwest, Wales. Because Lieutenant Rees was frequently away from home serving on various Royal Navy packet ships, he and Mary sent their son William to Prospect Place

Early Queenstown, c. 1865.
Courtesy Lloyd Carpenter collection

Academy, a boarding school in Bristol.[3] It was here that William received a stimulating education from his maternal grandfather George Pocock, inventor, poet and lay minister schoolmaster. It was probably George who broke the news to 12-year-old William that his father had died at sea from yellow fever while on a return trip from Mexico in 1839. After leaving the boarding academy, William completed his education at the Royal Naval School at Camberwell, London, an institution catering for the sons of naval officers. School holidays were usually spent at Bristol, where there was ample opportunity to play cricket under the watchful eye of his uncle, Dr Henry Mills Grace.

When Grace's son, the famous cricketer W.G. Grace, wrote his autobiography, he recalled: 'About the year 1845 the Mangotsfield [cricket club] was much strengthened by the appearance of two nephews of my mother, Mr William Rees and Mr George Gilbert, who came to stay with us during the holidays … Both were almost in the first class as batsmen, much above the average as bowlers and fielded with dash and certainty.'[4]

During one of the many trips William made between London and Bristol, a stop at Hungerford put him at the right place and time to save Mr R. Knight from drowning in the local canal. Although he was only 15 years old at the time, William was awarded the Royal Humane Society bronze medal for his actions. At the Royal Naval Dockyard on the Milford Haven in Pembrokeshire, William studied for his engineering apprenticeship and at the age of 22 accepted the position of assistant master at Mount Radford School in Exeter. Two of his students were brothers – Thomas and Charles Teschemaker. Years later, the three met up in New Zealand.

On 18 July 1848 William Gilbert Rees was named godfather to his cousin William Gilbert Grace (otherwise known in cricketing circles as W.G.), and the years 1848 to

1852 were interwoven with the lives of his many Pocock, Gilbert and Grace cousins. Cricket was forgotten, however, in 1852, when William and his cousin George Henry Bailey Gilbert, ready for adventures overseas, departed from England on board the 479-ton barque *Mary Ann*, bound for Australia.

Australia

After arriving in Sydney on 9 March 1852, William set off westward on a long journey over the Blue Mountains. His sketchbook shows that he visited Coolah in October 1852 and Mudgee in November.[5] Later in his life he mentioned visiting the Turon goldfields, but the lure of gold did not tempt him to tarry there; instead, he moved on to the Darling Downs, New South Wales, where on 24 July 1853 he drew two sketches at Stonehenge Station and annotated them with 'My first management, resident here for three months'.

The owner of Stonehenge was George Gammie. He and his brother John had established themselves as major landholders on 'The Downs'. Rees sketched his employer, adding to it the note, 'G.Gammie, Talgai 1853', possibly indicating that the two men had established a friendship, one that developed into a business partnership which determined Rees's future for the next 14 years.[6] When John Gammie died on 6 August 1853, George Gammie began selling his properties and eventually returned to England in 1855.[7] Before departing Australia, Gammie and Rees set plans in motion for a New Zealand venture, whereby Rees would act as Gammie's stockman manager and Gammie would be the financial backer. For this venture to succeed, the men needed to arrange the shipment of merino sheep to New Zealand and to secure suitable land there for grazing.

'William Gilbert Rees, July 1853', by W.G. Rees.

W.G. Rees' sketchbook, courtesy Alexander Turnbull Library, Wellington, Rees family donation

'Stonehenge Station, My first management, Darling Downs, 1853', by W.G. Rees.

W.G. Rees' sketchbook, courtesy Alexander Turnbull Library, Wellington, Rees family donation

'George Gammie of Talgai, 1853', by W.G. Rees.

W.G. Rees' sketchbook, courtesy Alexander Turnbull Library, Wellington, Rees family donation

'Frances Rees, Oct. 1858', by W.G. Rees.

W.G. Rees' sketchbook, courtesy Alexander Turnbull Library, Wellington, Rees family donation

Rees did not depart Australia until 10 February 1858, and then it was not to New Zealand but to England. He had committed himself to furthering the New Zealand project, but found much to fill his life in Australia between 1854 and 1858. He was a member of the New South Wales Cricket XI during the first intercolonial cricket match played at the Outer Domain in Sydney.[8] His cousin George Gilbert played with him, and another cousin, William Lee Rees, played in the opposing Victoria Cricket XI. A letter that Sampson Yeo Marshall of Goondiwindi Station wrote in October 1856 confirms that Rees was also heavily involved with managing sheep stations in the Macintyre River region, where his horsemanship, prowess as a boxer and skill at managing stock were held in high esteem.[9]

Before leaving Australia for England, Rees busied himself organising not only the purchase of the merino sheep that were to go to New Zealand but also the first New Zealand land deal for the Gammie/Rees partnership. Meanwhile, Colonel William Lewis Grant, late 7th Foot Royal Fusiliers, whom George Gammie met on his return to England, had joined the two men as a financial partner. The Grant/Gammie/Rees partnership signed up their first land deal at the end of October 1857 when runholder John Anderson sold them the lease of Dalvey Run (Run No. 140) at Pomahaka, Southland, with the lease to begin 29 April 1859.[10]

Rees arrived back in England in early June 1858. Although his stay there was short, it was long enough for him to play cricket for the Bath XXII against the touring United England XI. He also presented his godson and cousin W.G. Grace with his first cricket bat, which Grace described in his autobiography as 'not full size. But it had what I had long wished for, a cane handle.'[11] William spent much of his time with another cousin, Frances Rebecca Gilbert (born 27 November 1838 in Holloway, Middlesex). After a short courtship, William and Frances married on 20 July 1858.

New Zealand

Two months after the wedding, the clipper *Equator* sailed from London for New Zealand with William and Frances on board, along with John Gilbert, Frances' brother. On 22 January 1859 the *Equator* arrived at Wellington's Port Nicholson, and the Reeses lost no time in carrying on to Dunedin.

The 3000 merinos William had shipped from Australia were grazing at Johnny Jones' Coal Creek Station in the Shag Valley near Palmerston, Otago.[12] Frances was five months pregnant, and she and William were able to stay in the cottage at Matanaka, which Jones also owned. Rees visited Dalvey Run on 29 April 1859, the date on which the Grant/Gammie/Rees partnership took over the lease. On 14 May Frances gave birth to her first child, Mary Rose, at Dunedin.

Rees was keen to look for grazing country for his merinos, so he, William Anderson Low (a fellow passenger on the *Equator*), Charles Hopkinson, Nicholas von Tunzelmann and one other set off from Moeraki at the end of January 1860 to explore the hinterland of Otago. Because of their perseverance, Rees and von Tunzelmann discovered an expanse of suitable sheep country, now known as the Wakatipu Basin. In the middle of March, Rees and von Tunzelmann arrived back in Dunedin, starving and exhausted after six weeks of exploration. The editor of the *Otago Witness* wrote in the 24 March issue:

> We learn from a gentleman lately returned from an expedition into the interior, that the Wakatip Lake, along the banks of which he was by great perseverance, enabled to get (after navigating the lake on a moggie,[13] [sic] for two days) to a point from where he obtained a view of the northern end of the lake, and took observations from which he ascertained that the lake must extend a distance of 80 miles from one end to the other; the Northern end being within about 25 miles of Milford Haven, on the West Coast.[14]

A week later Rees wrote a letter giving a full description of the exploration into the interior, signing himself 'W.G.R.'.[15] Rees also wrote to the Otago Waste Land Board requesting licences for four runs in the Wakatipu Basin to be established under the Grant/Gammie/Rees partnership. As depicted on the map below, these were the Shotover Run, the Peninsula Run, the Bucklerburn Run, and the Staircase Run.[16] The board, however, did not grant licences until it was assured that the runs were properly stocked.

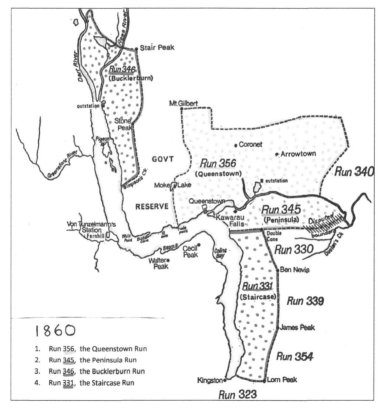

Sketch map of the four sheep runs in the Grant/Gammie/Rees partnership 1860–65, in George J. Griffiths, *King Wakatip* (Dunedin: John McIndoe Ltd, 1971, p. 92).

At a meeting of the board on 4 April 1860, Rees applied on behalf of Messrs Grant and Gammie to have an extension of time to stock Shotover Run, which would later become known as the Queenstown Run. (The name of the first run was a reference to the river running through the property – the Shotover. Rees named the river after partner George Gammie's estate back in England.) The board granted the request. All Rees had to do now was get his sheep from Shag Valley to the Wakatipu. The 3000 merinos finally arrived at the Wakatipu at New Year 1861. Rees was then able to supply stock not only to the Queenstown Run but also to the three other runs established held under the partnership. But in the eight months preceding the arrival of the sheep from Shag Valley, changes had been taking place at what was to become known as the home station at Queenstown Bay.

Just before August 1860, Rees made contact with Lewis Ackers of Otatara, near Invercargill. Ackers, well known as a whaler, trader, farmer, sawmiller and boat builder, sold Rees one of his whaleboats. The *Otago Witness* reported in October that 'Mr Rees ... started from Invercargill ... with a dray load of provisions and stores, weighing 24 cwt for his intended station and also a five-oared whaleboat with which he arrived at the southern end of the lake ... The boat is now on the lake.'[17] Five people accompanied Rees: boatman Bob Fortune, carpenters Harry Posselthwaite and George Washington McGaw, McGaw's wife Elizabeth, who was the cook, and another carpenter known simply as 'Chips'.

At Queenstown Bay the men immediately began work on completing the buildings for Rees's home station. These included a rodent-proof food storehouse set up on tin-covered poles, a long narrow hut consisting of three rooms, and (eventually) a calf shed, stockyard and milking yard. On the foreshore, where Eichardt's Hotel is today, Rees built his woolshed and a small wharf. In January 1861 he built a wattle and daub house at the mouth of what is now Horne Creek.[18]

Frances gave birth to George Manning Rees, her second child, at Dunedin on 26 January 1861. He died at Invercargill when only three months old, probably when Frances was on her way to the lake. She shifted into her new home at Horne Creek in April of that year. She was coping with the death of her baby when her younger brother John Gilbert drowned on 28 April while crossing the Clutha River with some cows at Wilkins Station near Lake Wanaka. Early in March 1862, Frances left Lake Wakatipu with servant girl Lizzie and two-year-old Mary Rose for the Dalvey Run at Pomahaka, where she gave birth on 22 April 1862 to Cecil Walter Rees. Frances, now 23 years old, stayed at Pomahaka over the winter. On her return to Queenstown she wrote a letter to her friend Louisa Fleming:

> We reached home ten days ago after being on the road nearly three weeks. I was
> heartily tired of it as you may imagine. We were delayed by the drays and then
> by the New River which was flooded and to crown it all, fancy my boxes were
> all upset in the middle of the New River. You never saw such a drying out as we
> had. All my beautiful books just out from home all spoilt. I was dreadfully upset
> about it ... dear baby is as jolly as ever, none the worse excepting that he has lost
> a little of his fat. He was very good but did not sleep much in the cart. I rode

after the first day to the foot of the lake from [the station of] Mr Wills to Mr McKellars – the distance is 32 miles – I was very tired with that ride.[19]

Gold

The dispute as to who was the first to discover gold in the Wakatipu Basin continued well into the end of the nineteenth century. William Fox stated: 'I was the first man that got gold in the Wakatipu district',[20] whereas Thomas Low and his brother-in-law John MacGregor were sure that it was them.[21] Goldfields secretary and later Wakatipu warden Vincent Pyke gave these two men the credit for being the first goldminers on the Arrow,[22] while prior to October 1862, Thomas Arthur and Harry Redfern, two of Rees' shearers, were reputedly the first panning for gold in the Shotover River.[23] Many years later, Vincent Pyke wrote to Rees, asking him who he thought was the first to discover gold in the Wakatipu. Rees replied:

> I think it was early in August 1862 that Maori Jack, also known as Jack Tewa and a companion made their appearance at the station … Jack on the evening he arrived, showed me a sample of gold which he had washed with his shovel from the bed of the Arrow, I then felt certain (for I had been at the Turon, NSW, in 1852) that it was only a question of a few months before I should be surrounded with diggers. At the end of September McGregor [sic] and party found gold in large quantities at the Arrow, just at the back of the present township. I know for a fact that McGregor got a hint about Maori Jack's find from a cadet I had

William G. Rees, c. 1860.

Courtesy Toitū Otago Settlers Museum, Dunedin

at the time. McGregor and party were getting at least 20 oz. a day with cradles alone. Fox and mate were next on that spot, and gradually some thirty men were at work there; but no 'rush' set in, as I managed quietly to supply all with tucker, even whilst my shearing was going on; and not one of my hands betrayed the fact to the shearers. I was most anxious to get my bit of wool off before the rush, which I knew must set in. Fox however, like a fool, must needs go to Dunstan; and the consequence was that he was watched and followed.[24]

Once word was out that gold had been found in the Wakatipu, miners poured in from neighbouring goldfields. By late November and on into December 1862, it was not unusual for 200 to 300 miners to be camped on the foreshore in front of Rees' home station waiting for the next shipment of flour, tea and 'baccy' to arrive in the *Undine*, Rees' whaleboat.[25] Starving miners relied on Rees bringing them their supplies from Saint John, later renamed Kingston. Rees' shepherd Alfred Duncan describes in *The Wakatipians* how he took 2/6d from each miner in acceptance of a pannikin of flour while Rees stood by with a pistol in his belt in order to maintain order. Rees never had to use the pistol, but one day he did have to deal with a stroppy Irishman who called him a liar. Rees dealt with the remark with a flurry of blows that left the Irishman spread-eagled on the ground, moving eyewitness Duncan to comment that Rees' name as an amateur pugilist rose above all others on the goldfields.[26]

Canvastown/Queenstown

Canvas and calico structures went up all around the Rees family's wattle and daub home. What was once called The Camp was now Canvastown, until on 1 January 1863 the settlement officially became Queenstown, with an estimated population of 500.[27] A year later, this number had risen to 1000.[28] Queenstown became a typical gold-mining town, noisy and bustling with activity. Along newly formed Camp Street as many as 100 to 200 horses could be seen tied to rail posts.[29]

As early as January 1863, Rees realised that the gold rush had ruined his prospects of continuing as a runholder on the flats between Arrowtown and Queenstown. However, there was one channel open to him whereby he hoped to salvage some of his run for himself, so on 11 February 1863 he attended a Waste Land Board meeting in Dunedin, where he requested pre-emptive right to retain blocks of land on his Queenstown Run, including 80 acres around his home station at Queenstown Bay. In attendance were Chief Commissioner William Cutten and board members James Howarth, Provincial Secretary Charles Logie, and Otago Provincial Government Superintendent Major John L.C. Richardson. When Howarth said, 'We have not allowed any one to exercise pre-emptive rights on a gold field,' Rees replied, 'True, but this is not declared a gold field.' Further discussion led Mr Cutten to opine: '… it is our intention Mr Rees to refuse to allow you any pre-emptive right, on the ground that the spots selected, if not now, will immediately be, within a gold field – that they are auriferous'. He concluded the hearing with the words: 'We refuse the application.'[30] On 17 February 1863 Otago's provincial government extended the Wakatipu goldfield to include the whole of the Wakatipu Basin.

Rees was now slaughtering his stock in order to supply the ever-hungry miners with fresh meat. Resentment and criticism of Rees' monopoly rights to the procurement of fresh meat brought forth many letters to the editor of the *Lake Wakatip Mail*. Charles Thatcher even wrote a song about it:

> *Now Rees has been playing a nice little game*
> *If in his position p'raps we'd do just the same.*
> *It's natural for him or for 'Any other Man'*
> *To get for his cattle as much as he can.*[31]

It's true that Rees was charging £3-12s-6d for a sheep, but in reply to condemnation of this sum and other stinging comments, he wrote to the *Wakatip Mail*:

> From the constant traffic through every part of my run, it is quite destroyed for all breeding purposes; indeed, owing to this, my lambing this summer has been a sad contrast to what I have heretofore experienced; for in place of three thousand I can only number as many hundred lambs. I have been obliged to remove all my breeding sheep, and make use of the country for the running of purchased fat stock to supply the butchers. The run is now carrying many hundred horses as well as many milch cows for the comfort of the diggers etc and I have never objected.[32]

In the same letter he went on to say that during his recent trip to Dunedin he'd informed the superintendent, Major Richardson, that whatever his legal rights to the title of the land around his home on which the township of Queenstown was now built, he would seek compensation rather than press his claim to the land. In the next edition of the paper, its editor informed the public that 'Mr Rees said that he

Queenstown Wharf, c. 1867.

Courtesy R.W. Murray collection, Cromwell Museum

intended to shift to Frankton, as the land about Queenstown was useless for pastoral purposes … He would not fight any more about the land and only expected fair compensation.'[33] Perhaps that is why Thatcher ended the last verse of his 'Golden Days at Lake Wakatipu' with

> *There's an old saying and it's true as it's quaint.*
> *The devil is not quite so black as folks paint.*
> *Thatcher rambles about and he frequently sees*
> *Lots of squatters that ain't half so decent as Rees.*[34]

Provincial government surveyors then set up offices on the banks of Horne Creek and surveyed the new towns of Queenstown, Frankton and Arrowtown.[35] In October, Rees applied to the Otago Provincial Executive for compensation for the Waste Land Board's decision to refuse him pre-emptive rights. The application prompted a proclamation, issued on November 6, cancelling the Grant/Gammie/Rees licence for Run 356 and stating that £10,000 compensation would be paid to the partnership for loss of the Queenstown Run.

On 19 January 1864 sale of the first sections in Queenstown took place, raising around £5000. But for the Rees family, any dream of remaining at Queenstown had been dashed: new plans were needed. The situation for the 25-year-old mother of two young children, Frances Rees, was very different from when she and William had first arrived at the lake. She no longer felt safe to wander down to the lakefront with her infants. Of greater worry, miners were in the habit of leaving their gold at Rees' house prior to the bullion being transported down to Kingston on the *Undine*. As much as 5000 ounces was sometimes left in Rees' charge. Reluctantly, in late spring 1863, the family moved to Kawarau Falls, where they built a permanent home of native beech from Rees' mill at the head of the lake.[36]

Rees was still managing the Bucklerburn, Peninsula and Staircase Runs at this time, although his life had become increasingly busy with his involvement in public affairs. He now had five boats operating on the lake, but they could barely keep up with the amount of cargo being shipped between Kingston and Queenstown.[37] He was also keeping up his community involvement: on 15 March 1863, Bishop Henry Harper had signed Rees' licence to be lay reader in the Church of England. When a church committee decided to build a church in Queenstown, Rees agreed to supply the timber at cost. On 8 August 1863 the *Wakatip Mail* reported: 'The Church of England at Queenstown is now opened, and divine service takes place every Sunday morning and evening, Mr. Rees officiating as lay reader on these occasions.'[38]

With the increasing number of buildings being established at Queenstown, the Otago Provincial Government decided that Frankton would not be the main town site,[39] even though Otago superintendent Sir John Richardson had originally favoured it.[40] In August 1863 Rees suggested that Frankton would be the ideal place for a hospital, and after a plea to the populace for funds, the community established a hospital there. It opened on 2 September 1863. The community also elected Rees chairman of the hospital committee, a role he remained in until he left the district.

That same month, Rees was elected chairman of the Queenstown Cricket Club, and in October chairman of the Wakatipu Jockey Club. He also became a foundation member of Ophir Masonic Lodge. By the end of 1863 he had interests in 14 different businesses,[41] and on 30 June 1865 Warden Richmond Beetham administered the oath to make William Rees a justice of the peace.[42]

If life was busy for William Rees, it was also for Frances. Three more daughters were born at Kawarau Falls: Ethel Grace, Mabel and Sarah Isabel. In 1865 the seven-year Grant/Gammie/Rees partnership contract came to an end. The partners did not apply for a renewal, and a notice advertising dissolution of the partnership appeared in the *Otago Provincial Gazette* in August 1865. A new opportunity then presented itself to Rees when Berkshire-born land baron Robert Campbell, owner of Otekaieke, Station Peak and Benmore stations[43] offered Rees a managerial position. Rees accepted.

At the end of 1866 Rees sold Kawarau Falls Station to the Boyes brothers,[44] and on 23 April 1867, William and Frances attended a farewell celebration, where they were presented with a purse of sovereigns and an illuminated address signed by 91 of Queenstown's male residents. Mr F. Hallenstein read out the document:

> It is with feelings of the deepest regret we learn you are so soon to leave the Wakatipu district. To you belongs the honour of having been its first Colonist and to your energy it is mainly due that a Country a few years ago alone in its native grandeur is now yielding its treasure of Wool and Corn and Gold. The interest you have at all times shown in the welfare of the District cannot be too highly estimated and the services rendered by your charity and kindness too warmly appreciated by us. Desirous that you should not depart from amongst us without bearing with you some token of the esteem and respect with which you are regarded by those amongst whom you have so long resided, we pray you to accept this purse of Sovereigns with which we hope you will purchase something that will remind you wherever you may be, you have with you the kindest wishes of many friends. Trusting that by the Blessing of God health happiness and prosperity may ever attend you, with our best wishes for Mrs Rees and your family,
>
> We are, Dear Sir, Your sincere Friends[45]

Mr Rees replied with a lengthy speech:

> It is now more than seven years since I was in a party of five formed for the purpose of exploring the unknown country west of the Upper Molyneux. After an unsuccessful attempt to push over the Crown Range, near the head of the Arrow, my companions gave up and returned; my friend Mr von Tunzelmann alone consenting to accommodate me in my further exploration. We were fully repaid for our trouble by the discovery of this beautiful district. Not being able to get horses farther than the present site of Queenstown, we built a raft of driftwood, and by means of it fully determined the shape of the Wakatip Lake, and the country in its immediate neighbourhood. You can form but little idea of the difficulties we experienced in getting into and through much of this district,

William Rees, c. 1870s.

Courtesy Rosemary Marryatt collection

now generally of easy access – constant firing having nearly destroyed the mass of speargrass and tumati-gora [sic[46]] which at that time nearly covered it ... In the course of the following spring I succeeded in getting a dray with supplies, and a whaleboat on a sledge up from Invercargill to the foot of the Lake; and the same summer stocked the run (the present Arrow flats) with sheep. Little did I think that within two years that same old whaleboat would take down to Kingston the first Wakatip escort of 25,000 ounces of gold ... The largest rush that Otago ever saw set in to this district, and my once solitary head station became the present Queenstown ...

During all this time my position amongst you has been a peculiar one. Rees was a member of that 'bloated squatocracy' and as such was, I fancy, at first looked by the diggers with no favourable eyes. But this day has shown me that, in my case at least, he has lived down all the antagonism of feeling. True, I have done no public good – if by that is meant – the good that I might have done by taking part in politics ... I fancy I am too outspoken to have made a politician. But I trust that my voice has never been unheard when the interest of the Wakatip district could be by any means advanced. No, I recognise in this, your kind testimonial, your estimation of me as a man; and I would humbly say that I trust I have striven 'to do unto others as I would have done them unto me' ... I shall always strive to spend on the lake any spare time that my duties may allow me; and God willing we shall all meet again. But if it be His good will

Statue by sculptor Minhal al Halabi of William Gilbert Rees at Queenstown Bay.

Photograph by Rosemary Marryatt

that we should never meet again on earth, I hope I shall be remembered by you – not as the public character – not as 'the jolly good fellow', but as a Christian gentleman.[47]

William and Frances purchased a silver tea and coffee set in remembrance of their Queenstown friends.[48] Rees used the £10,000 paid out by the Otago Provincial Government in compensation for the loss of Run 356 to reimburse his financial backers, Colonel W.L. Grant and George Gammie.[49]

After spending 16 years managing Campbell's Waitaki Valley sheep stations (where Frances gave birth to Mildred Gertrude and Charles Gilbert) and later Galloway Station in Alexandra, Rees was employed by the New Zealand Agricultural Department as a stock inspector. In this role he visited many high country sheep runs, such as South Canterbury's Mesopotamia Station and Tekapo's Lilybank. He painted scenes from both in 1886 and 1884 respectively. William died at the age of 71 in Wairau Hospital from complications following a gallstone operation and is buried alongside his wife, who died in March 1926, in the Owaka Cemetery, Blenheim.

William Gilbert Rees had a dream to be a runholder in the Wakatipu. His dream was short-lived, thanks to gold. However, his positive energy, his foresight, his integrity and courage left a mark on the developing town of Queenstown. Such human qualities will always outlive the value of gold.[50]

15.

The Merchants of the Rush:
The proto-bankers of the goldfields

Lloyd Carpenter

THE BELIEF THAT ONLY merchants benefited from the gold rush has a strong and persistent hold on popular imagination. Early legends of free-spending and lucky miners shouting for all occurred from San Francisco to Ballarat to Otago (hence 'Champagne Gully' in the Cromwell Gorge), and no goldfields' hotelier missed the opportunity to profit from such extravagance. But the behaviour of celebratory miners was neither coerced nor the product of trickery, nor did it persist as the authorities, presence of women and creation of permanent towns and villages civilised the new fields. The idea of poor-but-honest, free-spending-and-hearty miners exploited by a venal merchant class of traders makes for a good class struggle trope, but like most myths of the rush, the evidence refutes facile conclusions.

The relationship and the boundaries between miners and merchants were not as dichotomised as is widely believed. Miners became merchants; merchants became miners; miners and merchants developed mining claims together, and miners relied on merchants for finance, credit and their commercial networks and inter-business relationships. Merchants built their businesses and urban centres where the miners worked their claims.

In each of the new goldfields around the world, merchants built canvas premises, securing these against storms, dust and heat, and were the first to import glass, corrugated iron and pit-sawn timber with which to build permanent structures. They ran temporary gold-buying agencies for miners, even issuing temporary currency and cheques if the banks were tardy with building their establishments. Merchants sourced stock from London, Melbourne, New York, China and Dunedin, and organised carrier services to outlying areas. But they did much more than engage in commerce. Merchants worked with the miners to build schools, athenaeums and hospitals.[1] They were sworn in as justices of the peace, acted as temporary gold wardens and served as the mayors and counsellors for nascent rush towns.[2] It was merchants who advocated for

The newly built Cromwell School with pupils and members of the school committee, 1865. Miners on the committee included Thomas Logan, James Beare, James Corse (a doctor who was also working several claims as a miner) and Pat Kelly (who would later buy the Victoria Hotel). Merchants included butcher James Dawkins, hoteliers John Marsh and George Goodger, timber merchant Lewis Grant and bakers James Lawrence and James Scott.

Courtesy Lloyd Carpenter collection

land reform,[3] who spoke up when gold revenues were not spent on local infrastructure and who built the centres that allowed miners to settle down in their new country.

'The Oft-Quoted Shibboleth'

The imbalanced, dichotomised merchant/mining society idea is not new. In 1879 Californian historian Theodore Hittell said, 'the man who did not live [on the goldfields] by actual physical toil was regarded as a sort of social excrescence',[4] while Dunedin lawyer Alexander Bathgate, in an account of his goldfields experience as a bank clerk, called 'those who furnish the digger's requirements for his sustenance or amusement … [a] parasitic class'.[5] In his contribution to the 1933 *Cambridge History of the British Empire*, Australian historian Jerry Portus wrote that at Bathurst 'the diggers' precipitancy was the speculators' opportunity',[6] and in Victoria 'often the storekeepers, the smiths and the carriers made far more money than the miners'.[7] He also quoted Australian jurist Sir Roger Therry's observation that 'a penniless lollipop seller made £6000 a year by opening a public house on the road to Ballarat'.[8] Portus, possibly as a reflection of his earlier theological training,[9] wrote disapprovingly of diggings' townships, saying that there was no lack of 'the usual social parasites in these assemblages, where demand was all the more riotous because it was backed by unaccustomed purchasing power'.[10]

According to John Condliffe, writing in the New Zealand volume of the *Cambridge History of the British Empire*, 'the gold diggers as a body were not prosperous, but endured great hardships for little reward. As always, the chief gains were made by those who catered for their needs.'[11] Portus and Condliffe influenced Alexander McClintock, who in his 1949 centennial *History of Otago* quoted from both and concluded that 'there also congregated those who, in the legitimate pursuit of business, sought to fleece the reckless mining population whose undisciplined demand for the more doubtful commodities of commerce was sustained by an unrestricted purchasing power. Consequently in Otago, as in California and Australia, it was the merchant, the storekeeper, the carrier and the itinerant entertainer, who reaped the golden harvest.'[12]

Historian Matthew Wright calls the idea that constructs a goldfields society as one of merchants made wealthy at the expense of miners 'an oft-quoted shibboleth'.[13] It is a pervasive idea: Philip Ross May, in his *West Coast Gold Rushes*, commented that storekeepers tend to be 'regarded as a predatory class on the goldfields',[14] while the

Typical anti-trader rhetoric: 'His Silent Partners' by Louis Dalrymple shows a Klondike prospector working next to a stream surrounded by vultures labelled Gin Mill Keeper, Card Sharp, Dance House Keeper, Gambling Den, Dive Keeper and Opium Joint.

Source: *Puck*, vol. 42, no. 1069, September 1897, by Keppler & Schwarzmann

declaration that 'only the merchants profited at the goldfields' is repeated on websites and at goldfield heritage sites in New Zealand, California and across Australia, and is widely asserted in the historiography.

For Australian historian Robyn Annear, the idea 'that the storekeepers were the most successful gold-diggers is a truism',[15] while New Zealand's J.H.M. Salmond highlighted the case of Peter Jeffrey, who was 'typical of many intending miners who turned to the secondary occupation of storekeeping, and found greater wealth in this than in the wash pan and the cradle'.[16] In their 2008 'Migrating to riches?' study of the California rushes, Karen Clay and Randall Jones claim, in keeping with the frequently held conclusion of others,[17] that their results 'support the contention of miners and historians that merchants and other service providers reaped most of the profits from mining.'[18] These conclusions draw much of their evidence from observed phenomena in the earliest periods of each gold rush and cannot be taken as indicative of long-run profitability.

It is easy to understand the persistence of the myth: the idea is supported by the invocation of famous wealthy merchant names from the gold rushes such as Californian blue jeans inventor Levi Strauss, wagon manufacturer John Studebaker, bankers Henry Wells and William Fargo and general store owners Leland Stanford and Sam Brennan. Australians quote coaching magnate Freeman Cobb, retailer David Reid, storekeeper James Burns and shipping agent Robert Philp, while New Zealand celebrates retailer Bendix Hallenstein and brewers Speight and Kuhtze in Otago, and shoemaker Robert Hannah on the West Coast. All are discussed to prove the assertion that the merchants profited disproportionately to the miners they served.

Otago – 'Diggers in Town to Spend Their Gold on Having a Good Time'

Money flowed freely in new towns, creating the impression of rapidly acquired wealth.[19] When possible, storekeepers could – and did – make windfall profits in the early days of a rush. In September 1849 an Australian wrote from San Francisco to a relative in Melbourne. The letter was published in various Australasian newspapers, including the *Launceston Examiner* and, in abbreviated form, the *Otago News*: 'H-----, a cabin passenger, who never did a day's work in his life, a very gentlemanly fellow, worked as a day labourer on landing at 7 dollars per diem, and with the proceeds started a grocery store; he was only in business six weeks, and realised 800 dollars.'[20] This observation from California resonates with the observations of widely published letter-writer Amos Steck, who said: 'the men who are making the money in California, are the traders and rancheros on the lines of travel from the cities to the mines ... the keepers of hotels and eating-houses, are "coining money".'[21] Another American, General John C. Gilman, remarked in a letter to his hometown of Watertown, Wisconsin, that 'a man with some means can make a fortune here quicker than to dig for it; one or two thousand invested rightly in goods in N.Y. [to sell in California] ... is the chance to make fortunes.'[22]

Early merchants to Bathurst (NSW) were similarly opportunistic: 'Messrs Meyers and Twaddle have commenced a store in a bark building, with an excellent prospect of success … mobs are constantly arriving here, without food, money or implements.'[23] In his recollections of storekeeping at Bendigo in Victoria, Henry Brown admitted that in the early days 'business did not require any very nice calculations, the plan was usually to double and treble the Melbourne price',[24] while Gabriel's Gully storekeeper Alan Houston said 'the first few weeks of a "new rush" is the time for traders to make money. Many have done so.'[25] Rueben Waite found that when he set up the first store with 'provisions and every requisite for the diggings' at Mawhera Quay in Greymouth in 1864, 'the goods were going out as fast as I could possibly sell them, making handsome profits'.[26]

In late 1862 William Jackson Barry demonstrated the profits made early in a rush when he purchased two dray-loads of flour at Lawrence for £3.0 per 200-pound bag and resold them to the desperate miners at the Dunstan for £21-10s each. The arrival of 10 dray-loads of flour four days later ended his monopoly as quickly as it began.[27] Barry later broke the duopoly of Cromwell butchers by opening a butchery under the slogan 'The Right Man in the Right Place; No Monopoly' and using hot weather and arbitrage pricing to force competition.[28] His autobiography, *Past, Present and Men of the Times*, details the vicissitudes of running goldfields businesses from San Francisco to Ballarat and Central Otago, with occasional peaks of extraordinary profit inevitably followed by spectacular losses, extended troughs and skirmishes with creditors and bankruptcy.

The profit made by these first merchants to a new rush, where they could, however briefly, 'charge almost any price they choose',[29] has led the public and even historians such as James Belich[30] to infer a longer-term persistence in monopolistic pricing, profit levels and consequent merchant riches, and is the probable source of the persistent idea of merchant wealth. But this does not tell the full story. Alan Houston qualified his narrative of Gabriel's Gully storekeeping by admitting that the declaration of a new goldfield brought hard times, with the rush to the Dunstan nearly ruining him in 1865; an observer of the headlong migration of Kaniere miners to Okarito on the West Coast said 'storekeepers stand at the doorways with faces as long as their prices, and with tears in their eyes watched this end of the human tide … [as] the workings which but the other day was swarming with life and industry, now by comparison, appear almost deserted.'[31]

The Goldfields Urban Centres

Wherever gold was found, urban centres emerged; when the gold faded, the towns did too. As Bruce Rosenberg put it, 'the boom towns existed, to varying degrees, according to the momentary tides of anticipation, whim and rumour'.[32] Descriptions of ephemeral rush towns add to the idea of booming profits. Geoffrey Blainey described the gold town of Sofala in New South Wales as 'a camp of effervescent wealth'.[33] Charles Money's impressions on first viewing Gabriel's Gully township echo Blainey's words: 'here were canvas and galvanized iron stores, public-houses, restaurants, shanties of all descriptions and with every conceivable name, scattered around in all directions'.[34] Money's description of one store in the Tuapeka could have been located in any one of

The rapidly built goldfields 'boom' town of Clyde, Otago, February 1863 (six months after the discovery of gold).

Courtesy Clyde Historical Museum collection

500 rush towns around the world, and twins are found in Bayard Taylor's California[35] and in Clacy's[36] and Howitt's[37] Victoria. The image has become iconic in goldfields historiography:

> … a calico store, some 7 or 8 feet high, and about 10 by 12 feet in area; a few planks from old brandy and gin cases, nailed on saplings driven into the ground, formed the counter, on which were heaped the principal ingredients of a digger's domestic requirements – viz., sides of bacon, a tub or so of butter, one or two dry cheeses, sardines, lobsters, salmon, and other potted fishes and meats, bread, tobacco, clay pipes, and piled-up boxes of Letchford's vesta matches … the whole of this extensive warehouse was about as large as a reasonably-sized dog-kennel.[38]

Descriptions such as this have also been taken to infer profitability of the merchants at the expense of miners. However the assumption of long-term profiteering flies in the face of even the most basic of economics principles of long-run market behaviour and the unsustainability of monopolistic profits in a fully competitive market.[39]

Long-Run Patterns of Trader Profit

As rush towns matured, competition ensured non-sustainability of monopolist profiteering. Florence McKenzie said of the nine hotels in Queenstown: 'All did very well, but there was considerable competition among them.'[40] General Gilman, whose first letter had emphasised trader profitability on the Californian goldfields, wrote a few months later: 'A great change in prices of almost every thing has already taken place. All necessaries are much cheaper than heretofore, and the tendency of prices is still downwards.'[41] In 1860 a miner working at the Kiandra diggings on the Snowy River in New South Wales wrote to his storekeeper friend in Ballarat: 'There is a great many stores going up, and a great many on the road coming up to put up stores. I believe they will be selling things at first cost if something good does not come.'[42]

The crucible of sharp competition drove some merchants out of business. John MacGregor and Thomas Low, two prospectors sometimes credited as discoverers of the Arrow goldfield, took their pound's weight of gold hauled from Brackens Gully and ploughed it into a store in Queenstown in 1863, only to abandon the store a month later 'to return to the more profitable pursuit of mining'.[43] In September 1862 John Launder opened one of the first stores on the Maniototo Plains (New Zealand) at Alexander MacPherson's station, a transit point for miners heading to the Lake District.[44] At first, he reportedly earned £40 or £50 a day, but by mid-1864 his income had fallen to £2.0 a day and his credit was stretched. Competition and the building of roads changed a very profitable concern into one that was marginal at best.[45]

Nevertheless, gold brought wealth. Jim McAloon identifies Dunedin businesspeople who 'prospered considerably out of the gold-rushes',[46] and Erik Olssen describes a 'staggering prosperity'[47] for 'the merchants and professional men [of Otago]'. Dunedin's success followed the pattern in San Francisco and in Melbourne (which Blainey calls 'a second San Francisco'[48]), where the location of each as the main port of entry saw a rapid population increase, government spending on infrastructure[49] and a strong demand for foodstuffs and manufactured goods in the train of miners flooding into the hinterland seeking gold.

Philip May found that this pattern was not always true on New Zealand's West Coast, noting that even 'the big merchant importers in the three river ports were no less liable to sudden changes of fortune … [and] business failures were common'.[50] However, notwithstanding the potential for loss, the right mix of opportunity and good fortune could coalesce into business success, as Lyndon Fraser identifies in his *Castles of Gold*. Fraser found several West Coast Irish miners who invested gold earnings to become traders and who parlayed funds initially gained on the goldfields into fortunes in farming, coal-mining and transport in other centres such as Wellington.[51]

Dunedin businessmen even influenced the ethnic mix on the goldfields, since, as James Ng and Paul MacGregor's research has revealed, it was the invitation from Dunedin business leaders worried by losses of population and trade to the West Coast fields[52] that induced Lowe Kong Meng to recruit Chinese miners to Otago in 1865.[53] This was not the first time merchants influenced ethnicity on a goldfield: when the Foreign Miners' Tax of 1850 was enacted in California and led to armed bands driving off Hispanic and French miners, the resultant plunge in the price of supplies and land values saw merchants engage in a campaign to secure a policy of 'fair play' for foreigners and eventually a diminution in the tax levies, as well as acceptance of most ethnicities, even – in the early days – the Chinese.[54]

The idea that the gold-rush merchants made considerable profits is understandable, especially when the built environment provides such a strong visual reminder. The existence of magnificent gold-bought architecture in California's San Francisco and

Sacramento, Ballarat and Bendigo in Victoria, and Dunedin and Hokitika in New Zealand's South Island all testify to the wealth won in these regions. Yet each impressively built edifice hides stories of luck and loss in equal measure.

In Bendigo, Victoria, for example, the Shamrock Hotel has achieved iconic status in the local gold story, and the fact that it's still possible to have a drink at a bar once built and tended by the famous William Heffernan cements ideas of merchant wealth. What is not so obvious is that the Tipperary-born Heffernan, celebrated as the first white man to walk across the isthmus of Panama on his trip from New York to California (where he struck riches, depositing $20,000 worth of gold in the Philadelphia mint), died in Dunedin as the licensee of the Pier Hotel. He had suffered a severe reversal in fortune that saw large property holdings, the Shamrock and his remaining shares in mining companies all sold, leaving him 'in comparatively reduced circumstances'[55] with an estate worth a mere £374.[56]

Banker Merchants

Goldfields businessmen were more than retailers; they became the merchant bankers of the nineteenth-century mining economy. The legal environment of each country forced this outcome. In 1848/49 California was not yet part of America. In 1850s Australia and 1860s New Zealand, land tenure was insecure; town sections and farms – even when surveyed – were leasehold, and the property rights of mining claims were tenuous, so security for loans was problematic.[57] Additionally, the tools of modern financing in the form of useable credit did not exist, with banks existing to purchase gold, cash cheques, facilitate monetary transfers, and offer safe depository and savings services for business owners, investors and miners.[58] As each goldfield matured, some lawyers and accountants provided mortgage finance, but required legal instruments to do so.

The merchants had little choice but to become lenders: without available credit, the development of large-scale claims, expansion of commercial ventures and growth in their local economy would be limited, and the notoriously mobile mining population would move away to where new opportunities beckoned.[59]

Many 'new chum' miners arrived indigent or ill-equipped for the work they intended doing and needed finance to commence work. As each goldfield matured, the process of mining transitioned from individuals working their claim with pan or rocker, to collectivised, amalgamated claims that utilised Californian pumps, water races and sluice hoses, the 'paddocking' of alluvial claims, and quartz mines. For miners seeking financial support while spending a year digging water races in order to begin sluicing work, for syndicates constructing dams to lay the riverbed dry, or for companies developing promising auriferous quartz, this situation immediately established goldfields storekeepers and hoteliers as their only hope. By becoming investors, the merchants of the goldfields became venture capitalists of the gold rush, bankrolling many significant mining projects and commercial enterprises across each province. Sometimes they profited, mostly they covered costs, and on occasion they and all associated with a project paid a ruinous price for their gamble on miners' dreams.

Far from being a homogenous group, goldfield capitalists comprised distinct types.

Each reacted to a specific need and demand or identified opportunities and set these in motion. They included 'the grubstake merchants', 'the sleeper-shareholders' and 'the quartz merchants'.

The Grubstake Merchants

Miners gambled on finding riches in each new field; merchants gambled on miners finding gold and staying put once they found it. These were not passive profit-takers: they were active participants in each rush, and while they stood to profit from early opportunities, success was not guaranteed. At Nelson's Aorere field, William Lightband, reputed to have been the first man to find gold there,[60] commented that 'parties are weekly arriving from all quarters – some in destitute circumstances; these, through the kindness of the storekeepers, are enabled to get a few things on credit; and with this assistance numbers have made a good start, and in about a week have recovered themselves.'[61]

In every extant goldfields merchant journal, it is clear that the merchants' main role, apart from providing goods for sale, was extending credit to miners developing claims. Alan Houston did most of his business in his Gabriel's Gully store 'on account', to keep miners in supplies. Rarely knowing the actual names of his customers, he headed up his tabs with '"Little Bill", "Big Bill", "Black Bill" and "Sailor Jack"'.[62] According to James Ng, Chinese merchants performed a similar money-lending service to their community, and also employed their skills as bilingual traders to negotiate mining transactions.[63]

Even in the 1870s and 1880s most miners lived on provisions obtained by credit, regularly making payments from monthly wages to cover – or partly clear – the accumulated debt.[64] A law suit between a miner called Gibbs and two local storekeeping firms in Bendigo Gully showed a near-cashless society emerging in Otago, where store debt was covered by promissory notes issued against wages and cashed by mine employers, and where miners traded off part of their accumulated balance as payment in kind and worked for the businessmen for wages in their spare time.[65] A steady stream of Bendigo retailers suing mining company employees to have accounts paid[66] indicates that these outstanding debts were not the guaranteed source of profit that legend suggests.

Philip May was unequivocal about the potential for loss, stating that on the West Coast, storekeepers 'lost everything by extending credit to men they never saw again'.[67] Miles Fairburn concludes that 'to judge from the amount of litigation by storekeepers against miners who ordered goods on credit then decamped, credit must have been readily extended to almost every stranger who entered a goldfield'.[68] The storekeepers' lament can be heard in the recollections of Leonardo Pozzi, a Swiss-born gunsmith who opened a store at Yandoit, near Daylesford in Victoria: 'We carried on a large brisk business, and given plenty of credit to gold miners … you could not do any business without giving credit and nothing but tick business, and at the end found myself in queer street and rouined [sic] for bad business.'[69] The long-serving MP for Tuapeka, James Clark Brown, suffered a severe setback before he entered politics, losing his large store on Ross Street, Lawrence, and suffering near-bankruptcy, due to 'losses sustained through a too liberal credit system, which was, perhaps, in some degree a necessity of business in those ever changing and unsettled days'.[70]

The small-town storekeeper proto-banker was not just a goldfields phenomenon: David Hamer describes the provision of loans and credit for the supply of goods to local settlers[71] as not only a typical function of nineteenth-century New Zealand rural stores but also 'an essential source of short-term but very expensive credit for the struggling settlers who often needed loans to tide them over difficult times'.[72] In her study into Chinese in Australia after the gold had gone, Cora Trevarthen found an elaborate and highly structured system of credit existing among Chinese labourers that went 'far beyond simple bartering or exchange'.[73] Trevarthen's work reveals that this proto-banking sat alongside standard banking systems for even longer than is widely appreciated. Additionally, Allen Francis, the American consul in Victoria (British Columbia), observed the effects of the gold rush to Cariboo and other areas during the period 1862–70 and concluded that the system of credit jeopardised the entire economy: '… the miners lived on credit; when the gold did not "pan out" they could not pay their bills and thus ruined the creditors as well as themselves'.[74] He consequently advocated for tighter rules governing the giving of credit.

For merchants, grubstaking local miners was one means by which they could attract and keep trade. However, the process relied on the miners staying and earning, and it assumed that the merchants' own lines of credit were sufficiently robust to enable these men to pay their suppliers. The regularity with which storekeepers were bankrupted throughout the decades of the gold rush suggests that many could not pay their way, especially if the grubstaking extended to other merchants. As credit was stretched or as business decreased, retailers relied on one another for supplies or for bridging finance, all the while remaining hopeful that a mining, and therefore business, resurgence would occur. The files of most bankrupt Otago merchants[75] reveal high levels of inter-trader debt; in each of these cases, it was their fellow merchants who pursued them into bankruptcy.

This proto-banking could generate success though. Californian historians Larry Schweikart and Lynne Pierson Doti locate the genesis of the Bank of California in the grubstake lending that retailer Darius Ogden Mills offered miners.[76] In 1866, during the rush to Cerro Gordo high in California's Sierra Mountains, merchant Victor Beaudry built a blast furnace to process silver ore and extended credit to his miner customers, obtaining a significant portfolio of valuable mining claims when these men were unable to meet their payment obligations.[77] I have not found any equivalent to this predatory behaviour in Australian or New Zealand mining claims ownership, but I have found that some goldfields financiers, most notably Cromwell's Borthwick Baird, used foreclosure on mortgages to build an extensive farming, urban and business property portfolio.

The Sleeper-shareholder Merchants

Sleeper-shareholder merchants in Otago were exemplified by members of the Nil Desperandum Syndicate dam project at Quartz Reef Point in 1864,[78] Bendigo's Aurora Sluicing Syndicate of 1866, and many similar ventures across the goldfields of Australasia. These ventures reflect a system developed on the Victorian goldfields that delineated miners and merchants into 'sleeping' and 'active' shareholders.[79] It had the advantage of not necessarily requiring large amounts of 'up-front' capital. It also allowed miners who'd secured rights to mine promising claim ground – but who lacked the financial resources to adequately develop it – to build value in a large-scale enterprise through their own 'sweat equity'. These men brought to the concern their mining expertise, ownership of a potentially rich claim and a willingness to endure

Sluicing at the Blue Spur, Tuapeka, c. 1873. Every part of this operation required sophisticated financial structures to support it.

Courtesy R.W. Murray collection, Cromwell Museum

the harsh work of mining. The financiers brought their money but avoided the need to wield picks and shovels in dangerous or dusty claims, or to stand in the frigid waters of a gold-rich river to mine the alluvium. The model was elegantly simple: each shareholder held an equal-part ownership; the 'financial' shareholders worked at their businesses or trade and contributed the equivalent of a workman's wages to the company each week, while the 'working' (sometimes called 'active') shareholders drew a weekly wage from the company and did the physical work of mining or building.[80]

The Aurora Sluicing Syndicate was one such enterprise. In August 1865 Dunstan surveyor Julian Coates identified gold reserves in Bendigo's river terraces.[81] Henry Summers, Oswald Walker, brothers Arthur, William and George Barclay from Quartz Reef Point and Edward Barnes and William Gerrard from Amisfield Burn[82] pooled their resources to exploit the reserves through sluicing.[83] To obtain the capital they needed in order to build a water race to get sufficient water from a reliable source to where they required it on their claim, they approached businessmen and asked them to form a syndicate with them. The men who did so included Clyde-based butchers Thomas McMorran and William Grindley, storekeeper Thomas Hazlett, 'Old Bendigo Hotel' owner Edward Ryan, and John Perriam, storekeeper from Lowburn and Kawarau Gorge. With the requisite mix of financiers and miners, the group registered their claim and obtained the rights to the headwaters of Devil Creek.[84]

On completing the race, a 10-mile-long 'tremendous undertaking',[85] 13 months later (in April 1867) the miners of the syndicate immediately began sluicing,[86] yielding a weekly income of over £8.0 per shareholder. After four months the syndicate had fully repaid the cost of the race, and six months later the miners bought out the businessmen.[87] The investing merchants endured a year of strain on their cash flow and then enjoyed a year of returns that repaid their investment, made them additional money and created an asset that they eventually sold to their mining shareholders for a profit. The miners had their wages guaranteed as they worked, and so were able to build value in the company asset through their labour. The merchants could engage in gold mining without breaking a sweat, pursue their mercantile endeavours and share in the eventual riches of the project. Nevertheless, if such a project failed, as did Otago's Nil Desperandum project (during 1864 to 1866) to dam the Clutha River, the investing merchants could be left in a state of near bankruptcy.[88]

The businessmen of the syndicate did not blindly act as venture capitalists; like any modern equivalent, the financiers appraised the proposals from the miners, recognised their knowledge, competence and experience, and had the benefit of the corroborative report from Surveyor Coates. Each made an informed decision to invest and made a profit or a loss on the deal. The Aurora men profited; the Nil Desperandum's business shareholders collectively lost around £4000[89] and nearly bankrupted Cromwell's merchants in 1865.

The Quartz Merchants

The first quartz mine at Bendigo (NZ) was the Cromwell Quartz Mining Company, which began in 1866 when miners Jack Garrett and Thomas Logan found and secured

George Wellington Goodger, c. 1870.

Courtesy Hocken collections, Uare Taoka o Hakena,
University of Otago, Dunedin, File S04-007c

Swan Brewery, Cromwell, c. 1883.

Courtesy Lloyd Carpenter collection

a claim there. They developed it over 18 months with the support of Brian Hebden, who mined at Quartz Reef Point.[90] On finding payable stone, the men brought in Cromwell hotelier George Goodger as financier. By 1869 the newly formed company had purchased, shifted and erected a quartz-crushing plant, built a road and raised several hundred tons of stone from their mine for processing.[91]

Swan Brewery advertisement, c. 1878.

Courtesy Cromwell Museum collection

George Wellington Goodger makes an exemplary case study of the goldfields merchant. The Canadian-born Goodger mined in California and Victoria and began mining at Hartley's Beach and Duffer's Point near Cromwell after arriving in Otago in 1862.[92] He also mined at Quartz Reef Point in 1864, where he was briefly involved with the Nil Desperandum project.[93] In 1863 he built the Cromwell water supply race, erected yards and stables for storing and trading in livestock, and leased 30 acres on the Cromwell flats, where he ran the region's first dairy herd.[94] He co-owned a butchery and timber business and worked as a builder.[95] In 1864 he had accumulated sufficient capital to set up his Junction Commercial Hotel.[96]

Goodger was the first of several goldfields merchant boosters of Central Otago: in 1866 he was appointed to Cromwell School's first committee, he found and developed the Cromwell lignite pit, harvested the region's first crop of hay,[97] and in 1867 even became Cromwell's mayor after William Jackson Barry forgot to sign official papers confirming his re-election.[98] In the 1870s Goodger bought and developed the Swan Brewery[99] on the outskirts of town, erected commercial rooms opposite his hotel[100] and, with Thomas Logan and John Perriam, was one of the driving forces behind the funding and building of Cromwell's hospital.[101]

Throughout the 1870s, as the first person to turn to for investment capital, Goodger backed various ventures in the region, ranging from coaching services[102] and new mining ventures to large-scale water-race developments at Bannockburn.[103] The last of these led to Goodger's ruin, when the project failed.[104] At the time of his death in 1883, his assets were close to zero and others were running the businesses he'd started. Goodger was typical of many goldfields merchants: he was an experienced miner who worked claims, invested earnings and diversified to accumulate sufficient capital to open his own establishments.

At Bendigo (NZ), the local storekeepers and hoteliers were involved as quartz company investors. Examination of bankruptcy and newspaper records reveals why so many merchants and companies failed. Josiah Mitchinson was the financier of the Morning Star Claim.[105] When it became the Reliance Quartz Mining Company Limited, Mitchinson was its largest shareholder,[106] until it failed in 1877.[107] The miners who worked the claim, which offered hints of auriferous stone without ever yielding payable ore,[108] were effectively on his payroll for all those years, a financial strain that contributed to his bankruptcy in 1876.[109] Charles O'Donnell, Bendigo's longest-serving businessman (1864–1906), invested in several ventures, but avoided being the cornerstone financier for any of them. That said, he was involved in several claims, some simultaneously, for most of the 42 years he was resident at Bendigo. In 1869 he was prominent as 'O'Donnell & Company',[110] and as late as 1888 bought into the Jubilee Syndicate mine in the Rise and Shine Valley.[111] After 1878 he was Bendigo's only remaining retailer, whose home, hotel, bakery (which he added in 1876),[112] butchery and general store[113] operated from stone premises until 1906.[114]

Other Bendigo merchants included the proprietors of the Provincial Hotel, William Kelsall and John Wilson, who in 1870 developed an aerial ropeway to get ore from their claim across the gully to the Aurora Battery,[115] and William Smith, proprietor of the Solway Hotel who, with his partner Mrs Elizabeth Reid, financed the Try Again Syndicate for three years in the mid-1870s. James Patterson, hotelier of the Old Bendigo Family Hotel at Logantown, who originally backed the Aurora men in 1866, supported three different claims through 1870/71. None made any money, an outcome that for Smith, Kelsall, Wilson and Mrs Reid contributed to their bankruptcy.

A different pattern emerged as each goldfield matured. A prospector would find auriferous quartz, test it and secure it by registered claim before selling out to moneyed investors. The 'windfall' development of a quartz claim and its sale to capitalists was the ultimate reward for the quartz prospectors: the lonely days they spent picking their way over vast hillsides were rewarded with finding a reef, proving it, becoming small-scale 'boosters' of the claim's prospects and finally selling to investors and pocketing the proceeds. The later investors tended to be lawyers, accountants, merchants and industrialists from larger urban centres and eventually the United Kingdom, and were therefore similar to professional investors of today.[116] This type of investor was especially true of the dredging companies in the last decades of the nineteenth century,[117] but for the earliest days of quartz-mine development on Australasian fields, it was the local merchants who provided the working capital as the mines got underway.

The Wealthy of the Goldfields

Some retailers made a comfortable living on the goldfields, but many lived a hand-to-mouth, hardscrabble existence. In her survey of women on the Central Otago goldfields, Jennifer Dickenson notes that many of the sly grog shanty operators and boarding-house owners were women who were also forced into prostitution 'to supplement their meagre income',[118] suggesting that these businesses were no goldmine for their owners. Dickenson also lists several women business owners who ran stores or hotels in order to add to their husbands' mining income.[119] The retailers, hoteliers and merchants who made a comfortable – even good – living at the goldfields did not do so through opportunistic pricing to their miner customers. While Bendix Hallenstein did reasonably well as a multi-outlet retailer in Queenstown, Wanaka, Cromwell and Alexandra, it was his foray into clothes manufacturing in Dunedin that secured the family fortune and saw the name endure down to today.[120]

One of the most successful of the Central Otago merchants was storeowner and Clyde mayor[121] Benjamin Naylor,[122] but his fortune was not just a mercantile one; he accumulated his wealth by developing an extensive mixed farm[123] and then achieving vertical integration by selling his own dairy products, bread (made from his own wheat), meat and smallgoods through his store.[124]

It's easy to forget amidst all the stories of hardship and misfortune just how profitable mining could be for some miners. Stories of wealth found at Bendigo, Australia, abound, with miner E. Bright remembering:

> I got the first alluvial gold at Sandy Creek, and my brother the first surface gold in January, 1853 … The dirt gave about 2 dwt to the dish. I also picked up a piece of surface gold on the hill nearly 3 lb weight. We joined two mates and worked at Peg-leg Gully, where we got from 8 to 12 oz of gold per day. We used to just break the dirt and every second blow of the pick used to reveal gold.[125]

Early reports of the New South Wales Turon field laconically mentioned '71 ozs in the hands of one group, another 40 and several 10, 12, and 20 ozs … [and] considerable quantities of gold were taken out of Sofala Reach last week' as the result of just a few day's work.[126] G. Butler Earp's breathless travelogue of 1853 listed examples of miners' wealth in late 1851, such as that obtained at the Victorian fields:

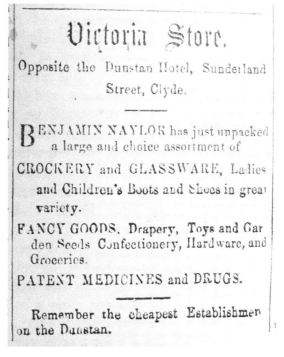

Benjamin Naylor's Victoria Store advertisement, in *Cromwell Argus*, February 1880.

Lakes District Museum, Arrowtown

Seven men obtained nine pounds of gold in one day; four got four pounds; another party of four, three and three-quarter pounds, &c.; every stream turning out a Pactolus … The whole dividing range between New South Wales and Victoria, known as the Snowy Mountains, was one vast gold field … a *ton and a half of gold* was waiting in Commissioner Powlett's tent for the escort. At Mount Alexander, a man obtained eighty pounds weight of gold in a single hour! and on the 20th of December, there had been collected, in Victoria alone, *ten tons, two hundred weights, eighty-two pounds, ten ounces of gold!*[127]

The haul that started the Otago rush was Hartley and Reilly's 87-pound find in August 1862, but subsequent reports show that theirs was not the only success, nor was it the biggest, given comments in newspapers such as 'miners are earning in a few days amounts as large as Hartley and Reilly did in months'[128] and 'your genuine Dunstan miner won't listen to [reports of fresh discoveries] unless they rise to pounds weight'.[129] Other comments reveal the richness of the Dunstan: 'The finds obtained by many of the miners would even astonish those who have seen the "jewellers shops" of Ballaarat [sic], or the results of a day's washing from claims in the far-famed Eaglehawk, Bendigo.'[130]

Comparisons are problematic, however. As a writer at a New South Wales rush commented, 'None of the miners like to make known the proceeds of the labours – the

Benjamin Naylor's Victoria Store, Clyde, 2013.

Photograph by Lloyd Carpenter

most communicative are the very fortunate and the unfortunate, the latter because they have nothing to be robbed of, and the former because they take great pleasure in talking of their luck.'[131] Many miners quietly extracted immense golden wealth from their claims across Australasia, taking their fortunes 'home' to Britain, Australian cities, America or onto farmland in New Zealand.[132] William Jackson Barry observed at the Arrow field that 'gold was being obtained in immense quantities, and many miners went home with their piles from the Arrow', while the journals of Watmuff,[133] Houston, Money and other writers were unequivocal when stating that many of their contemporaries were striking gold in incredible quantities.

Miners who were successful often secretly sold their claim while it was still pro-ducing good gold returns and then left, sometimes returning to where they had come from in Europe or Britain. The presence of settlements called 'Bendigo' in South Africa, Orkney and Pennsylvania, and estates called 'Clutha' in Yorkshire, 'Ballarat' in California and 'Tuapeka' near Edinburgh all testify to the migration of successful miners who invested their gold winnings in property, farmland and businesses.

A facile conclusion, too often drawn, is that the miners who worked claims in California for small success, shifted to New South Wales and Victoria for equally mixed results and then pursued their dreams of striking it rich in Tuapeka, Dunstan, the West Coast and Thames were the majority. Equally facile is the notion that lack of persistence, perpetual migration and eventual death with a small accumulation to their name was the experience of these miners. Most miners regarded mining as the means to an end – an end that would enable them to invest the wealth accumulated in agriculture or business, rather than engage in a preferred lifestyle per se. When Charles O'Donnell of Bendigo Gully died, leaving an estate worth £1111, his occupation was listed as 'farmer', reflecting where he had invested his gold and business earnings. In the late nineteenth century, many farmers, small business owners and merchants of various kinds who led a life of successful enterprise, and who died leaving significant sums from their life's work, did not necessarily show that they got their start mining gold from the freezing waters of an Australasian goldfield. This hidden facet of goldfields' wealth makes it highly unlikely that we will ever discover the truly wealthy of the goldfields.

Conclusion

Although a divide existed between miners and merchants on the goldfields, the divide was not one of wealth or even of the degree to which earnings were hard-won. The divide was simply along the nature of urban resident and mining-cottage dweller, of business-owner and miner. The nature of their respective operations produced a naturally dichotomised society, but the relationship between each was more symbiotic than adversarial. Through investments and shareholdings, the goldfields merchants shared in the work and rewards of the miners, in addition to making some retail profit off their spending, but the simple economic law of arbitrage attenuated any attempts at excessive profitability in pricing. Like most generalisations, the myth that only the merchants made money on the goldfields can be proven in the exception but disproved in general.

16.

The Early Central Otago Goldfield Lawyers

Jeremy Finn

IN THIS CHAPTER I consider 15 identifiable lawyers who practised in the Otago goldfields from 1862 to 1877. The group includes four lawyers who practised in Lawrence, two of whom definitely extended their practice to the Central Otago area. It is probable the other two did as well. However, I have excluded those lawyers based in Dunedin who came to Central Otago only rarely, or who were involved in goldfields-related litigation in the courts in Dunedin itself and did not appear in the regional courts.

The literature on the Central Otago gold rushes – indeed, on Central Otago history generally – rarely says much about the legal profession. I therefore drew heavily on the listings of lawyers in surviving editions of *Mackay's Almanac*,[1] newspaper reports of cases in the lower courts (Warden's Court, District Courts and Resident Magistrate's Courts) in various towns in the region, various official records, and some Otago District Law Society records. The limitations of these sources must be acknowledged. Some lawyers may simply not have appeared in the cases that made the newspapers (although the detail in the reporting of cases is generally high), and certainly much legal work would not have involved litigation. It is also clear that in these lower courts, the majority of cases did not involve lawyers. Whether this absence reflected a lack of access to legal services or a general reluctance to bear the expense of engaging a lawyer is unknown.

Reliance on the *Almanac* is also problematic, as some entries are demonstrably incorrect in detail as to names, and on some occasions lawyers may have practised so briefly as not to be listed at all, or for their location data to be incorrect. For example, *Mackay's Almanac* for 1875 lists three solicitors in Queenstown: G.B. Barton, W. Turton and G.F. Fynn.[2] The first two, George Burnett Barton and Wesley Turton, are familiar names, and I discuss their careers later in this chapter. Identifying the third listed person, G.F. Fynn, is more difficult. A lawyer with that surname appears not to have been admitted to practice at any time in New Zealand. Three possibilities exist, however. First, 'Fynn' was not a lawyer, but perhaps a mining agent. Second, if he was a lawyer, he may have registered in the *Almanac* in the expectation of joining the profession but for some reason was unable to do so. Third, and by far the most likely reason, is that the almanac is in error. The *Almanac* entry is probably best read as an inaccurate reference to Hugh Joseph Finn, who is known to have been in practice in Queenstown in the mid-1870s.

Some archival records are also problematic, as with the records of Henry Wirgman Robinson. Robinson was warden of the Mount Ida/Naseby/St Bathans area in the late 1860s and early 1870s and a resident magistrate sitting there and at Hyde. In the documents preserved, Robinson set out the details of cases heard, but very few of them had any reference to lawyers appearing. Robinson's records for 1869 indicate only one instance where a lawyer was involved, namely when 'Mr Stewart barrister of Dunedin' appeared in one case.[3] During the following year, at most three cases recorded the presence of counsel. One was in the Resident Magistrate's Court at Hyde, where 'Mr Main' appeared in what seems to have been a mining-related action. The others were both in the Warden's Court: one at Naseby, where 'Mr Bathgate' appeared, and the other at St Bathans, where Robinson recorded that 'W L Bailey' appeared for a plaintiff called McConnochie.[4]

Mr Stewart is easily identified as William Downie Stewart, a leading Dunedin lawyer. Mr Main is almost certainly David Forsyth Main of Dunedin, and Mr Bathgate must be Alexander Bathgate of the same city. However, W.L. Bailey cannot be identified. No other record of any such practitioner could be found. It is possible that Bailey was not a lawyer but was nevertheless permitted audience in the case, as a mining agent would perhaps have been. It is less likely that he was a lawyer practising without having been

Mr Hugh Joseph Finn.

Source: *The Cyclopedia of New Zealand*, vol. 2, Auckland District, 1902 (Christchurch, The Cyclopedia Company), p. 980

formally admitted to the profession. That did happen on occasion, though. When Walter Taylor applied for admission in 1870, his admission was opposed, unsuccessfully, on the basis he had been practising law without being admitted.[5] Taylor practised in South Otago until 1880, but moved to Gore in Southland early in 1881 for health reasons. He died there in October 1881, aged 39.[6] As we will see, similar issues about practice before admission may be evident for two of our Central Otago cohort.

The Early Years

One of the earliest lawyers – possibly the first – resident and practising in Central Otago was John Patten. Patten was admitted to the New Zealand profession as a solicitor in 1860 and as a barrister the following year. His admission was on the basis of having served articles in Victoria. Patten had first been articled to his father in Melbourne, but when his father died just short of the required five years of articles, Patten moved to Geelong to complete his time there. No record can be found of Patten actually being admitted in Australia, and when he first came to New Zealand in 1860 he worked as a clerk for John Dean Bamford in Lyttelton and went into partnership with him as a solicitor after admission. However, Bamford dissolved the partnership in March 1861 'for breach and non-observance of the covenants in their articles of partnership' and, perhaps pointedly, requested debtors of the firm to make payments to Bamford and not to Patten.

Patten must have moved to Dunedin shortly after that and very quickly got into difficulties. He was suspended from practice in January 1862 after he was intercepted while in a rowing boat heading to an Australia-bound steamer in Port Chalmers. He had in his possession £13 that he had obtained from a client on the basis he (Patten) would pay the money to the client's creditor and so get the bailiffs out of the client's premises. Patten was charged with fraudulent appropriation of the money but was acquitted. However, because he had admitted the wrongful application of the money, the Supreme Court judge suspended him from practice and ordered him to show cause as to why he should not be struck off.[7] Despite this outcome and according to a letter published in the *Otago Daily Times* in 1865,[8] Patten, then resident in or near Dunstan/Clyde, had acted as solicitor to John McCormack, charged with attempted arson, at a bail hearing on or just after 28 February 1863. This representation would clearly have been in breach of his suspension from practice. And it would have come after the Court of Appeal had struck him off the rolls of barristers and solicitors on 26 February 1863, although Patten probably did not receive the result of that hearing.[9]

The next evidence of other lawyers practising in the central Otago area is a report that a 'Mr Campbell, the barrister' spoke at a public meeting in Queenstown in 1863.[10] There is also a record of him appearing as counsel in the Resident Magistrate's Court in Arrowtown in September 1864.[11] Campbell can be identified with confidence as Henry Elmes Campbell, who had been admitted as a solicitor and attorney in England in 1843 after serving articles in Nottingham and passing the examination required for admission as an attorney.[12] He later cited his address at the time of his admission as '10 New Millman St in Middlesex and Maidstone in Kent'.[13]

Campbell moved to Australia in 1853 and sought admission first in Victoria and then in New South Wales, apparently settling at Albury on the New South Wales/Victoria border. His practice there did not thrive, and Campbell became insolvent, owing over £3300 as against assets of under £2400.[14] He must have come to New Zealand quite soon after that, as he was admitted as a barrister and solicitor in Dunedin on 18 July 1862.[15] Campbell is listed as 'M H E' Campbell in *Mackay's Almanac* for 1865,[16] as both a solicitor and conveyancer in the Tokomairiro area, and as being in practice in Queenstown. However, the reference to Tokomairiro suggests that the reference may have been to a branch office managed by a clerk because it refers to 'R Jones Manager'. Jones was to appear in later years as the manager for 'J W Macgregor' [sic]' practice in the same area. Campbell was not a long-term settler, though, as he clearly followed the path taken by many miners (and a few lawyers) from Central Otago to the West Coast. In 1866/67 he was practising as a barrister and solicitor in Hokitika.[17]

Campbell is one of only two lawyers listed for the Central Otago area in *Mackay's Almanac* for 1865; the other was 'W W Wilson' in Queenstown. William Wilfrid Wilson also had a chequered career, which started in England, where he was articled to a solicitor in Warrington.[18] He appears to have been admitted as a solicitor in 1846 and an attorney in 1847 and then to have practised for some years in London, given that he is listed in 1848 as the junior partner in a London firm. In 1850 he ceased practice in England and went to Australia, arriving in Victoria in December 1850, but then going on to South Australia for about 21 months where he was admitted to the profession and practised as a solicitor. He then returned to Melbourne and was employed as the secretary to the Chamber of Commerce in Melbourne and as a clerk in a Melbourne law firm. He was admitted to the legal profession in Victoria in April 1855.

At some point, Wilson was the solicitor for the Trades Protection Society, which probably required him to act for various small traders seeking to recover money owed to them. However, he did not prosper, and in 1861 was declared bankrupt with assets of only £99 against liabilities of £646. He reportedly attributed his insolvency to 'a falling-off of business and pressure from creditors'.[19] In April 1862 former clients sued him for moneys he had received from defendants but had not passed on to the clients. He did not contest those claims. This incident must have acted as a spur to leave Melbourne.

In October 1862 Wilson was admitted as a barrister and solicitor in Dunedin where he practised for some years, initially on his own account and then in partnership with Michael Kidston and John Stamper. In 1865 he was an unsuccessful candidate in the inaugural election of a mayor for Dunedin, his lack of success perhaps being foreshadowed by having to second his own nomination.[20] Certainly, any practice at Queenstown must have been short-lived, as by 1868 Wilson was again in practice in Dunedin.[21] His later movements and history are not known.

1866 to 1871

There seem to have been no new legal practitioners on the Central Otago scene in the years 1866 to 1867. *Mackay's Almanac* for 1868 lists not one lawyer practising in any of the Central Otago areas. The most likely candidate to be doing so, though, is 'J W Macgregor [sic] in Milton'[22] (probably J.A.J. MacGregor), but his practice was apparently run by a manager rather than MacGregor being a resident in the town. Nor are there any records of lawyers practising from goldfield towns in 1869. Indeed, in 1872 the *Tuapeka Times* specifically contrasted the absence of lawyers from the area in 1869 with the dozen in the goldfields in 1872.[23]

A new lawyer appeared in Central Otago in 1870. Frederick John Wilson opened a solicitor's practice in Clyde in January 1870 and a branch in Cromwell in March 1871.[24] He was the first solicitor to have such a practice in Cromwell. Wilson had qualified by serving articles with James Smith in Dunedin from 2 July 1863. The date when he opened his practice is hard to reconcile with the data in his admissions file, which records him as being admitted as a solicitor in January 1872 and a barrister in March of that year. Either the admissions information is wrong (but it is repeated in Wilson's entry for the members of the Otago District Law Society in 1874), or Wilson began his practice before he was admitted to the profession, or the secondary sources are wrong. Wilson later moved to a government position. Between 1897, at the latest, and 1907, he was solicitor to the Public Trustee, with a salary in the later year of £525.[25]

The first recorded resident lawyer in Naseby appears to have been George Frederic Rowlatt, who was admitted as a solicitor in Dunedin on 24 August 1871 and as a barrister some months later. He had qualified by serving articles with Joseph O'Meagher from May 1866 and was listed as practising in Naseby on an Otago District Law Society membership list for 1874 and in *Mackay's Almanac* for 1875.[26] We know little more about his practice. However, because he filed for bankruptcy in November 1880, with assets of £265 as against liabilities of £570 odd,[27] it is unlikely that his practice provided a generous income. He may have later sought to return to practice in Wellington, given the correspondence about him between the Otago District Law Society and its Wellington counterpart in 1877.[28]

A new lawyer made his first appearance, it seems, in 1871. The record book of the Warden's Court at Clyde shows that on 28 March 1871 Anthony Brough, a local solicitor, appeared on behalf of an objector to an application for authority to create a head race.[29] This entry in the record book is the first mention of a lawyer appearing in that court despite the records going back to 1866.

Anthony Brough is definitely the Anthony Brough who was admitted as a solicitor in Dunedin in August 1868 and as a barrister three months later after having served three years in articles with James Smith. He seems to have remained in New Zealand for only a short time after admission and his brief sojourn at Clyde, because in late 1872 he sought admission as a solicitor in New South Wales. His admission was confirmed two years later. He appears to have practised in rural New South Wales from that time, with the sojourn including a period in Cobar, where he served as an

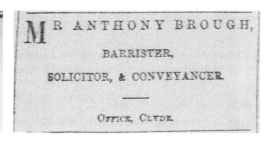

These advertisements promoting the services of Mr Anthony Brough, Clyde, appeared on (left-hand photo) page 4 of the *Cromwell Argus*, 15 December 1869, and page 3 of the *Dunstan Times*, 24 June 1870.

alderman in 1884 before moving to Hay in the Riverina district in 1886. In 1888 he was elected to the municipal council and as mayor of the town. He died of a sudden illness on 1 October 1889, leaving a widow and at least one son and a very small estate, the principal asset apparently being an insurance policy for £200.[30]

By 1871 the presence of lawyers in at least some of the local civil litigation appears to have become more common. For example, in the case of *Goodyear v Joel* in the District Court at Clyde in May 1871, W. Nolan appeared as solicitor for the plaintiff and 'Mr Barton' as solicitor for the defendant.[31] Identifying either of these lawyers was difficult. This is the only mention I could find of a solicitor called Nolan, and no one of that name seems to have been admitted to the profession before 1880. As with some other records of 'lawyers' in this area, we can assume that either the lawyer was practising without having been admitted or that the source was, for some reason, inaccurate.

The problem with the other lawyer is quite different. Two well-known Otago lawyers called Barton were practising in the 1870s. They were George Elliott Barton and his unrelated near namesake George Burnett Barton. The latter was born in Sydney and received part of his education in that city. He left Sydney University under a cloud after clashes with university authorities and went to England, where he was called to the bar at the Middle Temple on 16 November 1860, having enrolled as a student in 1857. He soon returned to Sydney but did not practise law there (he was apparently deaf, which would have been a significant hindrance). Instead, he was active in journalism, briefly held a government appointment and then for some time was Reader in English at the University of Sydney, where he wrote a number of books and articles on literary issues.

George Burnett Barton relinquished these two positions to move to Dunedin as editor of the *Otago Daily Times*, a move made for financial reasons. He later resigned the editorship after a major political controversy, sparked when he alleged the government was manipulating the provision of news telegrams so as to disadvantage his newspaper. He was sued for libel as a result, but the case never came to judgement.[32] During his time in Dunedin Barton was not admitted as a solicitor until July 1871. He was resident in Queenstown for a brief period, and certainly appears to have been well in funds at this time. In 1873 he contracted to have a house built in the town for £761, although he sued the builder for substantial damages for not having it completed by the due date.[33] He stood unsuccessfully for the local parliamentary electorate in 1873.

Barton also appears to have been a defendant in a suit brought by Albert Eichardt, owner of Queenstown's best-known hotel, as in 1876 Eichardt sued Wesley Turton, solicitor, to recover the amount of verdicts and costs for two earlier actions against Barton, the verdicts totalling almost £100. Eichardt sued Turton at the same time for an unpaid liquor bill, and it seems highly possible Barton's liability was for the same kind of debt.[34] Barton then practised in Dunedin, but by 1878 was in Christchurch. Papers were filed in 1880 to have him struck off the roll of solicitors, but the reasons, and the outcome, are not known.[35]

While in Otago Barton edited New Zealand's first legal periodical, the *New Zealand Jurist*. In later years he returned to Australia, where he resumed journalism, wrote on literary and historical issues and was active in the Federation campaigns. He died in 1901 in a country town in New South Wales where he was editing the local newspaper at the time. Barton has certainly been somewhat overshadowed by his far better-known younger brother, Edmund Barton, the first prime minister of the Commonwealth of Australia.[36]

Our other candidate for the 1871 appearance, G.E. Barton, had a leading place as a barrister in Dunedin. It seems unlikely – although it is possible – that counsel of George Elliott Barton's stature would have been engaged for a dispute over £120 worth of allegedly undrinkable beer. In contrast, we know that George Burnett Barton later settled in Central Otago and practised there. However, he was not admitted as a barrister and solicitor of the Supreme Court until 21 July 1871, more than two months after the hearing at Clyde. We can only leave the matter as unresolved until further data can be found.

The 1872 Snapshot

According to the *Tuapeka Times* of June 1872, the goldfields hosted 12 lawyers: four in Queenstown, one in Cromwell, three in Lawrence, three in Clyde, and one in Naseby.[37] Unfortunately, that claim cannot be confirmed; nor can the lawyers be conclusively identified. Two were Brough and (probably) Frederick Wilson. A civil case at Clyde in 1872 records Anthony Brough appeared for the plaintiff but that the defendant initially was not represented. However, it turned out that 'Mr Wilson' was acting as solicitor for the defendant but had been engaged in Cromwell on the first day of the trial. Both lawyers appeared when the case was later fully heard.[38]

It is clear, though, that more lawyers were active – and resident – in the area. Several cases in Queenstown involved Barton and 'Macgregor' as counsel, both in the District Court and the Warden's Court.[39] The latter, Joseph Alexander James MacGregor, had relocated from Dunedin. He had been admitted as an attorney in England at some point before 1843 and practised in London. He moved to Victoria, was admitted in Melbourne in 1853, and then came to New Zealand in 1862. In 1863 he is listed as practising in Dunedin, and in 1865 he stood as a candidate for mayor of Dunedin.

He appears to have followed the gold rushes to the West Coast, as he is listed in 1866 as practising in partnership with George Harvey (a former law clerk of McGregor's) at Hokitika.[40]

MacGregor was back in Dunedin in early 1867. The following year he was declared bankrupt. The papers filed in relation to his affairs showed a man very deeply in debt with liabilities of over £12,000 and assets of just under £500. MacGregor appears to have allowed credit to many clients who failed to pay; his solicitor indicated that over £4200 of bad or doubtful debts had not been included in the assets. His creditors were also many and varied, the largest being the Bank of New South Wales to whom he owed over £9000 for principal and interest on a £6000 loan taken out in 1857. Among the various smaller creditors were many Dunedin tradespeople.[41] There is more than a hint of fraud on his creditors, as his Trustee in Bankruptcy stated that:

> [T]he bankrupt recently built a house at Anderson's Bay which is mortgaged
> to the Building Society and has conveyed the equity of redemption to his wife.
> The ground on which the house is built is only partially paid for, as is the house.
> The furniture etc belonging to the Bankrupt is mortgaged to his wife's sister for
> the sum of £250 who is in possession and living with the bankrupt. The Trustee
> has no funds to contest these to all appearances fraudulent transactions and no
> creditors oppose the Bankrupt's discharge as far as I am aware.[42]

MacGregor's then law clerk, Joel Barnett Lewis, tendered the sum of £5 to purchase the debts and other claims MacGregor had against his debtors. That arrangement too might seem suspicious to modern eyes. However, MacGregor continued on in practice, as did many other insolvent lawyers of the time.

Developments 1873 to 1874 and the Lawyers from Lawrence

During 1873 no new practices appear to have been established in Central Otago. Three lawyers are reported as appearing as counsel at a sitting of the Resident Magistrate's Court in Naseby in 1873 – Messrs Barton, Chapman and Smith.[43] The Barton referred to may be either George Burnett Barton or George Elliott Barton; most likely the former. The other two are probably Frederick Revans Chapman and James Smith, both based in Dunedin, and so their careers need not be traced further here.

In 1874 the first definite report of a lawyer based in Lawrence appearing in the Central Otago courts is that featuring 'Mr McCoy', who presented as counsel in the Resident Magistrate's Court at Roxburgh that year.[44] He and another lawyer based in Lawrence, John Copland, also appeared at a court hearing in Alexandra in 1876.[45]

Both of these individuals can be identified. Mr McCoy was Frederick Henry McCoy, another of our cohort who had come from Australia. He was the son of a professor at Melbourne University and had been admitted as a barrister in Victoria in 1868. He was admitted in Dunedin as a solicitor in August 1870 and as a barrister in March 1871.[46] This separation in time is a little odd, as he would have been entitled to seek admission in the dual capacity in 1870, and many migrant lawyers chose that option. Shortly after his admission as a barrister, McCoy employed an articled clerk in Dunedin, but by 1874 at the latest he was in practice in Lawrence. He died there on 17 October 1887, leaving an estate of 'over £100', a formula sometimes used as a signal that estate duty would be payable but that the estate had not been calculated. The inventory of his assets suggests that, unless he had very significant debts or other liabilities not mentioned, the estate must have been significantly more than £100 because he had life insurance policies totalling more than £1400, some freehold land in Lawrence and shares in a mining company.[47]

John Cornish Copland had a different background and an unusual one. He was first admitted to the legal profession in British Columbia in 1864 and practised there for five years before he came to New Zealand in 1869.[48] He is, as far as is known, the only nineteenth-century New Zealand lawyer to come from Canada. Like many other travelling lawyers, he was admitted first as a solicitor (in February 1870) and then as a barrister some weeks later. In 1874 he was in regular practice in Lawrence.[49] Unfortunately, as yet, the details of his later life are not known.

It seems possible that two other Lawrence-based lawyers may also have been active in Central Otago. Little is known of the first – William Nott Gooday. He was admitted as an attorney in England in 1865, as a solicitor in New Zealand in May 1870 and as a barrister a year later (an unusually long gap). Gooday was in practice in Lawrence by 1874. Few traces of him can be found over the next two decades, other than that he was practising in Eltham and Hawera in Taranaki in the mid-1890s.[50]

The other lawyer of interest, John Mouat, had a most interesting career. He was a rarity, perhaps even unique, because he was a miner who became a lawyer. Born in November 1830 in the Shetland Islands, he left there for Victoria in 1852. He mined on the Victorian goldfields until 1861 and then came to Otago, where he mined for gold for a further four years at Gabriel's Gully. In 1864 he was elected to the Otago Provincial Council. Two years later he briefly held office in the provincial government before starting his training in November 1867 to become a lawyer while in the offices of (Bryan) Cecil Haggitt, a very prominent Dunedin lawyer.

Mouat spent at least some of this period in Lawrence, as court documents in 1871 describe him as 'an articled clerk of Lawrence'.[51] He was admitted as a barrister and solicitor in April 1872, briefly practising in Dunedin before returning to Lawrence. His reasons for doing so were revealed in successful proceedings for judicial separation from his wife Maria Theresa on the grounds of her cruelty.[52] Mouat alleged Maria was addicted to alcohol and was violent towards him and their children when she was under its influence. He claimed to have done everything he could to assist her to give up excessive drinking, including having her committed to an asylum for a year's treatment.[53] When that failed to effect a cure, he 'removed to Lawrence with the view of removing his said wife to that place where being a stranger she would be less likely to obtain intoxicating liquor'.[54] In 1874 he was back on the lower Clutha as a lawyer in practice in Lawrence. At some later time he moved back to Dunedin, where in the 1890s he practised in partnership with one of his sons. Mouat died in July 1902.[55] The *Cyclopedia of New Zealand* records him as 'a Freemason, an Oddfellow, and a Druid of long standing'.[56]

1875 to 1877

By the latter half of the 1870s several lawyers were resident in Queenstown. They regularly appeared in opposition to one another in the town's District Court. On 26 April 1875, for example, the court heard four civil cases, with Wesley Turton serving as counsel for the plaintiff in three of them. A 'Mr Finn', who must be Hugh Joseph Finn, appeared for the defendant in three cases and the plaintiff in the fourth.[57] Two further cases were held over, with these two lawyers again appearing for the opposing parties.

Wesley Turton was from an Auckland family but came to Otago where he was articled to Gibson K. Turton in August 1864. A number of lawyers with that surname practised law in Otago and elsewhere through the second half of the nineteenth century. Wesley Turton was admitted to the profession in February 1870. He appears to have been in Dunedin in 1872 because in February of that year he employed Spence Hardy Turton as articled clerk. However, by 1874 Wesley Turton was practising in Queenstown. Newspapers of the time refer to a 'Mr Turton' appearing in the Queenstown District Court in May 1875, and giving a speech 'as senior counsel in the district' to a new judge.[58] In the late 1870s he was involved in the creation of the Southland District Law Society, but he may have done this while resident in Queenstown. He was certainly practising there by the late 1890s, and was the Crown prosecutor for the Otago goldfields.[59] Wesley Turton died in October 1922, leaving an estate of under £3000. The estate papers indicate that for many years he had been the Queenstown agent for the Perpetual Trustees Executor and Agency Company of New Zealand, presumably undertaking this role in addition to his legal practice.[60]

Archival records reveal that actions over water-race licences for the diggings were a constant source of business for Wesley Turton. Between 1886 and 1893 he appeared as plaintiff in 20 cases in the Arrowtown or Queenstown Warden's Court, bringing actions against rights holders (the actions asked that these men be fined for not paying renewal fees for their water-race licences) and then presenting the court with letters from the respective licence-holder seeking to have a fine imposed rather than the licence being revoked. It seems clear that, in all cases, the licensees were Turton's clients and that the actions were simply a way of ensuring the licence was not revoked after non-payment.

The essentially sham nature of the proceedings is best illustrated by an 1892 case where Turton sued Horatio Nelson Firth, receiver of gold revenue and also warden in the Warden's Court at Arrowtown. Firth was sued in his capacity as 'Receiver in the partnership suit of James Colghan v John Murchase and John Mackay Nicol' and thereby holder of the licence. Not only did Firth give judgement in favour of Turton in the case and therefore against himself, but he also provided a cheque to cover renewals of the licences, a cheque dated before the matter came to the court.[61] Not all Turton's cases ended so well. In 1901 he was the subject of a complaint to the Otago District Law Society, alleging he was improperly acting for a mining company against a former client. However, Turton appears to have satisfied the society that he had not breached his professional obligations.[62]

Other records tell us a little more of Turton as an individual. As briefly noted above, he was sued in the Otago Goldfields District Court in 1876 for £128-19s-0d by Albert Eichardt, the local hotelier. The itemised claim, covering the period 1872 to 1876, is for liquor and 'refreshments', the former being by far the dominant element. Eichardt's claim noted Turton had at times paid instalments to a total of £35 off his liquor bill; the claim therefore was for the balance. The matter was apparently settled through arbitration.[63] On another occasion Turton sued a former client, one McCaffrey, £31-6s-0d for work done in advising and carrying through McCaffrey's bankruptcy and discharge, to be met with the resolute defence that because McCaffrey had been bankrupted and discharged, any former debts were not enforceable.[64] The resolution of the case is not known.

Turton's regular sparring partner, Hugh Joseph Finn, was born in Ireland in 1847, educated in Dublin and France and then at the Melbourne Grammar School before attending the University of Melbourne. He apparently practised in the goldfields area of Victoria, as he was gazetted as an officer in the Sandridge Volunteer Artillery in August 1873.[65] He came to New Zealand in early 1874 and was admitted as a barrister and solicitor in August 1874.[66] He appears to have settled quite quickly in Queenstown, where he practised law and was for a time the manager of a gold-mining company. There is little to indicate the size and scope of his practice, but in 1878 he is recorded as suing a local storekeeper for payment for professional services as defence counsel when the storekeeper was charged with various liquor-sale offences.[67] In 1879 Finn was elected as the member of the House of Representatives for Wakatipu but served only a single term, because by the expiry of that term he had moved to Gisborne, where he practised as a barrister and solicitor for many years.[68] He died in Tauranga in 1927.

The 26 April 1875 list can be seen as a good indication of the kind of litigation involved in the District Court at that time.[69] The four cases heard were *Barry v Powell* (summons for security for costs), *Cotter v Gallagher* (bill of exchange and interest), *Le Suer v Miller* (action for £200 unpaid wages) and *McClaghan v Scott* (a claim for £130-15s-0d, where the defendant, who was not legally represented, accepted he was liable to pay £124 and where in consequence Mr Finn accepted no costs). On 14 June of that year two civil actions took place in the same court. In both, Wesley Turton appeared for the plaintiff and Finn for the defendant. There were also five bankruptcy hearings. Finn appeared in four of them and Turton in three.

While the bulk of cases for the remainder of 1875 were contests between Turton and Finn, other lawyers were briefly featuring in the court by August of that year. On 17 August a 'Mr Wilson' (probably Frederick Wilson) appeared in two civil cases and a bankruptcy hearing. One of the civil cases involved litigation against Wesley Turton – for whom Wilson appeared – but the case was discontinued, for reasons unknown, in October.[70] By that time, Turton was represented by a 'Mr Johnston'. In 1876 Johnston appeared more regularly – in both civil and criminal cases.

Mr Johnston is almost certainly the 'W Johnston' listed in *Mackay's Almanac*[71] as practising as a solicitor in Cromwell in 1875. Johnston was admitted as a barrister and solicitor in Dunedin in January 1862, and entered practice there almost immediately. He is listed in a directory for 1866 as practising in Princes Street, Dunedin, and appears to have been practising in that city as late as 1874, but his earlier or later careers are not recorded. Some hints come from a libel action Johnston brought against a firm of land agents in 1869 in Dunedin.[72] Johnston's counsel suggested Johnston was at that time the oldest established lawyer in Dunedin, having practised there for 17 or 18 years and having been in practice for 28 years overall. The counsel also hinted that Johnston had originally come from Ireland. The 'turnabout' nature of legal practice with a small number of lawyers is demonstrated by criminal sittings on 11 April 1876, where Johnston appeared for the Crown in one criminal case, with Finn as defence counsel; the next case involved Turton as prosecutor and Johnston as defence counsel.

Conclusion

Although generalising from the relatively small sample that these 15 lawyers comprise must be done with care and some reservations, two matters deserve comment. First, there is the strong Australian connection in that many lawyers practised in Australia before coming to New Zealand. However, it is striking that of our cohort only two, Finn and Mouat, had close connections with the goldfields areas of Australia, and Mouat was not then a lawyer. Many Australian goldfields lawyers came to Otago, but it appears they stayed in Dunedin and practised from there.

The second and more important point is that a high proportion of these early lawyers appear to have chosen the goldfields area because few other choices were fully open to them. Even leaving to one side the singular case of John Patten, it is likely that a substantial number of our cohort were practising in rural Otago because they saw themselves as having little opportunity to build a worthwhile practice in a more competitive environment. This perceived lack may be because, as was the case for George Burnett Barton, a physical disability put them at a disadvantage. It is possible (though this is simply speculation) that some lawyers went to the region because they considered it to be healthier. For example, the dry climate may have attracted those with 'consumption' (tuberculosis) or other lung-related disorders. In a few cases, a rural town in the goldfields may have seemed to be a place where a young lawyer without connections could build a practice. This notion may have been behind the decisions that George Rowlatt and Frederick Wilson made to move to Naseby and Clyde respectively.

For many of the other early lawyers, however, it is clear that recent financial disasters and bankruptcies or practice-related problems drove them from their earlier spheres of practice. Central Otago provided a place where they could get away from creditors and hope that their histories and reputations would not travel with them. A different push factor applied with John Mouat, but his move to Lawrence to try to solve his matrimonial problems is again the result of perceived need and not a matter of free choice.

Of our 15 lawyers, one was a criminal, two may have practised illegally, and four were insolvent at some point in their careers. Seven of 15 with dubious aspects to their practice is a high proportion. If we exclude the apparently less trouble-prone Lawrence lawyers, seven of the remaining 11 had practices with questionable elements. This proportion suggests that setting up a legal practice in the Otago goldfields in the 1860s and 1870s was a gamble that those with little capital or little to lose were content to take in the hope that good fortune would come of the decision. In this, the lawyers were similar to many of the miners from whom they attempted to profit.

17.

Wooden Rails and Gold: Southland and the demise of the provinces

André Brett[1]

IN 1864 SOUTHLAND BECAME the second province of New Zealand, after Canterbury, to open a public railway.[2] New Zealand's provinces, formed under the auspices of the 1852 Constitution Act that granted the colony representative government, were charged with two of the key tasks of colonisation – immigration and public works. Because of their modest revenue, however, most provinces had made little public works progress by 1864, and immigration was handled more by the pulling power of gold rushes than by effective provincial initiatives.

The opening of Southland's first eight miles of railway, from Invercargill to Makarewa, should have been a momentous occasion in the history of both the province and the entire colony. Instead, it was a calamity. The railway was constructed of wooden rails, and as if that was not farcical enough, poor-quality wood was used. Two separate opening days had to be held; the latter ended with many travellers from Invercargill stranded in Makarewa as the locomotive strained for traction on muddy, splintered rails. It would be an exaggeration to suggest that this was the day New Zealand's provinces died, but it inflicted a serious wound on their prospects.

The railway was constructed so that Southland could secure a share of the Central Otago gold rush, but the failure of Southland's attempt to tap that region's wealth played a significant role in the demise of New Zealand's provinces. This inability was a critical juncture in the series of events that led to the provinces being stripped of powers from 1865 and then consigned to the dustbin of history by the Abolition of Provinces Act in 1875. Southland's awareness that the gold rush would not last forever led it to experiment with wooden rails rather than iron. Construction costs exceeded the province's means, and the inadequacy of the short operational section compounded its financial woes. By the time Southland could accept any traffic for carriage by rail, the peak of the gold rush had passed, leaving the province to persevere for increasingly little gain. The resulting bankruptcy of Southland was the most spectacular example of provincial failure to pursue the business of colonisation and provide basic public works. These failures provided justification for the central government to assume key provincial powers and then to abolish the provinces entirely.

In 1872 Otago's district railway engineer, William Newsham Blair, wrote an incredulous letter to MP William Reeves, then Resident Minister for the Middle (i.e. South) Island, about Southland's wooden railway. Blair described the railway's history as 'not only instructive but amusing'.[3] Yet historians have given little attention to the broader context of the embarrassing failure of Southland's railways. The province has been the subject of two theses, both considerably outdated. The older thesis, by Helen A. Henderson under the pseudonym 'Alpaca', is an effective narrative for orienting those unfamiliar with Southland's history but provides little analysis.[4] A.R. Dreaver scrutinised the superintendency of James Menzies, under whom the province embarked on the railway scheme, yet reached the baffling conclusion that Southland's 'story was not one of vivid colourful incident … [or] dramatic scenes'.[5] Even though Dreaver associated colour and drama with success, it is impossible to describe Southland's railway tribulations as anything other than colourful and dramatic. W.P. Morrell is more thorough and exact in his history of the provincial system, but he recounts the key points of Southland's public works-related debt as a kind of subplot, peripheral to the operation and demise of provincialism.[6] By writing from the top–down perspective of the central government and focusing on matters of law and 'high' politics, he failed to grasp the full magnitude of Southland's failure.

A local history might be expected to provide deeper coverage, yet *Murihiku: The Southland Story*, an otherwise thorough history of the Southland region to 2006, does not.[7] Erik Olssen astutely links Menzies' profligate spending to Invercargill's ascendancy over other leading settlements and to the province's reunification with Otago in 1870, but not to the demise of the whole provincial system.[8] Vince Boyle and Jim Brown's chapter in *Murihiku* on land transport barely mentions the railway's broader social effects, nor does it draw out the theme of provincial governments struggling to manage public works. In fact, it is oddly celebratory, praising the 'bold decisions by brave men with vision and pride in their region' and arguing that they 'would surely have been accused of weakness and a lack of foresight' had they not seized the opportunities of these 'exciting, wild times'.[9] Such accusations have not been levelled at politicians in provinces that did not embark on railway schemes. Boyle and Brown go even further, claiming that Southland was 'very fortunate' in the quality of its railway engineers – the men behind one of New Zealand's greatest public works failures.[10] If these men displayed 'very fortunate' expertise, it is hard to imagine what blunders would have made them unsatisfactory.

Even the rare works on Southland's early railway history fail to capture its full significance. A brief article by K.C. McDonald provides a lively account of the railway's misfortunes and emphasises technical errors of construction, but does not link the railway to Southland's bankruptcy and loss of independence.[11] The most detailed publication about Southland's railway woes is a short book by J.O.P. Watt, *Southland's Pioneer Railways*. Although an able and detailed publication, it is written primarily for rail enthusiasts and provides only a tentative and incomplete examination of the political implications of the railway's construction and failure.[12] It is remarkable that a story full of interest, tragedy and excitement has been so neglected within New Zealand historiography. It has not even proved a fertile ground for fiction. Donald Offwood briefly hints at its potential in his historical novel *Camerons of the Glen* but does not fully develop the tangent; his novel is concerned more with the role of the railway in transforming the daily lives of hinterland settlers.[13]

Southland was cursed with tremendously unfortunate timing. Separation from Otago was sanctioned by an order-in-council on 25 March 1861, effective from 1 April, mere weeks before Gabriel Read made his famous gold discovery at Gabriel's Gully near Lawrence. Southland could only watch enviously in August 1862 as Horatio Hartley and Christopher Reilly registered in Dunedin their discovery of the Dunstan River's gold. However, a few months later on 23 November, the province's fortunes appeared to change dramatically. When gold was struck on the Arrow River, the successful prospectors did not make for Dunedin but for Invercargill. For the people of Southland, it was as if Christmas had come early. The *Invercargill Times* was jubilant: '[The prospectors] were strangers to Invercargill, they went up to the Dunstan *via* Dunedin, and they were consequently acquainted with that route; their interests

The port of Invercargill at the height of the rush to the Queenstown Lakes District, c. 1864.

Courtesy Southland Museum and Art Gallery collection

were connected with that city, and yet ... they make for Invercargill in order to obtain supplies.'[14] It was clear that Invercargill, closer to the Central Otago goldfields than Dunedin, was best placed to supply the rush with its needs. Southland was not to be blessed with a goldfield half as significant as those on the Arrow or Clutha, but a lot of money could be made by diverting the goldfields' trade to Invercargill and its port at Bluff.

Suddenly, the construction of a railway became a point of urgency. The goldfields could not be supplied without reliable transportation. Unfortunately, reliable transportation did not exist in Southland. Organised Pākehā settlement was less than a decade old. The first 18 or so miles of the route to Central Otago from Invercargill was through swamp, the route to Bluff was similarly difficult, and the rudimentary roads were dire. Various methods of road construction had been tried, but the roads kept sinking into Southland's voracious soil and were notoriously impassable in winter.[15] Even before the gold rush, Superintendent Menzies had forecast at the provincial council's second session in January 1862 the necessity of a railway.[16] He reiterated the theme as news of Central Otago's wealth reached Southland.[17] However, when he prorogued the council less than three weeks before the excitement of late November, he warned that railway construction was 'of too serious importance to be entered into hurriedly' and urged caution in business dealings.[18] This careful approach evaporated in the euphoria of presumed wealth.

In February 1863 Invercargill's political set were occupied with animated discussions about the best infrastructure to build across the swamp to the small town of Winton, from where an all-weather road could easily be made to Lake Wakatipu and thus serve the goldfields. At a special sitting of the provincial council Menzies proposed two related projects: the first would be to build a conventional railway between Invercargill and Bluff to provide a much-needed link between capital and port, and the second to build a light horse-drawn tramway north to the gravelly plains beyond Winton. For Southlanders, the need to improve transport was especially acute. They believed they had been too cautious in seeking permission from Otago's provincial government to provide a gold escort from Central Otago to Invercargill, and they had already lost much trade and wealth to Dunedin.[19] The provincial council approved the Bluff railway but was unwilling to support the horse tramway, instead voting money for the upkeep of a road through the swamp. This decision was largely a product of Menzies' administration providing the council with a hastily prepared, poorly detailed measure. Tellingly, neither Theophilus Heale, the province's chief surveyor, nor his assistant, Robert M. Marchant, nor Otago's provincial engineer, Charles Swyer, supported the scheme.[20] Its deficiencies created sufficient opposition that the cause was lost; travellers between Invercargill and the north had to endure another muddy winter.[21]

Menzies did not give up his railway plans. At the end of July, Heale presented a preliminary report on the construction of a northern railway. A well-regarded surveyor and capable mathematician, Heale had been one of the first settlers in Wellington in January 1840 and would later serve as a Native Land Court judge.[22] He emphasised that time was of the essence, as the 'primary object [was] ... securing to this Province the great traffic which has sprung up with the Whakatipu [sic] Lake'.[23] Southland did not want to suffer through another winter without a railway because the road would become an 'adhesive bog' and gravel supplies were insufficient to macadamise it.[24] Work had to be completed by May 1864 not only to beat the winter but also to avoid losing any more traffic to Otago.

Although the Bluff railway was being constructed with iron rails, Heale thought it would not be possible to obtain a sufficient quantity from England in time to build a railway all the way to Lake Wakatipu. Rather conveniently, James R. Davies, who had recently arrived from Victoria to construct part of the Bluff railway, said that he could quickly and cheaply build a railway made of wooden rails.[25] Davies imported a demonstration locomotive to run on a short length of track, and Heale endorsed the plan in the belief that it 'involves no danger, and affords every probability of success'.[26] The locomotive, *Lady Barkly*, became the first to raise steam in New Zealand when it shuttled back and forth along the Invercargill jetty on 8 August 1863. The demonstration, under the watchful eye of Menzies and other government officials, was 'extremely gratifying'.[27] Enthusiasm subsumed scepticism; the demonstration was all the impetus Southland needed to make the fateful choice of wooden rails. Heale, in particular, was hopelessly optimistic about the ease of construction, believing that the use of wooden rails would allow 83 miles of railway to be built before the winter.

The first steam locomotive built in Ballarat was the Lady Barkly, which was manufactured by Hunt and Opie in 1860. This photograph shows the newly completed engine in the Hunt and Opie yard.

Courtesy Southland Museum and Art Gallery collection

Davies' patent locomotive engines, carriages, trucks and wagons advertisement, showing the *Lady Barkly* engine.

Courtesy Southland Museum and Art Gallery collection

By October preliminary works were underway and a bill was before the provincial council to authorise a loan of £100,000. Southland had already taken advantage of the relaxed attitude that Alfred Domett's central ministry held towards provincial loans and had received authority in April to raise £140,000 for construction of the Bluff railway.[28] The new loan, it was anticipated, would cover all expenses for the first 30 miles to Winton. The provincial council's opposition pushed heavily for the railway's route to be diverted via Wallacetown, but when a monster public meeting denounced the proposal, some members of the opposition experienced a change of heart. And so the government's proposal, complete with a direct line from Invercargill to Winton, was passed.[29]

Now all the project needed was Governor George Grey's assent. At the same time that the Domett ministry advised Grey to approve the Bluff railway loan, Domett wrote to Menzies stating that any northern railway proposal would receive a favourable hearing in Auckland. He believed Southland was pursuing advisable 'good policy' on sound reasoning.[30] At the end of October 1863 the government changed to a ministry headed by Frederick Whitaker and William Fox. Although less in favour than its predecessor of provincial loans, the new government upheld Domett's promise, and Grey duly assented to a loan for the northern railway.[31] Both April's and October's debentures had an interest rate of six per cent; these were handed over in full to banks to cover advances: the first £140,000 to the Bank of New South Wales and then £110,000 to the Bank of Otago. The banks charged Southland seven per cent interest on the advances and sold the debentures on the London market.[32] In the absence of Menzies, who was attending the Legislative Council in Auckland, Deputy Superintendent Nathaniel Chalmers received the honour of turning the first sod at a ceremony on 25 November 1863.[33] In acknowledgement of the occasion's significance, many businesses closed for the day; Southlanders believed the wealth of Otago's goldfields would soon enrich their province.

The cost of construction spiralled out of control. When Menzies returned from Auckland in January 1864, he found that the Bluff railway had exceeded costs by over £35,000, primarily because the engineer had expanded works to ease gradients and to allow for mainline sections of double rather than single track. He'd also undertaken other improvements. Worse still, the construction of roads and the railway to the north had led to liabilities of almost £100,000.[34] Roadworks had secured trade with Central Otago during the summer, but completion of the railway by winter was necessary to retain this trade while avoiding costly road maintenance. In February the provincial council approved two new loans to cover these debts and, they believed, the remaining costs necessary to complete both railways – loans of £40,000 for Bluff and £120,000 for the north, repayable over 20 years. However, the Whitaker–Fox ministry was more cautious than Domett in advising Grey's assent to provincial loans, especially as the ministry was seeking its own loan for £3 million to cover the costs of war and settlement in the North Island. Fox advised Menzies that the central government would only sanction a further loan to cover the completion of railway works for which the cost had already been incurred or contracted.[35] Thus, in late April, the £40,000 loan received reluctant assent but the £120,000 loan was categorically rejected.[36]

Despite provincial finances hanging in the balance during April, no impression was conveyed to the public that construction of either railway was anything but smooth. A report from commissioners appointed by the provincial council even touted the changes made to the Bluff line as improving its quality, and stated that it was free from 'the suspicion of being a job or an engineering failure'.[37] At a banquet celebrating Southland's secession from Otago, Heale spoke glowingly of the railway. He forecast that the first 10 miles of railway in New Zealand would soon open in Southland, ignoring the fact that railways had already opened in Nelson and Canterbury.[38] He also voiced his hope that 36 miles would be open within three months.[39] The tone of the banquet was extremely optimistic, with those attending looking forward to toasting even greater progress in 1865. On 9 April the *Daily News* observed that the main Invercargill railway station was nearing completion, would be equipped with commodious passenger and goods facilities and would serve as the meeting place of the two railway projects. The paper echoed the belief that the lines to Bluff and Winton would open within three months. In line with Heale's blinkered localism, the newspaper saw Southland as 'steadily and rapidly … progressing towards the consummation of the first great railway scheme in New Zealand. At present nothing threatens any untoward delay in opening the line.'[40] In hindsight, the latter statement is ludicrous in its inaccuracy.

Outside Invercargill, frustration grew throughout Southland over the province's lavish expenditure. In the west, the people of Riverton – a settlement older than Invercargill and still bitter about being passed over for the status of capital and principal port – took a particularly poor view of Invercargill's dealings.[41] When Riverton learned in February that the provincial council would seek further railway loans, there was disquiet. The mouthpiece of the town's interests, the *Riverton Times*, angrily denounced Southland's 'course of reckless and unwarrantable expenditure', especially as 'a pressing necessity exists for a still larger expenditure'.[42] The paper captured Southland's folly by asking pointedly, 'are the goldfields at the Wakatip [sic], unlike all other goldfields yet discovered, inexhaustible, and is the lead of the gold always sure to follow the line of the railway?'[43] A few weeks later, it lamented the impossibility of stopping the railway.[44] For better or worse, Southland was stuck with its debts.

Rumours about provincial insolvency were afoot among Southlanders by late April, and in May work ground to a halt. The northern railway was nowhere near completion to Winton, let alone Lake Wakatipu, and the Bluff railway was similarly incomplete. The *Daily News*, which initially maintained a discrete silence, finally called in early May for 'a Treasurer, possessing something of the quality of statesmanship' to deal with provincial finances, but it calmed public nerves with the assurance that 'the Government has fulfilled its engagements and maintained its credit, and we have no reason to apprehend that it will fail to do so'.[45] At this critical juncture, the *Daily News* was the only public voice in the provincial capital. The *Invercargill Times*' offices had been recently destroyed by fire, and the paper would not return until June, under the new name of the *Southland Times*. Throughout the following fortnight, the *Daily News* espoused optimism while demanding, increasingly aggressively, an emergency meeting of the provincial council to resolve the province's finances. It struggled to understand how there could be a crisis in funds when the money required to complete the railways was a 'mere bagatelle' compared to the millions of acres of land the province could offer as security.[46]

Behind the scenes, the provincial executive scrambled desperately to avert a financial collapse under the weight of railway costs and misappropriated expenditure, but only succeeded in scandalising the province at the hands of the *Otago Daily Times* (*ODT*). The *ODT* broke the story that the banks had refused any further overdraft or accommodation to the Southland government, so the executive 'prepared to issue Treasury notes, printed in imitation of Bank notes, and which the unwary might mistake for them'.[47] The *Daily News*, horrified by this allegation of fraud, demanded the *ODT* reveal its source.[48] Soon, more details emerged. Samuel Beaven, a member of the executive, had been despatched to Dunedin on an emergency mission – ultimately unsuccessful – to secure more funds from the Bank of Otago. Southland's treasurer, William Tarlton, confirmed to the *Daily News* that the executive had briefly contemplated, as a last resort, an issue of 'convertible Treasury notes'; however, 'they never *entertained the question of actually issuing them*'.[49] Beaven apparently felt himself authorised to order a note plate for a test pressing. He allowed the design to closely resemble bank notes and had copies struck in blue and pink. One of the notes found its way to Julius Vogel at the *ODT*.[50] News of this venture was possibly the least helpful information the province could have received at this moment. Instead of careful negotiations to win emergency concessions, the executive had committed a calamitous, if not quite criminal, blunder.

A few days later, on 20 May, the *Daily News* was reduced to announcing that 'The public works are now actually stopped! The result will be an enormous loss to the province. It will throw hundreds of labouring men out of employment, it will ruin innumerable tradesmen. It will leave the very works on which we have spent so many thousands of pounds, to go to waste for want of completion.'[51] Invercargill was already entering a commercial depression, and the collapse of public works that had employed many men and kept numerous businesses afloat was felt acutely. Recriminations were forceful and severe. The *Daily News* was incapable of understanding how a few thousand pounds could not be found to complete the railway eight miles north to Makarewa to meet the road north to Central Otago, or 16 miles south to Mokomoko jetty, a site offering deep water, even if it wasn't quite the calibre of Bluff harbour. Upon its revival, the *Southland Times* remained insistent that the railways were affordable, if expensive, and blamed the collapse of provincial finances on wasteful expense and mismanagement of provincial funds.[52]

Not only had the two railways created considerable debt, but because neither was close to finished, the government was starved of revenue with which to repay its loans. Southland's provincial bonds were essentially unsaleable in England, banks were unwilling to negotiate further loans, and the Whitaker–Fox ministry was unwilling to approve new loans anyway. The province was therefore reliant on the central government reluctantly advancing money – £15,000 per month for four months – on the security of Southland's waste-land revenue.[53]

More bad news was to come, and it would imperil the success of the wooden railway when work finally resumed. The contracts were poorly written, and earlier confusion during construction of the Bluff railway about the meaning of 'black pine' (the inspector of works interpreted it as miro, which had not been intended) had exacerbated matters.[54] A terse and damning exchange in the provincial council revealed that Deputy Superintendent Chalmers had authorised, in an attempt to save money, the use of inferior but cheaper wood for the northern railway. Kahikatea (white pine), a soft wood best known as the material for butter boxes in the early days of refrigerated exports, had been used in lieu of the contractually mandated and more expensive options of kauri, matai, totara and Tasmanian blue gum.[55] This decision had dire consequences.

In August 1864 construction resumed in a desperate attempt to open at least the first eight miles to Makarewa, to generate income and to salvage some dignity from the province's mess. The goldfields were already past their peak, and the feverish excitement of a rush would soon move to the West Coast, well beyond the reach of any Southland infrastructure. But even before construction began, Heale emphasised another important reason to build a railway. It would, he said, open prime agricultural land where 'the best means of communication' – railways – 'are required for purely local purposes'.[56] It would also drain the produce from the province's north and northeast, and open up the northwest and Fiordland. If Southland could not have Otago's gold, it might at least use the railway to exploit its own resources.

Unfortunately for Southland, the railway's calamitous opening showed just how much it had failed. The railway had to be opened twice. The original grand opening on 18 October 1864 was meant to be one of the most glorious days in the province's brief history – a day of achievement and celebration. However, the train to Makarewa was reserved for invited guests, leaving the rest of the populace on the platform, furious.[57] Invercargill was in an uproar. To calm popular dissatisfaction, the authorities planned a second grand opening for a week later, this time with trains open to the general public. However, a cloud was cast over proceedings when the celebration was preceded by the first death of a railway worker in New Zealand: a young employee Alfred Gasket fell beneath a train shunting in Makarewa three days before the planned festivities. He died instantly.[58]

When the big day came, Southlanders enjoyed a public holiday and turned out in large numbers to ride to Makarewa, where a picnic and sporting events were held. The morning passed without incident as a horde of Southlanders were conveyed to Makarewa. However, afternoon rain soon left the tracks coated in clay. The locomotive, in a shower of sparks and smoke, struggled to gain any traction as it hauled trainloads of tired passengers home to Invercargill. The train was too heavy for the poor-quality wood used to make the rails, and its weight had already been carving out splinters.

Invercargill railway station, c. 1864, showing wooden rails.

Source: Joyce Garlick, 'The first engine employed on a public railway', *New Zealand Railways Magazine*, vol. 12, no. 6, 1937, p. 29

Inevitably, some disgruntled passengers were left to fend for themselves. They either walked home to Invercargill damp and tired or stayed the night in Makarewa.[59] The wooden railway was clearly a massive folly. Despite the optimism of the *Southland Times*, which believed the rails would soon be laid all the way to Winton, the line was not yet ready to handle regular traffic of any sort.

What was a province to do? Southland drifted into a malaise and rarely used the wooden railway for the rest of the 1860s. During brief operational periods, the railway was beset by problems, such as cinders from the locomotive setting fire to the wooden tracks in December 1866.[60] The opening of the Bluff railway in 1867 did little to salvage the province's pride or prosperity. It, too, was accompanied by controversy, notably when police seized government property to repay unpaid debts on 20 December 1864. The contractors who constructed Bluff's railway pier received a judgement of over £15,500 against the provincial council. To pay the debt, the Invercargill sheriff took possession of the government offices, books and railway plant and did not return them until two days later when Menzies indemnified the sheriff personally.[61] The incident highlighted a discrepancy between national and provincial law: central government property could not be seized, but provincial property could.

The spectre of further litigation over Southland's debts hung ominously in the air. Because the province's anniversary of separation from Otago fell on 1 April, the *Southland News* in 1865 sarcastically wondered whether an 'All Fool's Day' separation banquet would be held.[62] Numerous private creditors were clamouring for payment, and Southland's debts to the bank and central government were not disappearing. Both creditors and province looked to the General Assembly for a solution. In October 1865 the assembly passed the Southland Provincial Debt Act, an action that had far-reaching consequences. The central government took on Southland's debt, but under the terms of the act impounded Southland's waste-land revenue to cover costs. A final clause required all future provincial loans to be approved through acts of the General Assembly so as to avoid any further disasters.

The failure of Southland province at the hands of its gold ambitions and railway debts began to convince its residents – and people throughout New Zealand – that not only was Southland's separation a failure but so too was provincialism; an adjustment of New Zealand's political organisation was clearly necessary. The *Southland News* despondently argued that if the only way Southland could prolong its 'wretched existence' was by delaying repayments to its creditors with tedious applications of the law, then 'the sooner our individual being as a Province is blotted out, the better'.[63] The *Lyttelton Times* feared that '[n]ot a debenture will be saleable [in England] if Southland be left to perish … [and] become notoriously bankrupt'.[64] This argument was meant to promote the establishment of the South Island as a separate colony from the war-torn and supposedly irresponsible North through flimsy claims that Southland could only be rescued if the South Island stood alone. However, the editor had a point about Southland damaging New Zealand's standing on the London money market. New Zealanders outside Southland did not want their public works and borrowing capacity inhibited by Southland's sins. South Island separatism faded with the passage of the 1860s, but discontent with the provincial system did not. In Invercargill the *Southland Times*, once so proud to defend its province, by 1867 was arguing that Southland 'emphatically repudiates the provincial system'[65] and lamented its 'utter uselessness'.[66]

Southland was not the only province to falter with public works, but it provided the most dramatic case, and its massive debts led to the first central government legislation that concretely pointed towards the end of the provinces. Auckland embarrassingly abandoned construction of a railway to the Waikato amidst accusations of financial incompetence. Wellington struggled to maintain communication with its Wairarapa hinterland, and the city lacked basic public works. A private industrial railway in Nelson flopped; the governor vetoed not one but two Marlborough railway bills. Of course, some provinces were poor and indebted for other reasons. Taranaki, suffering under the weight of war, notably tottered on a financial precipice.

By 1867 the central government had little choice but to revoke the ability of provinces to raise loans by any means. It passed two acts that consolidated all of New Zealand's loans, provincial and national, into one national loan.[67] The preamble to one of these acts, the Public Debts Act, emphasised Southland's debts and poverty as the most significant justification for the government's action. Suddenly, the provinces, even successful and prosperous ones such as Canterbury, could not borrow for major public works, and revenue alone was insufficient to fund major projects. Most provinces during 1867 to 1869 struggled to earn annual revenue greater than £100,000 and rarely showed a profit greater than £10,000; a rudimentary railway typically cost over £3000 per mile, exclusive of rolling stock or land purchases, so even a province turning a modest profit could not afford to commence short lines. With the provinces unable to perform key tasks, the way was cleared for their abolition.

Opinion in favour of abolition did not arise overnight and did not occur consistently throughout New Zealand, but as it developed, Southland's folly featured prominently. Some commentators tried to defend provincialism and felt Southland should not be used to condemn the entire system. This was especially the case in Timaru where its media advocate, the *Timaru Herald*, sought secession from Canterbury and believed the dire straits of Southland and other provinces were due to individual mismanagement rather than flaws of provincialism itself.[68] Southland slowly imploded, cutting down its political machinery ahead of reunion with Otago by abolishing its executive council and vesting additional power in its superintendent and a permanent treasurer. The *Grey River Argus* in 1869 noted this development approvingly, believing Southland would soon adopt the county model employed in Westland.[69] This was a region where anti-Canterbury rather than provincialist sentiment was strong, but those feelings reflected a wider phenomenon: in a transient society that had grown dramatically since the dawn of provincialism in 1853, New Zealanders were no longer so attached to their provinces. This was especially the case in the light of failures such as Southland's. New Zealanders simply desired local control of local affairs, thus importing British attitudes to decentralisation and developing a dizzying array of road and harbour boards and other local institutions.[70] During 1868 alone, the central government received

30 petitions from communities large and small requesting the abolition or alteration of the provincial system. Although the *Lyttelton Times* noted that the petitions were signed by only 'one fifty-fifth' of the Pākehā population, they consistently originated from dissatisfied hinterlands and reflected similar demands from diverse corners of the country.[71]

On 28 June 1870, Julius Vogel, the treasurer of William Fox's government, announced in his financial statement that the central government would implement a national scheme of public works and immigration, with emphasis upon trunk railways. The whole scheme was forecast to cost £10 million, of which £6 million would be provided by a loan. Although Vogel did not speak specifically of Southland, the province's bankruptcy had contributed to his proposal. The colony's financial position in 1867 and the prohibition on provincial borrowing was clearly influenced by Southland accruing a massive debt while trying to secure gold-rush trade. Circumstances elsewhere meant some sort of financial adjustment was necessary anyway, but it was Southland that most thoroughly trashed the standing of provincial loans. Had the provinces not been barred from further borrowing, public works could have proceeded, at least in the wealthier provinces, and Vogel would not have been able to speak of needing to start 'afresh' to address the colony's 'anxious desires expressed for a renewal of immigration and of public works'.[72] I am not proposing a counterfactual history, or suggesting that Vogel's Great Public Works Policy would not have occurred had Southland not gone bankrupt; rather, it is necessary to recognise that Southland's actions were central to what happened rather than an amusing footnote.

The Great Public Works Policy unleashed abolition. It usurped key provincial functions. The provinces had already been delegating some purely local functions to local bodies such as road boards and town municipalities, and now their key regional functions had been stripped from them.[73] Provinces were initially forecast as partners in the scheme, recommending routes for the central government to build, for example, but it was clear which tier of government held the purse strings and the power. Furthermore, the Great Public Works Policy compressed the time and space within which provincialism existed. Provinces were justified by the scattered and separate nature of New Zealand's early settlements. Now they were being connected and brought together by railway lines built with the express intention of crossing provincial boundaries. Provincialism could not survive this constriction of its space. That it vanished so fast, when the national network was largely still on the drawing board rather than a reality, is a testament to the energy of the abolition movement, to the fierce disapproval of provincialism held in hinterlands and some major centres, and to the crumbling financial arrangements that barely sustained provincial governments. Yet, at the heart of the whole process, poorly acknowledged and half forgotten, were eight useless miles of wooden rails straining to link Invercargill with Central Otago.

Epilogue

Once the Vogel era commenced, Southland's railway fortunes improved rapidly. In 1871 the northern railway as far as Winton finally opened, after which construction to Kingston proceeded apace. The whole line was formally opened on 10 July 1878, almost 15 years after work on it began, eight years after the body that commenced it ceased to exist, and two years after the entire provincial system was abolished. Scenes of revelry and excitement greeted the grand opening. A free train of 23 carriages hauled by four locomotives carried over a thousand Invercargillites to Kingston. Little mention was made of the railway's inauspicious start during the festivities. The glowing media reports detailed the scenery of the route, the activities on board the first train and the banquet held for dignitaries in Kingston – but avoided the issue of the wooden railway.[74] A rare reference appeared in the *Southland Times*' account of the speeches at the banquet; one of the speakers mentioned his attendance at the opening to Makarewa.[75]

This replica of the *Lady Barkly* was made by Bluff Engineering in 2003 and is part of a display on the Invercargill wharf. The Davies' patent system of angled guide wheels can be seen at the front. These were a major factor in the engine's declared ability to run on standard-gauge wooden rails.

Photograph by Anne Scott, Invercargill

Southland's railway network ultimately expanded to be one of the densest in New Zealand, with branch lines radiating to almost every corner of the region. Most traces of the wooden railway were swiftly obliterated, and the only known remnant to survive into the twenty-first century was McCallum's Shed, a farm building made out of wood salvaged from the railway and located between Makarewa and Winton at Wilsons Crossing.[76] The province also led the nation in bush tramways – rough lines built through dense forest for sawmilling purposes. Some of these lines employed wooden rails, and this time those laying them achieved much greater success than their forebears had in the 1860s. Southland's tramways pioneered the use of steam haulers in the 1880s and internal combustion engines in rail tractors in the 1920s. The Port Craig tramline featured the Percy Burn viaduct, the second largest wooden viaduct in New Zealand and still a landmark in western Southland.[77] The start of Southland's railway history may have been dismal, but the region swiftly rebounded, and the line between Invercargill and Makarewa remains operational to this day. In 2014, although much altered from the wooden rails of its infancy, the line marked its 150th anniversary.

5

GOLDFIELDS HERITAGE

18.

Challenges in Story-based Interpretation: Gold-rush heritage and visitors

Warwick Frost

IN 1929 THE INHABITANTS of the former mining town of Tombstone (Arizona, USA) staged the Helldorado Festival to commemorate the fiftieth anniversary of their founding. The combination of the evocative words Hell and El Dorado humorously signified the dual nature of many mining boomtowns, as did the town's name itself (allegedly its founding prospector had been warned he would find only his tombstone). To mark the occasion, the townsfolk dressed as miners and cowboys, re-opened the notorious Bird Cage Theater, staged mock hold-ups and re-enacted the infamous gunfight at the OK Corral. Perhaps only intended as a one-off commemoration, the annual festival continues today with very much the same mix of activities (see the illustration on the following page).

While looking back to their colourful past, the people of Tombstone also took the opportunity the festival provided to look forward and imagine future directions. The town's newspaper, the *Tombstone Epitaph*, predicted: 'Tombstone is entering a new era in the history of its developments. Climate, scenery and the attraction of the great outdoors will take the place of silver and gold. Thousands of Americans seeking these things will find them at their best in Tombstone and it is not hard to visualize the day when this city will come again into its own ... A new hotel, new homes, possibly a sanatorium would inevitably follow.'[1]

Half a world away and a year earlier, the former gold-mining town of Beechworth (Victoria, Australia) had entered and won a newspaper competition for the Ideal Town. The angle Beechworth took was that the town was an ideal tourism resort given its healthy mountain air, walking trails and idyllic scenery. Little mention was made of its mining history and none at all of its connections with the notorious bushranger Ned Kelly. Indeed, on the outskirts of town, the old workings of the Rocky Mountain Extended Gold Sluicing Company had been recently flooded to form a recreational attraction in picturesque Lake Sambell.[2]

The West gets Wild at the Helldorado Festival in Tombstone, Arizona. Amateur re-enactors relive past shootouts in the main street.

Photograph by Warwick Frost, 2012

Tombstone and Beechworth are two instructive examples of how former mining towns started to *reimagine* their past and package it for visitors. While we might think of this process as a modern one, the two examples illustrate that reimagining and the form it should take has been an issue for nearly a century, more or less starting once mining began to decline. These examples also demonstrate the diversity and dynamism of the process. For Beechworth, the strategy of positioning itself as a nature-based tourism resort and ignoring its mining past perhaps made sense in the 1920s and 1930s, but from the 1960s onwards, a different reimagining occurred. Fanned by a range of forces, including increasing nationalism resulting in an interest in Australian history, the town's historic buildings and townscape came to the fore.[3] In recent years there has been a further reimagining. As is evident in many country towns, there has been a shift towards marketing Beechworth as a *village*, with an emphasis on food, artisans and boutique accommodation.[4]

For Tombstone, presentation of its image has been more consistent. Across the United States, the 1920s saw a range of former mining towns begin to celebrate their past in order to attract tourists. These beginnings were partly due to the realisation that the pioneers were disappearing. Wyatt Earp, for example, died early in 1929. But they were also the product of new technologies that encouraged tourism, such as cars, radio and the cinema.[5] Since then, events such as Helldorado Days have reinforced the view that Tombstone was once a *wide-open* mining town, characterised by daily gunfights and lawlessness. In sticking to that image, Tombstone provides an interesting contrast to nearby Bisbee, which has used its impressive architecture as a foundation for food, craft and artisans.

These processes of reimagination are central to how the goldfields of the nineteenth century are experienced today. They affect not only what the visitor understands and enjoys, but also what communities and governments choose to value and protect. They furthermore underpin the sustainability and identities of the former goldfields. In this chapter, I aim to build on my previous work in extending our understanding of how gold-rush heritage is interpreted for visitors and how that process influences heritage conservation.[6] In undertaking this project, I consider a range of examples from Australia, New Zealand and the United States, in recognition of the heritage that the nineteenth-century goldfields around the Pacific share.

Freeman Tilden and Interpretation

The pioneering work on interpretation is by Freeman Tilden, and it is still highly influential today, particularly in the United States.[7] Tilden is often presented as a wise and experienced national park ranger who developed his innovative ideas over decades of presenting guided tours, before finally writing them down. In such a mythologised image, he is a latter-day incarnation of the nineteenth-century Scottish-American naturalist and advocate for the establishment of Yosemite and Sequoia National Parks, John Muir, with the exception, most importantly, that his (Tilden's) development was the result of his experience as a national park ranger. The reality is unfortunately not that romantic. Tilden was an experienced newspaper journalist and fiction writer rather than a crusty park ranger. In 1941, the Director of the US National Park Service (NPS) hired Tilden to work on public relations and publicity. One particularly important task was that of writing a handbook that the NPS could give to potential sponsors. Moving on from that effort, Tilden realised that what was missing within current NPS practice was a basic philosophy to guide interpretation planning. The absence of this intellectual foundation meant that those overseeing heritage sites tended to dismiss interpretation as lightweight entertainment for visitors and therefore of little value.[8]

Tilden conceptualised interpretation as a service integral to both natural and cultural heritage (the NPS managed both types of site). This service was provided by 'thousands of naturalists, historians, archaeologists, and other specialists … engaged in the work of revealing, to such visitors as desire the service, something of the beauty and wonder, the inspiration and spiritual meaning that lie behind what the visitor can with his senses perceives'.[9] More formally, Tilden defined interpretation as 'An educational activity which aims to reveal meanings and relationships through the use of original objects, by firsthand experience, and by illustrative media, rather than simply to communicate factual information'.[10]

Personally, I find Tilden's first explanation more powerful and instructive than his second dictionary-style definition. The first more successfully captures the notion of a profound experience – of the visitor getting something far better than they expected. However, there's a tinge of sadness in reading Tilden's insightful work over half a century after it was written. Central to his premise was the idea that interpretation went beyond what visitors could see by themselves. This idea is one often lost in contemporary interpretation practice and rhetoric. The trend towards minimising interpretation – most obvious in zoos, for example – is in direct contradiction of Tilden's argument. Furthermore, Tilden's warnings about the overuse of gadgetry, particularly in terms of his idea that technology can never better a good human performance of interpretation,[11] now seem forgotten.

Tilden's great success was in distilling a range of ideas into six core principles of interpretation. This set of numbered commandments was easy for a wide variety of employees, volunteers and other stakeholders to remember. Like their Biblical equivalent, the commandments had an authoritative status. Set in stone, they were both enduring and unchallengeable. Paraphrased for simplicity, they can be understood as follows:

1. Interpretation must be related to the visitor as a person, either their personality or experience.
2. Interpretation must be based on and include factual information, but interpretation is not simply information.
3. Interpretation is an art and must be approached from a multidisciplinary perspective.
4. 'The chief aim of interpretation is not instruction, but provocation.'
5. Interpretation should aim to present a whole rather than a part.
6. Programmes for children should be separately developed and not be simply a dilution of the adult version.[12]

In the 60-plus years since Tilden's work was published, it has been highly influential in heritage studies and practice.[13] While subject to modifications, its core tenets have not been challenged. Today, its legacy can be seen in the continued emphasis on story-telling and persuasive messaging in a wide range of heritage contexts. It's certainly regularly applied in goldfields heritage, even though (I would argue) there is a need to remain vigilant in ensuring its consistent and effective application. An unevenness in how people use Tilden's principles is often apparent. The public governance of many heritage sites comes with many advantages, but also, unfortunately, with a strong tendency towards under-resourcing, which results in deficiencies in the quality and maintenance of interpretation programmes.

Adapting Interpretation to Cultural Heritage

In considering the application of interpretive principles to cultural heritage, it is important to make a qualification in order to secure understanding of differences within the field of natural heritage. In cultural heritage studies, interpretation has two meanings; these sometimes conflict. The first, as outlined above, is *visitor interpretation*. The second is *historical interpretation*. History is more than a collection of facts and dates. Historians try to understand the past. They do this by theorising about issues such as why certain things occurred and the implications of historical events. In such cases, there may be multiple historical interpretations.

Historians have no problems with this multiplicity, but it is often confusing for government agencies and other stakeholders who prefer to have history presented in clearer and more certain forms. This matter is especially worrying for designers of visitor interpretation because of their awareness that multiple interpretations might lead to controversy, disagreement and dissatisfaction. The temptation is to simplify – to go for an *official* interpretation that fits in with the views of the decision-makers paying for the interpretation project. Such developments are unfortunate because we need to realise that heritage is dissonant by its very nature and that debate and disagreement is healthy for society. Our gold-rush heritage, in particular, needs this edgier and more diverse interpretation.[14]

Complementing the trend towards avoiding conflict is one of sanitising and romanticising the past. Often against historical evidence, interpreters reimagine the past in the light of modern-day concerns. One example illustrates this problem. At

Interpretive panel depicting neighbouring Chinese and European families exchanging produce, Columbia State Historic Park, California.

Photograph by Warwick Frost, 2012

the Columbia State Historic Park in California, an interpretive panel shows two families at work in their gardens (see the illustration above). One is Chinese, the other European. Over a white picket fence, a European woman and a Chinese man exchange produce. In the background, their spouses and children look on. The Chinese family has a vegetable garden, the Europeans do not, but they do have fruit trees and chickens. Accordingly, the exchange suggests the two families are seeking mutual benefits from their different comparative advantages. The picture is an idyllic one, firmly rooted in twenty-first-century ideals of multiculturalism. Was gold-rush Columbia like this? Most likely not. Nearby interpretation tells the visitor that the Chinese were marginalised into a distinct camp on the outskirts of the European township. Historical research into Chinese–European relationships in this period provides a far more complex picture of exchange and dependency than simple over-the-fence bartering.[15] The challenge for interpreters is to incorporate that historical research into their displays for visitors.

Some Case Studies

In order to illustrate some of the challenges and issues in providing interpretation for goldfields visitors, I present the following case studies. To give them order, I've divided them into three categories based on the style (or method) of interpretation provided. In examining these different approaches, my intention is not to present some as better than others, but rather to highlight how the strategic design of interpretation affects the quality of the visitor experience.

Trails

The most common approach is that of trails, with interpretation provided sequentially at various stops. For reasons of cost and logistics, interpretation is commonly provided through a self-guided tour rather than through a face-to-face encounter with a guide. These self-guiding interpretive media include brochures or booklets carried by the visitor and associated numbered markers and information panels along the trail. Recent years have seen a tendency to use new media, such as podcasts downloadable from websites, though in essence this development is a change in delivery format rather than function.[16]

Gold-heritage trails come in two forms. The first links various towns and sites within regions and is designed for visitors to explore by car. An example is the Otago Goldfields Heritage Trail containing 22 sites, in New Zealand.[17] The second is contained within specific sites and caters for walkers. Examples include trails at the Arrowtown Chinese settlement, Bendigo, the Bannockburn sluicings and Stewart Town (Central Otago, New Zealand), and Coloma State Historic Park and the Castlemaine Diggings National Heritage Park (Australia). Interpretation is provided either by numbered markers linked to a guidebook or brochure, or by a series of panels.[18]

Many of these trails wind through the ruins of diggings, a landscape character-ised by 'piles of rocks and holes in the ground' that may be difficult for visitors to comprehend, especially if they compare them to intact or reconstructed mining towns such as Tombstone, Beechworth and Sovereign Hill.[19] In such cases, the challenge for interpretation is to provide answers for what these ruins were and how they related to the larger landscape. The two illustrations below provide contrasting examples of how interpretive panels facilitate understanding of the landscape.

Despite the ubiquity of trails, it is frustrating that the effectiveness of the interpretation they provide is often limited. Spatially, they are designed to follow a linear path through a series of fixed heritage sites, views and points. But this approach restricts

An interpretive panel helps to make sense of ruined stone buildings on a walking trail at Bendigo, Otago.

Photograph by Warwick Frost, 2011

There is no interpretive panel for these ruins at Castlemaine Diggings National Heritage Park, Victoria. The purpose and history of these buildings, each larger than a miner's hut, are unknown.

Photograph by Warwick Frost, 2011

their flexibility; the story each tells must be hammered into the shape of the trail and its immovable features. Narrative structure and the highlighting of important elements are usually lost because the visitor is funnelled along the numbered trackway or circuit. In addition, when designed as a way of providing interpretation within the restraint of limited resources, they are often further compromised by the lack of ongoing funding for maintenance or updating. Markers fall over and are not replaced; brochures and booklets run out.[20] At the time of writing the Otago Goldfields Heritage Trail still utilised interpretative panels from the 1980s Otago Goldfields Park, while the current booklet for the Mount Alexander Diggings in Australia predated the establishment of the national park in 2001.[21] At Columbia State Historic Park, the walking trail through the overgrown alluvial mining area is constructed and promoted as a nature trail.

Living History

Living history is a broad term applied to efforts to interpret the past for a modern audience by simulating historical characters, situations and technology. This approach occurs in a range of contexts. It can be found at outdoor museums, historic buildings and sites, theme parks and at commemorative events. A critical element of living history is re-enactment, wherein people dress in the costume and character of a past period. While such display is often undertaken by paid actors, it is also highly popular with large numbers of enthusiastic amateurs.[22] For these people, interest in immersing themselves in what they may perceive as a better and simpler time could be a reaction to the ills of modernity. Although living history is usually viewed as a recent phenomenon, early manifestations of this approach occurred in nineteenth-century Scandinavia and in the 1920s' development of Colonial Williamsburg in the US state of Virginia.[23]

The exemplar of the living history approach to the gold rushes is Sovereign Hill (Ballarat, Australia). Its aim has been to provide a recreation of the diggings from the period 1851 to 1860. This approach of representing gold-heritage sites and towns at their nineteenth-century peak is commonplace, though it raises the issue of ignoring other periods and the continuance of an enduring community.[24] A highly successful visitor attraction, Sovereign Hill draws in around 500,000 visitors per year. Re-enactments are staged by a core of paid actors and 300 volunteers. Authenticity is highly valued, with no buildings or costumed performances represented unless they can be verified as truly from Ballarat during that period.[25] Accordingly, when the character of a young gypsy girl was introduced, her tearaway hijinks were seen as highly entertaining. However, the role was eventually retired when it became apparent that no such person existed during the gold rushes. Another difficult issue is how best to represent Aboriginal people. They were present on the goldfields, but their society was in disarray. Should the negative results of European settlement be fully represented to visitors?[26]

Sovereign Hill, like many living history projects, receives a great deal of criticism for its interpretation and performances. David Goodman, for example, argues that it diverts serious historical researchers away from the gold rushes, 'for the creation of Sovereign Hill … only confirmed a sense that interest in the gold rush was mostly for

Tourists take photographs with costumed staff at Sovereign Hill, 2012.

Photograph by Lloyd Carpenter, 2012

School groups visiting Sovereign Hill are required to behave in period style, not just wear the costumes.

Photograph by Lloyd Carpenter, 2012

children and tourists'.[27] As with criticism levelled elsewhere, commentators critique Sovereign Hill for too strong an interest in the exact reproduction of clothing and for performers playing their roles for laughs.[28] Certainly, the least satisfying part of the Sovereign Hill production is the comic opera police troopers, suggestive of Blackadder rather than the deeply mistrusted 'Joes' of Eureka. In contrast, Sovereign Hill's performers are at their best with pathos – playing with the realisation that travelling across half the world for gold was not necessarily transformative and reminding us of the risk and edginess of their adventures.[29]

Surprisingly, there is no equivalent of Sovereign Hill in the United States. Despite being known for its living history successes, ranging from Colonial Williamsburg (Virginia) to Old Tucson (Arizona) to various Civil War battlefields, the concept has not really been extended to gold-rush heritage.[30] And yet, as I have found on a number of fieldwork trips to the US, there is widespread knowledge and admiration of Sovereign Hill. The closest venture to the Ballarat enterprise is Columbia State Historic Park in California. Established in 1945, it comprises 33 original buildings in situ within that 1850s gold town. Although managed by California State Parks, that organisation provides neither living history performances nor active interpretation.

The 'Joes!' of the goldfields or Blackadder's police? Sovereign Hill's constabulary, 2012.

Photograph by Lloyd Carpenter, 2012

Tourists are encouraged to 'try their hand' in gravels 'salted with gold dust' each morning. This group was visiting Sovereign Hill in 2014.

Photograph by Lloyd Carpenter

A concessionaire's employee in costume outside the saloon where he works, Columbia State Historic Park, California.

Photograph by Warwick Frost, 2012

Instead, these come from volunteer groups and some of the concessionaires operating businesses within the town. Particularly on weekdays, the result is a quiet and flat experience for visitors. There is little sense of the bustle of activity of a gold town.

Events

Staging events at heritage sites has become an increasingly popular way of providing engaging and immersive interpretation. The advantage of such an approach is logistical. Marketing can be focused on attracting visitors to the time and place for performances, displays and re-enactments. Furthermore, the lure of a golden heritage can be used to sustain community festivals. An example of this is the Go for Gold Chinese Festival in Nundle (New South Wales, Australia).[31] In this section, I will focus on just one event, the annual commemoration of the Monster Meeting at Chewton, near Castlemaine, Australia.

The Monster Meeting occurred on 15 December 1851. Over 10,000 diggers assembled to successfully protest against a decision to double the gold licence fee. Inspired by the British Chartist tradition, the assembly was a monster meeting not so much for its size but because of the miners' idea that they could 'monster' the authorities, that is, be so rowdy in their agitation that officialdom would give in.[32] Today, the local community commemorates the event annually.[33] I attended the 2010 event, which was co-incidentally filmed by British documentary-maker Tony Robinson.[34] There were two components. The first was a march from the Chewton pub to the original site of the meeting. The second was a re-enactment, in which costumed volunteers delivered the speeches made in 1851. Each performer started by introducing themselves and stating their connection to modern-day Chewton. They then entered into their character and spoke as them. Interspersed with the verbatim historical speeches were musical performances.

It's intriguing that the re-enactment takes place within the Castlemaine Diggings National Park. In the United States, commemorative re-enactments involving conflict are usually banned from National Park Service land. These include re-enactments of the Battles of Gettysburg and Little Bighorn, which instead take place on private property. Such a ban is partly due to possible physical damage from the large numbers of

The re-enactment of the 1851 Monster Meeting at Castlemaine Diggings National Heritage Park combines costumed locals delivering the historical speeches, interspersed with musical performances.

Photograph by Jennifer Laing, 2011

people participating and watching, and partly due to avoidance of controversy.[35] In the Monster Meeting case there is no such problem, as national park staff are enthusiastic supporters. Nor is there much dissonance; we are all on the side of the miners. There is only mild amusement that Governor Charles La Trobe, usually portrayed as liberal and moderate, is here the villain of the piece.

Where the Monster Meeting engages visitors is in allowing them to participate. No one is just a spectator. Everyone is encouraged to march, and no costume is required. As the procession unfolds, communal singing, chanting and flag-waving create a sense of communitas. At the protest site, visitors are part of the crowd, cheering and jeering in response to cues from the performers. This is not a pantomime; participants are engaged in a protest (and, I suspect, easily able to see parallels to modern protests and issues). As Terry Wallace outlines in his work, two groups are at play. The minority are costumed re-enactors, reading from the historical script. The majority are dresser-ups, without a script, but still playing their roles.[36] Most importantly, this anarchic performance allows us a peek into the political life and aspirations of the goldfields.

However, dissonance can certainly be a factor in gold-rush commemorative events. The most noted are concerned with the Eureka Stockade (Ballarat, Australia). In recent years, different groups have been highly outspoken in demanding greater recognition for their views and a consequent rejection of others.[37] While this development is of concern to organisers and stakeholders, it can also be viewed as healthy debate over the contested meanings of this conflict.

Principles of Interpretation for Gold-rush Heritage

Fifty years on, Freeman Tilden's six principles of interpretation still apply, although their use tends to be a bit haphazard. Unfortunately, while Tilden is widely known, many decision-makers and heritage practitioners have only heard his message second hand; very few have actually read him. As we look forward to how we will interpret and conserve gold-rush heritage in the future, it's important that we resolve to re-engage with Tilden and his wisdom.

Tilden's principles are intended to be generally applicable to both natural and cultural heritage. In concluding this chapter, I want to take the opportunity to propose some further principles – ones that complement and extend Tilden but are specific to gold-rush heritage and visitors. The overview of sites in Australia, New Zealand and the United States provided in this chapter demonstrates a lack of evenness in interpretation. Some things work and some do not. To continue successfully engaging with visitors, we need to be strategic in planning how we best do that. We already have too many gold-rush sites that are sterile and uninteresting and consequently little visited and with limited public support for conservation. Challenging and evocative interpretation is needed to engage visitors and turn them into supporters of gold-rush heritage initiatives. My six principles therefore are:

1. Interpretation should be based on stories of *people*. Machinery and technical aspects do appeal to some visitors, but not enough that they should be central to interpretation.
2. In line with Tilden's idea of provocation, interpretation should be surprising or challenging. Visitors need a sense of new ideas or perspectives that make them see different ways of viewing stories they might have thought they already knew.
3. The gold rushes were a global phenomenon, with major impacts on the world's economy and movements of people. That sense of a major event needs to be communicated.
4. Care needs to be taken in overlaying modern concerns. Relevance is important, but we still need to convey that the past is different from the present.
5. The message is more important than the method or form of interpretation. New technology still needs to be engaging and – very importantly – needs to be maintained.
6. Immersion through commemorative events and re-enactments is a powerful way of engaging with visitors. Such special events are an effective way of using limited resources.

19.

Central Otago Goldfields Archaeology

Neville Ritchie

THE CENTRAL OTAGO GOLD rushes have been celebrated in word, song and imagery and are recognised as integral to the historic landscape of Central Otago.[1] In many places, goldfield relics are the dominant visual component, from old dwellings and settlements to the infrastructure of mine-water reticulation and management in the form of water races and dams, or work sites associated with alluvial and hard-rock mining. Although the goldfield relics are not generally regarded as 'archaeology', they are certainly evidence of past events and practices.

While individual towns and places in Central Otago had connections to and identified with nearby goldfield sites, it was the advent of the Otago Goldfields Park that saw the first systematic approach to recording and evaluating goldfield sites. Unlike the extant national parks in New Zealand, the Otago Goldfields Park began as a concept. With no reserves or Crown land to form the nucleus of a park, the starting point was simply an idea. That idea was to create a complex of scattered historic reserves throughout Central Otago, despite acknowledgement that this task would be complicated by the need to incorporate some key sites on privately owned land into the proposed park's structure.[2]

In 1971 the then director of National Parks and Reserves, Mr P.H.C. (Bing) Lucas, produced a paper outlining the broad purpose of the park.[3] It was 'to serve as a prime visitor attraction while preserving as a permanent cultural asset a cross section of the history of the goldrush era of a century ago'.[4] Bing Lucas also envisaged that the park would embrace sites of gold discoveries, techniques of gold winning, one or two deserted mining towns, parts of existing goldfields towns, and mining trails linking sites. Lucas's paper provided a thematic basis for site selection through the adoption of 'goldfield themes' – discovery, access methods, social life and major events.[5]

After consultation involving the New Zealand Historic Places Trust and territorial local authorities as well as considerable publicity, support for the concept was sufficiently robust to convince the minister of lands to approve the park's establishment, which he did in 1973. From the outset, those involved in the project realised that the single conceptual entity of 'park' could only exist if its widely scattered components were linked historically and thematically. To this end, the nascent park employed a ranger, Tony Perrett, to investigate, record and evaluate some 350 locations that came, to varying degrees, within the terms of the park concept.

Five main criteria were used to provide a basis for site evaluation: historical significance, physical evidence remaining, visual setting, vulnerability to deterioration, and interpretation opportunities. Perrett, with the support of an advisory committee, scored each site against a five-point scale, but as work progressed, Perrett and his advisors found it necessary to refine the system, by changing the emphasis away from the initial gold rushes of the 1860s to the later mining era (1870–1914), given that most of the remaining relics and mining landscapes of Central Otago are from that latter era.

Eventually, the team devised the following system of categories to embrace the full span of goldfields sites from 1861.[6]

Theme	Sub-theme
1. Discovery	Pre-rush, rushes
2. Communications	Trails, accommodation, river crossings, supplies, shipping
3. Mining Techniques	(a) Alluvial mining – paddocking, ground sluicing, hydraulic sluicing, hydraulic elevation dredging, diversions, dams, water races (b) Quartz mining – excavation, ore transportation, milling, motive power, gold recovery
4. Lifestyle	Settlement, dwellings, cemeteries, notable events, monuments

This method determined rankings for each site, which in turn created priorities for inclusion in the park. Ten areas were recommended for immediate inclusion, another 20 were seen as a secondary priority, and 20 further sites were deferred indefinitely. By April 1983, 22 sites and historic areas (more or less the present number) had been incorporated into the park. The inclusion of Cromwell's 'Chinatown' was always going to be short-lived because it would eventually be inundated by the waters of the Lake Dunstan hydro reservoir, but it proved the catalyst for including the Arrowtown Chinese settlement in the park.

The process of trying to capture the Central Otago gold rushes in a few key sites cannot be equated with archaeology per se. This is because archaeology is a process of 'pattern recognition' gained from the detailed recording and study of structures, features and information inherent in archaeological deposits and manmade landforms that allow us to determine the time and disposition of human activities. Goldfields archaeology is a specialised aspect of historical archaeology, and it has a long history in New Zealand.[7] It is somewhat ironic that the beginning of goldfields archaeology in Central Otago was a positive spin-off from the controversial Clutha Valley 'Clyde Dam' hydro-electric power project, which commenced in 1975.

As a result of the then recently passed Historic Places Amendment Act 1975, the Ministry of Works, on behalf of the New Zealand Electricity Department, was obliged to commission archaeological surveys of the Cromwell Gorge area, which would be flooded upon completion of the dam. During the summer of 1975/76, the University of Otago's Professor Charles Higham and Graeme Mason along with students from the university's Anthropology Department completed a number of surveys.[8] In 1977 Mary Newman conducted a further survey along the route of the new gorge highway.[9] These surveys revealed that the proposed dam would affect over 150 (mainly gold-mining) sites in the Cromwell Gorge.

Although the Anthropology Department would have been well placed to run an archaeological mitigation project, its academic interests at the time focused more on pre-European sites in New Zealand and other projects in South-East Asia and Oceania, so it passed on the opportunity to complete further work in and around Cromwell. Instead, Professor Higham persuaded the newly formed New Zealand Historic Places Trust that the best way to mitigate the impact of the dam on archaeological resources was to appoint an archaeologist to lead an archaeological and historic research project centred on the areas affected by the dam, that is, the Cromwell Gorge, the Kawarau Gorge and the Upper Clutha Valley near Luggate. After engaging in discussions in 1976/77, the Historic Places Trust and the Ministry of Works and Development reached agreement on the way forward. The agreement had two main features:

1. The Ministry of Works and Development and the New Zealand Electricity Department would fund a structured five-year archaeological and historic research project.
2. The project, to be known as the Clutha Valley Archaeological Project, would be conducted under the direction of a resident archaeologist seconded to the Ministry of Works and Development centre at Cromwell but employed and overseen by the New Zealand Historic Places Trust.

The agreement between the ministry and the trust was notable from an archaeological perspective, in that it was the first attributable to the Historic Places Amendment Act 1975. Without the legislation, there would have been little or no funding for archaeological mitigation work and few resources to ensure it was recorded properly. Legislation does not automatically protect sites, but the advent of the act lessened destructive impacts. By securing funding for mitigation work, the act also ensured some discouragement of and compensation for the physical loss of sites. By mid-1977, negotiations between the Historic Places Trust and the Ministry of Works and Development had been concluded and a project archaeologist employed, initially for a term of five years. The archaeological project officially commenced in December 1977 with my arrival in Cromwell, where I remained as the project archaeologist until the project's termination in June 1987.

The Clutha Valley Archaeological Project provided the wherewithal to maintain an effective archaeological presence in Central Otago for a decade (the original five-year

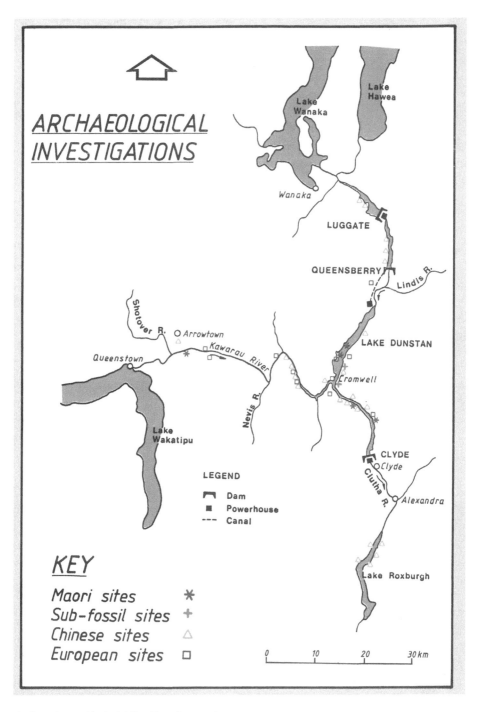

Archaeology: Clutha Valley Development.

Source: Cromwell: Electricity Division, Ministry of Energy, New Zealand Historic Places Trust, and Ministry of Works and Development, n. d.

project was extended to 10 years after significant finds and to allow sufficient time to complete reports). The decade-long duration of the project has yet to be exceeded by any other archaeological project in New Zealand, and with a total cost of about $100,000 per annum at the project's conclusion in 1987, it set new records for longevity and for expenditure on archaeological mitigation.

A Chronological Summary

Because of the general lack of knowledge at project inception about the sites in the area (most known ones were associated with mining), my job was initially defined loosely in terms of research objectives, but these gradually crystallised as the ground surveys that I and other team members conducted progressed. The immediate objective was to carry out systematic surveys of the entire Upper Clutha Valley and its tributaries. This aim possibly created an important precedent, in that there was informal agreement that the whole valley, from the floor to the mountain tops, would be surveyed (i.e. beyond the extent of the proposed reservoirs), so that the real impact of the losses caused by the hydro projects could be assessed. My presence as a fulltime Historic Places Trust archaeologist based in Cromwell also enabled participation in tangential projects in Fiordland, the Mount Aspiring and Aoraki Mount Cook National Parks, and the Waitaki Valley.

Initial fieldwork priorities were governed by the Ministry of Work and Development's need to gain resource consents for the construction of the Clyde Dam, so the first project work centred on the Cromwell Gorge and Lowburn areas. In the summer of 1978 I conducted an extensive test-pitting programme, the primary focus of which was on the 44 recorded rock shelters in the gorge. This work led to identification of two broad site-types for further investigation and research. These were the sites associated with the activities of the Chinese miners, and the few sites identified as pertaining to Māori before the arrival of Europeans.

By the end of 1979 I had investigated seven of the rock shelters. Two of these were pre-European Māori,[10] and five were used by Chinese miners between 1866 and 1890.[11] I also completed major surveys in the Kawarau Gorge,[12] the Upper Clutha Valley around Luggate[13] and in the Shotover valley, the latter completed at the behest of the Ministry of Works and Development as part of their work investigating possible silt-retention schemes for the valley.

Cromwell's Chinese camp, known locally as Chinatown, was targeted for excavation in the summer of 1980.[14] This excavation attracted the attention of both the New Zealand public and overseas researchers to the archaeological project. Interest was particularly evident among people in the United States where, in the early 1980s, the history and archaeology associated with that nation's many Asian migrant groups was gaining traction. Before I and my team got underway with the Cromwell Chinatown part of the project, our archaeological excavations had been relatively small, and while they were informative, they had not provided a large volume of material to work on. Chinatown changed that and had a major influence on the direction of the project for the next few years.

Cromwell Gorge rock shelter (now under Lake Dunstan).

Photograph by Neville Ritchie, 1984, courtesy Department of Conservation

After we had finished the Chinatown excavation, A.P. Harrison conducted a survey of the Roxburgh Gorge,[15] and it went some way towards redressing what had become a sorry situation. The formation of Lake Roxburgh after completion of the Roxburgh hydro dam in 1956 had not been prefaced with an archaeological survey or investigation of any sort, despite the fact that the gorge was an important mining area, had probably been the site of pre-European Māori moa hunting and had likely provided Māori with a route into the interior.

The situation is understandable when considered in historical perspective: the New Zealand Archaeological Association had been created only the year before, and even its members, like the rest of the population, probably knew little about the resources of the old gorge or its location, so there was little effort to record or salvage anything before it was lost, although two historic burials were relocated. Harrison's Roxburgh survey recorded about 150 sites, including 87 rock shelters with occupation material. Corresponding surveys in the Cromwell Gorge and the Kawarau Gorge found 44 and 25 such shelters respectively. The surviving sites in the Roxburgh Gorge represent less than half the number existing before the gorge's inundation by the hydro lake.

During 1980 I conducted survey work in the area affected by the Queensberry–Luggate

Chinatown, Cromwell (now under Lake Dunstan), looking west (top) and east (bottom).

Both photos courtesy Department of Conservation

low-dam proposal,[16] while Chris Jacomb and Sheridan Easdale completed a tangential survey of the Bendigo goldfield.[17] Associated surveys were also conducted, which in some cases yielded surprising results. In mid-1980, during survey work on the Slip Stream nephrite deposit, completed in conjunction with the Southland Museum and Mount Aspiring National Park, we found a nearly complete *Dinornis* moa skeleton in a rock shelter in the Dart Valley. Athol Anderson and I excavated the site a month later; the skeleton is now on display in the National Park Visitor Centre at Glenorchy.[18]

The summer of 1980/81 was devoted to excavations on the threatened pre-European Māori sites.[19] The largest of these was at Owens Ferry, which we located after a bottle collector brought in a bag of pieces of coloured rock for identification. The rock fragments proved to be flakes of silcrete and porcellanite, and the bag also contained bits of moa bone that bore clear cut marks. We located the eroding source of this material between Chard Road and the Kawarau River, and the ensuing excavation proved that the site had been a medium-sized moa-hunting camp.

The other pre-European Māori sites included Rockfall Shelter II in the Cromwell Gorge and two oven complexes at Park Burn and Tinwald Burn on the Clutha River bank above Lowburn.[20] Rockfall Shelter II contained sparse remains of a butchered

Recording in the Roxburgh Gorge, site G42/114, on the true left bank of the lake near Butchers Point.

Source: 'Archaeological baseline survey and management plan of the Clutha River Mata-au', report prepared for The New Zealand Historic Places Trust by Southern Pacific Archaeological Research, Department of Anthropology, University of Otago, Dunedin, p. 18.

moa, silcrete and porcellanite flakes, chips of green argillite adzes, and a shallow oven pit. The Park Burn site consisted of four virtually undisturbed oven pits (another eight had been destroyed by ploughing), and it furnished radiocarbon dates of 1500AD. Unfortunately, no artefacts or middens were uncovered during the Park Burn ovens excavation, and likewise the excavation of the single-oven Tinwald Burn site, so we were unable to positively ascertain the role of the sites. Because both oven complexes are sited beside backwaters of the Clutha River, they were probably associated with eeling or duck-catching.[21]

In addition to the pre-European Māori sites, we uncovered and excavated two substantial sub-fossil deposits at Firewood Creek and at the nearby Cromwell railway station during the construction of the new Cromwell Gorge highway. These sites, which predate human occupation in the area, contained the remains of moa, tuatara and several extinct bird species, including the giant South Island flightless goose (*Cnemiornis calcitrans*), the laughing owl, Finsch's duck and locally extinct species such as kiwi and weka.[22]

Excavations during the summer of 1981/82 centred on four Chinese hut and shelter sites in the upper Clutha, selected after assessment of the Luggate and Queensberry survey data.[23] These surveys enabled us to establish a descriptive terminology for tailing sites, which in turn enabled their recording in a more meaningful way the terminology-facilitated comparison of key features.[24]

Investigating, surveying and recording Rockfall Shelter II in the Cromwell Gorge. The site was initially occupied by moa hunters, later by Chinese miners and later still by rabbiters.

Photograph by Neville Ritchie

Five off-project jobs were also undertaken in this period, one of which was an eleventh-hour survey of the Ruataniwha depression, completed less than a month before Lake Ruataniwha, part of the Upper Waitaki power scheme, was created. Our presence in the Waitaki Valley also allowed us to carry out an inundation-effect study of partially submerged sites around Lake Waitaki and to work briefly on Barry Fankhauser's oven excavations in South Canterbury.[25] After completing this work, we did surveys for the Lands and Survey Department of two Lake Wakatipu sites: the Bobs Cove lime kilns and the Twelve-Mile Creek catchment.[26]

The summer of 1981/82 concluded with a rescue excavation at the Dart Bridge site near Glenorchy,[27] undertaken because of continuing erosion of the site by the Dart River. Our final field work for the season involved a survey of the Carrick goldfield, during which we recorded about 100 sites, including remnants of the nineteenth-century reef-mining operations.

The following year, 1982/83, saw further historic site excavations in the upper Clutha and Kawarau Gorges, including the Hanging Rock and Riverside Chinese shelters and a forge site. We excavated the latter two principally to provide the Otago Goldfields Park with the information it needed for interpretative purposes. We also removed a historic European burial (an unknown miner) from the route of the new Cromwell Gorge highway. By the end of 1982 the major surveys and associated reports were finished, and analysis of excavated materials and writing up of findings could begin in earnest. During the year, Simon Holdaway and Debbie Foster, working under the direction of the Historic Places Trust's Cromwell office, completed a major survey of the areas affected by the Lower Clutha hydro proposals.[28]

From the initiation of the Clutha Valley Archaeological Project, our team maintained a close working relationship with the Otago Goldfields Park administered by Department of Lands and Survey (forerunner to the Department of Conservation) staff. After the Cromwell Chinatown excavation, the department had somewhat reluctantly accepted responsibility for managing and maintaining the Chinatown site. It was understandably reluctant to spend money and energy on a site that would shortly be inundated. However, the site proved to be by far the most frequently visited site in the park, even more so after one of the huts was restored.

By early 1983 the Goldfields Park team required little convincing that the park needed a replacement for Chinatown. As most of the former Chinese settlements in Central Otago had been destroyed, the Arrowtown Chinese settlement was the obvious choice. Although the settlement was smaller than the one at Cromwell, it had two significant advantages – a standing Chinese store and easy access for foot traffic.

The funds the Department of Lands and Survey provided made excavation of the Arrowtown Chinese settlement and store the major project for the summer of 1983/84.[29] As well as the work on the Arrowtown project, excavations continued at other historic sites, including the Ledge (a European house) and the Rapids, a Chinese miners' campsite in the Kawarau Gorge. For me, off-project fieldwork included assisting Atholl Anderson and Lyn Williams with the Lee Island (Lake Te Anau) excavation, working on an assessment excavation at Ackers Cottage on Stewart

Excavation of miners' huts in the Queensberry–Luggate area, Upper Clutha River, 1981/82.

Photograph by Neville Ritchie

Island[30] and collaborating with Russell Beck and Karl Gillies (Southland Museum) and Brian Ahern (Mount Aspiring National Park) to complete a site survey of Lake Wakatipu's Pig and Pigeon Islands.

In 1984 additional off-project work included excavations on the site of a newly discovered moa-hunter site at Coal Creek near the Roxburgh hydro project[31] and at the sites of the first Hermitage and Ball huts in Mount Cook National Park.[32] Meanwhile, Stuart Bedford directed a major investigation specified within the Clutha Valley Archaeological Project brief and based on the site of the Halfway House Hotel in the Cromwell Gorge.[33]

In 1985 our work commenced with excavations at the Phoenix Quartz Mining Company's dynamo site in Skippers Creek, up the Shotover valley, a prelude to reconstruction on the site a year later.[34] The site is nationally significant because the first major industrial use of hydro-electricity in New Zealand occurred at this remote location. This work was followed by excavations of four further Chinese sites – the Platform and Flax Grove shelters in the Kawarau Gorge, the Willows hut site in the Upper Clutha and the horticultural terraces associated with Cromwell's Chinatown. The Flax Grove excavation remains especially notable for the number of paper artefacts recovered.[35]

We also endeavoured at this time to remove the remains of one of the old gold dredges from the Kawarau River so that a dredging interpretation display could

Restoration of Ah Lum's Store, Arrowtown Chinese Village, 1983/84.

Photograph by Neville Ritchie, Department of Conservation

be established on the Otago Goldfields Park. Despite having two extremely large bulldozers, a diver, a jet boat and backhoe, and skilled operators on each, several steel cables snapped and we could not budge the major components. We decided that the river could retain its treasure for now. Efforts to recover from the depths of the Kawarau Gorge one set of the huge turbines and pumps from the old Ripponvale irrigation-scheme pump house was more successful. Although the pump house would be flooded, the Otago Goldfields Park team re-erected the pumps in a static display on what would be the future shoreline upstream of the old pump-house site.

About mid-1985 we began the first of a series of test excavations on former business sites in the old main street of Cromwell. This work took place at the same time the sites were being cleared of structures prior to the hydro lake being filled. The 'downtown' Cromwell excavations continued intermittently into the summer of 1986/87. Only four sites proved particularly productive: the Bridge Hotel site (the first hotel in Cromwell, dating from 1862, where we uncovered a bottle dump), the sites of the adjoining White Hart and Commercial Junction hotels, and areas behind the former store sites associated with Cromwell's Chinatown.

With the end of the Clutha Valley Archaeological Project in sight, we conducted only one small investigation, on a Chinese hut at Horseshoe Bend, Upper Clutha, during the summer of 1986, although test excavations continued in downtown Cromwell as the Ministry of Works and Development cleared individual building sites. Horseshoe Bend was the twenty-third Chinese site to be excavated as part of the project, but we tested another 40 to some degree. During 1987 Alexy Simmons completed photographic, structural and historical documentation of the old Cromwell Bridge.[36]

Material Culture Studies

The chronological summary of the fieldwork reflects the nature and diversity of the Clutha archaeological project. However, from the outset, the intention was to achieve considerably more than just documentation of the affected sites, rescue excavations and completion of the associated reports. The duration of the project and the presence of a fulltime archaeologist with a fulltime assistant enabled much more in-depth research on the main artefact categories (glass and tin containers and European and Chinese ceramic containers and domestic wares) than had previously been possible on any project in New Zealand. The detailed studies of various artefact types broke new ground in historic archaeology in New Zealand, particularly with regard to dating tin matchboxes[37] and analysing the glass and tin containers[38] along with the wide range of European and Chinese artefacts we found in the Central Otago sites.[39] In addition to completing these specific studies, we were able to thoroughly document the artefacts from several major site assemblages, with the aim, in part, of providing baseline data for future studies.

Excavation of the Chinese Village at Arrowtown, 1982.

Photograph by Neville Ritchie, Department of Conservation

Site Management

The duration of the project enabled much greater emphasis on long-term site management in the area through the establishment of a productive working relationship with the Otago Goldfields Park team and direct liaison with government agencies such as Lands and Survey, Mines Department, Ministry of Works and Development, the New Zealand Electricity Department and, more distantly, with Fiordland, Mount Aspiring and Mount Cook National Parks. Together, our team produced a good number of papers on various aspects of site management, encompassing reservoir archaeology, goldfields, and public lands.[40]

Public Relations

Before I was stationed as the resident archaeologist in Cromwell, the surrounding region was an 'archaeological vacuum' because of the lack of a major museum or recognised archaeologists whom people could contact in the area. Some people did get in touch with Otago Museum, but for most interested parties the museum was too far away. The establishment of a regional archaeological facility undoubtedly resulted in a greater awareness of matters historic in the area, particularly archaeological resources. This heightened awareness came about simply because the Historic Places Trust agreed to base an archaeologist in Central Otago who was therefore in a position to talk to people directly about sites of potential archaeological interest on their properties.

Information, Reports and Publications

My team and I disseminated the information we derived from the archaeological investigations and surveys in three main ways (and please note that many of these documents are now available online):

- *Scientific papers* (mainly excavation reports and material culture studies), which we published in established archaeological journals.
- *Managerial/advisory papers, including survey reports and papers on specific aspects of site management.* These were produced and released by the Cromwell office of the Historic Places Trust. Some were initially presented as conference papers. We also produced for our client agencies (New Zealand Electricity Department and the Ministry of Works and Development) survey reports outlining the nature, distribution and likely impact on the sites in each area. All of these reports serve as a permanent record of the sites in the Upper Clutha and should be useful long-term management tools, as do the records of all sites that we entered into the national site-recording scheme maintained by the New Zealand Archaeological Association. We furthermore sent copies of all survey reports detailing the sites likely to be affected by the dam proposals to the Ministry of Works and Development head office in Wellington for inclusion in their library.
- *Public relations activities*, most notably public talks and field trips. The most popular (with the public) of the publications we produced was a free booklet

on the Clutha Archaeological project.[41] We made sure copies of all our reports were deposited in the local public libraries, as well as the Ministry of Works and Development library in Cromwell and the Hocken Library in Dunedin. The Historic Places Trust also housed copies of every publication. Other public relations activities included talks, field trips and laboratory tours. We furthermore set up displays, complete with handout materials, in the Ministry of Works and Development Clyde Dam Information Centre and the Cromwell and Lakes District (Arrowtown) museums. The project's addition of around 2000 sites to the national site-recording scheme and our systematic survey of nearly every farm in the Upper Clutha also brought widespread attention to our work and its outcomes.

Post-Project

The Clutha Valley Archaeological Project was a major catalyst for 'goldfields archaeology' in Central Otago, and throughout its duration saw material assistance from many individuals and agencies. Listing everyone who provided information or services would be a formidable task, so all that is possible here is to acknowledge their work. Many students assisted with the surveys, excavations, lab work and compilation of reports and site records. Over 150 worked on the project, some several times. Without their efforts and camaraderie, much less would have been achieved. Institutional support was provided by the Ministry of Works and Development, especially Cromwell-based staff, the New Zealand Historic Places Trust and the Otago Goldfields Park. A good working relationship with the staff of these organisations helped ensure that the archaeological project was productive and effective.

Since the project's completion in 1986 and my departure from the area, other researchers have taken up the baton, most notably Dr Jill Hamel and Dr Peter Petchey, both of whom have made major contributions, including writing many significant publications. Jill Hamel's work began with a series of site surveys undertaken as part of the government's tenure review of high-country station leases. Between 1985 and 1999 she completed at least 28 surveys and associated reports on large pastoral runs as part of their tenure reviews. The runs included significant Central Otago mining areas, among them Naseby, Old Man Range, Upper Pomahaka, Nokomai and the Upper Nevis, Morven Hills, Lindis Valley, Lauder, Cambrians, the Gowburn, Whitcombe and Upper Waikaia, Macraes, Criffel, Roaring Meg, Cardrona Valley, Serpentine, Doctors Point, Roxburgh Gorge, Bendigo, Earnscleugh, the Lammermoors and the Shotover River.[42]

Peter Petchey has been no less productive. Since 1994 he has produced at least 16 reports for the Macraes mine and completed reports on the Serpentine water wheel and battery, the Mount Aurum Recreation Reserve (including Bullendale and the first power-station site), water wheels in Otago, a survey of Macetown and the Arrow River, Bannockburn, the Round Hill goldfield, the Longwood mining water races and the Port Pegasus tin mines. His doctoral thesis involved a detailed analysis of historic mining battery sites in New Zealand.[43] Other major surveys include Brian

Sorting, analysing and recording the materials found at the various sites.

Photograph by Neville Ritchie, Department of Conservation

Vincent's investigations in Gabriel's Gully and Waipori[44] and Sheridan Easdale and Chris Jacomb's studies in the Lindis Pass and Nenthorn areas.

Another significant goldfields-related project has been the purchase and planned development of the Lawrence Chinese Camp. To date, the University of Otago's Department of Anthropology has completed three seasons of excavations, and the project remains ongoing.[45] Aerial photography of Central Otago gold-mining sites (and other historic sites across the country) by Kevin Jones has made another very useful contribution to the record of historic mining sites in Central Otago. For nearly two decades, Kevin has photographed New Zealand archaeological sites from the air, work that led to publication of his book *Nga Tohuwhenua mai Te Rangi: A New Zealand archaeology in aerial photographs*. The book includes a chapter on gold-mining sites in Central Otago.[46]

The Clutha Valley Archaeological Project's combined field work over three decades and the associated research and ensuing reports from each undertaking have resulted in a substantive record of the field remains of historic goldmining in Otago and Southland. The project allowed identification of the most significant historic places and a much better understanding of the operation, extent and diversity of gold-mining systems throughout the region. It is very unlikely that such a comprehensive archaeological survey of a region will ever again be completed in New Zealand, but opportunities remain to do further detailed studies of land parcels incorporating historic mining sites.

20.

Thatcher, Vitelli and Small

A play by Fiona Farrell
with music compiled by Robert Hoskins

CHARLES THATCHER, 'THE INIMITABLE THATCHER' (1830–1878), played the flute in London music hall bands before emigrating to Australia and the Victorian diggings. As an entertainer he became a colonial legend, documenting goldfields life by singing topical songs set to well-known tunes. After his marriage in 1861 to Annie Vitelli ('Madame Vitelli'), a young widow supporting herself by singing, Thatcher followed the rush to Otago. The couple embarked on three tours of New Zealand over the next decade accompanied by Joe Small, a sidekick entertainer whose specialty was woebegone songs that made people laugh. In the late 1860s Thatcher continued to mine his experiences with a retrospective diorama titled 'Life on the Goldfields'. He returned to England in 1870 to set up as a curio dealer. Thatcher travelled extensively to import items but died in Shanghai on 17 September 1878 during a cholera epidemic.

This play, based on Robert Hoskins' *Goldfield Balladeer*,[1] was first performed in 1989 at Massey University, with Paul Lyons (baritone), Valerie Wycoff (soprano) and Bruce Sinclair (tenor). Thatcher, the renowned balladeer, entrepreneur and capital-ist-adventurer, having contracted cholera while on a curio-collecting expedition in China, recalls glimpses of his career as he lies, feverish, in a hotel bedroom.

Thatcher, Vitelli and Small

(Darkness. Fade up slide collage – Central Otago/Shanghai 1870s – to a tin whistle rendering of the tune 'The Pirate King', which Thatcher used for his song 'Look Out Below!'. The performers enter, Small DR, Thatcher UC by the gong and Vitelli DL. As the tune fades to a close, Thatcher strikes the gong and erupts full volume DC into the 'performance area'.)

Thatcher: LADIES AND GENTLEMEN! Diggers and dignitaries, troopers and tradesmen, magistrates, ministers, grogsellers and grocers, bargirls and barbarians of all nations! You, the providers of provender! You, the protectors of privilege and the prominent possessors of property! You, particular and pious professors of parochial

Look out below!
(The Pirate King)

Wistfully

A young man left_ his na-tive shores, For trade was bad at home; To seek_his for-tune in this land, He crossed the bri_ny foam. And when_ he got to the Ar-row, It put_ him in a glow; To hear the sound of the windlass, And the cry, "Look out_ be-low!"_

Camp life at Drury
(King of the Cannibal Islands)

Spirited

The war draws its slow length a-long And I___don't think that I'll do wrong If I tell you now in a song, of the vo-lun-teers at Dru-ry. These Auck-land Rif-les had to tramp out there and live in a wret-ched camp, A prey to dy-sen-try and cramp, And ly-ing on blan-kets mud-dy and damp; Ris-ing as soon as the day did dawn, Pa-rades at five o'-clock in the morn, And all com-plaints re-gar-ded with scorn, And that's camp life_ at Dru-ry!

Chorus

Tak-ing coves for sol-diers is a shame On me I hope_they've got no claim, But I'll ex-pose the lit-tle game of camp_ life out_ at Dru-ry!

Presbyterianism! You, persuasive politicians! You, the peregrinating pursuivants of plenty with your pans, your packs and your pickaxes and your attendant publicans, prostitutes, pugilists and preachers! You, who are poor, and you, the pompous, petty potentates of this purloined paradise, pray: Pause!

For tonight, we present for your delight and edification

(Lights up on each as they are introduced.)

that superlative southern songbird: Madame Annie Vitelli!

(Vitelli trills spectacularly.)

The Irish Comic Delineator: Mr Joseph Small!

(Small tootles a few bars from a jig.)

And New Zealand's satirical songster, the inimitable Charles Robert Thatcher himself

(He bows.)

in their renowned dioramic production: LIFE ON THE GOLDFIELDS!

An explosion of colour, light and movement. Vitelli moves UC waving a tambourine, Small blows a fanfare on his tin whistle and plays percussion during the song – horseshoe, spoons, frying pan, whatever comes to hand, while Thatcher moves SL to the bass drum. Because the Victorian diorama combined projections and song, slides and lights should be exploited to the full, and the music should be cheerful and rowdy, full of confidence.

SONG: TO THE WEST

Thatcher, Vitelli, Small:
To the West, to the West, where the diggers repair,
There're no flies about it, the gold is all there;
And chaps who've been digging a very short while
Walk into the bank and dispose of their pile.
Where the rain falls in torrents and leaves such a flood,
That you sleep on the ground and your mattress is mud;
Where a fresh in the river may come down some day,
And very near wash Hokitika away!

To the West, to the West, where the ships run ashore,
Of wrecks we have witnessed two dozen or more;
Where bush rangers congregate, as you've been told.
And simple bank clerks are deprived of their gold.
Where beef's eighteen pence and where diggers devour
Rusty bacon and bread made of vile damaged flour.
How pleasant to be here and get a nice rest,
'Stead of knocking it out in the land of the West!

(Thatcher beats a soft rhythmic roll on the bass drum while Vitelli speaks.)

Vitelli: Listen: we are at the mid-point in this, the most glorious of centuries, and across continents and oceans you can hear it: the stirring, the murmur of a million men gathering together pannikin, pick and shovel; of a million women putting aside the implements of domestic life for the rough accoutrements of a calico tent on a distant hill. For the cry on every lip is RUSH HO! And the glint in every eye is GOLD!

Small: And from the four corners of the globe they come: to Ballarat and Bendigo, Tuapeka, Hokitika, Coromandel, Kapanga, Skippers Reach and Māori Gully, Arthurs Point and the Arrow!

(Song builds once more.)
To the West! To the West! Where the diggers repair.
There're no flies about it, the gold is all there;
And chaps who've been digging a very short while
Walk into the bank and dispose of their pile.
Where the rain falls in torrents and leaves such a flood
That you sleep on the ground and your mattress is mud;
Where a fresh in the river may come down some day
And very near wash Hokitika away!

(Thatcher and Small continue with the performance, miming each 'character' as he is introduced and giving it all the excitement and energy they've got. The effect should be exaggerated, highly coloured. Vitelli meanwhile has moved to the rear to her dressing room and is preparing for another performance entirely, pinning up her hair, tying on her bonnet, flustered that time is running out. She attempts from time to time to catch Thatcher's attention but the two men are caught up in the diorama.)

Thatcher: The excitement has spread to all classes! Lawyers are special pleaders with their wives to be allowed to go; doctors are eager to trade scalpel for shovel and …

Vitelli: Thatcher!

Thatcher: … an undertaker breaks up his stock of coffins and turns them into cradles. Gold cradles.

Small: And on the way to the diggings you can meet them all! Here's the man from Tipperary with his wardrobe in his handkerchief, whistling 'Erin Go Braugh' and twirling his handy bit of schtick!

Thatcher: Here, the Englishman, fancying his country the proudest in creation, steps it out …

Small: And here, the heathen Chinee …

Thatcher: The American, proud son of liberty …

Vitelli: Thatcher!

Small: The grave and taciturn Scot …

(If Small can manage bagpipes, use them here.)

Thatcher: The new chum, with his clean boots, bun hat and sandwich box, and at his heels …

Vitelli *(over)*: Thatcher! The man's not taking a blind bit of notice.

Thatcher: … the old digger who came into town last month to spend his pile, married within the week and is off again already to try his luck. Here …

Vitelli *(ready now, hair done and in costume)*: Thatcher!

Thatcher: Here the …

Vitelli *(insistent)*: Thatcher! Are you ready?

Thatcher *(notices at last)*: What?

Vitelli: They're waiting. Are you ready yet?

Thatcher *(moves into his 'dressing room', finds his watch on the table, is flustered and a little confused)*: Good Lord. Is it that time already? Do we have a good house?

Vitelli *(makes the final adjustments to her costume, takes one last look in the mirror and comes down stage to join Thatcher)*: Packed to the rafters and keen for curtain up!

(Lights up on Thatcher's dressing room. He slumps in the chair, slightly and pleasantly drunk. Joe Small gets dressed and made up – heavy on the rouge – in his room, and Vitelli bustles, checking out the new song soundlessly at the harmonium.)

Vitelli: You've warned Joe about the new song? Thatcher? Are you listening?

Thatcher: Eh?

Vitelli: The new song? You've warned Joe? He knows the tune?

Thatcher: Of course.

Vitelli: Oh, Thatcher! You reek of whisky! I can smell it from here!

Thatcher: Just a drop to wet the whistle, Annie, that's all. *(Singing)* Ah ah ah …

Vitelli: A drop! Can you stand?

Thatcher: With the greatest of ease, my dear!

(Vitelli offers her hand to help him from the chair but Thatcher pulls her down onto his knee.)

You're a nag, Annie. Do you know that? A nag, a virago and a termagant.

Vitelli *(freeing herself and straightening her dress)*: And if I were not, where would we be today, I ask you? A few tots of Old Tom and you've a memory like a sieve. You'll dry, as sure as bacon. You'll dry as you did last night and look a fool.

Thatcher *(expansive)*: Not a bit of it. I shall rise to the occasion.

(He slumps into his chair.)

You are in the presence, my dear, of a seasoned trouper, and after a decade of demonstrable dexterity, I'll not dry.

Vitelli *(prodding him into action)*: Let's just see you rise from that chair to begin with. Come on. Up you get, so I can put on your coat and fix your cravat.

Thatcher *(getting up from the chair)*: Make it a double buck with a flyaway, Annie. Something extravagant to dazzle the gallery!

Vitelli: Your coat first …

(She helps him on with it and then sets to tying his cravat. Thatcher hums to himself the tune of 'Major Croker'.)

Thatcher: Is Joe ready to go on?

Vitelli: He's rouging up. Give him five minutes. Oh, hold still …

Thatcher: Annie, my Calliope, my poetic muse. A rhyme, if you please, for 'Croker'.

Vitelli *(teasing and a little irritated)*: Croker? Hmm … How about 'soaker'?

(She prods him.) Or 'joker'?

(Prod.) Or 'provoker'?

(Prod.)

Thatcher: Ah hah! I have it. Poker!

(Sings) 'But his blunder made his jaw drop, like a blow struck by a poker.'

Vitelli: And who is to be the object of this poetic attack?

Thatcher *(singing)*: 'That clever Major Croker!'

(He takes a towel from the table, folds it and puts it on his head like a judge's wig.) Major Croker, J.P. of the Tuapeka judiciary, who has been passing solemn judgement these past seven months on erring humanity. 'Drunk and disorderly, sir?'

(He takes up his cane and bangs the table.) Bam! Three months' imprisonment, not to mention a fine little lecture on the perils of indulgence in spirituous liquor. 'Selling grog, m' dear? And without a licence?'

(Vitelli joins in, playing the role of Poll-the-grogseller.) Bam! That'll be a few weeks behind another set of bars for you, and we'll trouble you for ten pounds too, just to cover our expenses. And the man, it now emerges *(removes the towel wig)* is not even gazetted a J.P. He's been practising without a warrant! And won't I take the rub of him!

(Centre performance spot up. Small plays the first bars of 'Major Croker' on the fiddle as intro and Thatcher launches a performance of the song.)

SONG: MAJOR CROKER

Thatcher:
On Tuapeka justice seems
Dealt out with some severity,
The J.P. on the bench I'm told
Views prisoners with asperity!
Up there in January last
A regular rum old joker
Himself 'committed' 'mongst the rest
And his name is Major Croker!

Oh my Croker!
My jolly Major Croker!
You've put your foot in it this time,
My jolly Major Croker!

(Violin continues under.)

Vitelli: And just how tall is this Major Croker? Is he a big fellow by any chance? Handy with his fists? Of a bellicose and aggressive disposition?

Thatcher *(brushes her aside)*: A mosquito! A mouse!

Vitelli: Do you remember Costello in Bendigo? He was a mouse – until you prodded him once too often with that wife of his and her intimate consultations with the bank manager.

Thatcher *(airily)*: Costello was a bar-room scrapper! I disposed of him in one round!

Vitelli: Just the same, you be careful with your Major Croker, lest you pinch him too close!

Thatcher *(sings)*:
He pounced on poor grog-sellers there,
Swooped on them like an eagle,
But one day they discovered
His convictions were illegal.
Not being gazetted a J.P.
Some lawyer told this joker
That his convictions were all 'bosh';
What 'nuts' for Major Croker!

Oh my, Croker!
My jolly Major Croker!
You've put your foot in it this time,
My jolly Major Croker!

(Music under.)
Thatcher: That's what the audience likes: one of Thatcher's Locals, Comic or Satirical! When I arrive in a town and walk about with my notebook, looking for material, marking the eccentricities of the place, don't they all squeal! Don't they all scatter! But don't they all come sneaking to me on the quiet …

(Vitelli and Thatcher huddle to playact the 'informers'.)
Vitelli: Watch him, Mr Thatcher.
Thatcher: Or him.
Vitelli: Or him. Or her.
Thatcher *(in a good broad Birmingham accent)*: Have you heard about his summons for misleading investors?
Vitelli *(an old woman)*: Do you know how old Poll there fooled the sly-grog detectives?
Thatcher *(an Australian digger)*: Anyone told you how Cockatoo Jack got Rees to put up the money for a moa hunt?
Vitelli: Have you heard this? Have you seen that?
Thatcher: Local scandals, my girl. That's what brings them in. That's what brings in the tin.

(Sings ponderously to the tune of 'Major Croker'):
To put down vice and humbug
Is really Thatcher's mission,
And he'll try to do his duty
In spite of opposition!

Vitelli *(giving him a slow hand clap)*: Yes, yes, very fine and noble – but just you remember Costello, and while you're about it, you might also recall Chudleigh and

Barnes and all the others who've been the texts of your sermons and who haven't responded in a noticeably Christian manner!

(She moves US.)

Thatcher: I'll remember.

(Pause.)

I'll remember.

(Pause.)

Remember …

(Lights dim DS. Thatcher moves into the hotel/dressing-room area SL, pours himself a whisky. Small begins intro for 'I Dreamt I Dwelt in Marble Halls', softly legato. The intro dies away. Lights up on Vitelli USC, her costume glittering. She sings beautifully, unaccompanied, while Thatcher listens, sometimes hums along and sometimes speaks over.)

Vitelli:

I dreamt that I dwelt in marble halls
With vassals and serfs at my side,
And of all those assembled within those walls
That I was the hope and the pride.
I had riches too great to count – could boast
Of a high ancestral name.
But I also dreamt; which pleas'd me most,
That you loved me still the same.

Thatcher *(over)*: Remember her? And our children asleep in a butter box at the back of the hall? And the audience stamping: Thatcher! Thatcher! Thatcher!

And before all that, Brighton. Do you know Brighton? Shingle beach, Regent's Pavilion? My father had an importing business there. Foreign curios, jade and lacquer. That's where I learned the trade, and it's been a good trade too. You get to see a bit of the world, travel out to Shanghai or Kwangchow, pick up the stuff for a few yuan and ship it back to London where it's quite the rage. You can name your price.

(Vitelli finishes the first verse. A pause. Thatcher drinks.)

Thatcher: But, I tired of the business, as the young will, and went haring off to Victoria after gold, and that's where I met her.

Vitelli:

I dreamt that suitors sought my hand;
That knights upon bended knee,
And with vows that no maiden hear could withstand,
They pledged their faith to me.
And I dreamt that one of that noble host
Came forth my heart to claim;
But I also dreamt …

Thatcher *(over)*: Bendigo in 1860. She was singing at the Shamrock. Oh, don't get me wrong: she was a lady. Merchant's daughter. There was nothing cheap about

Annie. And her voice! A few trills from the 'Mocking Bird', a couple of bars of 'Marble Halls', and she had them in the palm of her hand. And they were a tough audience, let me tell you: brawlers, rough-housers. In the palm of her white hand.

(Pause. Thatcher listens to Vitelli sing.)

Well, what could a man do but marry her?

(Vitelli breaks off in mid-verse, impatient and irritated.)

Vitelli: Marry? Met in December, wed by March. We were billed as 'Mister and Mistress Butterfly, a Sentimental Duo'.

(They join to sing a few bars of 'Sweet and Low', a syrupy number, hand in hand and in close harmony. Vitelli breaks off again in mid-verse, drops Thatcher's hand.)

Butterflies be damned. Marry in haste and repent at leisure, they say. And what did I marry? Ten years of tramping New Zealand. Ten years of existing in a tent. Two babies I had, and I was performing a week before each was born and within a week after. Dunedin to Christchurch to Nelson to Hokitika – and what was that but a row of tin pubs and banks on a spit of sand and the river mouth littered with wrecks ...

(Vitelli sits in her dressing room, moodily fiddling with her hair and reciting the litany of places visited, while Thatcher sings cheerfully of gold.)

Vitelli: Auckland to Thames to Napier to Nelson to Wakatipu to Tuapeka to Dunedin to ...

SONG: GOLD

Thatcher *(over)*:
Gold's a wonderful thing, what a change it can make,
'Tis the great civiliser, it is, no mistake;
It peoples the country, wherever it's found,
There's certain to be a great rush to the ground.
This place at one time was a Māori peach grove;
Now thousands of diggers all over it rove,
They mark out their claims on this marvellous rush,
And put up machinery quartz here to crush.

Vitelli: To Grahamstown to Greymouth to Waikouaiti to Oamaru ...

Thatcher: Oamaru! Pah! Where they wanted *(he mimics the prissy Scots correspondent to* The Times*)*: 'healthy entertainment – for example, lectures by talented clergymen and Band of Hope meetings instead of Mr Thatcher's vulgar songs'. Let them just try it! Let them endure a season of desiccated clergymen and they'd soon be calling for one of Thatcher's Locals again. I've no time for them, these pious little provincial potentates. All pleasures are sinful, all change for the worse. We had our noses at the trough first and, by God, we'll keep all others away!

(Small strikes up on the bagpipes, and Thatcher and Vitelli mimic these prissy Scots; towards the end of the song the air in the bagpipes runs out.)

SONG: THE OLD IDENTITY

Thatcher, Vitelli:
Mr Cargill in Dunedin
Made such a funny speech;
He got up and told the council
That it devolved on each
Of all the early dwellers
To preserve safe as could be,
Amid the Victorian influx,
The Old Identity.

Are we to hear the bagpipes
And each one wear a dirk?
And every Sabbath morning
Crowd to that little kirk?
While some quite grateful ponder
How they came with 'nae bawbee'?
And plan ways of preserving
The Old Identity.

(Vitelli takes off her bonnet and returns to the litany of towns visited.)
Vitelli: Coromandel, Thames, Napier, Wanganui …

Thatcher *(irritable once more)*: And Wanganui! Prim lot! *(He mimics the finicky editor.)* 'We confess to a considerable degree of disappointment with Mr Thatcher. There is in his songs nothing but coarseness.' Coarseness! God help them! Provincial gentry without vigour or vision …

Small *(cuts in over this)*: I'm ready, Mr Thatcher.

(Thatcher pauses in mid-stride.)

Thatcher: Oh. *(Pause. He fumbles for this watch, confused, caught off balance.)*
Is it that time already? Do we have a good house?

Vitelli: Packed to the rafters and keen for curtain up.
(Pause.) Come on, Thatcher. Stir your stumps.
(She pushes him out onto the performing area.)
The intro, please. *(Thatcher doesn't know what she means.)*
For the new song. *(He's still confused, uncertain.)*
You know … Ladies and gentlemen … diggers and dignit …
(Thatcher picks up the cue and builds up to a confident and ringing introduction.)

Thatcher: Dignitaries! We present for your entertainment this evening, that renowned comic delineator of Hibernian hilarity, Mr Joseph Small!

(Joe Small beats a deafening roll on the side drum and moves DS into the performance light.)

Small:
You may have heard of all the troubles
They've had up Auckland way?
How they're recruiting city folks
To take a soldier's pay?
They're a soft lot, a gentle lot,
Unused to discipline.
Green as grass, not army brass.
They're only in it for the tin!

(Vitelli sings a bugle call, and Thatcher fetches his bass drum. Lights up, colour, flags, the three actors in a parody of military movement against a background of slides of the Taranaki Wars, showing the reality of an orchestrated land-grab in counterpoint to the cheerful ironies of Thatcher's song.)

SONG: CAMP LIFE OUT AT DRURY

Thatcher, Vitelli, Small:
The war drags its slow length along
And I don't think that I'll do wrong
If I tell you now in a song
Of the volunteers at Drury.
These Auckland Rifles had to tramp
Out there and live in a wretched camp,
A prey to dysentery and cramp
And lying on blankets muddy and damp;
Rising as soon as the day did dawn,
Parades at five o'clock in the morn,
And all complaints regarded with scorn,
And that's camp life at Drury!

Taking coves for soldiers is a shame
On me I hope they've got no claim,
But I'll expose the little game
Of camp life out at Drury!

Thatcher *(over Small's side drum):* It's all in the presentation, you see. Goldfield or battlefield, the raw material's muck, and the art's to warm it through and serve it sweet.

Taking coves for soldiers is a shame
On me I hope they've got no claim,
But I'll expose the little game
Of camp life out at Drury!

(The song builds to a noisy climax then tails away to Thatcher's drumbeat alone, which takes on some of the quality of the drumbeat used to warn of plague.)

Thatcher: And they said they'd prefer the Band of Hope to that. Or a talented clergyman.

(He's left alone, despondent.)

Vitelli: Talented clergymen have their place, Thatcher.

Thatcher: They have their uses, as anybody does.

Vitelli: You seemed ready enough to confess to Reverend Harper back on the Coast. You talked to him, hour after hour. What did you talk about?

Thatcher: The price of bacon. The gold rate. Who knocked out McCreedy. The possibilities of a field south of the Buller. The chances of war in the north. Common chat.

Vitelli: You talked about more than that. Harper was a serious man, charged with straightening the edges in Hokitika. He had his work cut out. You'd not have held his attention for more than five minutes with who knocked out McCreedy and the price of flour.

Thatcher: Bacon.

Vitelli: Or bacon. So what did you talk about?

Thatcher: We traded.

Vitelli: Traded?

Thatcher: Of course. It's the business of a colony. These preachers talk nobly, but they're here for exactly the same reason as you or me or the most grasping merchant or the most misbegotten, vicious workhouse scraping panning for pebbles and living on thin air: we're all after investment and accumulation – only the preacher is laying up good works for redemption at some later date in heaven, while we seek a more immediate return. We traded: I lent Harper my soul for a week or two and he lent us the harmonium. And I think I got the better bargain.

(Thatcher plays a discord on the harmonium. Vitelli is not amused.)

Vitelli: Do you take nothing seriously? Or can everything be fashioned to a joke, turned to a witty line?

Thatcher: Annie, my pet, I take most things seriously. In fact, I have often thought that if I hadn't chosen the stage I'd have made a more than passable preacher myself.

(Thatcher stands, takes up the book on the table and moves DS. Lights up – a church window – Thatcher plays the preacher and Annie plays the harmonium, Sunday School style.)

SONG: OUR OWN CORRESPONDENT

Thatcher:
The veracious correspondent
Of the *Canterbury Times*,
It seems has got an awful down
On Thatcher's vulgar rhymes.

He gave this hall a rare rub up,
And this audience he vowed
Were a regular 'noisy, dirty, drinking, smoking, cursing crowd'.

My word! I've got a character,
By jingo! So have you.
A pretty mob I'm singing to
If what he says be true.
According to this scribbling cove,
I really should be proud
To sing to such a 'noisy, dirty, drinking, smoking, cursing crowd'.

My song just like a sermon
Into headings I'll divide,
And trust, unlike this scribbling cove,
That truth will be my guide.
To preach to you in local rhyme
Oh let me be allowed,
My text is 'noisy, dirty, drinking, smoking, cursing crowd'.

We'll first begin with 'noisy',
Now some you will allow
Come into this Corinthian Hall
And often make a row.
Some that should know better
Stand there and talk so loud,
But I really don't think, on the whole,
That you're a 'noisy crowd'.

This scribbler calls you 'dirty',
But that's a fib I hope,
Permit me, therefore, now to ask,
How are you off for soap?
In future you must wash yourselves,
You cannot be allowed
To come in here to hear us sing
If you're a 'dirty crowd'.

Then next, you're charged with 'drinking',
It's true sometimes at night
A cove comes here and pays his bob
And gets a little tight.
But lushingtons in future

In this hall won't be allowed,
Though the barman oft complains and says
You're not a 'drinking crowd'.

This scribbler then accuses
That you're a 'smoking' crowd,
But you're free to take your baccy out
And blow your little cloud.
He charges you with 'cursing',
But seldom have I heard
Frequenters of this hall make use
Of any wicked word.

To find who penned this letter,
I'll hit upon a plan,
P'raps it's a camp official,
Or Howard the sausage man.
He's had a rub from Thatcher,
Or he'd not complain so loud
About the 'noisy, dirty, drinking, smoking, cursing crowd'!

Thatcher: Yes. I'd have made as good a job of it as Reverend Harper.

Vitelli: I found him a comfort. I said to him, Mr Harper, no one knows the despair I am in. I must go on each night and perform as through I was the merriest of creatures, but all the time I bear a sad and unhappy heart.

Thatcher: Theatricals, Annie! What better life could you have than the life of the player? The change, the excitement, the pleasures of performance?

Vitelli: You liked that. For me it was always just a means to an end, an interval, necessary, perhaps, while we accumulated the capital for a comfortable life. I imagined us settled somewhere, in a villa house; I didn't mind particularly where. Dunedin, Bendigo, Brighton – it didn't matter. The children at school, learning civilised ways. Neighbours bowing on the street. 'Good afternoon, Mrs Thatcher. Fine weather we're having for the time of year.' An ordinary, unremarkable existence. And if I had to travel by steamer up and down some savage coast, fearing that at any minute we'd be on the rocks, or if I had to make do in some muddy camp for a season or two, a year or two even, well, I was ready and I was willing. But not for ten years. Not for a lifetime.

Thatcher: But the comfortable life's so ordinary. I admit that at times there was tedium in touring. When the reviewers carped and cavilled, the children were ill or fretful, the audience gone cold – but at least it was never ordinary.

Vitelli: That's the trouble, you see. You thrive on sensation and change. And without them, and an audience, I believe you doubt you're alive. I never have. I sang and I enjoyed the applause, but I didn't believe in it, ever. And now it's over, and I like living quietly here in Brighton, attending to the fine detail. It's taken me years to understand this: that you talk commerce and trade, but it's the thrill of the hunt that you like, not the dull business of husbanding investment. You like piracy and adventure, living on your wits, endless improvisation.

Thatcher: And this is what you discussed with Harper?

Vitelli: Mister and Mistress Butterfly in winter.

(Sings slowly, unaccompanied):

Listen to the mocking bird.

Listen to the mocking bird.

Singing in the valley there below …

Thatcher: Annie!

Vitelli: I was miserable. Why won't you understand? Reverend Harper understood.

(Vitelli moves off US, moody. Thatcher pours himself a drink, unworried.)

Vitelli *(sings to herself):*

Listen to the mocking bird.

Listen to the mocking bird …

Thatcher: Huh. Misery's commonplace. Why should Harper not understand? It's easily understood. Think of Joe there, wallowing in it, night after night, as 'The Unfortunate Man', and the audience applauding …

(Thatcher sits in the chair SL, and Small comes DS to the performance area spot, clowning with the attempt to find the right place to stand. He recites his comic monologue as the straight-faced, miserable clown in broad stage-Oirish.)

Small *(cutting over Thatcher with the title):*

THE UNFORTUNATE MAN

(He is standing in the dark. He tries again, finds the spot, coughs delicately, begins):

I'm really a very unfortunate man.

I try to be happy but nowhere I can.

At home or abroad, let me go where I will,

My unlucky luck is pursuing me still.

I've run through a fortune, been cheated by friends,

Who laughed when I spoke about making amends.

I'm sure of a failure whatever I plan.

I'm really a very unfortunate man.

My days are all passed amid sorrow and grief.

My mornings are mournings all lacking relief.

When second I stood for some troublesome elf

The shot of his rival by chance hit myself.

I'm sure to endure the direst of ills.

I'm plagued with a lawsuit and pestered by bills;

I'm a debtor though living as plain as I can.

I'm really a most unfortunate man.

Whenever I go to a party or ball,
Some shocking disaster is sure to befall.
I go to the races whenever I choose,
And whatever I bet I am sure to lose.
A crusty old bachelor shall I repine
Though loving a maid who agreed to be mine.
But somebody managed her heart to trepan
And left me a very unfortunate man!

(Lights down. Small withdraws to his dressing room, where he takes up the Chinese mask and changes. Thatcher is left sitting in the hotel bedroom in Shanghai.)
Thatcher: You see? So ordinary that Joe could make a living out of it. You can make a bob or two out of anything providing you've got the nerve for it.
(Vitelli strikes the gong. She and Small tumble and spring CS, masks on and stripped to Victorian underwear for a tumbling routine.)
It's all in the presentation.
Small: Sa che la! *(This approximates to the Cantonese version of Thatcher's name.)*
(Thatcher looks up.)
Small: Sa che la chien sin!
Thatcher: Eh?
(Vitelli brings Thatcher CS, theatrically, performing for the audience while Small goes to the chest and throws Thatcher two vases. Thatcher will combine the roles of auctioneer and songster, with the others joining in the singing. This is not intended to be an attractive number.)

SONG: JOHN CHINAMAN

Thatcher:
John Chinaman, my jo, John!
Oh what can you be at?
To stay there in Victoria
It strikes me you're a flat.
New Zealand is the place, John,
But to come you're very slow;
Why don't you try the diggin's here,
John Chinaman, my jo?

Thatcher: Ladies and gentlemen, we present for your consideration this evening, these exquisite exempla of the Oriental craftsman's art. Note the figuration. Note the lacquer, the patina, the delicate craquelure.
(The three performers begin a routine, juggling the vases, tumbling, balancing – something cheerful and spectacular – which involves Thatcher too while he keeps up the patter of the auctioneer, addressing the audience, ideally involving them in the bidding.)

John Chinaman, my jo, John,
Come here you really should;
If you could see the gold, John,
You'd cry out, 'Welly good.'
Why stay at Ballarat, John,
Or worked-out Bendigo;
When there're such pickings for you here,
John Chinaman, my jo.

And what am bid I for these exquisite pieces? Sir? Would you give me ten guineas? Twelve?

Madam? For a vase that will signify that you are a woman of taste and discernment? Fifteen? Do I hear fifteen? Opportunities to purchase such porcelain are rare … Fifteen! Do I hear fifteen? Thank you, Madam. Is there any advance on fifteen … Eighteen … etc.

John Chinaman, my jo, John,
You're not unmindful that
You had a queer reception
One day near Lambing Flat.
Perhaps you fear another dose,
If here yourself you show;
For we might your pigtail off
John Chinaman, my jo.

(The action has become increasingly close to hysteria and violence. Finally, the vases fall and shatter. Dead silence. Lights change. Thatcher picks up the pieces and drops them one by one into the chest.)

Rubbish. Bought them yesterday in a sweatshop over on the Woosung delta. The coolies' children have nimble fingers …

Small *(still in his Chinese mask, standing to one side. Lights change so he and Vitelli are visible only in narrow spots, as though their faces float in mid-air.)*: Sa che la chien sin!

Thatcher *(speaking over, taking no notice of Small)*: … They work nineteen hours a day and turn them out by the barrowload …

Small: Sa che la. Sanghai yu cho luan. *(= There is cholera in Shanghai.)*

Thatcher: … Cost me three yuan …

Small: Gin nee tzer taso fan de nyu zin ee jing tsla. *(= The woman you had breakfast with this morning is dead.)*

Thatcher: … That's about – oh, one and six. I'll ship them back to London in a week or two, where they'll fetch ten, fifteen guineas apiece. They're quite the rage. Buy cheap, sell dear. That's all there is to it.

Small: Sanghai yu cho luan.

Thatcher: … It's all a matter of presentation. What is that fellow saying?

Vitelli: I believe he's warning you. I believe he's saying there is cholera in Shanghai.

Small: Gin nee tzer taso fan de nyu zin ee jing tsla.

Vitelli: ... And the woman who shared your table at the hotel this morning has died of the disease.

Thatcher: Oh, there's always cholera in Shanghai. Or typhoid. Or plague, or some damn thing. The place is built on a mud bank. What else can you expect? It's not a spa; it's a trading port. Yes ... I've quantities of vases like this one. They'll sell well in London.

(He dumps the rest of the pieces in the chest, shuts the lid.)

Small: Cho luan! Cho luan!

Vitelli: Just you be careful, Thatcher!

Thatcher: It's all a matter of presentation.

Vitelli: Remember, Thatcher ...

(Lights dim on Vitelli and Small. Thatcher is left alone. He huddles into his jacket on the chair, cold.

Vitelli sings softly, pausing from time to time to speak to Thatcher, a dreamy counterpoint to Thatcher's thoughts.)

I'm dreaming now of Annie
Sweet of Annie, sweet Annie.
I'm dreaming now of Annie
Singing in the valley there below ...

Thatcher: But it's cold here. Chilly. Like that winter on the Arrow when ice split the stones and the melt smashed the dams to smithereens ...

(Vitelli and Thatcher speak over one another and lights fade from this point on to a spot on Thatcher alone and another, more pale, on Vitelli.)

Vitelli: Thatcher? Are you ready yet?

(She sings again, very slowly.)

Thatcher: They tramped in that winter from miles around through mud and snow for a tot of whisky and Joe mocking the miserable man ...

Vitelli: The man's not taking a blind bit of notice ...

Thatcher: ... Annie singing, and a few of Thatcher's Locals, comic and satirical. It brought in the tin.

Vitelli: Thatcher?

Thatcher: Is it that time already?

(Pause.) Do we have a good house?

(Vitelli's song fades away to nothing. Thatcher slumps in his chair, the glass falls from his hand. Fade to black, then to three pinhole spots on Thatcher, Vitelli and Small, like cameo heads in the darkness, with slides projected on the screens around them ...

Thatcher begins the song. They are strong and confident once more, singing as they used to sing, but unaccompanied, taking their time to tell the story.)

SONG: LOOK OUT BELOW!

Thatcher:
A young man left his native shores
For trade was bad at home;
To seek his fortune in this land
He crossed the briny foam.
And when he got to the Arrow
It put him in a glow
To hear the sound of the windlass
And the cry 'Look out below!'

Vitelli:
Wherever he turned his wondering eyes,
Great wealth did he behold,
And peace and plenty hand in hand
By the magic power of gold;
Quoth he, as I'm young and strong
To the diggings I will go,
For I like the sound of the windlass
And the cry 'Look out below!'

Small:
Amongst the rest he took his chance,
And his luck at first was vile;
But still he resolved to persevere,
And at length he made his pile.
So says he, I'll take my passage
And home again I'll go,
And I'll say farewell to the windlass
And the cry 'Look out below!'

Vitelli:
Arrived in London once again,
His gold he freely spent,
And into every gaiety
And dissipation went.
But pleasure if prolonged too much
Oft causes pain, you know,
And he missed the sound of the windlass
And the cry 'Look out below!'

Small:
And thus he reasoned with himself,
'Oh, why did I return?'
For the digger's independent life,
I now begin to yearn.
Here purse-proud lords the poor oppress,
But there it is not so.
Give me the sound of the windlass
And the cry, 'Look out below!'

Thatcher:
So he started for this land again
With a charming little wife,
And he finds there's nothing comes up to
A jolly digger's life.
Ask him if he'll go back again,
He'll quickly answer, no.
For he loves the sound of the windlass
And the cry, 'Look out below!'

(Lights fade finally. Only the slide of Otago – brown hills and blue sky – remains, reflected and misshapen by the corrugated surfaces on which it is projected.
Sound up – the tin whistle version of 'Look Out Below!' that opened the show. The performances leave the stage.)

Production Notes
The play is intended for performance on a set constructed from demolition materials, which echoes in its design the goldfields pub, the Victorian stage, and the Shanghai hotel bedroom: a box set created from old lengths of corrugated iron, timber and calico onto which slides can be projected, distorting on the uneven surfaces.

SR – Joe Small's dressing room: boxes or crates for table and chair, a piece of broken mirror, makeup (including rouge for Small's hallmark, the 'boozer's flush'), costume items (including an overly large bowler hat and a Chinese mask), and a variety of musical instruments. He'll need a choice of the following: tin whistle, flute, violin, concertina, bagpipes, side drum, percussion – horseshoe, spoons, frying pan. Small is a clown and a versatile musician.

USC – Vitelli's dressing room, on a raised dais draped Victorian fashion in bunting: a knocked-about cabin trunk for her brush, mirror, hat, hairpins, tambourine; costume items, including a Chinese mask. On or above the dais is a large oriental gong, which hangs like the sun over the set, catching the reflected light of the opening slides (central Otago in summer – brown hills, a slash of brilliant blue sky).

DSL – Thatcher's hotel bedroom in Shanghai/dressing room in some New Zealand shanty town: an easy chair, cane table, on which are a whisky bottle and glass, ewer and towel, book, fob watch, walking cane – a clutter. To one side, a harmonium and stool and a wooden packing crate (Chinese vase inside), and a bass drum.

Lighting – The lighting should be designed to alternately isolate and link these three areas, with a brightly lit performance area DC suggesting footlights and theatrical glitz.

The setting is not intended to be relentlessly 'authentic', but restless, glittering, the stuff of nightmare or dream, a blend of surfaces that catch and distort light. Somehow, it must suggest that this is gritty reality and simultaneously the delusion of fever.

Music Notes

The play chiefly includes Thatcher's topical songs, along with snippets from Annie Vitelli's parlour-song repertoire and Joe Small's popular song 'The Unfortunate Man' (converted into a monologue). Accompaniments include a choice of melodic and percussive instruments: tin whistle (or flute), fiddle (or concertina), bagpipes, harmonium, side drum, bass drum, tambourine, gong and horseshoe (or spoons or frying pan). Space prevents printing a full score, but the tunes of Thatcher songs not reproduced here are available in Robert Hoskins' *Gold's a Wonderful Thing: Charles Thatcher's songs of the New Zealand diggings* (Wellington: Steele Roberts, 2011). These, supplemented with script cues and the following notes, should suffice to stage a production.

'Look Out Below!' – solo, preferably played on tin whistle or flute.

'To the West' – Small's fanfare on tin whistle can be repeated Cs (to pitch the song) following the word-rhythm of the opening phrase. For each stanza have Vitelli shaking the tambourine lines 1 and 3 and Thatcher responding on alternate lines with a steady beat on the bass drum. Small strikes up on horseshoe (or frying pan or spoons) lines 5–6, following the word rhythm. Return to tambourine and bass drum alternation for lines 7–8, with all three instruments following the word rhythm of the chorus.

'Major Croker' – vocal line preferably doubled on fiddle.

'Gold' – unaccompanied.

'The Old Identity' – tune preferably doubled on bagpipes (air runs out of bagpipes towards the end).

'Camp Life at Drury' – Vitelli's bugle-call can be the opening two notes ('The war') repeated three times. Small plays a rhythmic tattoo on side drum and Thatcher marks time on bass drum.

'Our Own Correspondent' – harmonium with simple hymnal harmonies.

'John Chinaman' – unaccompanied (tune 'John Anderson, My Jo' is available on internet).

Notes

Chapter 1

1   Geoffrey Serle, *The Golden Age: A history of the colony of Victoria 1851–1861* (Carlton: Melbourne University Press, 1963) and *The Rush to be Rich* (Carlton: Melbourne University Press, 1971); Philip Ross May, *The West Coast Gold Rushes* (Christchurch: Pegasus Press, 1962); Weston Bate, *Lucky City: The first generation at Ballarat 1851–1901* (Carlton: Melbourne University Press, 1978) and *Victorian Gold Rushes* (Ringwood: Penguin, 1988); Geoffrey Blainey, *The Rush That Never Ended* (Carlton: Melbourne University Press, 1963); Ian McCalman, Alexander Cook and Andrew Reeves, eds., *Gold: Forgotten histories and lost objects of Australia* (Cambridge: Cambridge University Press, 2001); Keir Reeves and David Nichols, eds., *Deeper Leads: New approaches to Victorian goldfields history* (Ballarat: Ballarat Heritage Services, 2007). See also David Goodman, *Gold Seeking: Victoria and California in the 1850s* (St Leonards: Allen & Unwin, 1994).

2   See, for example, Keir Reeves and Benjamin Mountford, 'Sojourning and settling: Locating Chinese Australian history', *Australian Historical Studies*, vol. 42, no. 1, 2011, 111–25; Fred Cahir and Ian Clark, 'Aboriginal and Maori interactions in Victoria Australia, 1830–1900: A preliminary analysis', *New Zealand Journal of History*, vol. 48, no. 1, 2014, 109–26; Lyndon Fraser, *Castles of Gold: A history of the West Coast Irish* (Dunedin: Otago University Press, 2007); David Nichols, Dolly Mackinnon and Keir Reeves, 'Goldfields asylums: Anxieties, evasions and erasures', in Reeves and Nichols, *Deeper Leads*, 39–62; Steven Eldred-Grigg, *Diggers, Hatters and Whores: The story of the New Zealand gold rushes* (Auckland: Random House, 2008). For an entry point to the expanding literature on Eureka, see Clare Wright's prize-winning book *The Forgotten Rebels of Eureka* (Melbourne: Text Publishing Company, 2013). In regard to the growing environmental history of the goldfields, see, for example, Susan Lawrence and Peter Davies, 'The sludge question: The regulation of mine tailings in nineteenth-century Victoria', *Environment and History*, vol. 20, no. 3, 2014, 385–410. Eleanor Catton's Man Booker prize-winning novel *The Luminaries* (London: Granta, 2013) draws on new goldfields research and primary sources to paint a vivid picture of life during the West Coast gold rushes of the 1860s.

3   Lloyd Carpenter, 'Lighting a gen'rous, manly flame: The nostalgia for "dear old Bendigo"', *Journal of Australian Studies*, vol. 37, no. 1, 2013, 76–95.

4   Anonymous, 'A gold digger's notes', in *All the Year Round*, ed. Charles Dickens, vol. 10, no. 258, 2 April 1864, p. 186.

Chapter 2

1   Sigismund Wekey, *Otago: Its goldfields and resources; containing information to the end of August, 1862* (Melbourne: W.H. Williams, 1862), p. 14.

2   James Belich, *Paradise Reforged: A history of the New Zealanders from the 1880s to the year 2000* (Honolulu: University of Hawaii Press, 2001), p. 46.

3   Benedict Anderson, *Imagined Communities: Reflections on the origins and spread of nationalism* (London: Verso, 1983), pp. *xv–xvi*.

4   Belich, *Paradise Reforged*, p. 50, and generally on Australian east-coast inter-colonial shipping, see Department of Harbours and Marine Queensland, *Port and Harbour Development in Queensland from 1824 to 1985* (Brisbane: Harbours and Marine, 1986).

5   'Standardisation of railway gauges', in *Year Book of Australia* (Canberra: Australian Bureau of Statistics, 1967), pp. 1–25.

6   For one of the many disputes lasting right through the second half of the nineteenth century, see 'English mail services papers relating to, 1873', *Appendix to the Journal of the House of Representatives New Zealand*, 1873, Session 1, F-06.

7   G.R. Quaife, 'Pyke, Vincent (1827–1894)', from the *Australian Dictionary of Biography*: http://adb.anu.edu.au/biography/pyke-vincent-4423/text7223

8   'Otago', *The Argus*, 9 September 1861, p. 4.

9   Mel Watkins, 'A staple theory of economic growth', *The Canadian Journal of Economics and Political Science*, vol. 29, 1963, pp. 141–58.

10   John W. McCarty, 'The staple approach in Australian economic history', *Business Archives and History*, vol. 4, 1964, pp. 1–22; Geoffrey Blainey, *The Rush that Never Ended: A history of Australian mining* (Carlton: Melbourne University Press, 1963). See also C.B. Schedvin, 'Staples and regions of Pax Britannica', *The Economic History Review: New Series*, vol. 43, no. 4, 1990, pp. 553–59.

11   H.J. Dyos, *Exploring the Urban Past: Essays in urban history*, ed. David Cannadine and David Reeder (Cambridge: Cambridge University Press, 1982); C.B. Schedvin and J.W. McCarty, *Urbanization in Australia: The nineteenth century* (Sydney: Sydney University Press, 1974); Graeme Davison, *The Rise and Fall of Marvellous Melbourne* (Carlton: Melbourne University Press, 1978). See also Norman Harper, ed., *Pacific Circle: Proceedings of the Second Biennial Conference of the Australian New Zealand American Studies Association* (St Lucia: University of Queensland Press, 1968).

12   James R. Scobie, *Buenos Aires: Plaza to suburb, 1870–1910* (New York, 1974). See also Eric Lampard, 'The urbanizing world', in *Victorian City: Images and realities*, vol. 1, eds H.J. Dyos and Michel Wolff (London: Routledge Kegan and Paul: 1973), pp. 3–57.

13   Lampard, 'The urbanizing world', Tables 1.1, p. 5; 1.4, p. 21; and 1.7, p. 35.

14   Alan Mayne, *Fever, Squalor and Vice: Sanitation and social policy in Victorian Sydney* (St Lucia: University of Queensland Press, 1982).

15   Erik Olssen, *A History of Otago* (Dunedin: John McIndoe, 1984).

16   'Otago; or, a rush to the new gold-fields of New Zealand', *The Leisure Hour*, no. 554, 9 August 1862, p. 422.

17   'Editorial', *The Talbot Leader and North-Western Chronicle*, 11 July 1862, p. 4.

18   Alexander Don, *Early Central Otago: A Ballarat miner's reminiscences* (Dunedin: Otago Daily Times Print, 1931).

19   See, generally, J.M. Gandar, 'New Zealand net migration in the later part of the nineteenth century', *Australian Economic History Review*, vol. 19, no. 2, 1979, pp. 151–68.

20   'Our Australian letter', *Otago Daily Times*, 20 September 1893, p. 4.

21   'Our Melbourne letter', *Otago Daily Times*, 3 March 1892, p. 5.

22   J.A. Dowie, 'Inverse relations of the Australian and New Zealand economics, 1871–1900', *Australian Economic Papers*, vol. 2, no. 2, 1963, pp. 151–79.

23   G.A. Carmichael, *Trans-Tasman Migration: Trends, causes and consequences* (Canberra, 1983). See also Ian Pool, ed., *Trans-Tasman Migration: Proceedings of a workshop on population flows between Australia and New Zealand or vice versa* (Hamilton: University of Waikato, 1980).

24   Statistics New Zealand, *The New Zealand Official Year-Book 1910*. Digital yearbook collection: www3.stats.govt.nz/New_Zealand_Official_Yearbooks/1910/NZOYB_1910.html

25   See Richard Aitken, *Talbot and Clunes Conservation Study: For the Shire of Talbot and Clunes*

and Ministry of Planning and Environment (Talbot: Shire of Talbot and Clunes, 1988); Clutha District Council, *Planning Scheme: Register of heritage buildings* (Balclutha: Author, 2012), Table 13.1: www.cluthadc.govt.nz/district%20plan/sections/section%203%20general%20 section/heritage.htm

26   Michael Taffe, *Growing a Garden City: Ballarat Horticultural Society, 1859–2009* (Ballarat: Ballarat Heritage Services, 2014); Weston Bate, *Lucky City: The first generation at Ballarat, 1851–1901* (Carlton: Melbourne University Press, 1978), pp. 220–23.

27   'The unveiling of the Burns statue', *Otago Witness*, 27 May 1887, p. 12; 'Unveiling the statue of Robert Burns at Ballarat', *The Argus*, 22 April 1887, p. 13.

28   S.J. Butlin, *Australia and New Zealand Bank: The Bank of Australasia and the Union Bank of Australia Ltd 1828–1951* (London: Longmans, Green & Company, 1961), p. 181.

29   Wendy Jacobs et al., *Ballarat: A guide to buildings and areas 1851–1940* (South Yarra: Jacobs Lewis Vines Architects and Conservation Planners, 1981), pp. 32–35.

30   Fleur Snedden, *King of the Castle: A biography of William Larnach* (Auckland: David Bateman, 1997), p. 78.

31   Jonathon Mané-Wheoki, 'Early designs of Robert Lawson', *New Zealand Historic Places*, no. 33, 1991, pp. 35–38.

32   Jonathan Mané-Wheoki, 'Armson, William Barnett', from the *Dictionary of New Zealand Biography*: www.TeAra.govt.nz/mi/biographies/2a13/armson-william-barnett

33   Anna Crighton, 'Clayton, William Henry', from the *Dictionary of New Zealand Biography*: www.TeAra.govt.nz/mi/biographies/2c20/clayton-william-henry

34   Malcolm D. Prentis, 'Binding or loosing in Australasia; Some trans-Tasman Protestant connections', *Journal of Religious History*, vol. 34, no. 3, 2010, pp. 312–34: doi:10.1111/j.1467-9809.2010.00899.x

35   Candice Bruce, *Eugen von Guérard* (Sydney: Australian Gallery Directors Council and Australian National Gallery, 1980); Clune Galleries, *Eugen von Guerard: An exhibition of paintings and prints catalogue* (Sydney: Author, 1972).

36   Robert Hoskins, *Goldfield Balladeer: The life and times of the celebrated Charles R. Thatcher* (Auckland: 1977); Charles R. Thatcher, *Thatcher's Colonial Songster: Containing all the choice local songs, parodies, &c., of the celebrated Charles R. Thatcher* (Melbourne: Charlwood, 1865).

37   H. Garrett, *Recollections of Convict Life in Norfolk and Victoria* (Dunedin: Dunedin Public Library, 1973, first published 1886); Lance Tonkin, *The Real Henry Garrett, 1818–1885, Aus. and N.Z. criminal* (Dunedin: Author, 1980).

38   'Obituary: Mr Charles McQueen', *Grey River Argus*, 2 June 1906, p. 2.

39   D.R. Dickinson, *Gold Dredging in Victoria* (Melbourne: Mines Department of Victoria, 1939).

40   On Otago racing clubs, see W.A. Saunders., comp., *Historical Racing Records and the Inauguration of the Racing and Trotting Clubs in Otago and Southland* (Dunedin: Evening Star Company, 1949).

41   Chris McConville and Robert Hess, 'Forging imperial and Australasian identities: Australian Rules football in New Zealand during the nineteenth century', *The International Journal of the History of Sport*, vol. 29, no. 17, 2012, pp. 2360–71.

42   Acclimatisation Society of Victoria, *The Rules and Objects of the Acclimatisation Society of Victoria* (Melbourne: Author, 1861); R. McDowall, *Gamekeepers for the Nation: The story of New Zealand's acclimatization societies, 1861–1990* (Christchurch: Canterbury University Press, 1994).

43   Fred Cahir, *Black Gold: Aboriginal people on the goldfields of Victoria, 1850–1870* (Canberra: Australian National University and Aboriginal History Inc., 2012).

44   'Australian furs: The popular possum', *The Argus*, 21 April 1897, p. 7; Paul Star, 'Native forests and the rise of preservation in New Zealand (1903–1913)', *Environment and History*, vol. 8, no.1, 2002, pp. 275–90; Greg Gordon and Frances Hrdina, 'Koala and possum populations in Queensland during the Harvest Period, 1906–1936', *Australian Zoologist*, vol. 33, no.1, 2005, pp. 69–99.

45   'The protection of pests', *Otago Daily Times*, 8 August 1911, p. 10.

46   See, generally, 'The rabbits keep on running', *Otago Daily Times Weekend Magazine*, 15/16 July 2008, p. 3.

47   'The rabbiting industry', *Otago Daily Times*, 25 December 1902, p. 5.

48 See 'Unconquerable enemy or bountiful resource? A new perspective on the rabbit in Central Otago', *Australian and New Zealand Environmental History Network* (online), vol. 9, no. 1, 18 March 2014: http://environmentalhistory-au-nz.org/2014/03/unconquerable-enemy-or-bountiful-resource-a-new-perspective-on-the-rabbit-in-central-otago/

49 'Report on the manufacture and growth of *Phormium* or flax', in *Appendix to the Papers of the House of Representatives New Zealand*, 1890, paper H-36 p. 6, q. 72.

50 'The flax industry', *Otago Daily Times*, 5 February 1909, p. 2.

51 Ibid., 19 September 1906, p. 5.

52 *Report of the Royal Commission on Federation, Together with Minutes of Proceedings and Minutes and Evidence* (Wellington: Government Printer, 1901).

53 Ibid., p. *xviii*.

54 Ibid., p. *xix*.

55 Ibid., p. *xx*.

56 Ibid., p. 37.

57 Ibid., p. 60.

58 Ibid., p. 50.

59 Ibid., p. 61.

60 Davison, *The Rise and Fall of Marvellous Melbourne*, p. 56.

61 Ibid., p 71.

62 Olssen, *A History of Otago*, p. 102.

63 Erik Olssen, *Building the New World: Work, politics and society in Caversham 1880s–1920s* (Auckland: Auckland University Press, 1995), ch. 6.

64 Ibid., p. 125.

65 Robert Butrims, *The Phoenix Foundry: Locomotive builders of Ballarat. The history of a Ballarat engineering company* (Williamstown: Australian Railway Historical Society, 2013). See also Bate, *Lucky City*, p. 214.

66 H.O. Bowman, *Port Chalmers: Gateway to Otago* (Christchurch: Capper Press, 1948), p. 106.

67 *New Zealand Herald*, 24 November 1932, p. 12.

68 Gordon Parry, 'Hallenstein, Bendix', from the *Dictionary of New Zealand Biography*: www.TeAra.govt.nz/en/biographies/2h6/hallenstein-bendix

69 Moritz Michaelis, *Chapters from the Story of my Life* (Melbourne: Norman Bros), 1899.

70 Olssen, *A History of Otago*, p. 218.

71 Michael Bassett, *Working with David: Inside the Lange Cabinet* (Auckland: Hodder Moa, 2008), p. 135.

72 'F&P staff farewelled at "very personal function"', *Otago Daily Times* (online), 1 April 2009: www.odt.co.nz/news/dunedin/49853/fampp-staff-farewelled-039very-personal-function039

73 Ric Oram, *Pinot Pioneers: Tales of determination and perseverance from Central Otago* (Auckland: New Holland, 2004).

74 See the essays in the journal *Labour History*, no. 92, May 2007 and no. 105, November 2013.

75 Peter Hempenstall, 'Overcoming separate histories: Historians as "ideas traders" in a trans-Tasman world', *History Australia*, vol. 4, no. 1, 2007, p. 1.

76 Donald Denoon, Philippa Mein Smith and Marivic Wyndham, *A History of Australia, New Zealand, and the Pacific: The Blackwell history of the world* (Oxford: Wiley-Blackwell, 2000), pp. 30–31.

Chapter 3

1 John Henry Watmuff, diary, book 2, 5 December 1862, p. 252 (private collection).

2 Ibid., book 2, 13 April 1862, p. 320.

3 John Henry Watmuff, *The Journals of John Henry Watmuff, New Zealand Extracts, 1861–1864*, Entry 3/22, Manuherikia, 12 October 1862.

4 Watmuff exchanged monthly correspondences with John Halley and Henry Vikerman, both of whom were employed by the Nelson Reef Company at Bendigo. Upon describing the gloomy contents of the letters, Watmuff frequently restated that he would remain in Otago as it provided him with the best financial prospects. See, for example, book 2, 29 March 1862, p. 315; and 20 April 1862, p. 320.

5   Philip Ross May, *The West Coast Gold Rushes* (Christchurch: Pegasus Press, 1962); Lyndon
    Fraser, *Castles of Gold* (Dunedin: Otago University Press, 2007).
6   See Stevan Eldred-Grigg, *Diggers, Hatters and Whores: The story of the New Zealand gold rushes*
    (Auckland: Random House, 2008); Miles Fairburn, *The Ideal Society and Its Enemies: The
    foundation of modern New Zealand society, 1850–1900* (Auckland: Auckland University Press,
    1989); Jock Phillips, *A Man's Country? The image of the Pakeha male. A history* (Auckland:
    Penguin, 1996); Jock Phillips and Terry Hearn, *Settlers: New Zealand immigrants from England,
    Ireland and Scotland, 1800–1945* (Auckland: Auckland University Press, 2008).
7   William Parker Morrell, *The Gold Rushes* (London: Macmillan, 1941); J.H.M. Salmon,
    A History of Goldmining in New Zealand (Wellington: Government Printer, 1963).
8   See, for example, Geoffrey Serle, *The Golden Age: A history of the colony of Victoria, 1851–1861*
    (Carlton: Melbourne University Press, 1963), p. 228; Geoffrey Blainey, *The Rush That
    Never Ended: A history of Australian mining* (Carlton: Melbourne University Press, 1993),
    p. 59; Anthony Edward Dingle, *The Victorians: Settling* (McMahons Point: Fairfax, Syme
    & Weldon Associates, 1984), p. 99. For a historiography of the Australian gold rushes, see
    Iain McCalman, Alexander Cook and Andrew Reeves, 'Introduction', in *Gold: Forgotten
    histories and lost objects of Australia*, eds Iain McCalman, Alexander Cook and Andrew Reeves
    (Cambridge: Cambridge University Press, 2001), pp. 1–22.
9   Philippa Mein Smith, 'The Tasman world', in *The New Oxford History of New Zealand*, ed.
    Giselle Byrnes, (South Melbourne: Oxford University Press, 2009), p. 297.
10 Frank Thistlethwaite, 'Migration from Europe overseas in the 19th and 20th centuries', in
    A Century of European Migration, 1830–1930, eds Rudolph J. Vecoli and Suzanne M. Sinke
    (Champaign-Urbana, IL: Chicago University Press, 1991), p. 31.
11 Alan Lester, 'Imperial circuits and networks: Geographies of the British Empire', *History
    Compass*, vol. 4, no. 1, 2006, pp. 124–41; David Lambert and Alan Lester, 'Introduction:
    Imperial spaces, imperial subjects', in *Colonial Lives Across the British Empire: Imperial careering
    in the long nineteenth century*, eds David Lambert and Alan Lester (Cambridge: Cambridge
    University Press, 2006), pp. 1–31.
12 Alan Lester, 'British settler discourse and the circuits of empire', *History Workshop Journal*,
    vol. 54, no. 1, 2002, p. 25.
13 Geoffrey Blainey, 'A theory of mineral discovery: Australia in the nineteenth century', *Economic
    History Review*, vol. 23, no. 2, 1970, pp. 298–313.
14 David M. Emmons, *The Butte Irish: Class and ethnicity in an American mining town,
    1875–1925* (Champaign-Urbana, IL: University of Illinois Press, 1989), p. 18.
15 Serle, *The Golden Age*, pp. 225–28, 241.
16 Charles D. Ferguson, *The Experiences of a Forty-Niner During Thirty-Four Years' Residence in
    California and Australia* (Cleveland, OH: The Williams Publishing Company, 1888), p. 153.
17 William Crawford Walker, diary, 20 September 1862, State Library of Victoria, MS 11485.
18 *Mount Alexander Mail*, 9 September 1861.
19 Serle, *The Golden Age*, p. 228; Susan Lawrence, 'After the gold rush: Material culture and
    settlement on Victoria's central goldfields', in *Gold: Forgotten histories and lost objects of
    Australia*, p. 262.
20 Serle, *The Golden Age*, p. 228.
21 Lawrence, 'After the gold rush', p. 262.
22 *Bendigo Advertiser*, 28 January 1863, p. 2. See also the following: *Bendigo Advertiser*, 1 October
    1861, 15 October 1861 and 2 December 1862; *Inglewood Advertiser*, 9 December 1862; *Mount
    Alexander Mail*, 21 August 1861.
23 Enda Delaney, *Demography, State and Society: Irish migration to Britain, 1921–1971* (Liverpool:
    Liverpool University Press, 2000), p. 289.
24 Eric Richards, 'An Australian map of British and Irish literacy in 1841', *Population Studies*,
    vol. 53, no. 3, 1999, pp. 356–58; Angela McCarthy, *Irish Migrants in New Zealand,
    1840–1937: 'The desired haven'* (Woodbridge: The Boydell Press, 2005), pp. 2–3, 70–80; Fraser,
    Castles of Gold, pp. 16–17.
25 James Gascoigne, reminiscences (Toitū Otago Settlers Museum, Dunedin, DC-0483, not
    paginated).

26   Watmuff, diary, book 2, 2 December 1861, p. 251. See also Thomas Armstrong (Melbourne), 27 August 1869 (State Library of Victoria, Melbourne, MS-12164); William Jackson Barry, *Past & Present, and Men of the Times* (Wellington: McKee & Gamble, 1897), pp. 145–46.

27   Delaney, *Demography, State and Society*, pp. 289–92.

28   Watmuff, diary, book 2, 2 December 1861, p. 251. See also Archibald Henderson (Patea) to his niece, 2 December 1869, 'Archibald Henderson letters' (Toitū Otago Settlers Museum, Dunedin, DC-2399); John Lees (Melbourne) to his wife (Oldham, Lancashire), 21 January 1862, 'John Lees letters' (State Library of Victoria, Melbourne, MS 10083); Watmuff, diary, book 4, 27 December 1863, p. 44.

29   See Nancy L. Green, 'The comparative method and poststructural structuralism: New perspectives for migration studies', *Journal of American Ethnic History*, vol. 13, no. 4, 1994, pp. 3–22.

30   Serle, *The Golden Age*, pp. 229–41. Brinley Thomas draws a similar conclusion with respect to the flow of capital between Britain and the United States in his book *Migration and Economic Growth* (Cambridge: Cambridge University Press, 1954), p. 111.

31   In 1862 the *Hobart Town Mercury* complained that Tasmania's inability to establish a direct steam service to Dunedin allowed Melbourne merchants to buy up Tasmanian flour intended for sale in Otago and to re-export it more cheaply to Dunedin. See *Otago Daily Times*, 9 January 1862, p. 2. At Hobart, this frustration was intensified by the migration of many of the town's merchants to Otago. See R.G. Kellaway, 'Immigration from New Zealand: The Tasmanian Select Committee of 1864', in *Conference Proceedings 20th New Zealand Geography Conference, Massey University New Zealand, 1999* (Hamilton: Massey University, 1999), pp. 173–74. For products imported and sold on the diggings, see *Otago Daily Times*, 3 January 1862, pp. 2 and 4 and Supplement p. 1, as well as 6 July 1863, p. 2; 'Day book of Bendix Hallenstein' (Toitū Otago Settlers Museum, Dunedin, DC-1430).

32   Otago colonists frequently attributed the lack of a rush from Britain and Ireland to the lack of a direct gold shipment to Britain. See, for example, 'Original correspondence', *Otago Daily Times*, 20 May 1863, p. 5.

33   'Fortnightly communication with Melbourne', *Otago Daily Times*, 1 January 1862, p. 2.

34   Earl Pomeroy, *The Pacific Slope: A history of California, Oregon, Washington, Idaho, Utah, and Nevada* (Reno, NV: University of Nevada Press, 2003), p. *xviii*; Daniel Patrick Marshall, 'Claiming the land: Indians, goldseekers, and the rush to British Columbia', PhD thesis, University of British Columbia, Vancouver, 2000, pp. 8–18.

35   Thomas Burns, *Early Otago and Genesis of Dunedin: Letters of Rev. T. Burns, D.D., 1848–1865* (Dunedin: Evening Star Company, 1916), part 5.

36   *Otago Daily Times*, 3 January 1862 and 6 July 1863; 'Day book of Bendix Hallenstein', Toitū Otago Settlers Museum, DC-1430.

37   'Mining', *Bendigo Advertiser*, 10 March 1863, p. 2.

38   'The gold fields', *Otago Daily Times*, 19 March 1864, p. 5; 16 May 1864, p. 4.

39   'Dunstan', *Otago Daily Times*, 16 May 1864, p. 5.

40   Aled Jones, *Powers of the Press: Newspapers, power and the public in nineteenth century England* (Aldershot: Scholar Press, 1996), p. 5.

41   'Fortnightly communication with Melbourne', *Otago Daily Times*, 1 January 1862, p. 2.

42   May, *The West Coast Gold Rushes*, p. 125.

43   'Reports of the Postal Superintendent of New Zealand', *Appendices to the Journals of the House of Representatives New Zealand*, 1863–1865, D1–D2.

44   Frederic Ramsden, diary, 17 September 1861 (State Library of Victoria, Melbourne, MS-12522).

45   C.J. Coles, diary, 5 September 1861, 22 March 1862, 24 March 1862 (State Library of Victoria, Melbourne, MS-12398).

46   McCarthy, *Irish Migrants*, pp. 2–3.

47   Gascoigne, reminiscences, not paginated.

48   Watmuff, diary, book 2, 20 October 1861, p. 240; 27 October 1861, p. 241; and 2 December 1861, p. 250.

49   Henry Morgan, diary, 1 February 1863, National Library of Australia, M848M.

50   Phillips, *A Man's Country*, pp. 27–28.

51   Alexander Don, *Early Central Otago: A Bathurst miner's reminiscences* (Dunedin: Otago Daily Times Print, 1932), pp. 2–4.

52   Eldred-Grigg, *Diggers, Hatters and Whores*, p. 282.

53   Fairburn, *The Ideal Society*; Eldred-Grigg, *Diggers, Hatters and Whores*; John Milton Hutchins, *Diggers, Constables and Bushrangers: The New Zealand gold rushes as a frontier experience, 1852–1878* (Lakewood: Avrooman-Apfelwald Press, 2010); Phillips, *A Man's Country*.

54   David Fitzpatrick, *Irish Emigration, 1801–1921* (Dublin: Economic and Social History Society of Ireland, 1984), p. 30; Eric Richards, *Britannia's Children: Emigration from England, Scotland, Wales and Ireland since 1600* (London and New York: Hambledon & London, 2004), pp. 13–14, 298–99; McCarthy, *Irish Migrants*, p. 189; Colin Pooley and Jean Turnbull, *Migration and Mobility in Britain Since the Eighteenth Century* (London: UCL Press, 1998), pp. 180–213.

55   McCarthy, *Irish Migrants*, p. 188.

56   Lawrence, 'After the Gold Rush', p. 253.

57   David Fitzpatrick, *Oceans of Consolation: Personal accounts of the Irish migration to Australia* (Ithaca, NY and London: Cornell University Press, 1995), pp. 187–229. The Victorian prospector Charles Jarvis Coles also received letters from acquaintances and family members on the Otago goldfields. See Charles Jarvis Coles, diary, 5 September 1861, 22 March 1862, 24 March 1862 (State Library of Victoria, Melbourne, MS-10869).

58   See, for example, Watmuff, diary, book 2, 27 July 1862, pp. 359–60. See also book 2: 20 October 1861 p. 241; 21 February 1862, p. 306; 16 March 1862, p. 311; 23 March 1862, p. 312; 5 April 1862, p. 317; 23 August 1862, p. 371; and 31 August 1862, p. 374; book 3: 3 November 1862, p. 26; 9 November 1862, p. 28; 30 November 1862, p. 35; 7 December 1862, p. 37; 21 December 1862, p. 41; 18 January 1863, p. 52; 25 January 1863, p. 53; 1 February 1863, p. 57; 27 February 1863, p. 65; 27 April 1863, p. 90; 24 May 1864, p. 99; and 28 June 1863, p. 124; book 4: 27 July 1863, p. 6; and 22 November 1863, p. 4.

59   *Mount Alexander Mail*, 8 January 1863, p. 2.

60   Ibid., 27 December 1862, p. 2 and 10 March 1863, p. 2; 'Editorial', *Otago Daily Times*, 7 January 1863, p. 5 (continuation from p. 4).

61   'Court news', *Argus*, 28 May 1864, p. 5.

62   *Daily Telegraph* (Dunedin), 19 November 1863. It is unclear if Scott ever paid for the care of his wife and children.

63   Kellaway, 'Tasmania and the Otago gold rush, 1861–1865', *Papers and Proceedings: Tasmanian Historical Research Association*, vol. 46, no, 4, p. 172.

64   Fitzpatrick, *Oceans of Consolation*, p. 503.

65   Thomas Pierson, diary, 1 January 1862 (State Library of Victoria, Melbourne, MS-11646).

66   Ibid., 27 January 1862.

67   Ibid., 16 February 1862.

68   See D.H. Akenson, 'Reading the texts of rural immigrants: Letters from the Irish in Australia, New Zealand, and North America', *Canadian Papers of Rural History*, vol. 7, 1990, p. 402.

69   See Brian Roberts, *American Alchemy: The California gold rush and middle-class culture* (Chapel Hill, NC: University of North Carolina Press, 2000), especially pp. 69–92.

70   Cole Harris, *The Resettlement of British Columbia: Essays on colonialism and geographical change* (Vancouver: University of British Columbia Press, 2011), p. 162.

71   See for example, Peter Warren, diary, 1863 (Toitū Otago Settlers Museum, Dunedin, no call number); Watmuff, diary; Charles J.D. Robjohns, diary, 1864 (Alexander Turnbull Library, Wellington, MS-Papers-4913); John Penderick, diary (Lakes District Museum, Arrowtown, N-1901).

72   Andrew Bools, *The Wonders of Providence and Grace, as Illustrated in the Life of the Author, While Doing Business in Deep Waters, in Travels on Sea and Land, and over the Gold Fields of Australia and New Zealand* (London: F. Kirby, 1890), p. 71.

73   See, for example, *Mount Alexander Mail*, 13 September 1861 and 8 September 1862; *Inglewood Advertiser*, 9 September 1862 and 28 October 1862; *Bendigo Advertiser*, 30 October 1862.

74   'Annual Report of the Postmaster General of New Zealand', *Appendices to the Journals of the House of Representatives New Zealand*, 1863–1865, D-1.

75   Alan Atkinson, *The Europeans in Australia: A history* (New York: Oxford University Press, 1997), vol. 1, p. 242.

76   On migration and private correspondences, see McCarthy, *Irish Migrants*; Fitzpatrick, *Oceans of Consolation*; Angela McCarthy, ed., *A Global Clan: Scottish migrant networks and identities since the eighteenth century* (London: I.B. Tauris, 2006); Eric Richards, Richard Reid and David Fitzpatrick, eds, *Visible Immigrants: Neglected sources for the history of Australian immigration* (Canberra: Research School of Social Sciences, Australian National University, 1989).

77   'Editorial', *Otago Witness*, 12 October 1861, pp. 4–5.

78   'Editorial', *Otago Daily Times*, 20 December 1861, p. 4.

79   George Wakefield (Ballarat, Victoria) to his father (England), 23 September 1861, 'George Wakefield letters', State Library of Victoria, MS 6331.

80   'Editorial', *Mount Alexander Mail*, 9 September 1861, p. 2.

81   'Otago', *Age* (Melbourne), 9 September 1862, p. 4.

82   'Editorial', *Bendigo Advertiser*, 6 December 1862, p. 2.

83   'Editorial', *Bendigo Advertiser*, 12 March 1863, p. 2.

84   As cited in the *Otago Daily Times*, 13 February 1863, p. 4.

85   'The New Zealand gold-fields', *Argus*, 24 September 1861, p. 4.

86   'Dunedin', *Argus,* 22 October 1861, p. 5.

87   'New Zealand', *Argus*, 5 April 1862, p. 5.

88   'Dunedin', *Argus*, 22 October 1861, p. 5; 'New Zealand – Otago', *Argus*, 26 June 1862, p. 5.

89   'The New Zealand gold-fields', *Argus*, 28 October 1861, p. 5.

90   Mark Hampton, *Visions of the Press in Britain: 1850–1950* (Champaign-Urbana, IL: University of Chicago Press, 2004), pp. 43–44.

91   'The rush to New Zealand', *Argus*, 28 September 1861, p. 5.

92   Ibid.

93   *Ballarat Star*, republished in *Daily Telegraph*, 10 February 1863.

94   J. Reeve, correspondence written to Police Magistrate Mr McLachlan dated 5 October 1861 and published in 'The Otago goldfields', *Bendigo Advertiser*, 17 October 1861, p. 2.

95   Ibid., 2 October 1861, p. 2.

96   James Vallens, correspondence to Mrs Vallens dated 7 October 1862 from Kawara [sic] River, originally published in the *Ballarat Star* and then in the *Bendigo Advertiser*, 25 November 1862, p. 3.

97   'Editorial', *Otago Witness*, 14 September 1861, p. 5.

98   'Editorial', *Otago Witness*, 5 April 1862, p. 4.

99   'Editorial', *Daily Telegraph,* 10 February 1863, p. 2.

100   Ibid.

101   *Otago Daily Times*, 11 December 1861, p. 2.

102   Jones, *Powers of the Press*, p. 6; Hampton, *Visions of the Press in Britain*, pp. 19–39.

103   'Editorial', *Bendigo Advertiser*, 8 September 1862, p. 2.

104   Charles Clifford, 'Letter to the editor', *Argus*, 30 October 1861, p. 7.

105   'Letters to the editor', *Otago Daily Times*, 18 December 1861, p. 4.

106   Raewyn Dalziel, *Julius Vogel: Business politician* (Auckland: Auckland University Press/Oxford University Press, 1986), pp. 23–30.

107   Dirk Hoerder, 'Introduction. From dreams to possibilities: The secularization of hope and the quest for independence', in *Distant Magnets: Expectations and realities in the immigrant experience, 1840–1930*, eds Dirk Hoerder and Horst Rössler (New York and London: Holmes & Meier, 1993), pp. 1–32.

108   Patricia Nelson Limerick, *The Legacy of Conquest: The unbroken past of the American West* (New York and London: W.W. Norton, 1987), p. 44.

109   Hoerder, 'Introduction', p. 5.

110   David A. Gerber, *Authors of Their Lives: The personal correspondence of British immigrants to North America in the nineteenth century* (New York: New York University Press, 2006), p. 8.

Chapter 4

1   See William Parker Morrell, *The Gold Rushes* (London: Adam and Charles Black, 1940); Alexander Hare McLintock, *The History of Otago* (Dunedin: Whitcombe and Tombs,

1949); Erik Olssen, *A History of Otago* (Dunedin: John McIndoe Limited, 1984); Stevan Eldred-Grigg, *Diggers, Hatters, and Whores: The story of the New Zealand gold rushes* (Auckland: Random House, 2008). For present purposes, the Tuapeka rush is defined as June 1861 to July 1862.

2   Vincent Pyke, *History of the Early Gold Discoveries in Otago* (Dunedin: Otago Daily Times and Witness Newspapers Company Ltd., 1887), p. 52.

3   The letters from which excerpts have been taken form part of a collection held by the writer. Unless otherwise stated, quotations in this chapter are from this source.

4   Contrary to the established view, Read did contemplate keeping news of the discovery private. See George Munroe's account in Pyke, *History of the Early Gold Discoveries in Otago*, pp. 40–41.

5   'Official report on the Tuapeka Gold Fields, by J.T. Thomson, Chief Surveyor, 6 July 1861', *Otago Witness*, 13 July 1861, p. 5.

6   'The gold fields', *Otago Witness*, 27 July 1861, p. 5.

7   'Our gold fields', *Otago Witness*, 3 August 1861, p. 5.

8   T.B. Gillies, 'A visit to the Tuapeka gold fields', *Otago Witness*, 20 July 1861, p. 5.

9   'A trip to the diggings', *Otago Witness*, 20 July 1861, p. 5.

10   'Monthly summary', *Otago Witness*, 31 August 1861, p. 4.

11   'Passenger lists – Victoria, Australia outwards to New Zealand', on the New Zealand Society of Genealogists' website: www.genealogy.org.nz/Products_48.aspx?CategoryId=11&ProductId=387

12   Based on 1579 males and 163 females for whom ages were given.

13   The sources for the immigration graphs are 'Statistics of the old year', *Otago Witness*, 4 January 1862, p. 3; 'Emigration returns for the Port of Dunedin, from January 1 to September 16 1862', *Otago Daily Times*, 19 September 1862, p. 6, and 'Immigration and emigration', *Otago Daily Times*, 6 October 1862, p. 4.

14   See Rodney Maddock and Ian McLean, 'Supply-side shocks: The case of Australian gold', *Journal of Economic History*, vol. 44, no. 4, December 1984, pp. 1047–67. The anti-Chinese feeling was manifest in the Lambing Flat riot, a series of incidents that took place between November 1860 and September 1861, perhaps the most notorious being that in Burrangong on 30 June 1861.

15   'The philosophy of rushes', *Bendigo Advertiser*, 21 August 1861, p. 2.

16   Section XII of the Gold Fields Act 1858.

17   Commissioner Strode to Superintendent, 7 September 1861, in Otago Provincial Government Series 6, Hocken Library, Dunedin.

18   Otago Provincial Council, *Votes and Proceedings*, Session XIII, 1861, Appendix, p. *xviii*.

19   Charles L. Money, *Knocking about in New Zealand* (Melbourne: Samuel Mullen, 1871), p. 8.

20   Thomas Murray, 'Influx of diggers', *Otago Witness*, 28 September 1861, p. 6.

21   'Summary', *Otago Witness*, 12 October 1861, p. 4.

22   'The New Zealand gold-fields,' *Argus*, 14 October 1861, p. 5.

23   'Ballarat miners at Tuapeka', *Star* (Ballarat), 2 October 1861, p. 1.

24   Special Correspondent, 'The New Zealand gold-fields', *Argus*, 14 October 1861, p. 5.

25   'Thirteen days later news from New Zealand', *Star* (Ballarat), 14 October 1861, p. 3.

26   'Otago the gold fields', *Lyttelton Times*, 9 October 1861, p. 4.

27   Keen is the writer's great-great grandfather.

28   'Tuapeka gold-field', *Argus*, 24 September 1861, p. 6.

29   'Summary for Europe', *Argus*, 26 September 1861, p. 5, and 25 October 1861, p. 5.

30   'The New Zealand rush,' *Bendigo Advertiser*, 1 October 1861, p. 3.

31   'New Zealand: The gold-fields', *Argus*, 29 November 1861, p. 5.

32   'The fever abates', *Bendigo Advertiser*, 24 September 1861, p. 2.

33   'Editorial', *Argus*, 18 October 1861, p. 4.

34   See Gavin McLean, *Sam's Grief: A true tale of the goldrushes* (Dunedin: Otago Heritage Books, 1989).

35   'New Zealand, Otago', *Star* (Ballarat), 22 January 1862, Supplement p. 1.

36   'The Waipori', *Otago Daily Times*, 3 Januray 1862, p. 2; 'Waipori', *Otago Daily Times*, 27 January 1862, p. 2; 'New Zealand. Otago', *Argus*, 11 April 1862, p. 6.

37   'New Zealand', *Bendigo Advertiser*, 19 December 1861, p. 3.

38   'The gold-fields', *Otago Daily Times*, 3 March 1862, p. 2.

39   'The gold fields Tuapeka', *Otago Daily Times*, 13 May 1862, p. 5.

40   'The gold fields Tuapeka', *Otago Daily Times*, 26 July 1862, p. 5.

41   See, for example, 'The gold fields Tuapeka', *Otago Daily Times*, 31 July 1862, p. 5.

42   Admissions to Dunedin Hospital during the year ended 30 September 1862 included 122 for typhoid, 141 for inflammatory diseases and 36 for bowel disorders. These admissions included miners brought down from the Tuapeka.

43   'Gold fields', *Otago Daily Times*, 19 April 1862, p. 4.

44   Historians have long claimed that merchants and other service providers reaped most of the profits from mining. See, for example, Karen Clay and Randall Jones, 'Migrating to riches? Evidence from the Californian gold rush', *Journal of Economic History*, vol. 68, 2008, pp. 997–1027; Keir Reeves, Lionel Frost and Charles Fahey, 'Integrating the historiography of the nineteenth-century gold rushes', *Australian Economic History Review*, vol. 50, no. 2, July 2010, pp. 111–28.

45   'Tuapeka diggings', *Otago Witness*, 12 October 1861, p. 5.

46   Patrick O'Farrell, review of Philip R. May's 'The West Coast Gold Rushes', *New Zealand Journal of History*, vol. 3, 1969, pp. 89–90.

Chapter 5

1   This description of events is based on John Angus, *One Hundred Years of Vincent County 1877–1977* (Clyde: Vincent County Council, 1977), pp. 31–35.

2   *Dunstan Times*, n.d., quoted in Angus, *One Hundred Years of Vincent County*, p. 32.

3   'Cromwell (from our correspondent)', *Otago Daily Times*, 9 February 1877, p. 3.

4   Number cited in Angus, *One Hundred Years of Vincent County*, p. 19, and taken from Statistics New Zealand, *Census of New Zealand 1878*: www3.stats.govt.nz/ historic_publications/1878-census/1878-results-census.html

5   See John H. Angus, 'City and country: Change and continuity', PhD thesis, vol. 1, University of Otago, Dunedin, 1976, pp. 19–157.

6   This change is described in most gold-mining histories. See, for example, J.H.M. Salmond, *A History of Goldmining in New Zealand* (Wellington: Government Printer, 1963), pp. 102–10. For an account of the changes in a nearby field, Cardrona, see John H. Angus, *Aspiring Settlers: European settlement in the Hawea and Wanaka region to 1914* (Dunedin: John McIndoe, 1981), pp. 27–31.

7   Explicit references were made in the debate to the need to pre-empt the democratic contagions of Victoria. See Neill Atkinson, *Adventures in Democracy: A history of the vote in New Zealand* (Dunedin: University of Otago Press, 2003), pp. 44–46.

8   In 1861 Major J.L. Richardson, fearing miner radicalism, had the colonial governor send down 100 troops from the North Island in anticipation of security problems (they were not needed). See Graeme Morton, 'Gold, law and Freemasonry: A biographical analysis of Vincent Pyke as a goldfields administrator in Otago 1862–1867', BA Hons essay, University of Otago, Dunedin, New Zealand, 1994, p. 29.

9   For the franchise, see D.M. Wylie, 'Representation and the franchise in New Zealand, 1852–1879', MA thesis, University of Otago, Dunedin, 1951, pp. 53–56; S.E.R. O'Sullivan, 'Political effects of gold in Otago, January 1862–January 1864', MA thesis, University of Otago, Dunedin, 1959, pp. 1–19.

10   Protests about the requirement to register for provincial elections were part of a petition by Wakatipu miners for administration to be transferred to central government. See O'Sullivan, 'Political effects of gold', p. 15.

11   Similarly at Queenstown, a warden was in post within three months of the discovery of gold on the Arrow. Wayne Angus, 'Queenstown 1862–1864: The genesis of a goldfield's community', BA Hons essay, University of Otago, Dunedin, New Zealand, 1987.

12   A.P.F. Browne, 'The Otago goldfields 1861–1863: Administration and public life', MA thesis, University of Canterbury, Christchurch, 1974, pp. 223–24.

13   Ibid., p. 210. See also Salmond, *A History of Goldmining*, pp.103–04; Vincent Pyke, *History of Early Gold Discoveries in Otago* (Dunedin: Otago Daily Times and Witness Newspapers Co. Ltd., 1962), pp. 61–67. With respect to the establishment of order, by far the most common

offence was that of drunk and disorderly (117 out of 175 cases in 1863 in the Queenstown Warden's Court).

14   A contemporary account of the Eureka Stockade incident emphasises the local and spontaneous nature of much of the action and the roles of petitions, crowds and deputations. One difference from events on the Otago goldfields was the sending in of troops, which changed the dynamic completely. See Raffaello Carboni, *The Eureka Stockade* (Melbourne: J.P. Atkinson and Co., 1855): www.hereticpress.com/Dogstar/History/Carboni.html#.VhL1lys-VCE

15   Browne, 'The Otago goldfields', p. 192. This account of the nature of politics in the 1860s draws extensively on Browne, pp. 192–230. See also Angus, *Queenstown 1862–1864*, pp. 30–32; Salmon, *A History of Goldmining*, p. 103.

16   Browne, 'The Otago goldfields', p. 197.

17   See discussion of the failure to generate a democratic movement in Stevan Eldred-Grigg, *Diggers, Hatters and Whores: The story of the New Zealand gold rush* (Auckland: Random, 2008), pp. 351–58.

18   W.R. Mayhew, *Tuapeka; The Land and its People: A social history of the borough of Lawrence and its surrounding districts* (Dunedin: Otago Centennial Historical Publications, 1949), pp. 68–78; Robin Marks, *Hammer & Tap: Shaping Tuapeka County 1876–1976* (Lawrence: Tuapeka County Council, 1977), pp. 336–40. Like Pyke, Brown was an elected member and from time to time chief executive of the county council. He did not have a county named after him but did have three Tuapeka ridings invested with his given and family names: James, Clark and Browns.

19   See Angus, *100 Years of Vincent County*, pp. 28–34.

20   Marks, *Hammer & Tap*, p. 340, citing the *North Otago Times* of 1887.

21   The principal sources for Pyke's life are Angus's 'City and country' and *100 Years of Vincent County*; Morton, 'Gold, law and Freemasonry'; Terry Hearn, 'Vincent Pyke', from Te Ara – Encyclopedia of New Zealand: www.teara.govt.nz/en/biographies/2p33/pyke-vincent

22   Hearn, 'Vincent Pyke', para. 10.

Chapter 6

1   Vincent Pyke, *History of the Early Gold Discoveries in Otago* (Dunedin: Otago Daily Times and Witness Newspapers Co. Ltd., 1887), p. 5. Note that although the spelling 'Maoris' or 'Maories' in this and other historical sources is incorrect because the Māori alphabet has no letter 's', I have retained the spellings used in them.

2   James T. O'Leary, 'The colonising pen: Mid-nineteenth-century European writing about Māori', PhD thesis, Victoria University of Wellington, 2001, pp. 26–91.

3   'Editorial', *Otago Daily Times*, 15 August 1862, p. 4; 'Editorial', 21 August 1862, p. 4.

4   For example: 'Native politics', *Otago Daily Times*, 17 March 1862, p. 4; 'Editorial', 13 April 1863, p. 4; 'The Native War', 17 June 1863, p. 5; and others.

5   'Mining intelligence', *Star* (Ballarat), 24 August 1861, p. 2.

6   Duperrey's second-in-command, Jules Sébastien César Dumont d'Urville, returned to New Zealand in 1826 in the *Coquille* (re-named *Astrolabe*) and mapped much of New Zealand's coast.

7   Leslie R. Marchant, 'Blosseville, Jules Poret de (1802–1833)', from Australian Dictionary of Biography: http://adb.anu.edu.au/biography/ blosseville-jules-poret-de-1799/text2041

8   John Hall-Jones, 'Caddell, James', from Te Ara – the Encyclopedia of New Zealand: www.TeAra.govt.nz/en/biographies/1c1/caddell-james

9   R. McNab, *Murihiku: A history of the South Island of New Zealand and the islands adjacent and lying to the south, from 1642 to 1835* (Invercargill: William Smith, 1907), p. 306.

10   Translation: 'Essay on the manners and customs of the inhabitants of the southern land of Tavai-Poénammou [Te Wai Pounamu]'.

11   Jules de Blosseville, 'Mémoire géographique sur la Nouvelle-Zélande'. In *Nouvelles annales des voyages de la géographie et de l'histoire* (Paris: MM. J.B. Eyriès and Malte-Brun, 1826), vol. 24, p. 32. Translation by R. McNab, *Murihiku*, p. 227.

12   Hilary Mitchell and John Mitchell, *Te Tau Ihu o Te Waka a Maui: A history of Māori of Nelson and Marlborough. Vol I. Te tangata me te whenua – the people and the land* (Wellington: Huia Publishers, 2004), pp. 134–37.

13   Pyke, *History of the Early Gold Discoveries*, p. 3.

14   Eva Wilson, *Hakoro Ki Te Iwi: The story of Captain Howell and his family* (Orepuki: Wilson Family, 1976), pp. 26–27.

15   '"Mararoa", Maori miners' amazing expedition voyage to California in search of gold', *Evening Post*, 18 December 1937, p. 10.

16   MaraeMelbourne, '*Pasifika Victoria "The way forward"*': www.maraemelbourne.net/thereport. php

17   'Coroner's inquest', *Empire*, 20 December 1855, p. 2.

18   'Magistrate's Court', *Sydney Morning Herald*, 25 January 1854, p. 4.

19   'A Black Man's Life', *Empire*, 11 June 1855, p. 4.

20   'Newcastle', *Sydney Morning Herald*, 19 November, 1855, p. 3.

21   'Newcastle Regatta', *Maitland Mercury*, 26 May 1857, p. 5.

22   David 'Fred' Cahir, 'Black gold: A history of the role of Aboriginal people on the gold fields of Victoria, 1850–70', PhD thesis, Ballarat University, Victoria, pp. 94–122.

23   'Advertisement: A first rate chance', *Bendigo Advertiser*, 27 July 1857, p. 3.

24   'Maori Gully', *Bendigo Advertiser*, 5 September 1857, Supplement p. 1.

25   'Puddling machines for sale', *Bendigo Advertiser*, 14 August 1856, p. 3.

26   'Bendigo mining intelligence', *Bendigo Advertiser*, 18 October 1858, p. 2.

27   'Whipstick', *Bendigo Advertiser*, 1 June 1858, p. 2.

28   'Elysian Flat, Whipstick', *Argus*, 16 December 1857, p. 4.

29   'Whipstick', *Bendigo Advertiser*, 9 February 1858, p. 2.

30   'The 71-pound nugget', *Bendigo Advertiser*, 13 April 1858, p. 3.

31   'A Red Jacket nugget', *Bendigo Advertiser*, 11 November 1863, p. 2.

32   'John Chinaman at the diggings', *Argus*, 23 May 1855, p. 6.

33   *Age* (Melbourne), quoted in 'Fallacies with reference to the natives', *Otago Witness*, 1 March 1862, p. 8.

34   'Editorial', *Otago Daily Times*, 1 December 1862, p. 4.

35   'Old Identiana, being a compilation of incidents and anecdotes of the pioneer days', *Otago Witness*, 31 March 1898, p. 19.

36   Ibid.

37   'The story of the early gold discoveries in Otago, chapter I', *Otago Witness*, 5 November 1886, p. 14; Pyke, *History of the Early Gold Discoveries*, p. 3.

38   F. Tuckett, entry dated 'Saturday & Sunday May 4 & 5th, 1844', in 'The survey of Otago, the future site of Dunedin, part of Frederick Tuckett's diary, from March 28th to June 1st 1844'. Diary transcription courtesy of Winterbourne Family History Online: www. frenchaymuseumarchives.co.uk/FrederickTuckettLetters.htm

39   'Biographical sketches of the colonists of the first decade', *Otago Witness*, 17 March 1898, p. 27.

40   'Editorial', *Otago Daily Times*, 27 December 1862, p. 4.

41   'Old Identiana', *Otago Witness*, 31 March 1898, p. 19.

42   'Rakiraki's sketch of the great lagoons near the source of the Matou River, 1844', in J.W. Barnicoat's journal 1844 (Hocken Library, Dunedin, reference HM 882).

43   'Provincial Council', *Otago Witness*, 6 December 1856, p. 3.

44   'The gold dredging industry', *Otago Witness*, 31 August 1899, p. 18.

45   'Latest from Tuapeka', *The Otago Colonist*, 19 July 1861, p. 3.

46   'The rush to New Zealand', *Bendigo Advertiser*, 30 September 1861, p. 3.

47   'The New Zealand goldfields, No. IV', *Argus*, 14 October 1861, p. 5.

48   'A Yankee gold-digger', quoted in J.M. Hutchins, *Diggers, Constables, and Bushrangers: The New Zealand gold rushes as a frontier experience, 1852–1876* (Lakewood, CO: Avrooman-Apfelwald Press, 2010), p. 53.

49   'News of the week', *Otago Witness*, 15 August 1863, p. 5.

50   'Waitahuna', *Otago Witness*, 28 June 1862, p. 3.

51   W. Ayson, *Pioneering in Otago* (Dunedin: Reed, 1937), p. 58.

52   'Old memories of Southland', *Southland Times*, 4 September 1889, p. 3.

53   A.H. Duncan, *The Wakatipians or Early Days in New Zealand* (Arrowtown: Lakes District Centennial Museum, 1969; reprinted from the 1888 original), p. 32.

54   Quoted in Pyke, *History of the Early Gold Discoveries*, p. 82.

55   Duncan, *The Wakatipians*, p. 32.

56   Vincent Pyke, Secretary of Goldfields, 'Report on the gold fields of Otago', *Otago Daily Times*, 17 October 1863, p. 10.

57   'Fatal boat accident on Lake Wakatip', *Otago Daily Times*, 28 August 1862, p. 5.

58   'Editorial', *Otago Daily Times*, 25 September 1862, p. 4; 'The natives', *Colonist*, 14 October 1862, p. 3; 'Mr Rees', *The Southland News*, 5 November 1862, p. 3; Duncan, *The Wakatipians*, p. 41.

59   'Editorial', *Otago Daily Times*, 6 October 1863, p. 4. The medal is now on display at the Lakes District Museum, Arrowtown.

60   'Death of Mr Rees', *Otago Daily Times*, 3 November 1898, p. 4.

61   Duncan, *The Wakatipians*, p. 41.

62   Philip Ross May, *The West Coast Gold Rushes* (Christchurch: Pegasus Press, 1962), p. 140.

63   'Old Identiana', *Otago Witness*, 31 March 1898, p. 19.

64   F. MacKenzie, *The Sparkling Waters of the Whakatipua* (Dunedin: Reed, 1948), p. 78.

65   Pyke, *History of the Early Gold Discoveries*, p. 82.

66   'Passing notes', *Otago Witness*, 6 April 1888, p. 21.

67   Thomas Low, 'Correspondence', *Otago Daily Times*, 26 January 1899, p. 3.

68   T.J. Hearn, 'Fox, William', from Te Ara – the Encyclopedia of New Zealand: www.TeAra.govt. nz/ en/biographies/1f16/fox-william

69   See, for example: 'The West Canterbury goldfields', *Lyttelton Times*, 16 February 1866, p. 3.

70   Hearn, 'Fox, William'.

71   'Editorial', *Otago Daily Times*, 7 September 1865, p. 4; 'Dunstan', 30 October 1865, p. 5; 'Lake Wanaka to the West Coast: Mr Pyke's report', *Otago Witness*, 4 November 1865, p. 7.

72   Pyke, 'Report on the goldfields of Otago'.

73   District Coroner (Oamaru), 'Accidents and fatalities', *Star*, 28 July 1898, p. 3.

74   'The Kyeburn murder', *Otago Daily Times*, 24 September 1880, p. 3.

75   William Grumitt, letter to the editor, 'Discovery of the Wakatipu goldfield', *Otago Witness*, 24 November 1898, p. 19.

76   W. Grumitt, 'Correspondence', *Otago Daily Times*, 17 November 1898, p. 2.

77   Thomas Low, 'Correspondence', *Otago Daily Times*, 26 January 1899, p. 3; Hearn, 'Fox, William'.

78   'The goldfields', *Otago Daily Times*, 17 January 1863, p. 5.

79   'Lake Wanaka to the West Coast', p. 7.

80   'Facts and scraps', *Nelson Examiner and New Zealand Chronicle*, 23 November 1865, p. 3.

81   Duncan, *The Wakatipians*, p. 59.

82   'Editorial', *West Coast Times*, 10 December 1866, p. 2.

83   'Local and general news', *Wellington Independent*, 21 March 1867, p. 3.

84   'Editorial', *Otago Daily Times*, 19 September 1870, p. 2.

85   Ibid., 19 May 1874, p. 2.

86   'A new rush', *Evening Post*, 16 February 1880, p. 3.

87   'The Gympie diggings (from the Gympie Times)', *West Coast Times*, 9 June 1869, p. 3.

88   'The gold fields', *Otago Daily Times*, 18 April 1863, pp. 5, 5b.

89   'The Lake Country', *Otago Daily Times*, 2 April 1863, p. 5.

90   Ibid., 27 March 1863, p. 5.

91   'The gold fields', *Otago Daily Times*, 18 April 1863, p. 5.

92   'The Lake Country', *Otago Daily Times*, 5 February 1863, p. 4.

93   Ibid., 6 April 1863, p. 5.

94   'Narrative of current events for transmission to Melbourne', *Otago Daily Times*, 7 February 1863, p. 5.

95   Ibid.

96   Reported as per newspaper: John H. Salmon, *History of Goldmining in New Zealand* (Wellington: Government Printer, 1963), p. 91; H.A. Glasson, *The Golden Cobweb: A saga of the Otago goldfields, 1861–64* (Dunedin: Otago Daily Times, 1957), pp. 68–69; haka: R. Gilkison, *Early Days in Central Otago* (Dunedin, Otago Daily Times, 1930), p. 45; additional weapons and a haka: D.A. Knudson, *The Story of Wakatipu* (Christchurch: Whitcombe and Tombs, 1968), p. 80; Hutchins, *Diggers, Constables, and Bushrangers*, p. 72;

additional weapons, a haka, violence and 'one at least was killed': MacKenzie, *Sparkling Waters of the Whakatipua*, p. 84.

97   'Otago, latest', *Taranaki Herald*, 25 April 1863, p. 3.

98   'Our lake correspondent', *Otago Daily Times*, 30 April 1863, p. 4.

99   Pyke, *History of the Early Gold Discoveries*, p. 88.

100   Vincent Pyke (Secretary of Goldfields), 'Report on the Goldfields of Otago', *Otago Daily Times*, 17 October 1863, p. 10.

101   Gilkison, *Early Days in Central Otago*, p. 43.

102   Vincent Pyke, 'The story of the early gold discoveries in Otago', *Otago Witness*, 21 January 1887, p. 14.

103   T.A. Pybus, *Maori and Missionary: Early Christian missions in the South Island of New Zealand* (Wellington: Reed, 1954), p. 169.

104   Gilkison, *Early Days in Central Otago*, p. 43.

105   Atholl Anderson, 'Ellison, Thomas Rangiwāhia', from Te Ara – the Encyclopedia of New Zealand: www.TeAra.govt.nz/en/biographies/2e7/ellison-thomas-rangiwahia

106   'News of the week', *Otago Witness*, 13 February 1875, p. 15.

107   'Advertisements: Farm to LET', *Otago Daily Times*, 28 July 1882, p. 1.

108   Anderson, 'Ellison, Thomas Rangiwāhia'.

109   For example: 'Estate of Hemi Koraku Karetai, Puketeraki, 20 November, 1906' (Archives New Zealand, Dunedin office, Otago Testamentary Register 1904–1907, C 720 961, Reference DAGI D247 9010 Box 7, record 7, and others).

110   'Our lake correspondent', *Otago Daily Times*, 30 April 1863, p. 4.

111   George Magnus Hassing, *Pages from the Memory Log of G.M. Hassing: Sailor; pioneer; schoolmaster* (Invercargill: Southland Times, 1930), p. 30.

112   'The gold fields' warden's report', *Otago Witness*, 25 September 1863, p. 2.

113   'Waipori', *Otago Witness*, 11 January 1862, p. 7.

114   'Reconnaissance survey of the Lake District', *Otago Witness*, 9 May 1863, p. 7.

115   'Southland', *Otago Witness*, 11 October 1862, p. 2.

116   'Southland, the Nokomai diggings', *Otago Witness*, 11 October 1862, p. 5.

117   'Later news, from the Nokomai', *Otago Witness*, 11 October 1862, p. 5.

118   'Arrow River', *Otago Daily Times*, 11 August 1863, p. 5.

119   'Tuapeka to Wakatipu', *Otago Daily Times*, 26 March 1863, p. 5.

120   'The Lake Country', *Otago Daily Times*, 4 September 1863, p. 6.

121   'Arrow River', *Otago Daily Times*, 11 August 1863, p. 5.

122   See L. Carpenter, 'A 35-year endeavour: Bendigo's Rise and Shine Sluicing Syndicate, *Australasian Historical Archaeology*, vol. 30, 2012, p. 10.

123   W.G. Mouat, *Devonport Ahoy! Recollections of Gilbert & Dick Mouat* (self-published, with copies held at Dunedin Public Library, Hocken Library, and other repositories).

124   D. Fetherling, *The Gold Crusades* (Toronto: Toronto University Press, 1997), p. 141.

125   Michael Gates, 'Rooting out the family tree can reveal fascinating history': http://yukon-news.com/opinions/columns/24185/

126   Margaret Orbell, trans., *He Reta Ki Te Maunga Letters to the Mountain* (Auckland: Reed, 2002), pp. 24–44.

127   Keir Reeves, 'Tracking the dragon down under: Chinese cultural connections in gold rush Australia and Aotearoa, New Zealand', *Graduate Journal of Asia-Pacific Studies*, vol. 3, no. 1, 2005, p. 56; Cahir, *Black Gold*.

128   For example, J.J. Rawls, 'Gold diggers: Indian miners in the California gold rush', *California Historical Quarterly*, vol. 55, no. 1, Spring 1976, pp. 28–45.

129   John Walton Caughey, *Gold Is the Cornerstone* (Los Angeles: University of California Press, 1948), pp. 27, 193; J.S. Holliday, *The World Rushed In: The California gold rush experience* (New York: Simon & Schuster, 1981), pp. 38–41, 328.

130   West Coast 1860s–1880s: J. Halket Millar, *Westland's Golden 'Sixties* (Wellington: Reed, 1959), pp. 9–15, 31–33, 36, 52, 55, 91–94, 112, 192; May, *The West Coast Gold Rushes*, pp. 66–69, 84–85, 89, 92–94, 152, 157, 160, 298; Salmon, *History of Goldmining in New Zealand*, pp. 129, 132, 134. Salmon also discusses Māori mining in Nelson in 1857 (pp. 36–37), updated in Hilary Mitchell and John Mitchell, *Te Tau Ihu o Te Waka: A History of Māori of*

Nelson and Marlborough. Vol II, Te ara hou – the new society (Wellington: Huia Publishers, 2004), pp. 186, 272, 299–309, 328, 444. Hauraki: Paul Monin, *Hauraki Contested 1769–1875* (Wellington: Bridget Williams Books, 2001), pp. 140, 178, 181, 206; Philip Hart, 'Maori and mining: A case study of Hone Werahiko and Te Aroha', *Journal of Australasian Mining History*, vol. 1, no. 1, 2003, pp. 79–94.

Chapter 7

1 Select Committee on Chinese Immigration, *Appendix to the Journals of the House of Representatives New Zealand*, 1871, H-5A, p. 13. The 1871 West Coast Chinese population was 24.

2 They were Mrs Lock Wah and Mrs Kwok Wah Siu. Mrs Lock, aged 44, arrived in 1892 to join her husband, the Panyu storekeeper in Naseby. Mrs Kwok spent six months in Alexandra in 1907. Her young (naturalised) Zengcheng Cantonese husband petitioned parliament with the help of Reverend Alexander Don to have her entry poll tax refunded in 1907. The couple moved from Dunedin to Alexandra to open a store, but this closed within months.

3 James Ng, *Windows on a Chinese Past* (Dunedin: Otago Heritage Books, vol. 1, 1993), chapter 1A, pp. 11–36.

4 In the 1874 census, 62 could read and write English out of the total New Zealand Chinese population of 4743. In the 1901 census, the Chinese population was 2857, of whom 385 could read and write English, 823 could read and write Chinese, and 17 could read Chinese.

5 To give a sense of the value of these amounts, a trained school teacher earned just over £2.0 per week in 1863 (£120 per year, including a school house), and a trained 'master' stonemason earned just under £3.0 per week until 1870. In the 1870s–80s, 'leading hand' quartz miners employed by the larger companies earned £3-10s per week. For more on this matter, see Lloyd Carpenter, 'A petty and spiteful spirit on the part of the company: The 1881 Cromwell Company strike at Bendigo, Otago', *Labour History*, no. 105, November 2013, pp. 187–210.

6 James Ng, *Windows on a Chinese Past*, vol. 1, Section 2A, p. 83.

7 The Chinese were threatened with being thrown overboard (J.A. Ewen and W.A. Tolmie, 'The Chinese question', *Otago Witness*, 30 September 1865, pp. 13–14; A. Mei Ho, 'The pioneer Chinaman on the Otago goldfields', *Otago Witness*, 10 June 1871, p. 9. One of these men was Louis Gaytan, a Siyi man (A. Don, *Roll*, no. 9, p. 54), who later was an intermarried (i.e. married to a European woman) storekeeper in Naseby and Macraes Flat and a prominent miner and leader of his Looi clan at Macraes.

8 'Editorial', *Otago Daily Times*, 23 February 1864, p. 4; 'Fifth report of the secretary of the gold fields', 30 January 1866, p. 5; 'The history of gold discoveries', 31 January, 1866, p. 5.

9 Ewen and Tolmie, 'The Chinese Question', pp. 13–14; 'Chamber of Commerce', *Otago Witness*, 14 October 1865, p. 17.

10 Ewen and Tolmie, 'The Chinese Question', pp. 13–14.

11 The Siyi (Seyip in Cantonese) were from a cooperative of four adjacent counties southwest of Guangzhou and Hong Kong. The Sanyi (Samyip in Cantonese) were from three adjacent counties to the west of Guangzhou.

12 Eric Wong Tape, 'Wong Tape papers', Hocken Library, Dunedin, 1969, MI++870m. The Siyi were the prime faction in Victoria. Wong founded the Kum Yoon Lee store in Dunedin, sold it in 1873 to three Zengcheng men representing a Hong Kong store with Sydney and Melbourne branches, and then opened a new Dunedin store named Hip Fung Taai. The merchant Wongs in Cromwell may have been relations.

13 Lee Mow Tai headed a partnership of five men, including Lowe Kong Meng ('Letters of administration', Archives New Zealand, Dunedin office, A1859 in DAAC, AccD239, 119), who operated the Sun War On store in Dunedin: 'The Chinese – singular superstition', *Otago Witness*, 29 November 1873, p. 20. Sun War On closed in 1874, to be replaced by the Sanyi store Kwong Shing Wing in Stafford Street.

14 'Obituary', *Outlook*, 19 August 1905, p. 5; 'Obituary', 27 December 1915, p. 7.

15 'News of the week', *Otago Witness*, 23 December 1865, p. 13; 'The pioneer Chinaman on the goldfields', *Otago Witness*, 10 June 1871, p. 9. See also Pauline Rule, 'The transformative effect of Australian experience on the life of Ho A Mei, 1838–1901, Hong Kong community leader and entrepreneur', *Journal of Chinese Overseas*, vol. 9, no. 2, 2013, pp. 107–34. Ho, a young

Nanhai interpreter, came to Dunedin in November 1865 to ascertain the arrangements made to receive incoming Chinese on 'behalf of influential countrymen', who most likely were Sanyi.

16   The Siyi Cantonese spread in an anti-clockwise arc to the Naseby, Cardrona and then Arrowtown, Cromwell, Clyde and Roxburgh districts. The big increase in numbers of Panyu Cantonese in 1871 enabled them to spread and consolidate in a clockwise arc from Tuapeka through Roxburgh, Alexandra and the Manuherikia Valley to Naseby, and then to the Queenstown area and the Southland goldfields.

17   The Siyi claims were at Blackstone Hill: *Otago Daily Times*, 26 January 1866, p. 4. The Sanyi claims were at Wetherstones and an unknown locality: *Tuapeka Recorder*, 23 February 1866, p. 3. See also 'The pioneer Chinaman on the goldfields', *Otago Witness*, 10 June 1871, p. 9.

18   The provincial secretary said: '… at first let them come and look around': 'The Chinese', *Otago Witness*, 18 May 1867, p. 9. The miner's right was required in 1868, and this stipulation was enforced equally on Europeans: 'Waitahuna', *Tuapeka Times*, 24 October 1868, p. 3.

19   Alloo, recruited from Victoria, rose to sergeant before being invalided out with rheumatism in 1878. Ng, *Windows on a Chinese Past*, vol. 1, pp. 201–04. Blewitt, educated in India and China, came from Australia. He was a scholarly bachelor and a Sinophile who lived in the Lawrence Chinese Camp. He was temporarily employed by the provincial government in 1867, rehired but made redundant in the 1869/70 slump, re-employed later in 1870 and finally lost his job in December 1876. See ibid., pp. 201–04. Charles Wong Gye replaced Alloo and Blewitt in 1878.

20   'Outrage on a Chinese', *Otago Witness*, 8 February 1868, p. 5.

21   'Dunstan', *Otago Witness*, 18 April 1868, p. 13; 'Bendigo', *Dunstan Times*, 16 April 1872, pp. 2 –3.

22   In 1867 Governor George Grey approved the ports of Auckland, Wellington, Nelson, Greymouth, Hokitika, Lyttelton, Dunedin, Invercargill and Bluff for the importation and warehousing of opium (*Southland Gazette*, 1866–70). That European traders stocked opium is inferred from the Chinese explanation that European stockists thwarted the Chinese campaign in 1888 to halt opium smoking by ceasing sale of the drug: Young Hee, 'Anti-opium meeting', *Outlook*, 29 July 1899, p. 4.

23   'Editorial', *Dunstan Times*, 7 October, p. 2; 'The Chinese', 16 December 1870, p. 2. The key element in early Chinese competition in New Zealand was that they discounted their labour and profit, so their cheapness probably applied to a range of goods and services. Accordingly, Europeans patronised them, and that may be one reason why European shopkeepers initially welcomed the Chinese and then tended to turn against them by 1871 ('The Chinese question', *Otago Witness*, 15 July 1871, p. 18). The Select Committee on Chinese Immigration recorded 96 Chinese stores in Otago in 1871. Competition from Chinese stores led to the 1867 Lawrence by-law banning Chinese premises in the borough, and was partly the reason for the Chinese shops in Alexandra being acted against in 1895.

24   'Waitahuna', *Bruce Herald*, 17 June 1868, p. 5; 'Lawrence', 30 December 1868, p. 5.

25   'Editorial', *Bruce Herald*, 10 April 1867, p. 5; 'Alexandra', *Otago Witness*, 18 October 1867, p. 11; 'Dunstan', *Otago Witness*, 25 August 1867, p. 2. In the 14 May 1869 issue of *The Dunstan Times*, the editor wrote (p. 2) that Chinese market gardeners had decreased the price of their vegetables.

26   For instance, at Kyeburn in 1870, vegetables were 'almost worth their weight in gold while fruit is altogether unobtainable': 'News of the week', *Otago Witness*, 9 July 1870, p. 15.

27   Ng, 'Table 8: Earnings', *Windows on a Chinese Past*, vol. 1, pp. 349–50.

28   European protagonists of the invitations probably regarded the Chinese willingness to work second-rate auriferous ground as positive because it minimised competition with other miners yet produced significant gold: 'The Chinese', *Dunstan Times*, 19 October 1867, p. 2, and 'Mining', 9 December 1870; 'Among the Celestials', *Otago Witness*, 18 September 1869, p. 11.

29   General labour: 'Wages at Weatherstones', *Tuapeka Times*, 14 March 1868, p. 3; 'The labour question', *Tuapeka Times*, 4 August 1870, p. 6; 'The dearth of labour', *Otago Witness*, 1 November 1873, p. 1; *Dunstan Times*, 28 March 1873. Mining employees: 'Dunstan', *Otago Witness*, 18 October 1867, p. 6. Harvesting: *Dunstan Times*, 30 January 1874 and 23 October 1874. Sheep station: *Dunstan Times*, 14 and 21 November 1873. Fencing: 'Local intelligence', *Tuapeka Times*, 26 June 1875, p. 2; *Outlook*, 13 April 1901, p. 22. Roading: 'Chinese labourers: To the editor', *Otago Witness*, 4 May 1872, p. 8.

30   Chinese could be hired at a cheaper rate: 'The Chinese question', *Tuapeka Times*, 5 October
      1871, p. 7. See also Select Committee on Chinese Immigration, H-5A, p. 14. Parties of
      Chinese were hired for roading projects, railway construction and rabbiting drives on contract
      rather than wages.

31   'Clutha railway', *Otago Witness*, 16 November 1872, p. 11; 'Warden's report', *Tuapeka Times*,
      20 May 1874, p. 3; *Appendix to the Journals of the House of Representatives New Zealand*, 1874,
      H-9, p. 24.

32   'Local and general', *Dunstan Times*, 11 August 1871. In Invercargill, Reverend Don recorded
      'about 20 Chinese cooks': Alexander Don, diary, 1881–83, entry of 30 August 1883, p. 116
      (diary held in James Ng's personal collection). Chinese domestic cooks and servants were also
      employed. See Joe Yue Sing, *A Brief History of the Overseas Chinese in New Zealand* (Palmerston
      North: New Zealand Twin Star, 1996), pp. 26–27.

33   Hong Kong law of 1858 required a Chinese doctor on emigrant ships. Because these doctors
      were not paid for the return trip, some left the ships for the goldfields, which meant that most
      concentrations of Chinese miners had one or two Chinese doctors: James Ng, *Windows on a
      Chinese Past* (Dunedin: Otago Heritage Books, vol. 2, 1995), pp. 44–47; *N.Z. Presbyterian*,
      2 April 1883, p. 185. After the gold rush, Chinese-trained doctors and herbalists became a
      longstanding feature in New Zealand cities.

34   'Editorial', *Otago Witness*, 9 December 1871, p. 12; 'The Chinese', *Dunstan Times*, 7 October
      1870, p. 2; 'Editorial', 18 November 1870, p. 2; 'Editorial', 9 December 1870, p. 2.

35   Select Committee on Chinese Immigration, H-5, H-5A, H-5B.

36   C.E. Haughton's Report in *Appendix to the Journals of the House of Representatives New Zealand*,
      1876, H-3, p. 4: 'It is a subject of regret that these inoffensive and industrious people are not
      likely to become permanent colonists …'

37   New Zealand Parliament, 1878, Parliamentary Debates (Hansard), vol. 28, pp. 417–22.

38   In the 1874 census, 1861 out of 4012 Chinese miners were sluicers, that is, 46 per cent.

39   In California, this was the 'Chinese pump'. In Victoria, it was the 'Californian pump'. These
      pumps could be worked by hand, pedals or waterwheel. Chinese used the pumps for mining
      and for low-lying market garden land such as at St Kilda in Dunedin: Don, diary, 1899–1907,
      entry c. 14 February 1902, item 413.

40   C.E. Haughton's assessment is representative: 'They set a valuable example by their industry
      and thrift to the European population. Their undoubted success in mining operations is
      mainly owing to their thoroughly understanding and carrying out the system of cooperation
      labour and applying to its direction great intelligence and an almost instinctive knowledge
      of hydrodynamical laws which enable them to apply the water at their disposal in the most
      economical manner'. C.E. Haughton, *Appendix to the Journals of the House of Representatives
      New Zealand*, 1876, H-3, p. 4.

41   *Dunstan Times*, 25 May 1877 and 28 February 1868.

42   Ng, *Windows on a Chinese Past*, vol. 2, chapters 3A–3D.

43   Ng, *Windows on a Chinese Past*, vol. 1, chapter 2F, pp. 349–50.

44   £100 was likely to have been the benchmark sum. See, for example: *N.Z. Presbyterian*,
      1 November 1892, p. 83; Don, 'Diary, 1899–1907', 1904, item 622; *Outlook*, 20 September
      1910, p. 14. In the 1870s, if a miner made £1-10s weekly and saved half, he accumulated £187
      in five years, paid off any remainder debt and grubstaking money, bought his passage home for
      some £20 and took over £100 away and paid for stopovers at Sydney and Hong Kong: *Outlook*,
      23 March 1901, p. 21.

45   William F. Spalding, *Eastern Exchange, Currency and Finance* (London: Pitman, 4th edn, 1924),
      p. 331.

46   Annual living expenses for a family in Guangzhou required £8.0 in 1906: *Outlook*, 16 June
      1906, p. 13.

47   For instance, 'Chinese immigration', *Otago Witness*, 23 September 1865, p. 9; 'Editorial', *Otago
      Witness*, 30 September 1865, pp. 10–11.

48   The progress to eventual settlement is the subject of a forthcoming book by James Ng with the
      working title of *From Sojourner to Settler*.

49   The first arrivals 'direct from the Flowery Land' came in 1869 to Tuapeka Flat and Horse Shoe
      Bend: 'Lawrence', *Otago Witness*, 8 May 1869, p. 5. Three shiploads were expected: '"Measures,

not Men''', *Tuapeka Times*, 28 August, 1869. In 1869, 'wealthy Chinese firms' left Lawrence to commence operations in Dunedin as part of preparations to receive more men direct from China: *Dunstan Times*, 14 May 1869. For population statistics, see James Forrest, 'Population and settlement on the Otago goldfields, 1861–1870', *New Zealand Geographer*, vol. 17, no. 1, 1961, pp. 74, 78–80.

50 Otago Provincial Council, 'The immigration report', *Votes and Proceedings*, 1865–66, session XX1, p. 12.

51 Forrest, 'Population and settlement on the Otago goldfields, 1861–1870', pp. 64–86.

52 'The pioneer Chinaman on the Otago goldfields; a letter from Ho A Mee', *Otago Witness*, 10 June 1871, p. 13. This letter describes Mr Ho's role in the first two Sanyi parties to arrive in early 1866, and then in the 2000 arrivals in 1871–72, when he was responsible in Hong Kong for chartering the ships.

53 The lintel of Choie Sew Hoy's second (still existing) store bears the date 1869. This two-storied brick store was built in 1896. His first (wooden) store was by Flinder's Lane and the Red Lion Hotel.

54 Forrest, 'Population and settlement on the Otago goldfields, 1861–1870', pp. 79–80.

55 'Gold and other mineral products' [tables showing the quantity exported from the colony], *Appendix to the Journals of the House of Representatives New Zealand*, 1890, I, C-03a, pp. 1–4.

56 'Inquest', *Tuapeka Times*, 11 January 1879, p. 3.

57 'The governor in Otago', *Otago Witness*, 3 January, 1874, p. 4.

58 James Ng, *Windows on a Chinese Past* (Dunedin: Otago Heritage Books, vol. 3, 1998), chapter 7A, pp. 9–36. In 1891, the population of Alexandra was 310 with 84 Chinese; in 1896, the figures were respectively 454 and 52.

59 The Hon. R. Pharazyn in the Legislative Council said: '… this agitation … arises from a small section of the community, and from the determination of a small number of shopkeepers and others who dislike the Chinese not because of their vices but because of their virtues': New Zealand Parliament, 1895, *Parliamentary Debates* (Hansard), vol. 91, p. 809.

60 'Chinese Immigration', *Otago Witness*, 23 September 1865, p. 9; 'Editorial', *Otago Witness*, 30 September 1865, pp. 10–11, 14; 'Manorburn', *Otago Witness*, 11 November 1865, p. 6; 'The Chinese Question', *Otago Witness*, 15 July 1871, p. 18; 'The Chinese question: To the editor', *Otago Witness*, 22 July 1871, p. 4.

61 Ng, *Windows on a Chinese Past*, vol. 1, pp. 313–14, 334–35. Of these mines, five were quartz mines; the sixth mined scheelite. The latest was the Hop Fong Li quartz mine at Bendigo. See, in this regard, James P. Parcell, *Heart of the Desert: Being a history of the Cromwell and Bannockburn Districts of Central Otago* (Christchurch: Whitcombe & Tombs, reissued 1976), p. 143; 'Mining intelligence', *Cromwell Argus*, 4 May, 1880, p. 5.

62 Ng, *Windows on a Chinese Past*, vol. 1, pp. 317–18.

63 James Ng, 'Choie Sew Hoy, dredging pioneer', in *Buckets of Gold: A conference on the historical development of gold dredging in New Zealand*, ed. Nicol Allan MacArthur (Alexandra: Central Otago Dredge Trust, 2006), pp. 29–42.

64 Ng, *Windows on a Chinese Past*, vol. 3, pp. 280–83.

65 The Tobacco Act 1879 gave New Zealand manufacturers using New Zealand-grown tobacco significant advantages over imports. Hong (Hang) Long and L. Ah Quie grew tobacco near Queenstown from 1883 to 1885. In 1886 Hong Long and Chau Mong began to grow tobacco in the microclimate at Lawrence. The two founded Wong Sing's Bonded Tobacco Manufactory in Dunedin, staffed entirely by Europeans. The factory made cigarettes and cigars from Lawrence tobacco under the licensed brand 'Royal Navy'. Customs and excise duties were raised for many items, including tobacco in 1888. The tobacco venture begun by Hong Long eventually failed: 'In bankruptcy', *Lake Wakatip Mail*, 22 April 1887, p. 5; 'In bankruptcy', 29 April 1887, p. 5; 'Bankruptcy meeting', 12 October 1894; 'Latest cable news', 19 October 1894, p. 2; 'Advertisements', 2 November 1894, col. 1, p. 2.

66 Ng, *Windows on a Chinese Past*, vol. 3; see specifically 'Chew Chong (1828–1920)' on pp. 304–19. In relation to his son Gerald McN. Chong winning the Military Medal, see Alistair Kennedy, *Chinese Anzacs: Australians of Chinese descent in the defence forces 1885–1919: Revised to include New Zealand-born Chinese of the New Zealand Expeditionary Force 1949–1919* (Canberra: Author, 2nd edn, 2013), chapter 7, pp. 125–49.

67   *Outlook*, 20 April 1901, p. 19.

68   Ng, *Windows on a Chinese Past*, vol. 1, section 2E, p. 299.

69   Select Committee on Chinese Immigration, H-5A, p. 11.

70   Ng, *Windows on a Chinese Past*, vol. 1, section 2F, pp. 345–50, including Tables 6–8.

71   Incidentally, the annual *arrival* figures could give a rough estimate of the number of Chinese who came to New Zealand during the gold era – analysis that is enabled by the poll tax of 1881, which differentiated newcomers from returnees to New Zealand. The total number is about 8000: James Ng, 'The sojourner experience', in *Unfolding History, Evolving Identity: The Chinese in New Zealand*, ed. Manying Ip (Auckland: Auckland University Press, 2003), p. 28.

72   A full copy of the roll is available: James Ng, *Windows on a Chinese Past* (Dunedin, Otago Heritage Books, vol. 4, 1993).

73   The mass exhumations of the Ching Shing Tong completed in 1883 and 1902 totalled 704 bodies. Men of Panyu and Hua counties were 69 per cent of the entries in Reverend Don's *Roll* in 1896. In the 25 February 1899 issue of *Outlook*, Don wrote: 'Our New Zealand Chinese are fully three-fourths [pure] Cantonese [Panyu] speakers' (p. 11). After the gold era ended, an unknown number (probably several hundred) of elderly Chinese gold seekers who could not or would not leave for China died in New Zealand. A few bodies were sent back, but the remainder lie in goldfields or other cemeteries; some in unmarked paupers' graves and others with grave markers decayed or lost.

74   'Benevolent Institution', *Otago Daily Times*, 3 June 1905, p. 2; 'Maintenance of aged Chinese', 14 May 1907, p. 2.

75   In 1897 the Chinese in Dunedin and inland Otago donated £142-9s. In 1900 the Dunedin Benevolent Institute went back to the Chinese community for more donations. In 1903 Reverend Don collected £67-9s from Dunedin residents for the Benevolent Institute. In 1904 he collected £115-14s in Dunedin and inland: *Otago Witness*, 17 June 1897, p. 16; 7 October 1903, p. 28; 5 May 1904, p. 6. By 1900 the fare to China fell from an earlier £20 to around £12, and the practice of sending Chinese patients to China became established in Dunedin and other Benevolent Institutes. The cost to keep a Chinese in the Dunedin Old Men's Home was £16 per annum.

76   'Benevolent Institution', *Otago Daily Times*, p. 2; 'Maintenance of aged Chinese', p. 2.

77   *Outlook*, 13 April 1901, p. 22.

78   Miss Selia Jinhua Tan, a researcher in the Qiaoxiang Culture Research Center in Wuyi University, Jiangmen City, Guangdong province, advised on much of the countryside governance description. Kuomintang wording is from Ministry of Information, *China Handbook, 1937–1943* (New York: Author, 1943), pp. 103–05.

79   Don, 'Diary, 1899–1907', 1905, item 698.

80   See Ng, *Windows on a Chinese Past*, vol. 2, pp. 42–48.

81   Historic Cemeteries Conservation Trust of New Zealand, 2006: www.cemeteries. org.nz/conservationprojects.php

82   'Queenstown', 'Arrowtown', 'Casualties', *Otago Witness*, 20 April 1904, p. 30.

83   The remittances were customarily twice a year in my father's time. The sums remitted by the Chinese gold seekers were mostly small amounts of sovereigns, as seen in Don's *Roll*, pp. 45, 47: Ng, *Windows on a Chinese Past*, vol. 2, pp. 43–44.

84   The Australian shipwrecked SS *Catterthun* carried £10,800 in sovereigns for Chinese merchants and passengers: 'Wreck of the Catterthun', *North Otago Times*, 9 August 1895, p. 2.

85   Karen Stade, *Appo Hocton: New Zealand's First Chinese immigrant Nelson 1842–1920* (Nelson: Nelson Provincial Museum, 2009), p. 32. A man coming back to New Zealand carried letters for a *li shee* of two shillings. Appo Hocton was a Zhongshan Cantonese individual who was the lone Chinese man in Nelson. His letter probably went to Lau Oi Ming, the Zhongshan storekeeper in Dunedin, who may have traded in 'ear fungus' with him directly or indirectly via the Hip Fung Taai store.

86   *Appendix to the Journals of the House of Representatives New Zealand*, 1891, H-2, pp. 7–8 and 1892, A-1A, p. 4. The worst period of anti-Chinese prejudice in New Zealand occurred during the tenure of the Liberal Government (1891–1912), which largely led the discrimination. For nearly all this time, there was no Chinese consulate.

Chapter 8

1   Edward Beatty, 'Approaches to technology transfer in history and the case of nineteenth century Mexico', *Comparative Technology Transfer and Society*, vol. 1, no. 2, 2003, p. 183.

2   Warwick Frost, 'Migrants and technological transfer: Chinese farming in Australia, 1850–1920', *Australian Economic History Review*, vol. 42, no. 2, 2002, p. 117.

3   46ºF to over 99ºF: *Te Ara Encyclopaedia of New Zealand*: www.teara.govt.nz/en/climate.html

4   Reverend Alexander Don, *Chinese Mission Work in Otago: Annual inland tour 1896–1897* (Dunedin: J. Wilkie, 1897), p. 480; *Christian Outlook*, 3 July 1897, p. 268.

5   Reverend Alexander Don, *NZ Presbyterian Chinese Mission Inland Tours XXIII and XXIV, 1909–1911 and Westland Tour, 1911* (Dunedin: Otago Daily Times, 1911), p. 11.

6   Neville Ritchie, 'Traces of the past: Archaeological insights into the New Zealand Chinese experience in southern New Zealand', in *Unfolding History, Evolving Identity: The Chinese in New Zealand*, ed. Manying Ip (Auckland: Auckland University Press, 2003), pp. 32, 45.

7   Neville Ritchie, personal communication, February 2011.

8   Franklin Hiram King, *Farmers of Forty Centuries; or Permanent Agriculture in China, Korea and Japan* (Madison, WI: Mrs F.H. King, 1911), pp. 67–68: https://ia802707.us.archive.org/19/items/farmersoffortyce00kinguoft/farmersoffortyce00kinguoft.pdf

9   Jeffrey Fee, 'Idaho's Chinese mountain gardens', in *Hidden Heritage: Historical archaeology of the overseas Chinese*, ed. Priscilla Wegars (Amityville, NY: Baywood Publishing, 1993), pp. 65–66.

10   James Ng, *Windows on a Chinese Past* (Dunedin: Otago Heritage Books, vol. 1, 1993), p. 323; Neville Ritchie, 'Archaeology and history of the Chinese in southern New Zealand during the nineteenth century: A study of acculturation, adaptation, and change', PhD thesis, University of Otago, Dunedin, 1986, p. 641.

11   Ng, *Windows on a Chinese Past*, vol. 1, p. 323.

12   'The Chinese question', *Otago Witness*, 30 September 1865, pp. 13–14.

13   Reverend Alexander Don, 'Diary 1899–1907', entry dated 1 January 1883, p. 126, cited in Ritchie, 'Archaeology and history of the Chinese', p. 640.

14   James Ng, *Windows on a Chinese Past* (Dunedin: Otago Heritage Books, vol. 2, 1995), p. 36.

15   *Outlook*, 14 April 1906, p. 13.

16   *Outlook*, 11 May 1901, p. 26.

17   Ng, *Windows on a Chinese Past*, vol. 1, fn. 151a, p. 341.

18   *Dunstan Times*, 14 October 1898. Quoted in Ng, *Windows on a Chinese Past*, vol. 1, p. 321. Ah Lock sold his garden to another Chinese, Chan Tseung Pooi, in around 1900. The Matakanui garden was still in existence in 1911, when Don reported that there were five men working there: *Outlook*, 1 August 1911, p. 14.

19   'Local intelligence', *Tuapeka Times*, 26 September 1874, p. 2.

20   Helen Leach, personal communication, 4 February 2011.

21   'Vincent County Horticultural Show', *Otago Witness*, 1 March 1894, p. 4; 'Vincent County Horticultural Society's Fifth Annual Show', 4 March 1897, p. 26; 'Alexandra', 24 February 1898, p. 26.

22   'Omnium gatherum', *Otago Witness*, 12 April 1894, p. 34.

23   'News of the week', *Otago Witness*, 24 August 1867, p. 11.

24   Jock Collins, Katherine Gibson, Caroline Alcorso, Stephen Castles and David Tait, *A Shop Full of Dreams: Ethnic small business in Australia* (Sydney: Pluto Press, 1995), p. 58.

25   Roger Waldinger, Howard Aldrich, Robin Ward and associates, *Ethnic Entrepreneurs: Immigrant business in industrial societies* (Newbury Park, CA: Sage, vol. 1, 1990), pp. 21–22.

26   Lily Lee and Ruth Lam, *Sons of the Soil: Chinese market gardeners in New Zealand* (Pukekohe: Dominion Federation of New Zealand Chinese Commercial Growers, 2012), p. 39.

27   Charles Fahey, 'Gold and land', in *Making Australian History: Perspectives on the past since 1788*, eds. Deborah Gare and David Ritter (South Melbourne: Cengage Learning, 2008), pp. 206–08.

28   Ng, *Windows on a Chinese Past*, vol. 1, p. 123.

29   Lee and Lam, *Sons of the Soil*, p. 6.

30   Karen Clay and Randall Jones, 'Migrating to riches? The evidence of the California gold rush', *Journal of Economic History*, vol. 68, no. 4, 2008, pp. 997–98.

31   'Reminiscences of Gabriel's Gully', *Evening Post*, Wellington, 23 December 1899, p. 3.

32   Ng, *Windows on a Chinese Past*, vol. 1, p. 302.

33   Ritchie, 'Traces of the past', p. 35.

34   Ibid. See also Ritchie, 'Archaeology and history of the Chinese', pp. 640–41.

35   Ng, *Windows on a Chinese Past*, vol. 1, p. 321.

36   Ibid. Also, Ritchie, 'Archaeology and history of the Chinese', p. 641.

37   Lee and Lam, *Sons of the Soil*, pp. 26–27.

38   'Ah Lum's store', on the Heritage New Zealand website: http://www.heritage.org.nz/the-list/
      details/4366

39   Guohua Xu and L.J. Peel, *Agriculture of China* (Oxford: Oxford University Press, 1991), p. 66.

40   Ibid., pp. 66, 70–71.

41   King, *Farmers of Forty Centuries*, pp. 67, 73–74, 90–91, 171.

42   'Local intelligence', *Tuapeka Times*, 21 October 1874, p. 2.

43   Barry McGowan, 'Adaptation and organization: The history and heritage of the Chinese in the
      Riverina and Western New South Wales, Australia', *Chinese America: History & Perspectives –
      The Journal of the Chinese Historical Society of America*, 2007 issue, p. 238.

44   Ng, *Windows on a Chinese Past*, vol. 1, p. 137.

45   Ibid., fn. 77d, p. 167.

46   Barry McGowan, 'The economics and organisation of Chinese mining in colonial Australia',
      Australian Economic History Review, vol. 45, no. 2, 2005, p. 124.

47   'The goldfields', *Dunstan Times*, 7 December 1877, p. 2.

48   Don, 'Diary 1899–1907', item 413, cited in Ng, *Windows on a Chinese Past*, vol. 1, fn. 77b,
      p. 167.

49   John McCraw, *Mountain Water and River Gold: Stories of gold mining in the Alexandra District*
      (Dunedin: Square One Press, 2000).

50   Ibid., pp. 227–29.

51   Ibid., p. 229. The physical remains of Lye Bow's garden and orchard are listed on the register of
      Heritage New Zealand Pouhere Taonga as a historic area. The site includes the remains of the
      orchard and surrounding stone wall, the probable site of Lye Bow's house, and an adjacent area
      of gold workings that includes a section of the Alexandra Borough water race (HNZ, Register
      no. 7547).

52   Ng, *Windows on a Chinese Past*, vol. 1, p. 89; Charles Sedgwick, 'Politics of survival', PhD
      thesis, University of Canterbury, Christchurch, 1982, pp. 64, 445; C.F. Yong, *The New Gold
      Mountain* (Richmond, S.A., Raphael Arts, 1977), p. 54; C.Y. Choi, *Chinese Migration and
      Settlement in Australia, Sydney* (Sydney, NSW: Sydney University Press, 1975), pp. 11–13; Jane
      Lydon, *Many Inventions: The Chinese in the Rocks, Sydney, 1890–1930* (Clayton, VIC: Monash
      Publications in History, 1999), p. 66.

53   Reverend Alexander Don, 'Roll of Chinese', reprinted as vol. 4 of James Ng, *Windows on a
      Chinese Past* (Dunedin: Otago Heritage Books, vol. 3, 1999).

54   Charles Sedgwick, 'Politics of survival', p. 319; Niti Pawakapan, 'The Chinese in Dunedin
      between the 1920s and the 1930s', MA thesis, University of Otago, Dunedin, 1987, p. 54.

55   James Ng, *Windows on a Chinese Past* (Dunedin: Otago Heritage Books, vol. 3, 1999), p. 9.

56   'The Chinese', *Dunstan Times*, 14 May 1869.

57   'Roxburgh', *Tuapeka Times*, 26 May 1877, p. 3.

58   Interim report of Select Committee on Chinese Immigration, *Appendix to the Journals of the
      House of Representatives of New Zealand*, 1871, vol. II, H 5, H5A, p. 4.

59   See, for example, the evidence given to the Select Committee on Chinese Immigration by James
      Hector MD, p. 10; H. Robinson, warden, Naseby, p. 17; Vincent Pyke, warden, Clyde, p. 17;
      Mr C. Broad, warden, Charleston, p. 19; Sgt McCluskey, police officer, Naseby, p. 22; R.B.
      Shearman, Commissioner of Police, Christchurch, p. 25; Mr E.H. Hunt, Wellington, p. 26.

60   See, for example, Keir Reeves, 'Tracking the dragon down under: Chinese cultural connections
      in gold rush Australia and Aotearoa New Zealand', *Graduate Journal of Asia-Pacific Studies*,
      vol. 3, no. 1, 2005, pp. 49–66; Julia Bradshaw, *Golden Prospects: Chinese on the West Coast of
      New Zealand* (Shantytown, Greymouth: West Coast Mechanical and Historical Society, 2009).

61   Sedgwick, 'Politics of survival', Appendix VIII.

Chapter 9

1 I have used Chinese characters where these are known to me. However, some of the Chinese people referred to in this chapter are known about only through mention in English-language newspapers and documents.

2 'Chinese residence tax', *Argus* (Melbourne), 31 May 1859, p. 7; Charles Powell Hodges, 'Chinese in Victoria: Report by Mr Hodges, Chinese interpreter, to the Honorable the Premier, on the Chinese in Victoria, having special reference to their numbers and employment', Melbourne, 31 May 1880, reprinted in *The Chinese in Victoria: Official reports and documents*, ed. Ian F. McLaren (Melbourne: Red Rooster Press, 1985), pp. 59–64.

3 Andrew Markus, *Fear and Hatred: Purifying Australia and California 1850–1901* (Sydney: Hale & Iremonger, 1979), pp. 1, 45.

4 Geoffrey Serle, *The Golden Age: A history of the colony of Victoria, 1851–1861* (Carlton: Melbourne University Press, 1968 edition), pp. 216–48.

5 James Ng, *Windows on a Chinese Past* (Dunedin: Otago Heritage Books, vol. 1, 1993), p. 123.

6 'The Chinese question: Deputation to the government', *Otago Witness*, 30 September 1865, p. 13.

7 Keir Reeves, 'Tracking the dragon down under: Chinese cultural connections in gold rush Australia and Aotearoa, New Zealand', *Graduate Journal of Asia-Pacific Studies*, vol. 3, no. 1, 2005, pp. 49–66.

8 Serle, *The Golden Age*, p. 331.

9 Chinese Immigrants Regulation and Restriction Act 1861: see Markus, *Fear and Hatred*, p. 34; Michael Williams, 'Chinese settlement in NSW: A thematic history', report prepared for the NSW Heritage Office of NSW, September 1999, p. 5: www.environment.nsw.gov.au/resources/heritagebranch/ heritage/chinesehistory.pdf

10 Paul Macgregor, 'Lowe Kong Meng and Chinese engagement in the international trade of colonial Victoria', *Provenance*, no. 11, 2012: http://prov.vic.gov.au/publications/provenance/lowe-kong-meng

11 'Our oriental traders', *Argus*, 14 April 1863, p. 5.

12 Birth year 1830: 'Mr. Lowe Kong Meng', *Australian News for Home Readers*, 20 September 1866, p. 4; birth year 1831: 'The late Mr. Kong Meng', *Argus*, 24 October 1888, p. 16.

13 'The Chinese population; Kong Meng', *Weekly Herald*, 14 August 1863, p. 1. Citation courtesy Pauline Rule.

14 'Mr. Lowe Kong Meng', *Australian News for Home Readers*, 20 September 1866, p. 4.

15 H.M. Humphreys, comp., *Men of the Time in Australia: Victorian series* (Melbourne, 1878, 1882), p. 263 of 1878 edition.

16 'District Court Thursday, June 2', *Argus*, 3 June 1859, p. 5.

17 Victor Purcell, *The Chinese in Malaya* (Oxford: Osprey Publishing, 1948), pp. 58–60.

18 Roderick Matthews, *The Flaws in the Jewel: Challenging the myths of British India* (New Delhi: HarperCollins, 2010), pp. 83–104; Lakshmi Subramanian, *History of India, 1707–1857* (Hyderabad: Orient BlackSwan), 2010, pp. 161–68.

19 'A brief school history', Historical Society, Penang Free School: www.pfs.edu.my/documentations.htm

20 Geoff Wade, 'New ways of knowing: *The Prince of Wales Island Gazette*, Penang's first newspaper', paper presented at The Penang Story International Conference, Penang, Malaysia, 19 April 2002, pp. 27–28, https://web.archive.org/web/20130915055134/http://www.penangstory.net.my/main-oldpg.html

21 'The Chinese population; Kong Meng', *Weekly Herald*, 14 August 1863, p. 1.

22 Noorjahan Dauhoo, 'The history of sugar with reference to 19th century Mauritius': www.articlesbase.com/k-12-education-articles/the-history-of-sugar-with-reference-to-19th-century-mauritius-242868

23 'The late Mr. Kong Meng', *Argus*, 24 October 1888, p. 16.

24 Humphreys, *Men of the Time in Australia*, p. 263.

25 'The Chinese population; Kong Meng', *Weekly Herald*, 14 August 1863, p. 1.

26 In sources on Lowe Kong Meng, the name Goone is usually spelt with an 'e' on the end but sometimes without; see Humphreys, *Men of the Time in Australia*, p. 263.

27 'Mr. Lowe Kong Meng', *Australian News for Home Readers*, 20 September 1866, p. 4.

28   Humphreys, *Men of the Time in Australia*, p. 263.

29   'The Chinese population; Kong Meng', *Weekly Herald*, 14 August 1863, p. 1.

30   'District Court Thursday, June 2', *Argus*, 3 June 1859, p. 5.

31   Guangzhou (Canton), Xiamen (Amoy), Fuzhou (Fou-tchow-foo), Ningbo and Shanghai.

32   L. Blussé, 'Junks to Java: Chinese shipping in the Nanyang in the second half of the eighteenth century', in *Chinese Circulations: Capital, commodities, and networks in Southeast Asia*, eds. Eric Tagliacozzo and Wen-Chin Chang (Durham, NC: Duke University Press, 2011), p. 255.

33   Purcell, *The Chinese in Malaya*, p. 40.

34   'Mr. Lowe Kong Meng', *Australian News for Home Readers*, 20 September 1866, p. 4.

35   Humphreys, *Men of the Time in Australia*, p. 263.

36   'The Chinese population; Kong Meng', *Weekly Herald*, 14 August 1863, p. 1.

37   Humphreys, *Men of the Time in Australia*, p. 263.

38   'The late Mr. Kong Meng', *Argus*, 24 October 1888, p. 16.

39   By 1880 there were 456 newspapers in Victoria, New South Wales, South Australia, Queensland and New Zealand: 'Victoria possesses 141 newspapers …', *Inangahua Times* (West Coast), 3 September 1880, p. 2.

40   Search of Australian newspapers in Trove (http://trove.nla.gov.au/newspaper) for 'Kong Meng' for 1 January 1853 to 31 December 1880 listed 2121 results, of which 217 are articles.

41   'Mr. Lowe Kong Meng', *Australian News for Home Readers*, 20 September 1866, p. 4.

42   'Advertisements: Produce, provisions &c', *Argus*, 19 September 1856, p. 8.

43   Ibid., 22 September 1856, p. 6.

44   'Advertisements: Merchandise', *Argus*, 14 July 1858, p. 7.

45   'The Chinese population; Kong Meng', *Weekly Herald*, 14 August 1863, p. 1.

46   'Our oriental traders', *Argus*, 14 April 1863, p. 5.

47   'Mr. Lowe Kong Meng', *Australian News for Home Readers*, 20 September 1866, p. 4. The ship registers recorded *Joshua Bates*, Ship No. 43,309 (23 August 1865); *Spray*, Ship No. 10,285 (30 August 1866); *Caroline* (8 April 1867, William McHugh part owner): Public Records Office of Victoria, VPRS 38/P0, Unit 5, inwards shipping report, 1 June 1863 to 17 December 1867; Merchant Shipping Act 1854, Port Melbourne, 14 May 1855 to 22 January 1982, Public Records Office of Victoria, NAA Series A7609, vol. 2, microfilm roll 1. Citation courtesy Pauline Rule.

48   1859 import data is from 'Imports: General imports into the colony of Victoria, during the year ended 31 December 1859', *Statistics of the colony of Victoria, compiled from official records in the Registrar-General's Office*, Government Printer, Melbourne, 1859, pp. 147–221. Public Records Office of Victoria, VA 2889 Registrar-General's Department, VPRS 943/PO Blue Books and Statistics 1854–1873.

49   Sing-wu Wang, *The Organisation of Chinese Emigration 1848–1888, with Special Reference to Chinese Emigration to Australia* (San Francisco, CA: Chinese Materials Center, 1978), pp. 114–18; Ng, *Windows on a Chinese Past*, vol. 1, pp. 94–97.

50   James Dundas Crawford, 'Notes by Mr. Crawford on Chinese immigration in the Australian colonies', Great Britain Foreign Office Confidential Print 3742, National Library of Australia, 1877, p. 19.

51   'John's "Talkee"', *Otago Witness*, 23 September 1871, p. 16, quoted in Ng, *Windows on a Chinese Past*, vol. 1, pp. 96–97.

52   Paul Macgregor, 'Chinese political values in colonial Victoria: Lowe Kong Meng and the legacy of the July 1880 election', *Journal of Chinese Overseas*, vol. 9, 2013, pp. 149–51; Barry McGowan, 'The economics and organisation of Chinese mining in colonial Australia', *Australian Economic History Review*, vol. 45, no. 2, 2005, pp. 119–38; Barry McGowan, 'Kongsis, huis and clans: The economics and organisation of Chinese alluvial mining, with particular reference to the Braidwood, Kiandra and Adelong goldfields of southern NSW and the tin fields of Northern NSW', paper presented at the nineteenth annual conference of the Australasian Mining History Association, 29 September to 4 October 2013, Beechworth, Victoria, Australia.

53   *Sands & Kenny's Commercial and General Melbourne Directory for 1859* (Melbourne: Sands and Kenny, 1857–59), pp. 23–24; *Tanner's Melbourne Directory for 1859* (Melbourne: John Tanner, 1859), p. 102.

54   'Chinese residence tax', *Argus*, 31 May 1859, p. 7; see also Macgregor, 'Lowe Kong Meng and Chinese engagement', for an account of, and the context for, this meeting.

55   In the Melbourne shipping registers for 1856–67, the merchants recorded as agents for inwards goods from Hong Kong were: Kong Meng & Co., Ah Kum, Louis Ah Mouy, R. Towns & Co., J.J. Marshall & Co., B.B. Nicholson, W. White Co., McEwan & Co., Wilkinson Bros Co., E. Cohen & Co., W. Swan & Co., Oscar Cushing & Co., and Boyd & Currie. However, Kong Meng & Co. and R. Towns & Co. were the main importers. See Public Record Office of Victoria: VPRS 38/P0, inwards shipping reports, Unit 3 (July 1854 to 30 November 1858), Unit 4 (December 1858 to May 1863), and Unit 5 (June 1863 to December 1867); VPRS 22/P1, Unit 1, shipping index 1864–1867.

56   'In days of old; Victoria's first Chinaman; Story of the gold fever, *Sun* (Sydney), 12 May 1918, p. 5.

57   Shipping advertisements, *Argus*, 13 September 1855, p. 1.

58   Public Records Office of Victoria: VPRS 38/P0, inwards shipping report, Unit 4 (December 1858 to May 1863).

59   Serle, *The Golden Age*, p. 228.

60   'Chinese residence tax', *Argus*, 31 May 1859, p. 7; Kathryn Cronin, *Colonial Casualties: Chinese in early Victoria* (Carlton: Melbourne University Press, 1982), p. 141.

61   'Commercial', *Geelong Advertiser*, 10 December 1861, p. 2; 'Shipping advertisements: Oithona', *Argus*, 17 December 1861, p. 1; 'Shipping intelligence', *Star* (Ballarat), 6 January 1862, p. 2; 'Shipping', *Argus*, 25 February 1862, p. 4; 'Shipping' and 'Exports', *Age*, 29 March 1862, p. 4.

62   'Shipping' and 'Exports', *Age*, 2 April 1862, p. 4.

63   'Shipping advertisements: Joshua Bates', *Argus*, 21 March 1862, p. 1; 'Shipping intelligence', *Star*, 11 April 1862, p. 2.

64   Public Records Office of Victoria: VPRS 38/P0, inwards shipping report, Unit 4 (December 1858 to May 1863). See also 'Shipping intelligence' and 'Commercial intelligence', *Argus*, 22 February 1862, p. 4; 'Imports', *Star*, 24 February 1862, p. 2.

65   'Shipping advertisement: Joshua Bates', *Argus*, 21 March 1862, p. 1; 'Shipping intelligence', *Star*, 11 April 1862, p. 2; 'Shipping', *Otago Daily Times*, 23 April 1862, p. 4.

66   'Shipping', *Argus*, 24 May 1862, p. 4; 'Shipping', *Age*, 30 May 1862, p. 4; Public Records Office of Victoria: VPRS 38/P0, inwards shipping report, Unit 4 (December 1858 to May 1863). The *Joshua Bates* was the first ship he purchased, acquiring it on 30 July 1864 from Alfred Woolley for over £2000 ('*Joshua Bates*, Ship No. 43,309').

67   John Bach, *A Maritime History of Australia* (Sydney: Pan Books, 1976), p. 136; Richard Cotter, 'The golden decade', in *Essays in Economic History of Australia*, ed. James Griffin (Milton, Queensland: Jacaranda, 1967), p. 125; Geoffrey Serle, *The Golden Age*, p. 42. See also Keir Reeves, Lionel Frost and Charles Fahey, 'Integrating the historiography of the nineteenth-century gold rushes', *Australian Economic History Review*, vol. 50, no. 2, 2010, pp. 111–28.

68   'Chinese residence tax', *Argus*, 31 May 1859, p. 7.

69   'Monetary and commercial', *Herald* (Melbourne), 27 October 1862, p. 4.

70   Ibid., 27 November 1862, p. 4.

71   'Melbourne', *New Zealand Herald*, 14 June 1869, p. 4; 'Shipping for the month', *Illustrated Australian News for Home Readers*, 19 June 1869, p. 130.

72   Map: 'The ocean steam routes of the world', in N.B. Dennys, *The Treaty Ports of China and Japan: A complete guide to the open ports of those countries, together with Peking, Yedo, Hongkong and Macao. Forming a guide book & vade mecum for travellers, merchants, and residents in general: with 29 maps and plans* (London: Trübner and Co., 1867), p. 668.

73   'Victoria', *Colonist* (Nelson), 28 June 1861, p. 4; 'Victoria', *Wellington Independent*, 1 October 1861, p. 4; 'Burning of the Kate Hooper', *Southland Times*, 16 January 1863, p. 2; 'The Chinese in Melbourne', *Daily Southern Cross*, 25 June 1863, p. 4; 'Victoria', *Southland Times*, 30 September 1863, p. 2; 'Australian news: Victoria', *Colonist*, 20 October 1863, p. 3; 'Editorial', *Otago Daily Times*, 15 February 1864, p. 4; 'Melbourne', *New Zealand Herald*, 26 April 1864, p. 4; 'Latest Australian telegrams', *Press* (Christchurch), 9 November 1864, p. 3.

74   'The Chinese question: Deputation to the government', *Otago Witness*, 30 September 1865, p. 13.

75   'The agitation which recently took place …', *Evening Post*, 27 December 1865, p. 2.

76   'The Chinese in Victoria: To the editor of the Age', *South Australian Advertiser* (Adelaide), 29 March 1860, p. 3 (anonymous, but it is likely that Kong Meng was the author of the letter). Citation courtesy Pauline Rule.

77   Mr J.A. Ewen, quoted in 'The Chinese question: Deputation to the government', *Otago Witness*, 30 September 1865, p. 13. James Ng also cites an 1861 example: *The Leisure Hour*, 1862, p. 422, in Ng, *Windows on a Chinese Past*, vol. 1, fn. 6, p. 161.

78   'The Chinese question: Deputation to the government', *Otago Witness*, 30 September 1865, p. 13; Ng, *Windows on a Chinese Past*, vol. 1, pp. 125–32.

79   'Dunedin Election', *Otago Daily Times*, 7 October 1865; 'The agitation which recently took place …', *Evening Post*, 27 December 1865, p. 2; 'From Tuapeka we learn …', *Bruce Herald*, 10 April 1867, p. 4.

80   'The pioneer Chinaman on the Otago goldfields', *Otago Witness*, 10 June 1871, p. 9.

81   'The agitation which recently took place …', *Evening Post*, 27 December 1865, p. 2.

82   'The pioneer Chinaman on the Otago goldfields', *Otago Witness*, 10 June 1871, p. 9.

83   Ng, *Windows on a Chinese Past*, vol. 1, pp. 132–34; Pauline Rule, 'The transformative effect of Australian experience on the life of Ho A Mei, 1838–1901, Hong Kong community leader and entrepreneur', *Journal of Chinese Overseas*, vol. 9, 2013, pp. 108–35.

84   'Pleiades Gold Mining Company' [registration notice], *Victorian Government Gazette*, 29 June 1866, p. 1373 (http://gazette.slv.vic.gov.au/), cited in Rule, 'The transformative effect of Australian experience', p. 130.

85   'From Tuapeka we learn …', *Bruce Herald* (Otago), 10 April 1867, p. 4.

86   'Items of news', *Mount Alexander Mail* (Castlemaine), 10 August 1867, p. 2, cited in Reeves, 'Tracking the dragon down under', p. 57.

87   New Zealand Census 1867, cited in Ng, *Windows on a Chinese Past*, vol. 1, p. 45.

88   'The pioneer Chinaman on the Otago goldfields', *Otago Witness*, 10 June 1871, p. 9. The account in the paper does not state who asked him to arrange the charter.

89   Ng, *Windows on a Chinese Past*, vol. 1, pp. 134, 156, 164 (fn. 47), 348.

90   National Archives, Dunedin office: DAAC. 1874. Acc D239, 119, letters of administration, A1859.59. Relating to the estate of Lee Mow Tie, who died without a will in 1874. Citation courtesy of James Ng.

91   Crawford, 'Notes by Mr. Crawford', p. 30.

92   James Ng, 'Sew Hoy, Charles', *Te Ara – the Encyclopedia of New Zealand*: www.teara.govt.nz/en/biographies/2s14/sew-hoy-charles

93   Macgregor, 'Chinese political values in colonial Victoria', pp. 148–53.

94   'The Chinese population; Kong Meng', *Weekly Herald*, 14 August 1863, p. 1.

95   'Shipping intelligence', *Argus*, 6 April 1869, p. 4; Public Records Office of Victoria: VPRS 3506, outward passenger lists 1852–1923, Lyttleton, 5 April 1869. Citation courtesy Pauline Rule.

96   'Alphabetical list of members 1854–1872,' *Science and the Making of Victoria: Histories and views of the Royal Society of Victoria from its inception to the present day, and its role supporting science and technology in Victoria* (Australian Science and Technology Heritage Centre and Royal Society of Victoria, 2001): www.austehc.unimelb.edu.au/smv/164.html

97   'Acclimatisation: To the editor of the Argus', *Argus*, 20 May 1861, p. 5.

98   See Macgregor, 'Lowe Kong Meng and Chinese engagement in the international trade of colonial Victoria'; Subramanian, *History of India, 1707–1857*, p. 154.

99   '[Yarra] Distillery Company', *Gippsland Times*, 27 September 1864, p. 3; 'Prospectus of the South Crinoline Amalgamated Quartz-Mining Company', *Argus*, 19 December 1864, p. 7; 'Commercial Bank of Australia: Prospectus', *Empire* (Sydney), 4 April 1866, p. 8; 'The English, Australian, and New Zealand Marine Insurance Company: Prospectus', *Sydney Morning Herald*, 23 June 1866, p. 2; 'Pleiades Gold Mining Company' [registration notice], *Victorian Government Gazette*, 29 June 1866, p. 1373; 'Prospectus of the Hazelwood Coal-Mining Company', *Argus*, 12 December 1874, p. 8 (Thomas Bent and David Mitchell were also directors); 'Prospectus of the Melbourne Fishmongers' and Deep Sea Fishing Company', *Argus*, Melbourne, 6 May 1880, p. 6 (George Coppin and Louis A Mouy were also directors); 'Prospectus of the North Midas Gold-Mining Company', *Argus*, 10 July 1886, p. 14; 'Sixth

schedule ... application to register the Madame Kong Meng Gold-Mining Company', *Argus*, 11 February 1887, p. 8; 'Prospectus of the Outward Bound Consolidated Silver-Mining Company, *Argus*, 11 February 1888, p. 14.

100 'The late Mr. Kong Meng', *Argus*, Melbourne, 24 October 1888, p. 16.

101 'Kong Meng and Columbia G.M. Company, Majorca', news clipping (newspaper title not known), 11 April 1873, in possession of descendants of Lowe Kong Meng.

102 'Prospectus of the South Crinoline Amalgamated Quartz-Mining Company', *Argus*, 19 December 1864, p. 7.

103 Pauline Rule, 'The missionary, the interpreter and the mining capitalist: Two Chinese brothers in the Victorian gold rush', paper presented at the nineteenth annual conference of the Australasian Mining History Association, 29 September to 4 October 2013, Beechworth, Victoria, Australia.

104 Ibid.

105 Ng, *Windows on a Chinese Past*, vol. 1, pp. 315–17.

106 Macgregor, 'Lowe Kong Meng and Chinese engagement' (see text under subheading titled 'The wider social context of trade').

107 'The Mayor of Melbourne's fancy dress ball', *Examiner*, 3 September 1863, p. 3; 'The Duke of Edinburgh in Victoria: The corporation fancy dress ball', *Argus*, 24 December 1867, p. 5; 'Little Bourke-Street', *Illustrated Australian News for Home Readers*, 27 December 1867, p. 11; 'Victoria: Opening of the new town hall, Melbourne', *Cornwall Chronicle*, 20 August 1870, p. 16; 'Opening of the new town-hall: The return fancy ball', *Argus*, 26 August 1870, p. 5.

108 Letter from Lowe Kong Meng to Redmond Barry, 18 March 1869: Public Record Office Victoria, VPRS 927/P0000, correspondence relating to various exhibitions [Trustees of the Public Library, Museum and Exhibition Buildings], Unit 5, Intercolonial and Fine Arts Exhibition.

109 'The late Mr. Kong Meng', *Argus*, Melbourne, 24 October 1888, p. 16.

110 Ibid.

111 Personal communication with descendants of Lowe Kong Meng, 1996.

112 Charles Hodges estimated the population of Chinese in 1880 to be 13,000: Hodges, 'Chinese in Victoria', p. 63.

113 Personal communication 2005 with Peter Williams, descendant of the owners of Moran and Cato grocery, a main importer of tea into Australia in the late nineteenth to mid-twentieth centuries.

114 Will of Lowe Kong Meng, in possession of his descendants.

115 Betty Osborn and Trenear DuBourg, *Maryborough: A social history 1854–1904* (Maryborough, Victoria: Maryborough City Council, 1985), pp. 210–18; 'Kong Meng and Columbia Tribute Gold Mining Company' [registration notice], *Victorian Government Gazette*, issue 52, 9 August 1872, p. 1506: http://gazette.slv.vic.gov.au/

116 Ng, 'Sew Hoy, Charles'.

117 'Choie Sew Hoy family tree': www.choiesewhoy.com/pdf/choiesewhoy-familytree2.pdf; James Ng, 'Sew Hoy, Hugh', *Te Ara – The Encyclopedia of New Zealand*: www.teara.govt.nz/en/biographies/5s10/sew-hoy-hugh

Chapter 10

1 'Deaths', *Lake County Press*, 6 June 1918, p. 3.

2 See, for example, *Lake Wakatip Mail*, 6 January 1888, pp. 1 and 5, 6 July 1894, pp. 1 and 2, and 15 November 1901, pp. 1 and 7; *Lake County Press*, 6 June 1918, p. 3; probate file, John McBride, 1876, no. Q/76 (Archives New Zealand, Dunedin office, R13287952 DAAC 9074 D239 286/A2057); 'Queenstown licensing papers to 1881, Police report', 6 December 1880 (Archives New Zealand, Dunedin office, R21726530 AEPG 26045 D568 124/b). In addition, Jane McBride had purchased six Queenstown sections for a total price of £23-15s in July 1873: 'Town allotment book', series 69, vol. 2, p. 316 (Archives New Zealand, Dunedin office, R10302438 DAAK 9398 D450 406/).

3 Charles Smithers, *The Licensee's Manual: Being a guide to the liquor laws of New South Wales* (Sydney: Law Book Co. of Australia, 1932), p. 146, quoted in Clare Wright, 'Of public houses

and private lives: Female hotelkeepers as domestic entrepreneurs', *Australian Historical Studies*, vol. 32, no. 116, 2001, p. 61.

4   See, for example, Raewyn Dalziel, 'The colonial helpmeet: Women's role and the vote in nineteenth-century New Zealand', *New Zealand Journal of History*, vol. 11, no. 2, 1977, pp. 112–23. See also Wright, 'Of public houses and private lives'. This journal article is well worth reading in full.

5   Louise Asher, 'Women on the Ballarat goldfields: 1850s and early 1860s', BA Hons research essay, University of Melbourne, Carlton, Australia, 1977, pp. 35, 43.

6   Clare Wright, *Beyond the Ladies Lounge: Australia's female publicans* (Carlton: University of Melbourne Press, 2003), pp. 30–31.

7   Stevan Eldred-Grigg, *Diggers, Hatters and Whores: The story of the New Zealand gold rushes* (Auckland: Random House, 2008), p. 375.

8   New Zealand Parliament, 1880, Parliamentary Debates (Hansard), vol. 35, p. 112. For the reference to Seddon as a publican in his early adulthood, see Tom Brooking, *Richard Seddon: King of God's Own* (Auckland: Penguin, 2014).

9   Licensing Act 1873, sec. 22; Milton Lewis, *A Rum State: Alcohol and state policy in Australia 1788–1988* (Canberra: Australian Government Publishing Service, 1992), pp. 54–55; Licensing Act 1881; Susan Upton, *Wanted, a Beautiful Barmaid: Women behind the bar in New Zealand, 1830–1976* (Wellington: Victoria University Press, 2013), p. 73.

10   Leonore Davidoff and Catherine Hall, *Family Fortunes: Men and women of the English middle class, 1780–1850* (London: Hutchinson Education, 1987), p. 272; Paul Jennings, *The Public House in Bradford, 1770–1970* (Keele, Staffordshire: Keele University Press, 1995), pp. 40, 126, 181; Sandra L. Myers, *Westering Women and the Frontier Experience 1800–1915* (Albuquerque, NM: University of New Mexico Press, 1982), p. 7.

11   Bettina Bradbury, 'From civil death to separate property: Changes in the legal rights of married women in nineteenth-century New Zealand,' *New Zealand Journal of History*, vol. 29, no. 1, 1995, p. 51.

12   Ibid., p. 59; Licensing Act 1881 Amendment Act 1889, 53 Vict., no. 34.

13   Alcoholic Liquors Sale Control Act 1893, 57 Vict., no. 34, section 12(1); Sandra Coney, *Standing in the Sunshine: A history of New Zealand women since they won the vote* (Auckland: Viking Penguin Books New Zealand, 1993), p. 129.

14   Charles Thatcher, 'Poll the grogseller', in Robert Hoskins, *Goldfield Balladeer: The life and times of the celebrated Charles R. Thatcher* (Auckland: William Collins, 1977), p. 149.

15   Charles Thatcher, 'Changes on Bendigo', in Hugh Anderson, *The Colonial Minstrel* (Melbourne: F.W. Cheshire, 1960), pp. 53–54.

16   'Dunstan Magistrate's Court Judgements Book 1862–1864' (Archives New Zealand, Dunedin office, DADO Acc. D557 137a): 12 December 1862, Thomas Kidson vs Jessie MacLeod for £7; 23 December 1862, Kurtz vs Jessie McLeod for £2.5s; 13 January 1863, Robert Harmer vs Jessie McLeod for £15.

17   'Dunstan Magistrate's Court Judgements Book 1862–1864', 3 and 4 February 1863 (Archives New Zealand, Dunedin office, R15820033 DADO D557 130/c).

18   'Police intelligence: Police Court, Queenstown', *Lake Wakatip Mail*, 12 September 1863, p. 5.

19   'Police intelligence: Police Court, Queenstown', *Lake Wakatip Mail*, 27 June 1863, p. 5.

20   'Queenstown Court Records Book 1863–1872', 11 September 1863 (Archives New Zealand, Dunedin office, AEPG Acc. D568 10a); 'Police intelligence: Police Court, Queenstown', *Lake Wakatip Mail*, 12 September 1863, p. 5.

21   'Queenstown Court Records Book 1863–1872', 4 and 9 February 1864.

22   Ibid., 3 August and 1 September 1863; 'Police intelligence: Police Court, Queenstown', *Lake Wakatip Mail*, 2 September 1863.

23   'Clyde Magistrate's Court Judgements Book 1866–1869', 4 November 1868 (Archives New Zealand, Dunedin office, DADO Acc. D557 138a).

24   'Magistrate's Court', *Dunstan Times*, 12 February 1869, p. 3. McLeod was using her alias of Kate O'Reilly in this instance.

25   Anne Hutchinson, 'Weldon, Barbara', from the Dictionary of New Zealand Biography: www.teara.govt.nz/ en/biographies/1w11/weldon-barbara. My thanks to Rachel Dawick, who introduced me to Barbara Weldon on a cold night in Barrytown Hall in May 2013, via

the song she wrote about Barbara. Rachel Dawick travelled throughout New Zealand with her show called 'The Boundary Riders Tour', which told the stories of pioneer New Zealand women in song.

26   George Magnus Hassing, *Pages from the Memory Log of G.M. Hassing: Sailor, pioneer, schoolmaster* (Invercargill: Southland Times, 1930), p. 45. See also Lloyd Carpenter, 'Defining a date and place in the Otago gold rush: The problematic journal of George Magnus Hassing and Bendigo', *Journal of Australasian Mining History*, vol. 10, 2012, p. 35.

27   'Clyde Magistrate's Court Judgements Book 1866–1869', 1 January 1868, 5 and 25 March 1868, 1 and 9 December 1868, and 13 January 1869; 'R.M. Court', *Cromwell Argus*, 10 August, 1870, p. 2.

28   'Resident Magistrate's Court – Ann Box *v.* Lilian Cutler', *Cromwell Argus*, 12 May, 1874, p. 3.

29   Ibid.

30   Carpenter, 'Defining a date and place in the Otago gold rush', p. 36.

31   'Magistrate's Court', *Dunstan Times*, 6 November 1968, p. 3; 'Clyde Magistrate's Court Judgements Book 1866–1869', 4 November 1868; *Otago Police Gazette*, 4 December 1868 (Archives New Zealand, Wellington office, ACIS 17653 P 12 3/3–5/10). In regard to the Caversham Industrial School, see the entry on Te Ara – Encyclopedia of New Zealand: www.teara.govt.nz/en/photograph/26076/ caversham-industrial-school

32   'Cromwell R.M.'s Court', *Cromwell Argus*, 12 January 1870, p. 3; 'Clyde Magistrate's Court Judgements Book 1869–1871', 5 January 1870 (Archives New Zealand, Dunedin office, DADO Acc. D557 138b).

33   'Cromwell R.M.'s Court' *Cromwell Argus*, 27 April 1870, p. 2.

34   'Clyde Magistrate's Court Judgements Book 1869–1871', 1 February 1871; 'Cromwell Resident Magistrate's Court', *Cromwell Argus*, 7 August 1877, p. 4; *New Zealand Police Gazette*, 3 December 1877, p. 81 (Archives New Zealand, Dunedin office, DABS D77/1a–o); 'Courts', *Cromwell Argus*, 16 January 1883, p. 5; 'Cromwell Civil Record Book 1881–1887', 20 June 1884 and 24 April 1888 (Archives New Zealand, Dunedin office, AEOR Acc. D541 6a); 'Courts', *Cromwell Argus*, 24 April 1888, p. 5.

35   'Advertisements – late', *Cromwell Argus*, 25 December 1888, p. 2. This item describes a 'six-roomed iron dwelling house on a residence area of one acre, together with a two-stalled stable'. The furniture, which was to be sold at auction with the house, consisted of 'six iron bedsteads, three sofas, parlour and cooking stoves, bagatelle table, musical instruments, tables, chairs, cooking utensils, clock, tow lamps, sewing machine, etc.' which would be 'sold without the slightest reserve'.

36   'Clyde Magistrate's Court Judgements Book 1866–1869', 28 May 1866 and 8 March and 4 July 1867; 'Obituary, Mrs James Rivers', *Alexandra Herald*, 13 January 1909, p. 5.

37   'Apprehensions', *Otago Police Gazette*, 28 February 1871, p. 9. The Kofoed family were brewers at Wetherstones and later Milton.

38   *Cromwell Argus*, 12 June 1877 and 27 August 1878.

39   'Cromwell Civil Record Book 1881–1887', 17 November 1882 (Archives New Zealand, Dunedin office, AEOR Acc. D541 6/b no. 2); *Cromwell Argus*, 16 January 1883; 'Return of licenses cancelled', *New Zealand Police Gazette*, 17 May 1882, p. 78.

40   'Cromwell Civil Record Book 1881–1887', 17 November 1882; *Cromwell Argus*, 16 January 1883. In 1894, the Wakatipu Electoral Roll showed an Annie Shade of Mount Pisa, accommodation housekeeper.

41   'Police Court, Lawrence', *Tuapeka Times*, 18 April 1885, p. 3.

42   'Discharges', *New Zealand Police Gazette*, 7 July 1886, p. 130; '"Measures not Men"', *Tuapeka Times*, 23 June 1886, p. 2.

43   'Annual licensing meetings', *Lake Wakatip Mail*, 8 June 1888, p. 2.

44   'Sly-grog selling', *Tuapeka Times*, 28 July 1870, p. 6.

45   'Queenstown Court Records Book 1863–1872, 31 January 1865, 31 March 1865, 12 September 1865, [no precise date] September 1866, 22 November 1866, 5 December 1866, and 28 January 1867; probate file, Elizabeth Norrington, 1876 (Archives New Zealand, Dunedin office, DAAC Acc. D239 902). A certain fiction seems to have been maintained with regard to Norrington's marital status. When she died in 1876, the *Lake Wakatip Mail* noted

that Norrington's life was full of romance and that 'Her husband was recently drowned fording a river on the West Coast goldfields of this Island': 'Editorial', *Lake Wakatip Mail*, 30 November 1876, p. 2. This comment on Mr Norrington's demise is not supported by death records for the period.

46   'Kyeburn Committee: Hyde Hotel', *Mount Ida Chronicle*, 10 June 1886, p. 2; 'Licensing committees, Kyeburn District: Mrs Connolly's application', *Mount Ida Chronicle*, 9 June 1887, p. 3.

47   'Notice of application for a publican's license', *Mount Ida Chronicle*, 15 June 1889, p. 2; 'Licensing committees, Waihemo', *Otago Witness*, 10 June 1897; 'Licensing Committee meetings', *Otago Witness*, 9 June 1909, 17 July 1913.

48   Probate file, Maria Connolly, 1913 (Archives New Zealand, Dunedin office, DAAC Acc. D239 325 no. 2220).

49   'Albion Hotel', *The Cyclopedia of New Zealand: Vol. 4. Otago & Southland Provincial Districts* (Christchurch: The Cyclopedia Company, 1905), pp. 699–700; New Zealand electoral roll 1894, Tuapeka electorate; probate file, Catherine Lucas, 1905 (Archives New Zealand, Dunedin office, DAAC Acc. D239 196 no. 4938).

50   'Annual licensing meetings', *Lake Wakatip Mail*, 8 June 1888, p. 2.

51   Queenstown licensing papers to 1881, police reports, 2 March and 21 May 1880.

52   William and Emma George, Union Hotel: *Dunstan Times*, 6 January 1866; James and Kitty Holt, Vincent County Hotel: *Dunstan Times*, 6 January 1882.

53   'Licensing Board', *Cromwell Argus*, 12 June 1883, p. 3.

54   Lloyd Carpenter, 'Rich in myth, gold and heritage: Aspects of the Central Otago gold rush 1862–2012', PhD thesis, University of Canterbury, Christchurch, 2013, p. 295.

55   Family descendant information; Queenstown licensing papers to 1881, application for a temporary licence, 11 May 1878; Lake District police report, 31 March 1882; probate file, John Black Kerr, 1887 (Archives New Zealand, Dunedin office, DAAC Acc. D239 903 no. 3/87). See also Jim McAloon, 'Colonial wealth: The rich in Canterbury and Otago 1890–1914', PhD thesis, University of Otago, Dunedin, 1993, pp. 148–99, and Davidoff and Hall, *Family Fortunes*, p. 299. These three authors argue that the joint nature of hotel businesses in terms of work roles meant that widows of hotelkeepers were more likely to inherit the family hotel business outright than were the widows of men in other businesses.

56   'Licencing', *Dunstan Times*, 8 August 1873, p. 3; 'Clyde businesses', *Wise's Almanac and Otago Business Directory, and Gardeners' and Farmers' Calendar* (Dunedin: H. Wise & Co., 1875–76), p. 35; probate file, James Holt, 1891 (Archives New Zealand, Dunedin office, DAAC Acc D239 89 no. 2082); Dunstan Licensing District licensing papers 1891–1893, application for renewal of licence, 6 May 1892, and police report on licensed houses in the Dunstan District, 8 December 1892 (both from Archives New Zealand, Dunedin office, R12678003 DAEQ 21711 D573 31/aq).

57   Probate files: Edward Barber, 1871 (Archives New Zealand, Dunedin office DAAC Acc. D239 219 no. A51), and Emma Barber, 1887 (DAAC D239 65 no. 1522); [No title], *Mount Ida Chronicle*, 28 April 1871, p. 3; 'For sale by tender', *Mount Ida Chronicle*, 7 July 1887, p. 2; 'County of Maniototo, tenders', 18 August 1887, p. 2; 'Death', *Mount Ida Chronicle*, 20 August 1887, p. 2. For an example of Barber's church involvement, see 'Hamilton', *Mount Ida Chronicle*, 20 March 1879, p. 3. Acknowledgements of Barber's church work appeared frequently in the 'Hamilton' column of the *Mount Ida Chronicle*.

58   *Mackay's Otago, Southland and Goldfields Almanac Directory and Annual* (Dunedin: Joseph Mackay, 1867), p. 171; 'Queenstown Court Records Book 1863–1872', [no precise date given] September 1866, 4 December 1866, 12 October 1868, and 1 December 1868 (Archives New Zealand, Dunedin office, R21724915 AEPG 21734 D568 10/a); 'Licensing Court', *Lake Wakatip Mail*, 8 June 1876, p. 3.

59   Queenstown licensing papers to 1881, police report, 6 December 1880 (Archives New Zealand, Dunedin office, R12678003 DAEQ 21711 D573 31/aq); 'Annual licensing meetings', *Lake Wakatip Mail*, 8 June 1888, p. 2.

60   'Advertisements', *Lake Wakatip Mail*, 15 August 1866, col. 5, p. 1; 'Advertisements', 30 August 1871, p. 3; 'Advertisements', 27 April 1888, p. 1.

61   Queenstown licensing papers to 1881, police reports and licensing committee papers, 1878–1881.

62   Probate file, Albert Eichardt, 1882 (Archives New Zealand, Dunedin office, DAAC Acc. D239 902).

63   'Advertisements – New Zealand Licensing Act, 1873', *Lake Wakatip Mail*, 13 March 1874, p. 3.

64   Probate files, Julia Eichardt, 1892 (Archives New Zealand, Dunedin office, DAAC Acc. D239 904 no. 3/92 and DAAC Acc. D239 284 no. A1969).

65   'Tuapeka Licensing Committee Minute Book 1894–1909', 2 December 1886 and 12 December 1901 (Archives New Zealand, Dunedin office, R1337571 DADQ D132 1/b); 'Roxburgh – hotels', *The Cyclopedia of New Zealand: Vol. 4. Otago & Southland Provincial Districts*, p. 700.

66   Probate file, Catherine Lucas, 1905 (Archives New Zealand, Dunedin office, R22047229 DAAC 9073 D239 196/4938).

67   'Annual licensing meetings', *Lake Wakatip Mail*, 6 June 1890, p. 5. See also the reduction in Maria M. Lynch's licence fee for her Reefers Arms Hotel, *Lake Wakatip Mail*, 8 June 1888.

68   'District of Hawea – licensing', *Cromwell Argus*, 15 June 1886, p. 3. By 1886 quarterly police reports were a legal requirement anyway.

69   'Obituary', *Lake County Press*, 1 August 1912, p. 5. See also 'Queenstown Licensing Committee Minute Book 1894–1900', applications for licence renewal, 1 June 1894 (Archives New Zealand, Dunedin office, R21724915 AEPG 21734 D568 10/a); 'Advertisements: New Orleans Hotel, Arrowtown', *Lake Wakatip Mail*, 18 January 1901, p. 1.

70   'Deaths', *Dunstan Times*, 4 February 1876, p. 3. Her husband Robert Kidd held the licence. For evidence that Mary Kidd worked behind the bar, see 'Cromwell District – licensing', *Cromwell Argus*, 18 June 1872, p. 2.

71   'Pembroke', *Cromwell Argus*, p. 2; 'Social', 3 January 1883; 'Local and general', 11 January 1887, and 'Obituary', 28 August 1905, p. 5.

Chapter 11

1   *Otago Police Gazette*, 1 June 1866, p. 29; Fitzgerald family file, Lakes District Museum, Arrowtown.

2   Elizabeth Norrington and Eliza Jenkins both took out 'married woman's protection' orders to protect their earnings from their troublesome husbands: biographical files, Lakes District Museum, Arrowtown. For Eliza Pocock, see 'Serious charge against Mr Warden Williamson', *Lake Wakatip Mail*, 24 August 1864, p. 2. See also 'Resident Magistrate's Court: Charge of common assault', *Otago Daily Times*, 17 August 1864, p. 6; 'Pocock v. Williamson' and 'Charleston, Upper Shotover', *Otago Daily Times*, 3 September 1864, p. 5; 'The Lake District', *Otago Daily Times*, 5 September 1864, p. 6; 'Miss Pocock's case', *Otago Daily Times*, 10 September 1864, p. 5; 'The Lake District', *Otago Daily Times*, 23 September 1864, p. 5.

3   'Resident Magistrate's Court', *Otago Daily Times*, 15 June 1864, p. 5.

4   'Resident Magistrate's Court', *Otago Daily Times*, 26 June 1863, p. 4.

5   Births in the district of Ballarat, Mary Ann Tyree, register no. 359, 1855. Births in the district of Ballarat, Frederick James Tyree, register no. 21, 1862 (registers held at Ballarat Archives Centre, Ballarat, Victoria). Death of Frederick James Tyree registered 6 August 1863, Dunedin, information from descendant Pat Brocklebank.

6   'Marriages in the District of Wakatipu', no. 15, 1 February 1871 (Archives New Zealand, Dunedin office, R12071724 DAFH 3947 D485 468/).

7   Passengers on the *James Gibb*, 1849, State Records Authority of New South Wales, Kingswood, New South Wales, Australia; *Persons on Bounty Ships to Sydney, Newcastle, and Moreton Bay (Board's Immigrant Lists)*: series 5317, reel 2459, item [4/4909]; 'Family tree for Mary Bricheno 1825–1913', by noelinew153: http://trees.ancestry.com.au/tree/9216629/person/794412871?ssrc=&ml_rpos=4

8   'Lambing Flat', *Goulburn Herald*, 7 August 1861, p. 3 (Mary's surname is spelt Roles in this newspaper item); 'Riot and assault at Lambing Flat', *Goulburn Herald*, 21 September 1861, pp. 3–4; 'Goulburn Circuit Court', *Sydney Morning Herald*, 24 September 1861, p. 2.

9   Implied in 'Resident Magistrate's Court', *Mount Ida Chronicle*, 3 June 1870, p. 3; B. Burns

advertising Liverpool Arms Hotel for sale, *Otago Daily Times*, 1 April 1867, p. 3; 'Resident Magistrate's Court: Licensing meeting', *Mount Ida Chronicle*, 10 December 1869, p. 3 (Mary's surname is again spelt Roles).

10   'Marriages', *Mount Ida Chronicle*, 14 March 1873, p. 4.

11   Family tree for Charles Thomas Rolls: http://trees.ancestry.com.au/tree/13906724/ person/18018335133? ssrc=&ml_rpos=3. Intention to marry for Mary Rolls and Daniel Robertson, 20/18, 1873, in 'Register of births, deaths and marriages' p. 703 (Archives New Zealand, Wellington office).

12   'Deaths, Robertson, Mary', *Mount Ida Chronicle*, 3 October 1913; 'Family tree for Mary Bricheno 1825–1913'.

13   Family data for Charles Nicholson and Amalie Carlina Koch: http://trees.ancestry.com.au/ tree/38811747/ person/19287219980?ssrc=&ml_rpos=1. 'Supreme Court', *Otago Daily Times*, 21 September 1869, p. 2; *The Cyclopedia of New Zealand: Vol. 4. Otago & Southland Provincial Districts* (Christchurch: Cyclopedia Company Limited, 1905), p. 696.

14   'Arrow Police Court', *Lake Wakatip Mail*, 17 February 1864, p. 5.

15   'Arrow Police Court', *Lake Wakatip Mail*, 8 March 1865, p. 3.

16   'Magistrate's Court', *Arrow Observer*, 21 June 1876, pp. 2–3.

17   'Local', *Arrow Observer*, 21 June 1876, p. 3.

18   Marriage certificate for Daniel Quadri and Annie Young, 1 July 1863, registered at Dunedin 1863, folio 885, copy courtesy of Gaye Wilson.

19   'Action of ejectment at Arrowtown before a bench of magistrates', *Otago Daily Times*, 13 September 1864, p. 6; 'Dunstan', *Otago Daily Times*, 21 March 1865, p. 4; 'Supreme Court: Criminal session', *Otago Daily Times*, 3 June 1865, p. 5; *Otago Police Gazette*, 2 October 1865, p. 57; 'Advertisements', *West Coast Times*, 22 February 1866, p. 3.

20   'Resident Magistrate's Court', *West Coast Times*, 2 November 1866, p. 2.

21   'Examination of A.J. Carr continued', *West Coast Times*, 21 December 1866, p. 2.

22   'Correspondence: Rumor [sic] relative to Mrs Quadri', *West Coast Times*, 2 October 1867, p. 3; 'Advertisements', *West Coast Times*, 17 December 1868, p. 3; 'Notices: West Coast Hotel', *West Coast Times*, 17 December 1868, pp. 2, 3.

23   'Westport Resident Magistrate's Court minutes 1870–75', pp. 121–41 (Nelson Provincial Museum, Nelson); 'The Inangahua District', *Grey River Argus*, 19 September 1872, p. 2.

24   'Resident Magistrate's Court', *Inangahua Herald*, 23 November 1872, p. 2; 'The Inangahua District', *Grey River Argus*, 22 November 1872, p. 2; 'Magistrate's Court', *Inangahua Herald*, 26 March 1875, p. 3; 'Editorial', *Grey River Argus*, 10 May 1875, p. 2; 'Editorial', *West Coast Times*, 12 May 1875, p. 2.

25   'Resident Magistrate Court', *Westport Times*, 10 May 1878, p. 4.

26   'Resident Magistrate's Court', *Lyell Times*, 15 August 1885, pp. 2, 4 (Mindermann's surname is spelt Minderman in this newspaper item, while Annie Quadri reverted to using Annie Young for her name.)

27   I received the details in the entry for Annie Young (née Golightly) in the Westport deaths database from Norman Crawshaw in 2002. Daniel Quadri's death certificate 1907, folio 2974.

28   'Editorial', *West Coast Times*, 24 May 1881, p. 2. Place of birth from 'Hokitika Register of Prisoners 1865–1874', 29 November 1869 (Archives New Zealand, Christchurch office, CAUA CH306 4 9/1).

29   'Central Police Court', *Sydney Morning Herald*, 20 July 1855, p. 6; 'Sydney quarter sessions', *Sydney Morning Herald*, 18 August, p. 7.

30   'Supreme Court', *Sydney Morning Herald*, 28 December 1855, p. 5; 'Sydney quarter sessions', *Sydney Morning Herald*, 27 May 1856, p. 4.

31   'Police Court', *Star* (Ballarat), 19 January 1858, p. 2; Barbara Weldon, number 200, 'Victoria prisoner's index' (Public Record Office of Victoria, North Melbourne, VPRS 516/1).

32   'Editorial', *Argus* (Melbourne), 4 June 1862, p. 4.

33   Search on the Trove website for Barbara Weldon for a list: http://trove.nla.gov.au/

34   Entries for Barbara Weldon from *Otago Police Gazette*, listed in 'Otago nominal index': http://marvin.otago.ac.nz/oni/basic.php

35   'Resident Magistrate's Court', *Otago Daily Times*, 5 March 1864, p. 5.

36 Ibid., 21 January 1863 p. 5; 'The incorrigible again', *Otago Witness*, 10 September 1864, p. 9.

37 'Resident Magistrate's Court', *Evening Post*, 7 August 1869, p. 2; 'Gaol department report, 23 January 1874', *Westland Votes and Proceedings*, 1874, p. 11 (William Heinz Reference Collection, Hokitika Museum).

38 'Hokitika register of prisoners 1865–1874' (Archives New Zealand, Christchurch office, CAUA, CH306, 4, 9/1).

39 'Attempted suicide', *West Coast Times*, 13 September 1870, p. 2.

40 'Editorial', *West Coast Times*, 3 April 1873, p. 2.

41 Ibid., 28 October 1873 p. 2.

42 'Editorial', *Grey River Argus*, 1 November 1882, p. 2.

43 Certificate of marriage for John Watson and Janet Bailey, 5 January 1859, 1859/147, 'Victorian registry of births, deaths and marriages' (Department of Justice and Regulation, Melbourne).

44 Multiple entries can be found in the *New Zealand Police Gazette*'s 'Return of discharged prisoners, 1874–1885'. See also Janet Watson, 'Seacliff medical casebook', pp. 1–3 (Archives New Zealand, Dunedin office, DAHI19956 D264 46 6 patient 2755).

45 'Australian vital records index'. Isabella was born in 1859 at Campbells Creek; Elizabeth in 1861 at Kingower. John was born in 1864 at Emerald Hill but died at six months of age. The birth record for James (c. 1865) has not been located.

46 'Resident Magistrate's Court, Naseby', *Mount Ida Chronicle*, 2 April 1869, p. 2.

47 'Notice', *Mount Ida Chronicle*, 19 November 1869, p. 2; 'Editorial', *Mount Ida Chronicle*, 30 September 1870, p. 2.

48 'Resident Magistrate's Court', *Mount Ida Chronicle*, 26 April 1872, p. 5.

49 Ibid., 5 September 1873, p. 5.

50 Ibid., 2 April 1875, p. 5.

51 Ibid., 22 February 1877, p. 2; 'What is vagrancy', *Mount Ida Chronicle*, 1 March 1877, p. 2.

52 'Resident Magistrate's Court', *Mount Ida Chronicle*, 9 June 1877.

53 Birth index for John Watson, 1881/1304, 'Births, deaths and marriages online': www.bdmhistoricalrecords.dia.govt.nz/Home/

54 Birth index for Mary Jenkins Watson, 1878/9888, 'Births, deaths and marriages online'; 'The courts, Naseby', *Mount Ida Chronicle*, 14 November 1878, p. 3; 'The courts: Rape on Janet Watson', *Mount Ida Chronicle*, 28 May 1881, p. 3; 'The courts: Naseby', *Mount Ida Chronicle*, 4 June 1881, p. 3. The probable birth registration is 1881/1304: John Watson: mother Janet Watson, father not recorded.

55 'The courts: Naseby', *Mount Ida Chronicle*, 28 May 1881, 4 June 1881, and 9 June 1881, p. 3.

56 [No title], *Mount Ida Chronicle*, 1 September 1881, p. 2, and 'Inquest' p. 3; probate file Thomas Ford, also known as John Farmer and John Ford (Archives New Zealand, Dunedin office, DAAC 9074 D239 278 A1690).

57 'Warrants issued under the Industrial Schools Act 1882', John Farmer, p. 209 and Johanna Farmer, p. 94 (Archives New Zealand, Dunedin office, ACGB 8304 CW13 2 and ACGB 8304 CW13 4); 'Editorial', *Mount Ida Chronicle*, 30 September 1870, p. 2; 'Resident Magistrate's Court', *Mount Ida Chronicle*, 5 September 1873, p. 5.

58 'Resident Magistrate's Court, Naseby', *Mount Ida Chronicle*, 22 November 1883, p. 3.

59 Ibid., 26 December 1889, p. 5.

60 Ibid., 13 July 1893, p. 3.

61 Seacliff Hospital records for Janet Watson, pp. 1–3 (Archives New Zealand, Dunedin office, DAHI D266 1985 23-2755; DAHI 19956 D264 46 6 2755); Marriage of Isabella Watson and Alfred Thomas Price, online index registration number 1880/1117. Industrial School records for David Watson, p. 124 (Archives New Zealand, Wellington office, CW13/2). In 1911, Alfred Thomas Price (chemist) and Isabella Price married. They, along with James Watson, chemist's assistant, were living at 4 Richardson Street, Dunedin, according to Caversham Project records: http://caversham.otago.ac.nz/dbaccess/ index.php. The most likely Porirua burial is that of Janet Watson, age 86 (though she would have been only 76) in October 1916.

62 List of church register index cards at Christchurch City Library: http://homepages.ihug. co.nz/~ashleigh/ Library.BMDs/WILSON.Christchurch.City.Library.BMB.html

63 George Magnus Hassing, *Pages from the Memory Log of G.M. Hassing: Sailor, pioneer, schoolmaster* (Invercargill: Southland Times, 1930), p. 72; Lloyd Carpenter, 'Defining a date

and place in the Otago gold rush: The problematic journal of George Magnus Hassing and Bendigo', *Journal of Australasian Mining History*, vol. 10, 2012, p. 36.

64   Ibid., p. 72. The approximate date of the births of Jane and John Wilson's children are Louisa 1859, Eliza 1861, Ellen (Eleanor) 1862, Eva 1864, Eda (Ida) 1865: information taken from the 'Cromwell Magistrate's Court judgement record book', 3 November 1868 (Archives New Zealand, Dunedin office, DADO Acc D557 207c). Accessing registrations on the births microfiche and using the folio number to find where the births were registered yields Louisa 1859/288 Kaiapoi, Elizabeth 1861/393 Dunedin, Eleanor 1862/391 Timaru, and Eva 1864/504 Timaru.

65   'Cromwell Magistrate's Court judgement book', 3 November 1868 (Archives New Zealand, Dunedin office, DADO Acc D557 207c). Also 'Cromwell Watch-house charge book', 1864–1880 (Archives New Zealand, Dunedin office, DAKU 9248 D383 4); 'Magistrate's Court', *Cromwell Argus*, 6 June 1876, p. 3.

66   'Resident Magistrate's Court', *Dunstan Times*, 5 January 1870, p. 2.

67   'Local and general', *Dunstan Times*, 23 December 1870, p. 3.

68   'Cromwell Watch-house charge book, 1864–1880', 1 February 1871 (DAKU, 9248, D383, 4); 'News of the week', *Otago Witness*, 25 February 1871, p. 15.

69   'Cromwell Watch-house charge book, 1864–1880' (assault on Ann Box/Murley), 4 August 1874 (DAKU 9248 D383 4); 'Resident Magistrate's Court', *Cromwell Argus*, 28 August 1876, p. 5.

70   'Inquest', *Otago Witness*, 13 October 1892, p. 11.

71   Burial details for Jane Wilson: www.dunedin.govt.nz/facilities/cemeteries/cemeteries_search

72   'In memoriam', *Otago Daily Times*, 5 February 1910, p. 4.

Chapter 12

1   Catherine Bishop, 'Women on the move: Gender, money-making and mobility in mid-nineteenth-century Australasia', *History Australia*, vol. 11, no. 2, 2014, 28–59.

2   Philip Ross May, *The West Coast Gold Rushes* (Christchurch: Pegasus Press, 1962), p. 480.

3   This analysis is based on a study of 735 women whose deaths were registered on the West Coast between 1876 and 1915. These sources were linked systematically with cemetery records, probate files, genealogies, family histories and newspaper obituaries.

4   May, *The West Coast Gold Rushes*, p. 285.

5   David Noel Doyle, 'Review article: Cohesion and diversity in the Irish diaspora', *Irish Historical Studies*, vol. 31, no. 123, 1999, p. 419.

6   Descendant information and private family papers courtesy of Ron Patterson and Brian Nolan.

7   I am indebted to the late Ted Matthews for research on these women.

8   Gale Davidson Gibb, 'Memories of Red Jacks: Johanna Shanahan Weir', in *Women of Westland and Their Families*, eds. Yvonne Davison and Frankie Mills (Greymouth: Westland Branch, New Zealand Council of Women, 1998), pp. 185–86.

9   Descendant information and private family papers courtesy of Mary O'Connor (London).

10   Joanna Bourke, *Husbandry to Housewifery: Women, economic change and housework in Ireland, 1890–1914* (Oxford: Clarendon Press, 1993), p. 16.

11   May, *The West Coast Gold Rushes*, p. 310.

12   *Hokitika Evening Star*, 9 February 1866, quoted in 'Westland gold fields: Hokitika', *Nelson Examiner*, 17 February 1866, p. 3.

13   May, *The West Coast Gold Rushes*, pp. 323–34.

14   Mary P. Anderson, 'The Anderson family', unpublished manuscript (Hokitika Museum).

15   'Register of marriages', 2999/1887, Greymouth (Registrar-General of Births, Deaths and Marriages); descendant information, Ron Patterson.

16   'Register of marriages', 2975/1882, Charleston; 447/1889, Reefton; 1932/1881, Hokitika (Registrar-General of Births, Deaths and Marriages).

17   Gibb, 'Memories of Red Jacks', p. 187.

18   Will of John Cronin (Archives New Zealand, Christchurch office, HK 124/1914).

19   Mark Wallace, 'Memories of the early years in South Westland: Catherine Wallace (Markey)', in Davison and Mills, *Women of Westland*, pp. 276–83.

20   Descendant information, Ted Matthews; Ted Matthews, 'The Deverys and the Gillins: A brief

history', unpublished manuscript, n.d. (Westcoast Historical Museum, Hokitika).

21   Ellen Piezzi (Waimea) to Victer Piezzi (California), 3 June 1879 (courtesy of Julia O'Connor).
22   Ellen Piezzi (Waimea) to Victer Piezzi (California), undated c. 1880 (courtesy of Julia O'Connor).
23   Ellen Piezzi (Rimu) to Victer Piezzi (California), undated c. 1881 (courtesy of Julia O'Connor).
24   Ellen Piezzi (Waimea) to Mrs Piezzi (California), 6 June 1879 (courtesy of Julia O'Connor).
25   Descendant information, courtesy of Bill Nolan.
26   Ellen Piezzi (Waimea) to Victer Piezzi (California), 3 June 1879 (courtesy of Julia O'Connor).
27   Descendant information courtesy of Ted Matthews.
28   Anne Hutchison, 'Barbara Weldon', *Dictionary of New Zealand Biography*. Volume 1: 1769–1869 (Wellington: Bridget Williams Books and Department of Internal Affairs, 1990), p. 581.
29   Wallace, 'Memories of the early years', p. 282.
30   'Editorial', *West Coast Times*, 17 September 1894, p. 2.
31   Ibid., 18 September 1894, p. 2; 24 September 1894, p. 2; 25 September 1894, p. 2; and 26 September 1894, p. 2; Peter Ewen, 'Ann's "house rules" had their moments in the early pub game', *The Coaster*, 26 May 1999, p. 2; Gerard Morris, ed., *Waiuta, 1906–1951: The gold mine, the town, the people* (Reefton: Friends of Waiuta, 1986), pp. 81–85; descendant information courtesy of Peter Kerridge.
32   Peter Graham, 'Mrs Isabell Kathleen Graham', in Davison and Mills, *Women of Westland*, p. 273.
33   Ellen Piezzi (Waimea) to Victer Piezzi (California), 8 October 1881 (courtesy of Julia O'Connor): from a transcription of the lost original.
34   'Magee family' (Alexander Turnbull Library, Wellington, MS Papers 116); 'Notes from the journal of Pat Magee', in Davison and Mills, *Women of Westland*, p. 174.
35   Will of Michael Scanlon (Archives New Zealand, Christchurch office, WP 1/1894).
36   Wills of Daniel Falvey, HK 227/1884, James McInroe, GM 153/1890, James Corbett, HK 2172/1908, Bernard Rogers, RN 153/1904, and Patrick Healey, HK 23/1910 (all from Archives New Zealand, Christchurch office).
37   Donald Harman Akenson, 'Reading the texts of rural immigrants: The letters from the Irish in Australia, New Zealand and America', in *Canadian Papers in Rural History*, ed. Donald Harman Akenson (vol. 7, Garanoque, Ontario: Langdale Press, 1990), pp. 395–96.
38   WP 185/1915 (Archives New Zealand, Christchurch office).
39   WP 159/1914, GM 156/1914, GM 96/1912, and WP 197/1915 (Archives New Zealand, Christchurch office).
40   WP 9/1902 (Archives New Zealand, Christchurch office).
41   Bishop, 'Women on the move', pp. 38–43, 58.

Chapter 13

1   Vincent Pyke, *History of the Early Gold Discoveries in Otago* (Dunedin: Otago Daily Times and Witness Newspapers Company Ltd., 1887); R.T. Wheeler, *The Story of Wild Will Enderby* (Dunedin: Mills, Dick and Company, 1887); A.H. McLintock, *History of Otago: The origins and growth of a Wakefield class settlement* (Dunedin: Otago Centennial Historical Publications, 1949), pp. 447–48, especially 456; Frederick W.G. Miller, *Golden Days of Lake County: The history of Lake County and the boroughs of Queenstown and Arrowtown* (Christchurch: Whitcombe and Tombs Ltd., 1949); James Crombie Parcel, *Heart of the Desert: Being the history of the Cromwell and Bannockburn Districts of Central Otago* (Dunedin, Otago Centennial Historical Publications, 1951); J.H.M. Salmon, *A History of Gold-mining in New Zealand* (Wellington: Government Printer, 1963); W.P. Morrell, *The Gold Rushes* (London: Adam & Charles Black, 2nd edn, 1968); John Hall-Jones, *Goldfields of the South* (Invercargill: Craig Printing Company Ltd., 1982); Erik Olssen, with Tom Field, *Relics of the Goldfields: Central Otago* (Dunedin: John McIndoe, 1976); Erik Olssen, *A History of Otago* (Dunedin: John McIndoe, 1984), pp. 56–65, and 'Lands of sheep and gold: The Australian dimension to the New Zealand past', in *Tasman Relations: New Zealand and Australia 1788–1988*, ed. Keith Sinclair (Auckland: Auckland University Press, 1987), pp. 34–51; Terence John Hearn and Ray Hargreaves, *The Speculators'*

Dream: Gold dredging in southern New Zealand (Dunedin: Allied Press, 1985); T.J. Hearn, 'After the rush, Central Otago, 1860s to 1910s', in *Bateman New Zealand Historical Atlas/Ko Papatuanuku e Takato Nei*, ed. Malcolm McKinnon (Auckland: David Bateman, 1997), plate 45, 'They came for the golden pile: Otago gold miners 1867–1871 and their wives', in *Landfall in Southern Seas II: Proceedings of the 8th Australasian Congress on Genealogy and Heraldry held at Lincoln University, February 1997*, comp., Garry Jeffrey (Christchurch: New Zealand Society of Genealogists, 1997), pp. 121–39, 'Mining the quarry', in *Environmental Histories of New Zealand*, eds. Eric Pawson and Tom Brooking (Melbourne: Oxford University Press, 2002), pp. 84–99, and 'They came to the golden pile: Scots miners in the goldfields, 1861–1970', in *The Heather and the Fern: Scottish migration and New Zealand settlement*, eds. Tom Brooking and Jennie Coleman (Dunedin: Otago University Press, 2003), pp. 67–86; Jock Phillips and T.J. Hearn, *Settlers: New Zealand emigrants from England, Ireland and Scotland, 1800–1945* (Auckland: Auckland University Press, 2008), pp. 18, 19, 38–39, 41, 52, 57, 61, 87, 89, 96–97, 103, 111, 121–22, 130, 135, 147; James Ng, *Windows on a Chinese Past* (Dunedin: Otago Heritage Books, 4 vols., consecutively published 1993–1999); John McCraw, *Early Days on the Dunstan* (Dunedin: Square One Press, 2007); Grahame Sydney, *Promised Land: From Dunedin to the Dunstan goldfields* (Auckland: Penguin, 2009).

2   Key theses include: Robin Marks, 'Lawrence Athenaeum and Miners' Institute: A fragment of goldfields history', MA diss., University of Otago, Dunedin, 1973; T.J. Hearn, 'Land, water and gold in Central Otago 1860s–1921: Some aspects of resource use policy and conflict', PhD thesis, University of Otago, 1981; Wayne Angus, 'Queenstown 1862–1864: The genesis of a goldfields community', BA Hons diss., University of Otago, 1987; Angela Morton, 'Macetown: A community built on gold', BA Hons diss., University of Otago, 1987; Jennifer L. Dickinson, 'Picks, pans and petticoats: Women on the Central Otago goldfields', BA Hons diss., University of Otago, 1993; Graeme Morton, 'Gold, law and Freemasonry: A biographical analysis of Vincent Pyke as a goldfields' administrator in Otago, 1862–1867', BA Hons diss., University of Otago, 1994; Sandra Quick (for an account of women and the liquor industry) 'The colonial helpmeet takes a dram: Women participants in the Central Otago goldfields liquor industry 1861–1901', MA diss., University of Otago, 1997; Marc Phillip Ellison, 'A history of the Ellison whanua of Otakou', BA Hons diss., University of Otago, 2008; Nicol Allen MacArthur, 'Gold rush to gold dredge: The "evolution of alluvial gold mining technology in Otago, 1861–1898"', BA Hons diss., University of Otago, 2008, and 'Gold rush and gold mining: A technological analysis of Gabriel's Gully and the Blue Spur, 1861–1891', MA diss., University of Otago, 2013; Peter Petchey, 'The archaeology of the New Zealand stamp mill', PhD thesis, University of Otago, 2013; Lloyd Carpenter, 'Rich in myth, gold and heritage: Aspects of the Central Otago gold rush 1862 – 2012', PhD diss., University of Canterbury, Christchurch, 2013.

3   David Goodman, *Gold Seeking: Victoria and California in the 1850s* (Stanford, CA: Stanford University Press, 1994), and '"That dream of quiet was rudely broken on": Experiencing and remembering gold rushes', Otago Anniversary guest lecture, Dunedin, 24 March 2011; Graeme Wynn, *Canada and Arctic North America: An environmental history* (Santa Barbara, CA: ABC-CLIO, 2007).

4   Olssen, *History of Otago*, pp. 58–59; Sydney, *Promised Land*, pp. 69–85.

5   Sydney, *Promised Land*, p. 85.

6   Olssen, *History of Otago*, p. 59; Sydney, *Promised Land*, pp. 87–106.

7   Olssen, *History of Otago*, p. 59; Sydney, *Promised Land*, p. 145.

8   McCraw, *Early Days on the Dunstan*, pp. 125, 210.

9   Olssen, *History of Otago*, pp. 59, 61–65; Sydney, *Promised Land*, p. 145.

10   Olssen, *History of Otago*, pp. 59–64; T.J. Hearn, 'William Fox', in *Dictionary of New Zealand Biography*, ed. W. H. Oliver (Wellington: Bridget William Books and Department of Internal Affairs, vol. 1, 1990), p. 138.

11   Olssen, *A History of Otago*, p. 59.

12   Ibid., p. 60.

13   Ibid., pp. 59–64.

14   Angus, 'Queenstown 1862–1864'. The lodges included the Masons and the Ancient Order of Foresters.

15 Robert Pinney, *Early Northern Otago Runs* (Auckland: William Collins, 1981); Noel Crawford, 'Allan McLean', in *Dictionary of New Zealand Biography*, vol. 1, pp. 254–55; Jim McAloon, *No Idle Rich: The wealthy in Canterbury and Otago, 1940–1914* (Dunedin: University of Otago Press, 2002), pp. 35, 41, 45, 47.

16 Olssen, *A History of Otago*, p. 66; Peter Bristow, 'A brief history of mining at the Bendigo Historic Reserve', document OTACO-4053, Research, Development and Improvement Division, Department of Conservation, Wellington, 2007: www.doc.govt.nz/conservation/historic/by-region/otago/central-otago/bendigo-historic-reserve

17 Stevan Eldred-Grigg, *Diggers, Hatters and Whores: The story of the New Zealand goldrushes* (Auckland: Random House, 2008); Hearn, 'After the rush, Central Otago, 1860s to 1910s'.

18 Dickinson, 'Picks, pans and petticoats: Women on the Central Otago goldfields'.

19 Miles Fairburn, *The Ideal Society and its Enemies: The foundations of modern New Zealand society 1850–1990* (Auckland: Auckland University Press, 1989).

20 Angela Morton, 'Macetown'.

21 Miller, *Golden Days of Lake County*, p. 116.

22 A.H. Horn, 'Horn family papers' (Hocken Library, Dunedin, MS 1567/001-004), cited in Danny Knudson, *Skippers: Triumph and tragedy* (Queenstown: Otago and District Historical Society and Lakes District Museum, in press), chap. 2.

23 Ibid., p. 121; Olssen, *History of Otago*, p. 65.

24 Miller, *Golden Days*, p. 121.

25 Ibid., p. 122.

26 Knudson, *Skippers: Triumph and tragedy*, chap. 10.

27 Ibid., pp. 122–23; Olssen, *History of Otago*, p. 65; John Hall-Jones, 'Historic Bullendale hydro-heritage', Our Heritage: www.doc.govt.nz/conservation/ historic/by-region/otago/queenstown-wakatipu/bullendale-hydro-heritage/; 'Historic Mount Aurum Conservation Reserve, Department of Conservation', Our Heritage: www.doc.govt.nz/conservation/historic/by-region/otago/queenstown-wakatipu/mount-aurum/; Peter Petchey, *Gold and Electricity: Archaeological survey of Bullendale* (Wellington: Science & Technical Publishing, Department of Conservation, 2006): www.doc.govt.nz/documents/science-and-technical/sap237.pdf

28 Olssen, *History of Otago*, p. 65.

29 MacArthur, 'Gold rush to gold dredge'.

30 Hearn and Hargreaves, *The Speculators' Dream*, pp. 3–5.

31 Ibid., pp. 13, 78; Olssen, *A History of Otago*, pp. 126–27.

32 Hearn and Hargreaves, *The Speculators' Dream*, p. 12.

33 Ibid., p. 18.

34 Ibid., pp. 24–42.

35 Ibid., p. 51.

36 Calculated from the appendices in Ibid., pp. 79–87.

37 Ibid., pp. 55–57, 66.

38 Ibid., p. 59.

39 Morrell, *The Gold Rushes*, pp. 260–82.

40 Ministry for the Environment, *The State of the New Zealand Environment* (Wellington: Author, 1997), section 8, p. 41. The Clutha figure comes from *Appendices to the Journal of the House of Representatives of New Zealand*, 1920, D6B, cited in Hearn, 'Mining the quarry', pp. 92, 304. See also Hearn and Hargreaves, *The Speculators' Dream*, pp. 61–74.

41 Frederick W.G. Miller, *There Was Gold in the River* (Wellington: A.H. & A.W. Reed, 1969), pp. 22–54; Olssen, *History of Otago*, p. 183.

42 On this argument regarding the impact of the mythologies associated with the Great Depression in New Zealand, see Tony Simpson, *The Sugarbag Years: A people's history of the 1930s Depression in New Zealand* (Auckland: Random House, 4th edn, 2000), p. 16.

43 James Belich, *Replenishing the Earth: The settler revolution and the rise of the Anglo-World, 1783–1939* (Oxford: Oxford University Press, 2009).

44 Rebecca Lenihan, 'Diaspora or dispersion? Scottish settlement patterns in New Zealand', in *Unpacking the Kists: The Scots in New Zealand*, eds. Brad Patterson, Tom Brooking and Jim McAloon (Toronto/Dunedin: McGill-Queen's University Press/Otago University Press, 2013), pp. 66–72.

45   Hearn, 'Mining the quarry', pp. 84–99; Jim McAloon, 'The New Zealand economy', in *The New Oxford History of New Zealand*, ed. Giselle Byrnes (Auckland: Oxford University Press, 1995), pp. 206–12.

46   The Sydney-based Bank of New South Wales and the Auckland-based Bank of New Zealand benefited considerably from the Dunstan rush; the local Bank of Otago and the London-based National Bank likewise benefited but to a lesser extent. The fortunes of the National Insurance Company, the National Mortgage Association, and stock and station agencies such as Dalgety, Wright Stephenson, Rattray, and Donald Reid also gained from the discovery of gold in the Dunstan even if they gained much more from financing and servicing the pastoral farming stimulated by the rush. The Shiels family did especially well from brick manufacture, while the McLeod Brothers made a small fortune from their soap. See McAloon, *No Idle Rich*, pp. 38–39, 48–49, 59, 61.

47   Morrell, *The Gold Rushes*, pp. 260–82.

48   T.W.H. Brooking, *A History of Dentistry in New Zealand* (Auckland: New Zealand Dental Association,1981), pp. 56, 65.

49   Daniel Davey, 'Lost tailings: Gold rush societies and cultures in colonial Otago, New Zealand, 1861–1911', PhD thesis, University of Otago, Dunedin, 2014.

50   Marks, 'Lawrence Athenaeum and Miners' Institute'; Angus, 'Queenstown 1862–1864'; Morton, 'Macetown'.

51   Hearn, 'Land, water and gold in Central Otago'.

52   Hearn, 'After the rush, Central Otago, 1860s to 1910s', plate 45, 'They came for the golden pile: Otago gold miners 1867–1871 and their wives', and 'They came to the golden pile: Scots miners in the goldfields', pp. 67–86; Phillips and Hearn, *Settlers*, pp. 18, 19, 38–39, 41, 52, 57, 61, 87, 89, 96–97, 103, 111, 121–22, 130, 135, 147.

53   Papers Past: http://paperspast.natlib.govt.nz/cgi-bin/paperspast

54   Quick, 'The colonial helpmeet takes a dram'; Fabia Fox, 'Crime in nineteenth century Dunedin', MA in progress, University of Otago.

55   Ng, *Windows on a Chinese Past*.

56   James Beattie, 'The empire of the rhododendron: Reorienting New Zealand garden history', in *Making a New Land: Environmental histories of New Zealand*, eds. Pawson and Brooking (Dunedin: Otago University Press, 2013), pp. 241–60, and 'Expanding the horizons of Chinese environmental history: Cantonese gold-miners in colonial New Zealand, 1860s–1920s', draft article supplied with permission of the author.

57   I have attempted to do this for the West Coast in my new biography of Seddon: Tom Brooking, *Richard Seddon, King of God's Own: The life and times of New Zealand's longest serving prime minister* (Auckland: Penguin, 2014), pp. 29–86.

58   See Len Richardson, 'Parties and political change', in *The Oxford History of New Zealand*, ed. Geoffrey W. Rice (Auckland: Oxford University Press, 2nd edn, 1992), pp. 210–29; James Watson and Lachy Paterson, eds., *A Great New Zealand Prime Minister? Reappraising William Ferguson Massey* (Dunedin: Otago University Press, 2011). On the politics of Victoria, see Geoffrey Serle, *The Golden Age: A history of the colony of Victoria, 1851–1861* (Carlton: Melbourne University Press, 1963), and *The Rush to be Rich: A history of the colony of Victoria, 1883–1899* (Carlton: Melbourne University Press, 1971); Goodman, *Gold Seeking*; Stuart Macintyre, *A Colonial Liberalism: The lost world of three Victorian visionaries* (Melbourne: Oxford University Press, 1991).

59   MacArthur, 'Gold rush to gold dredge', and 'Gold rush and gold mining'.

60   Hearn, 'Land, water and gold in Central Otago 1860s–1921', and 'Mining the quarry'.

61   Simon Schama, *Landscape and Memory* (London: Harper Perennial, 1995), pp. 14–16.

62   John Hall-Jones, *Mr Surveyor Thomson: Early days in Otago and Southland* (Wellington: A.H. & A.W. Reed, 1971), *Goldfields of Otago: An illustrated history* (Invercargill: Craig Printing Co. Ltd., 2005), and *Gold Trails of Otago* (Cromwell: Otago Goldfields Heritage Trust, 2009).

63   See the society's *Queenstown Courier*: www.queenstownhistoricalsociety. org.nz/page7.html

64   On photographs and photography, see Joan M. Schwartz, 'The geography lesson: Photographs and the construction of imaginative geographies', *Journal of Historical Geography*, vol. 22, no. 1, 1996, 16–45. For an interesting recent example of how women can regain their place in

goldfield history, see Clare Wright, *The Forgotten Rebels of Eureka* (Melbourne: Text Publishing Australia, 2013).

Chapter 14

1 Robert Hoskins, *Goldfield Balladeer: The life and times of the celebrated Charles R. Thatcher* (Auckland: William Collins, 1977), pp. 169–71.

2 George J. Griffiths, *King Wakatip: How William Gilbert Rees, cousin and cricketing godfather of the incomparable W.G. Grace, emigrated to the colonies and founded the most beautiful township in New Zealand* (Dunedin: John McIndoe), 1971.

3 'Department of Agriculture: Mr William Gilbert Rees', *The Cyclopedia of New Zealand. Vol. 1: Wellington Provincial District* (Wellington: Cyclopedia Company Limited, 1897), p. 1500.

4 W.G. Grace, *Cricket* (Bristol: Arrowsmiths, 1891), p. 65.

5 'Rees, William Gilbert, 1827–1898: Original sketches/by W G Rees, 1852–1884' (Alexander Turnbull Library, Wellington, Reference Number E-199-q).

6 Ibid.

7 Mark Baker, *Southern Downs Cultural Heritage Study, Vol. 1: Main report* (Warwick, Queensland: Southern Downs Regional Council, 2010), p. 13

8 'William Rees, Australia', ESPN Cricinfo: www.espncricinfo.com/australia/content/player/7316.html

9 S.Y. Marshall to W.G. Rees, correspondence, 1 October 1856, Goondiwindi, in the author's personal collection.

10 Amanda Rodger Dickson, *West Otago: 150 years of farming and families, Book One, 1850–1875: Runholders, managers and shepherds* (Waikouaiti: Author, 2011), pp. 18–21, 166.

11 Grace, *Cricket*, p. 74.

12 'Death of a pioneer', *Otago Daily Times*, 1 November 1898, p. 2.

13 A 'moggie' is a mōkihi, a Māori raft fashioned from bundles of bulrushes tied with flax.

14 'Local intelligence – Wakatip Lake', *Otago Witness*, 24 March 1860, p. 5.

15 W.G. Rees, correspondence, 'Expedition to the interior', *Otago Witness*, 31 March 1860, p. 5.

16 Griffiths, pp. 91–94.

17 Editor, 'The Wakatip Lake', *Otago Witness*, 27 October 1860, p. 5.

18 Alfred H. Duncan, *The Wakatipians, or Early Days in New Zealand* (London: Simpkin, Marshall & Co.), 1888, p. 15.

19 Letter from Frances Rebecca Rees to Louisa Fleming, 15 October 1862 (Lakes District Museum collection, Arrowtown, File No. N1124).

20 William Fox, correspondence, 'The Arrow River diggings', *Otago Witness*, 6 December 1862, p. 5.

21 William Grumitt, letter under the heading 'Discovery of the Wakatipu goldfield', 1863, *Otago Witness*, 24 November 1898, p. 19.

22 Vincent Pyke, *History of the Early Gold Discoveries in Otago* (Dunedin: Otago Daily Times and Witness Newspapers Company, 1887), p. 84.

23 Duncan, p. 47.

24 Pyke, p. 82.

25 Duncan, pp. 51–52.

26 Ibid., p. 51.

27 Florence Mackenzie, *The Sparkling Waters of Whakatipua: The story of Lake Wakatipu* (Dunedin: A.H. & A.W. Reed, 1947), p. 86.

28 James Forrest, 'Population and settlement on the Otago goldfields, 1861–1870', *New Zealand Geographer*, vol. 17, no. 1, 2008, pp. 73–74.

29 Ibid.

30 'Runholders and pre-emptive rights: Mr Rees's claim', *Otago Witness*, 14 February 1863, p. 5.

31 Hoskins, pp. 169–71.

32 'Original correspondence', *Lake Wakatip Mail*, 10 June 1863, p. 5.

33 'Deputation to Vincent Pyke, Esq.', *Lake Wakatip Mail*, 17 June 1863, p. 4.

34 Hoskins, p. 171.

35 Alan J. De La Mare, *Wakatipu's Golden Days* (Arrowtown: Lakes District Museum, 2000), p. 19.

36 Mackenzie, p. 87.

37   Herbert A. Glasson, *The Golden Cobweb: A saga of the Otago goldfields 1861–64* (Dunedin: Otago Daily Times, 1959), p. 68.
38   'Monthly summary of current events', *Lake Wakatip Mail*, 8 August 1863, p. 5.
39   De La Mare, p. 20.
40   Mackenzie, p. 87.
41   Glasson, p. 68.
42   'Editorial', *The Otago Daily Times*, 18 July 1865, p. 5.
43   Otekaieke is on the south bank of the Waitaki River, North Otago. Station Peak is on the opposite bank, and Benmore is near the present Benmore hydroelectric dam at the head of the Waitaki Valley.
44   'Advertisements: Notice under provisions of "The Lost Licences and Leases Act, 1865"', *Otago Daily Times*, 21 September 1866, p. 6.
45   The address is now in the Lakes District Museum, Arrowtown.
46   Matagouri (*Discaria toumatou*). Known by early settlers and miners as 'Wild Irishman'.
47   For a full transcription of the speech, see 'Farewell supper to Mr. Rees', *Lake Wakatip Mail*, 27 April 1867, p. 3.
48   On display at the Lakes District Museum, Arrowtown.
49   Later known as George Gammie Maitland.
50   Rosemary Marryatt is the great-granddaughter of William and Frances Rees.

Chapter 15

1   Erik Olssen, *A History of Otago* (Dunedin: John McIndoe, 1984), p. 72.
2   Erik Eklund, *Mining Towns: Making a living, making a life* (Sydney: New South Publishing, 2012), pp. 43, 56, 112, 145, 178 and others; Susan Lawrence, *Dolly's Creek: An archaeology of a Victorian goldfields community* (Carlton: Melbourne University Press, 2000), pp. 29–30, 58–59; Barry McGowan, *Dust and Dreams: Mining communities in south-east New South Wales* (Sydney: University of New South Wales Press, 2010), pp. 190–93.
3   Hamer, David, 'Towns in nineteenth century New Zealand', *New Zealand Journal of History*, vol. 13, no.1, 1979, p. 14; Tom Brooking, 'Use it or lose it: Unravelling the land debate in late nineteenth-century New Zealand', *New Zealand Journal of History*, vol. 30, no. 2, 1996, pp. 145–53.
4   Theodore Henry Hittell, *History of California* (San Francisco: N.J. Stone, vol. 3, 1879), p. 174.
5   Alexander Bathgate, *Colonial Experiences or Sketches of People and Places in the Province of Otago, New Zealand* (Glasgow: James Maclehose, 1874), pp. 86–87.
6   Garnet Vere Portus, 'The gold discoveries, 1850–1860', in *The Cambridge History of the British Empire: Vol. VII, Part I: Australia*, eds. J.H. Rose, A.P. Newton and E.A. Benians (Cambridge: Cambridge University Press, 1933), p. 245.
7   Ibid., p. 251.
8   Roger Terry, *Reminiscences of Thirty Years' Residence in New South Wales and Victoria* (Sydney: Royal Australian Historical Society/University of Sydney Press, 2nd edn, 1974, first published 1863), p. 371, quoted in Portus, p. 251.
9   W.G.K. Duncan, 'Portus, Garnet Vere (Jerry) (1883–1954)', from the Australian Dictionary of Biography: http://adb.anu.edu.au/biography/portus-garnet-vere-jerry-8082/text14103
10   Portus, 'The gold discoveries', p. 251.
11   John B. Condliffe, 'Economic development', in *The Cambridge History of the British Empire, Vol. VII, Part II: New Zealand*, eds. J.H. Rose, A.P. Newton and E.A. Benians (Cambridge: Cambridge University Press, 1933), p. 153.
12   Alexander H. McClintock, *The History of Otago: The origins and growth of the Wakefield class settlement* (Dunedin: Otago Centennial Historical Publications, 1949), p. 448.
13   Matthew Wright, *Reed Illustrated History of New Zealand* (Auckland: Reed, 2004), pp. 166–68.
14   Philip Ross May, *The West Coast Gold Rushes* (Christchurch: Pegasus Press, 1962), p. 281.
15   Robyn Annear, *Nothing but Gold: The diggers of 1852* (Melbourne: Text Publishing, 1999), p. 101.
16   John H. Salmon, *History of Goldmining in New Zealand* (Wellington: Government Printer, 1963), p. 65.
17   See, for example, 'California': http://en.wikipedia.org/wiki/California_Gold_Rush

18   Karen Clay and Randall Jones, 'Migrating to riches? Evidence from the California gold rush', *Journal of Economic History*, vol. 68, no. 4, 2008, p. 998.

19   See Geoffrey Serle, *The Golden Age: A history of the colony of Victoria, 1851–1861* (Carlton: Melbourne University Press, 1963), p. 218.

20   'California (ex-*Launceston Examiner*)', *Otago News*, 10 March 1850, p. 4.

21   'Correspondence', *Democratic State Register*, 2 April 1850, p. 3.

22   Ibid., 9 April 1850, p. 5. The letter was addressed to the editor of the *Watertown Register*.

23   'Gold fields', *Sydney Morning Herald*, 6 June 1851, p. 2.

24   Annear, *Nothing but Gold*, p. 101.

25   Alan Houston, 'The goldfields of Otago, A.H.'s jottings, March 1865' (Hocken Library, Dunedin, Misc-MS-1413), pp. 3, 15; see also William Howitt, *Land, Labour and Gold; or, two years in Victoria with visits to Sydney and Van Diemen's Land* (London: Longman, Brown, Green & Longmans, 1855), p. 8.

26   Quoted in George Ogilvy Preshaw, *Banking under Difficulties or Life on the Goldfields of Victoria, New South Wales and New Zealand* (Melbourne: Edwards, Dunlop & Co., 1888), p. 99.

27   William Jackson Barry, *Past, Present and Men of the Times* (Wellington: McKee & Gamble, 1897), p. 149.

28   'Cromwell', *Otago Daily Times*, 27 September 1864, p. 5.

29   Keith V. Sinclair and William F. Mandle, *Open Account: A history of the Bank of New South Wales in New Zealand 1861–1961* (Wellington: Whitcombe & Tombs, 1961), p. 23.

30   James Belich, *Making Peoples: A history of the New Zealanders from Polynesian settlement to the end of the 19th century* (Honolulu: University of Hawaii Press, 1996), p. 347.

31   'Mining', *Press* (Christchurch), 19 August 1865, p. 2.

32   Bruce A. Rosenberg, 'The folklore of the gold rush', *Huntington Library Quarterly*, vol. 44, no. 4, 1981, p. 294.

33   Geoffrey Blainey, *The Rush That Never Ended* (Carlton: Melbourne University Press, 1963), p. 25.

34   Charles Money, *Knocking About in New Zealand* (Melbourne: Samuel Mullen, 1871), pp. 9–10.

35   Bayard Taylor, *Eldorado: or, adventures in the path of empire: Comprising a voyage to California, via Panama; life in San Francisco and Monterey; pictures of the gold region, and experiences of Mexican travel* (New York: G.P. Putnam's Sons, 1850), p. 55.

36   Ellen Clacy, *A Lady's Visit to the Gold Diggings of Australia in 1852–53, Written on the Spot* (London: Hurst and Blackett, 1853), p. 38.

37   Howitt, *Land, Labour and Gold*, p. 11.

38   Money, *Knocking About in New Zealand*, p. 10.

39   See, for example, J.K. Galbraith, 'Monopoly power and price rigidities', *The Quarterly Journal of Economics*, vol. 50, no. 3, 1936, pp. 456–75; V.E. Lambson, 'Competitive profits in the long run', *The Review of Economic Studies*, vol. 59, no. 1, 1992, pp. 125–42; P. Dutta, A. Matros and J.W. Weibull, 'Long-run price competition', *The RAND Journal of Economics*, vol. 38, no. 2, 2007, pp. 291–313 and others.

40   Florence McKenzie, *The Sparkling Waters of Whakatipua: The story of Lake Wakatipu* (Dunedin: A.H. & A.W. Reed, 1947), p. 115.

41   'Letters', *Watertown Chronicle*, 23 April 1851, p. 4.

42   'Snowy River goldfield, ex-*Melbourne Herald*, 10 August', *Lyttelton Times*, 12 September 1860, p. 4.

43   Salmon, *History of Goldmining in New Zealand*, p. 92.

44   George Magnus Hassing, *Pages from the Memory Log of G.M. Hassing: Sailor, pioneer, schoolmaster* (Invercargill: Southland Times, 1930), p. 45.

45   'Supreme Court', *Otago Witness*, 4 June 1864, p. 9.

46   Jim McAloon, *No Idle Rich* (Dunedin: University of Otago Press, 2002), p. 73.

47   Olssen, *A History of Otago*, p. 69.

48   Blainey, *The Rush That Never Ended*, p. 39.

49   Keith C. McDonald, *City of Dunedin: A century of civic enterprise* (Dunedin: Dunedin City Council, 1965), pp. 45–49.

50   May, *The West Coast Gold Rushes*, p. 281.

51   Lyndon Fraser, *Castles of Gold: A history of the West Coast Irish* (Dunedin: Otago University Press, 2007), pp. 60–62.

52   See Belich, *Making Peoples*, pp. 348–49.

53   James Ng, 'The Chinese Goldseekers in Otago', presentation at Monash University, Melbourne, Victoria, Australia, 19 June 2003: www.stevenyoung.co.nz/the-chinese-in-new-zealand/What-s-New/Chinese-goldseekers-in-Otago.html

54   Leonard Pitt, 'The beginnings of nativism in California', *Pacific Historical Review*, vol. 30, no. 1, 1961, pp. 27–37.

55   'William Heffernan', *Otago Daily Times*, 23 March 1891, p. 6.

56   'Heffernan, William, testamentary register 1886–1892' (Archives New Zealand, Dunedin office, C 720 957 DAGI D247 9010 Box 3).

57   'Advertisements', *Cromwell Argus*, 12 January 1870, p. 2.

58   Jim McAloon, 'The New Zealand economy', in *The New Oxford History of New Zealand*, ed. Giselle Byrnes (Melbourne/Auckland: Oxford University Press, 2009), p. 211.

59   'Warden's report', *Dunstan Times*, 4 December, 1874, p .2.

60   See 'Veteran goldminer', *Evening Post*, 16 January 1930, p. 15; 'Obituary', *Auckland Star*, 17 February 1931, p. 3. See also 'Collingwood', *Colonist*, 19 April 1861, p. 3.

61   'The Nelson gold fields', *Nelson Examiner and New Zealand Chronicle*, 13 June 1857, p. 3.

62   Houston, 'The goldfields of Otago, A.H.'s jottings', p. 14.

63   James Ng, 'Chinese goldseekers'.

64   'Warden's Court', *Dunstan Times*, 14 April 1871, p. 3 and others.

65   'Resident Magistrate's Court', *Cromwell Argus*, 10 August 1870, p. 3; C. Lawson, letter to his 11-year-old daughter and his son in Liverpool, 20 December 1882, copy held by author.

66   See, for example, from bankruptcy papers, Archives New Zealand, Dunedin office: 'Simpson, Bruce, miner of Bendigo, 14 July 1870, bankruptcy' (C705001 DAEQ D573 21570 4); 'William Grant, carpenter of Bendigo, 2 September 1870, bankruptcy' (C705002 DAEQ D573 21570 5); 'Barnes, Edward George, miner of Quartzville, formerly of Bendigo, 25 February 1875, bankruptcy' (DAEQD573 7d). See also *Cromwell Argus*, 8 February, 1871, p. 3; 'Philip Matthews, miner of Bendigo, bankrupt', *Dunstan Times*, 12 January 1876, p. 3; 'Edward Aldridge, miner of Bendigo, bankrupt,' *Cromwell Argus*, 6 June 1876, p. 5; 'Thomas Downey, miner of Bendigo, bankrupt', *Cromwell Argus*, 4 June 1878, p. 5; 'John Charlton, miner of Bendigo, bankrupt', *Cromwell Argus*, 11 June 1878, p. 3; 'William Henry Lidston, miner of Bendigo, bankrupt', *Otago Daily Times*, 9 February 1892, p. 8.

67   May, *The West Coast Gold Rushes*, p. 281.

68   Miles Fairburn, *The Ideal Society and Its Enemies: The foundations of modern New Zealand society 1850– 1900* (Auckland: Auckland University Press, 1989), p. 105.

69   L. Pozzi, letter to Josephine, 4 January 1905, Melbourne, International Service of the Swiss Broadcasting Corporation: www.swissinfo.ch/eng/-i-have-made-a-very-bad-calculation-/994482

70   'The death of Mr J.C. Brown', *Tuapeka Times*, 11 February 1891, p. 3.

71   Hamer, 'Towns in nineteenth century New Zealand', p. 7.

72   Ibid., p.12.

73   Cora Trevarthen, 'After the gold is gone: Chinese communities in north-east Victoria, 1861–1914', *Journal of Chinese Australia*, vol. 2, October, 2006: www.chaf.lib.latrobe.edu.au/jca/ issue02/09Trevarthen. html#_edn26

74   C.J. Fedorak, 'The United States Consul in Victoria and the political destiny of the colony of British Columbia, 1862–1870', *Journal of British Columbia Studies*, vol. 79, 1988, p. 7.

75   A representative sample from Clyde bankruptcy papers, Archives New Zealand, Dunedin office: 'Peyton, Neil, hotelkeeper of Bendigo, 25 October 1870' (DAEQ Acc 21570 D5735/c); 'Geer, J., storekeeper, 29 September 1870' (DAEQAcc21570D5733/n); 'Thormahlen, J., storekeeper of Clyde, 31 December 1869' (DAAC Acc 18116 D256532/352); 'Colclough, C.&W., v. Horrigan, T., storekeeper of Logantown, 16 February, 1872' (DAEQ Acc D5732168828bc57); 'Kelsall & Wilson, storekeepers of Bendigo, 15 February 1871' (R12677742 DAEQ Acc 21570 D5735/f); 'Mitchinson Josiah – formerly Bendigo now Dunedin – formerly storekeeper now traveller 1877' (DAAC 18118 D256 544/120).

76   Larry Schweikart and Lynne Pierson Doti, 'From hard money to branch banking: California banking in the gold-rush economy', in *A Golden State: Mining and economic development in gold rush California*, eds. R.J. Orsi and J.L. Rawls (Berkeley, CA: University of California Press, 1999), pp. 209–32.

77   G.L. Shumway, L. Vredenburgh and R. Hartill, *Desert Fever: An overview of mining in the California desert conservation area* (Riverside, CA: United States Bureau of Land Management, 1980), p. 26.

78   'Reminiscences by "Pioneer"', *Cromwell Argus*, 17 August 1908, p. 2.

79   Blainey, *The Rush That Never Ended*, pp. 50, 67; Serle, *The Golden Age*, pp. 219–21; 'Mining', *Star* (Ballarat), 12 September 1857, p. 2; R.M. Serjeant, 'A local court decision', *Bendigo Advertiser*, 28 September 1857, p. 3; Alexander Dick, 'Working and sleeping shares', *Bendigo Advertiser*, 21 May 1858, p. 3; 'Buninyong Court of Mines', *Bendigo Advertiser*, 24 March 1860, p. 4; 'Court of Mines', 6 September 1860, p. 2; 'A law wanted for mining on private property', *Bendigo Advertiser*, 10 June 1863, p. 2; 'Mining intelligence', *Argus* (Melbourne), 1 March 1864, p. 5; 'The goldfields, Junction Point goldfield', *Braidwood Independent*, 12 October 1867, p. 5; 'Latest mining news from Gympie', *Brisbane Courier*, 21 January 1869, p. 3; 'Country news, by mail, Gilberton', *Queenslander*, 2 September 1871, p. 11; 'Nuegummie and Talliewidgee Reefs', *Clarence and Richmond Examiner and New England Advertiser*, 27 May 1873, p. 6; 'Editorial', *Northern Miner*, 1 September 1877, p. 2 and others. See also 'Ballarat Mining District Bylaw XII', *Star* (Ballarat), 2 February 1861, supplement, p. 1; 'The new goldfields regulations', *Sydney Morning Herald*, 4 April 1872, p. 5 and others.

80   'Cromwell', *Otago Witness*, 12 August 1865, p. 7.

81   'Coates, J., report to Goldfields Warden Vincent Pyke', *Otago Witness*, 12 August 1865, p. 6.

82   'Cromwell', *Dunstan Times*, 6 January 1866, p. 3.

83   Ibid., 18 October 1867, p. 2.

84   'News of the week', *Otago Witness*, 17 February 1866, p. 11.

85   'Warden's report', *Dunstan Times*, 16 June 1866, p. 3.

86   'Cromwell', *Dunstan Times*, 26 April 1867, p. 3.

87   'Local', *Dunstan Times*, 18 February 1868, p. 2.

88   Lloyd Carpenter, 'The Clutha's first dam: The Nil Desperandum project at Quartz Reef Point, 1864–66', *The International Journal for the History of Engineering & Technology*, vol. 83, no. 2, 2013, pp. 266–70.

89   'Dunstan', *Otago Daily Times*, 8 March 1866, p. 5.

90   George M. Hassing, 'A reminiscence of Bendigo', *Otago Witness*, 22 August 1922, p. 63.

91   Lloyd Carpenter, 'Reviled in the record: Thomas Logan and the origins of the Cromwell Quartz Mining Company, Bendigo, Otago', *Journal of Australasian Mining History*, vol. 9, September, 2011, pp. 44–49.

92   John Cassels, 'Goldfields pioneers', *Otago Witness*, 7 June 1884, p. 13.

93   'G.W. Goodger, Clyde applications, memo to goldfields warden advising of share transfer' (Archives New Zealand, Dunedin office, Acc D98 7416).

94   'Mayor and Corporation of Cromwell vs. G.W. Goodger & Party, 1 April 1868, Cromwell Plaints 1865–67', (Archives New Zealand, Dunedin office, Acc D98 7440); 'Bendigo Gully', *Dunstan Times*, 4 March 1870, p. 1; Cassels, 'Goldfields pioneers', p. 11.

95   'Advertisements', *Dunstan Times*, 22 May 1868, p. 1.

96   Noel Kennedy and Ron Murray, *Early Pioneers in the Cromwell Area 1863–1880* (Cromwell: Cromwell and District Historical Society, 1999), p. 22.

97   'Cromwell', *Dunstan Times*, 27 January 1866, p. 2.

98   'Local', *Dunstan Times*, 30 August 1867, p. 3.

99   'The regions', *Otago Witness*, 22 August 1874, p. 6.

100   'Advertisements', *Cromwell Argus*, 20 January 1877, p. 3.

101   'Cromwell hospital opening', *Cromwell Argus*, 3 November 1874, p. 2.

102   Edgar M. Lovell-Smith, *Old Coaching Days in Otago and Southland* (Christchurch: Lovell-Smith & Veneer Ltd., 1931), p. 83.

103   'Mining', *Otago Daily Times*, 19 February 1872, p. 1; 'Warden's Court', *Otago Daily Times*, 11 January 1883, p. 1.

104   Olssen, *A History of Otago*, pp. 65–66.

105   'Advertisements', *Cromwell Argus*, 13 July 1870, p. 3.

106   'Warden's Court', *Otago Witness*, 29 November 1873, p. 9.

107   'In bankruptcy', *Otago Witness*, 12 September 1885, p. 19.

108   'Bendigo mining', *Dunstan Times*, 15 October 1875, p. 3.

109 'Bankruptcy', *Cromwell Argus*, 24 October 1876, p. 1.
110 'Warden's report', *Cromwell Argus*, 15 December 1869, p. 5.
111 'Mining', *Otago Witness*, 15 June 1888, p. 12; M.O. Broad, comp. and ed., 'William Gilbert Mouat 1863–1956: Land surveyor, mine surveyor, gold miner, gold dredge operator, designer & builder, engineering consultant' (Dunedin: Author, 2003): www.rgreen.org.uk/WGM.html
112 'Local', *Cromwell Argus*, 6 June 1876, p. 3.
113 'Bendigo', *Dunstan Times*, 8 March 1878, p. 2.
114 'Regions', *Otago Witness*, 5 August 1908, p. 55.
115 'Warden's report', *Dunstan Times*, 21 September 1870, p. 3.
116 See also Blainey, *The Rush That Never Ended*, p. 72.
117 Terry J. Hearn, and Raymond P. Hargraves, *The Speculators' Dream: Gold dredging in southern New Zealand* (Dunedin: Allied Press Ltd., 1985), pp. 1, 4, 12.
118 Jennifer L. Dickenson, 'Picks, pans and petticoats: Women on the Central Otago goldfields', BA Honours diss., University of Otago, Dunedin, 1993, p. 32.
119 Ibid., p. 45.
120 Charles Brasch and Colin R. Nicolson, *Hallensteins: The first century 1873–1973* (Dunedin: John McIndoe, 1973), p. 14.
121 'Country news', *Otago Daily Times*, 26 July 1873, p. 5.
122 When he died in June 1905, Benjamin Naylor's estate was worth £18,254 ('Naylor, Benjamin, testamentary register 1904–1907', Archives New Zealand, Dunedin office, C 720 961 DAGI D247 9010 Box 7).
123 'Chestermains Farm, Matakanui', *The Cyclopedia of New Zealand. Vol. 4: Otago & Southland Provincial Districts* (Christchurch: Cyclopedia Company Limited, 1905), p. 625.
124 'An Otago Central model farm', *Otago Witness*, 22 March 1905, p. 9; 'Manuherikia', *Otago Witness*, 10 June 1887, p. 17.
125 'Bendigo goldfields, an Adelaide pioneer – a story of the early days', *The Advertiser* (Adelaide), 29 January 1910, p. 10.
126 'Turon', *Sydney Empire*, 21 January 1854, p. 3.
127 G. Butler Earp, *The Gold Colonies of Australia, Their History & Progress, with Ample Details of the Gold Mines, How to Get to Them, and Every Advice to Emigrants* (London: Routledge & Co., 1853), p. 215, emphasis in original.
128 'The Dunstan', *Otago Witness*, 27 December 1862, p. 2.
129 Ibid., 2 December 1862, p. 5.
130 'Dunstan diggings', *Otago Daily Times*, 27 September 1862, p. 5.
131 'News from the interior', *Sydney Morning Herald*, 6 June 1851, p. 2.
132 'Dunstan', *Otago Daily Times*, 30 April 1868, p. 5.
133 John Henry Watmuff, *The Journals of John Henry Watmuff: New Zealand extracts, 1861–1864* (Hughesdale: Stephen J. Arnold, 2006), entries 2/310, 3/5, 3/8, 3/28 and others.

Chapter 16
1 Joseph Mackay, *Mackay's Otago, Southland, West Coast and Goldfields Almanac* (Dunedin: Joseph Mackay, published annually).
2 *Mackay's Otago, Southland, West Coast and Goldfields Almanac for 1875* (Dunedin: Mackay, 1875), p. 258.
3 Henry Wirgman Robinson, diary entry for 22 July 1869, in 'Henry Wirgman Robinson papers' (Hocken Library, Dunedin, Acc ARC-0546).
4 Ibid., entries for 19 January 1870, 3 March 1870 and 23 August 1870.
5 Taylor was born in Norfolk in 1811, was admitted as an attorney in 1865 and had moved to Auckland by 1858. He then went to Napier for a decade before settling in Balclutha, where, he said, people asked him to do their legal work business because there was no other lawyer available: 'Walter Taylor, admission papers' (Archives New Zealand, Dunedin office, Acc DAAC D140 273/LP 258).
6 'The late Mr Walter Taylor', *Bruce Herald*, 25 October 1881, p. 3.
7 For a full account of Patten's case, see Jeremy Finn, 'The early years of an unregulated profession: Lawyers in the South Island 1850–1869', *Canterbury Law Review*, vol. 6, 1995, pp. 56–65.
8 'Alleged extraordinary case of false conviction', *Otago Daily Times*, 14 October 1865,

republished in the *Otago Witness*, 21 October 1865, p. 15.

9   'John Patten, admission papers' (Archives New Zealand, Christchurch office, Acc CAHX 20160, CH244 Box 2/as). The dissolution and request to debtors appears as 'Notice', *Lyttelton Times*, 15 and 19 June 1861, p. 8 (in each case).

10 'Queenstown, 14th November, 1863', *Otago Daily Times*, 20 November 1863, p. 9.

11 'Resident Magistrate's Court', *Otago Daily Times*, 13 September 1864, p. 6.

12 'Examination for attorneys', *Law Times*, vol. 1, 1 July 1843, p. 278.

13 'Roll of barristers, solicitors, attorneys, proctors and conveyancers' (State Records New South Wales, Sydney, Acc 13364); 'Henry Elmes Campbell, admission document' (Public Record Office Victoria, Melbourne, Acc VPRS82 P0000/Box 1C).

14 'Insolvency Court', *Sydney Morning Herald*, 7 March 1861, p. 2.

15 Entry for H.E. Campbell, 'Roll of barristers, solicitors and articled clerks 1862–1903' (Archives New Zealand, Dunedin office, Acc DAAC D375).

16 *Mackay's Otago, Southland, West Coast and Goldfields Almanac for 1865*, p. 20.

17 *Stevens and Bartholomew's New Zealand Directory 1866* (Melbourne: G. Stevens & D.H. Bartholomew, 1866).

18 This account is drawn from material in the following sources: 'Applicants for admission as attorneys', *Law Times* (London), vol. 6, 14 February 1846, p. 401; 'Attorney examinations', *Law Times* (London), 23 May 1847, vol. 7, p. 167; 'Wilfrid Wilson, admission papers' (Public Record Office of Victoria, Melbourne, Acc VPRS82 P0000/Box 19); 'Admission papers, Wilfrid Wilson' (Archives New Zealand, Dunedin office, Acc DAAC D140 273/LP 271); *Stevens and Bartholomew's Directory 1867*; Otago District Law Society membership list 1874, in 'Otago District Law Society: Further records' (Hocken Library, Dunedin, Acc 01-209).

19 Quoted in 'J R P Stamper, Dunedin date: 1 November 1876. Subject: Report regarding charge against Mr William Wilfrid Wilson for perjury before Mr Justice Williams' (Archives New Zealand, Wellington office, R24349065 ACGS 16211 Ji 195/bv 1876/3135)

20 'The mayoralty', *Otago Witness*, 21 July 1865, p. 15.

21 In that year he employed John Archibald Duncan Adams as an articled clerk: 'Roll of barristers, solicitors and articled clerks 1875–1903' (Archives New Zealand, Dunedin office, Acc DAAC/ D375).

22 *Mackay's Otago, Southland, West Coast and Goldfields Almanac for 1875*, p. 176.

23 'Local and general', *Tuapeka Times*, 20 June 1872, p. 7.

24 James Parcell, *Heart of the Desert: A history of the Cromwell and Bannockburn districts* (Christchurch: Whitcoulls, 1976), p. 77.

25 'Nominal roll of persons employed in each department (other than postal and railways), giving length of service as at 31 March 1907 and salaries for financial year 1907–1908, chargeable on the consolidated fund', *Appendices to the Journals of the House of Representatives of New Zealand*, 1907 session I, H-05, p. 63.

26 'Otago District Law Society membership list 1874'; *Mackay's Otago, Southland, West Coast and Goldfields Almanac for 1875*, p. 268.

27 'George Fredric Rowlatt, Queenstown bankruptcy papers 1880' (Archives New Zealand, Dunedin office, Acc AEPG D568 22919 Box 112, item ref j).

28 Letter 27 October 1887 from Wellington, in 'Complaints 1879–1934, Otago District Law Society: Further records' (Hocken Library, Dunedin Acc 01-209, Box 7).

29 'Clyde warden's record book 1866–1886' (Archives New Zealand, Dunedin office, Acc DAEQ D574 21492 Box 3).

30 Data for this account are drawn from entries for Anthony Brough, 'Roll of barristers, solicitors and articled clerks 1862–1903'; 'Anthony Brough admission papers' (Public Record Office of Victoria, Melbourne, Acc VPRS 28, P0002, Unit 297); 'Roll of barristers, solicitors, attorneys, proctors and conveyancers' (State Records New South Wales, Sydney, Acc 13364); 'Death of Mr Anthony Brough, Mayor of Hay', *The Maitland Mercury & Hunter River General Advertiser*, 10 October 1889, p. 3.

31 'Notes of His Honour Wilson Gray Esq DCJ 15 May 1871' (Archives New Zealand, Dunedin office, Acc DAEQ D573 21550).

32 Entry for G.B. Barton, in 'Papers relating particularly to southern people' (Hocken Library, Dunedin, MS 1926/129).

33   *George Burnett Barton v George Oswald Clayton*, in 'Otago Goldfields District Court plaint book, Record no. 79, 1873' (Archives New Zealand, Dunedin office, AEPG D568 21034 Box 42).

34   *Albert Eichardt v Wesley Turton*, in 'Otago Goldfields District Court plaint book, record 22/76, 1876', (Archives New Zealand, Dunedin office, AEPG D568 21034 Box 43). It is interesting that Wesley Turton's brother Gibson Turton sought commitment for treatment for alcoholism in 1880. See, in this regard, 'Lunacy case file No L 187, Gibson Kirke Turton 1880' (Archives New Zealand, Dunedin office, DAAC D140 Box 272).

35   Letter from Smith Anderson, Solicitors of Dunedin, 27 April 1880, in 'Complaints 1879–1880 Otago District Law Society: Further records' (Hocken Library, Dunedin, Acc 01-209).

36   Barton's life is described, with minor inaccuracies, by John Ward in the Australian Dictionary of Biography: www.adb.anu.edu.au/biography/barton-george-burnett-2949. See also 'George Burnett Barton admission papers' (Archives New Zealand, Christchurch office, Acc CAHX 20160, CH244, box 1/f).

37   'Local and general', *Tuapeka Times*, 20 June 1872, p. 7.

38   'Notes of His Honour Wilson Gray Esq DCJ', notes of 13, 16 and 23 November 1871 (Archives New Zealand, Dunedin office, Acc DAEQ D573 21550 Box 1).

39   'Resident Magistrate's Court', *Lake Wakatipu Mail*, 27 November 1872, in 'H.W. Robinson clippings book' (Hocken Library, Dunedin, Acc MS-2908/001).

40   This account is based on 'Joseph MacGregor, admission papers' (Archives New Zealand, Christchurch office, Acc CAHX 20160, CH244, box 2/v); *Canterbury Directory, 1867*; *Stevens and Bartholomew's Directory, 1866* (Archives New Zealand, Christchurch office).

41   'Bankruptcy – J A G MacGregor' (Archives New Zealand, Dunedin office, Acc DAAC D256 18116 Box 525, record 44).

42   Ibid.

43   'Resident Magistrate's Court' *Tuapeka Times*, 16 January 1873, p. 6.

44   Ibid., 24 October 1874, p. 2.

45   Ibid., 16 December 1876, p. 2.

46   This paragraph is based on material from the entry for Frederick McCoy, 'Roll of barristers, solicitors and articled clerks 1862–1903'; 'Otago District Law Society membership list 1874'.

47   'Probate Frederick Henry McCoy' (Archives New Zealand, Dunedin office, Acc DAAC D239 9073 Box 66, record 1542).

48   'John Copland admission papers' (Archives New Zealand, Dunedin office, Acc DAAC D140 273/LP58).

49   'Otago District Law Society membership list 1874'.

50   'William Nott Gooday, admission papers' (Archives New Zealand, Dunedin office, Acc DAAC D140 273/LP95); 'Otago District Law Society membership list 1874'; *Wise's New Zealand Post Office Directory 1896–97* (Dunedin: H. Wise & Co., 1896).

51   'Marie Theresa Mouat, wife of John Mouat, 1871 lunacy case file No L125' (Archives New Zealand, Dunedin office, Acc DAAC D140 Box 271).

52   *John Mouat v Maria Theresa Mouat* (1884–1885), in 'Divorce file' (Archives New Zealand, Dunedin office, Acc DAAC D140 20681 Box 391, record 55). Mouat stated in an affidavit that Maria had 'violently struck and threatened to strike and injure' Mouat, and 'he dreads that she may at last provoke him to retaliate and so as to use undue violence toward her'. The use of 'undue' is interesting and perhaps telling.

53   The relevant documents are in 'Marie Theresa Mouat, wife of John Mouat, 1871 lunacy case file No L125'.

54   *John Mouat v Maria Theresa Mouat* (1884–1885).

55   Mouat's will gave priority to repaying his sons for moneys they had advanced to Mouat or spent for his benefit. Mouat then provided that 'none of my property or effects be given to my wife but that if there be any residue after payment of my debts the executors may apply a sum not exceeding 10/- a week for the support and maintenance of my wife during her widowhood': 'John Mouat, probate file' (Archives New Zealand, Dunedin office, Acc DAAC D239 9073 Box 164, record 4128).

56   *The Cyclopedia of New Zealand, Vol. 4: Otago & Southland Provincial Districts* (Christchurch: The Cyclopedia Company Limited, 1905), p. 390.

57 'Queenstown District Court Judge's notebook 1871–1880' (Archives New Zealand, Dunedin office, Acc AEPG D554 20949 Box 15, item B).

58 'Judge Harvey at Queenstown', *North Otago Times*, 6 May 1875, p. 2.

59 This account is based on the entry for Wesley Turton, 'Roll of barristers, solicitors and articled clerks 1862–1903'; 'Otago District Law Society membership list 1874'. For his later location, see *Wise's New Zealand Post Office Directory 1896–97*. For his estate, see 'Wills of the week', *Sunday Times* (Perth, Western Australia), 28 March 1926, p. 11 (noting exemplification of probate).

60 'Wesley Turton, probate' (Archives New Zealand, Dunedin office, Acc DAFG D328 9067 Box 55, record 149/22).

61 *Wesley Turton v the Official Assignee in Bankruptcy (of the property of Martin Birch)*, in 'Arrowtown Warden's Court, plaint book' (Archives New Zealand, Dunedin office, Acc AEPG D568 21789 Box 40, record 20). The 20 cases are listed in the plaint books for the Arrowtown Warden's Court (Archives New Zealand, Dunedin office, Acc AEPG D568 21789, Boxes 40 and 52), as well as the plaint book for the Queenstown Warden's Court (AEPG D568 22085, Boxes 52 and 53).

62 Letter from Shotover Quartz Mining Co No Liability Coy to ODLS, 19 January 1901, in 'Otago District Law Society: Further records', (Hocken Library, Dunedin Acc 01-209, Box 7, complaints 1879–1934, folder for 1901).

63 *Albert Eichardt v Wesley Turton*, in 'Otago Goldfields District Court plaint book, 29 November 1876', Archives New Zealand, Dunedin office, Acc AEPG D568 21034 Box 43, record 21-22/76.

64 *Wesley Turton v Edward McCaffrey*, in 'Otago Goldfields District Court plaint file 1874', Archives New Zealand, Dunedin office, Acc AEPG D568 21034 Box 42 record 95

65 'Untitled', *Argus* (Melbourne), 30 August 1873, p. 5.

66 Entry for Hugh Joseph Finn, 'Roll of barristers, solicitors and articled Clerks 1862–1903, Archives New Zealand, Dunedin office, Acc DAAC D375.

67 *Hugh Joseph Finn v Richard Howarth*, 'Otago Goldfields District Court plaints book', 29 November 1878, Archives New Zealand, Dunedin office, Acc AEPG D568 21034 Box 43 record 9/78.

68 *The Cyclopedia of New Zealand, Vol. 2: Auckland provincial district* (Christchurch: The Cyclopedia Company, 1902), p. 980.

69 'Queenstown District Court Judge's notebook 1871–1880', Archives New Zealand, Dunedin, Acc Dunedin AEPG D554 20949 Box 15, item b.

70 Ibid.

71 *Mackay's Otago, Southland, West Coast and Goldfields Almanac for 1875*, p. 261.

72 'Supreme Court – civil sittings', *Otago Daily Times*, 11 March 1869, p. 2.

Chapter 17

1 An early version of this chapter was presented at the 150 Years of Riches conference at the University of Canterbury in November 2011. The University of Melbourne provided grants to support my attendance and research; attendance was also made possible by Ian Frater kindly donating his time. I am grateful to Stuart Macintyre and Patricia Grimshaw for proofreading and advice. I received much encouraging feedback from conference attendees: you know who you are. In particular, Paul Mahoney made a couple of invaluable suggestions. Donald Offwood kindly sent me the relevant portion of *Camerons of the Glen* and I thank Eunice Frater for facilitating contact. Indeed, I would like to thank the entire Frater clan of Earnscleugh – my forebears – and it is fitting that Central Otago should feature within my work. I also appreciate the support provided at this time by Charlotte Whild. Finally, I request the indulgence of Southlanders: yours is a lovely region, and this chapter is written in a spirit of affection for its intriguing and entertaining history.

2 New Zealand's first railway, the Dun Mountain Railway, was a private industrial line from Nelson to Wooded Peak. It opened on 3 February 1862 and was worked as a horse-drawn tramway. See Mike Johnston, *High Hopes: The history of the Nelson mineral belt and New Zealand's first railway* (Nelson: Nikau Press, 1987).

3 W.N. Blair to William Reeves, 31 July 1872, in 'W.N. Blair letterbook' (Alexander Turnbull Library, Wellington, qMS-0246).

4   Helen A. Henderson ('Alpaca'), 'Historical account of Southland as a province, 1861–1870', MA thesis, University of Otago, Dunedin, 1919.

5   A.R. Dreaver, 'The Southland province of New Zealand in the days of Dr J.A.R. Menzies (superintendent 1861–1864)', BA Hons diss., University of Otago, Dunedin, 1929.

6   W.P. Morrell, *The Provincial System in New Zealand, 1852–76* (Christchurch: Whitcombe and Tombs, 2nd edn, 1964), especially pp. 144–46 and pp. 164–65 (first edition published 1932).

7   Paul Sorrell, ed., *Murihiku: The Southland story* (Invercargill: Craig Design and Print, 2006).

8   Erik Olssen, 'The peopling of Southland', p. 73, and Olssen, 'Loyalty and localism: Southland's political odyssey', pp. 85–86, both in Sorrell, *Murihiku*.

9   Vince Boyle and Jim Brown, 'Making tracks: The development of land transport in the south', in Sorrell, *Murihiku*, p. 108.

10   Ibid., p. 120.

11   K.C. McDonald, 'Southland's wooden railway: An experiment of the "sixties"', *New Zealand Railways Magazine*, vol. 13, no. 9, December 1938, pp. 15–16, 67.

12   J.O.P. Watt, *Southland's Pioneer Railways 1864–1878* (Wellington: New Zealand Railway and Locomotive Society Inc., 1965).

13   Donald Offwood, *Camerons of the Glen* (Christchurch: Caxton Press, 2008), p. 153.

14   'Editorial', *Invercargill Times*, 25 November 1862, p. 2.

15   Watt, *Southland's Pioneer Railways*, pp. 14–15.

16   James Menzies, opening speech of the second session, 17 January 1862, *Votes and Proceedings of the Southland Provincial Council, 1861–69*, p. 16.

17   James Menzies, opening speech of the third session, 23 October 1862, ibid., p. 32.

18   James Menzies, prorogation speech of the third session, 4 November 1862, ibid., p. 56.

19   'Opening of the provincial council', *Invercargill Times*, 24 February 1863, p. 2. For detailed coverage of Southland's gold-escort tribulations, see Richard S. Hill, *Policing the Colonial Frontier: The theory and practice of coercive social and racial control in New Zealand, 1767–1867* (Wellington: V.R. Ward, 1986), pp. 700-07.

20   'Southland', *Otago Daily Times*, 14 March 1863, p. 5.

21   'Provincial council', *Invercargill Times*, 6 March 1863, p. 2.

22   Bernard John Foster, 'Heale, Theophilus', Te Ara – the Encyclopaedia of New Zealand: www.teara.govt.nz/en/1966/heale-theophilus/1

23   Preliminary report of Theophilus Heale to James Menzies regarding the northern railway, 31 July 1863, in 'Menzies papers' (Alexander Turnbull Library, Wellington, MS-Papers-0055-03).

24   Ibid.

25   'Editorial', *Invercargill Times*, 14 July 1863, p. 2.

26   Preliminary report of Theophilus Heale.

27   'Editorial', *Invercargill Times*, 11 August 1863, p. 2.

28   James Menzies to Alfred Domett, 6 March 1863, and Domett's reply, 10 April 1863, *Appendices to the Journals of the House of Representatives of New Zealand (AJHR)* 1864, B-03, p. 33.

29   'Political – provincial', *Invercargill Times*, 17 November 1863, p. 2.

30   Alfred Domett to James Menzies, 11 April 1863, *AJHR* 1863 B-05, p. 27. The allegedly sound reasoning referenced by Domett was expressed in a letter to him by Menzies on 4 February 1863 in *AJHR* 1863 B-05, pp. 23–24.

31   William Fox to James Menzies, 20 February 1864, *AJHR* 1864 B-03, p. 43.

32   'Report on the financial condition of the province of Southland', *AJHR* 1865 B-03A, p. 5.

33   'Editorial', *Invercargill Times*, 25 November 1863, p. 2.

34   Two letters from James Menzies to William Fox, both 4 February 1864, *AJHR* 1864 B-03, pp. 39–40.

35   William Fox to James Menzies, 8 March 1864, ibid., p. 41.

36   William Fox to James Menzies, 27 April 1864, ibid., p. 42.

37   *Daily News*, 14 April 1864, p. 3. This paper was normally known as the *Southland News*, but went by the name of *Daily News* for a few months in 1864. Although the paper is sometimes referred to as the *Invercargill Daily News*, 'Invercargill' did not appear in the masthead.

38   Numerous Southland politicians promoted their railway as New Zealand's first, with no reference to Canterbury – the omission of Nelson's private horse-drawn industrial line is more understandable. It is impossible to be certain whether this ignorance, which was not far

removed from unbridled boosterism, was feigned or actual. However, it is hard to believe that Heale, in particular, was unaware of the Christchurch to Ferrymead railway, or to understand why he would choose to espouse a blatant untruth even to aid boosterism. It's possible that because the Ferrymead line was only a temporary route until the opening of the Lyttelton tunnel, Heale did not think it counted as a permanent railway.

39   *Daily News*, 2 April 1864, pp. 4–5.

40   *Daily News*, 9 April 1864, p. 4.

41   Olssen, 'The peopling of Southland', p. 73.

42   *Riverton Times*, 20 February 1864, p. 2.

43   Ibid.

44   *Riverton Times*, 2 April 1864, p. 2.

45   *Daily News*, 4 May 1864, p. 2.

46   *Daily News*, 17 May 1864, p. 3.

47   'Editorial', *Otago Daily Times*, 12 May 1864, p. 4.

48   *Daily News*, 14 May 1864, p. 2.

49   'William Tarlton to the editor', *Daily News*, 16 April 1864, p. 3 (emphasis original).

50   Ibid, pp. 2–3.

51   *Daily News*, 20 May 1864, p. 2.

52   'Editorial', *Southland Times*, 2 June 1864, p. 2.

53   'Provincial council', *Southland Times*, 18 August 1864, p. 2. The central government originally intended to advance the money for three months only.

54   *Daily News*, 14 April 1864, p. 3.

55   The debate is reproduced in 'Provincial council', *Southland Times*, 23 July 1864, p. 4. William Tarlton elaborated further on the matter at an October meeting of electors, printed in 'Mr Tarlton at the Theatre Royal', *Southland Times*, 8 October 1864, p. 3.

56   Preliminary report of Theophilus Heale, 'Menzies papers'.

57   'Editorial', *Southland Times*, 20 October 1864, p. 2.

58   'Fatal accident', *Southland Times*, 25 October 1864, p. 2.

59   'The Oreti railway, public opening', *Southland Times*, 27 October 1864, p. 2.

60   'Editorial', *Southland Times*, 5 December 1866, p. 2.

61   Ibid., 23 December 1864, p. 2.

62   *Southland News*, 1 April 1865, p. 2.

63   Ibid., 30 March 1865, p. 2.

64   'Editorial', *Lyttelton Times*, 28 February 1865, p. 4.

65   'Editorial', *Southland Times*, 15 April 1867, p. 2.

66   Ibid., 30 December 1867, p. 2.

67   Public Debts Act 1867 (31 Victoria 1867 No. 89) and Consolidated Loan Act 1867 (31 Victoria 1867 No. 90).

68   'Editorial', *Timaru Herald*, 13 May 1865, p. 4.

69   'Editorial', *Grey River Argus*, 5 January 1869, p. 2.

70   John Cookson, 'How British? Local government in New Zealand to c. 1930', *New Zealand Journal of History*, vol. 41, no. 2, 2007, pp. 146–47. Notably, although provinces could not borrow from 1867, local bodies could borrow modest amounts for local works.

71   *Lyttelton Times*, cited in 'Local self-government', *Otago Witness*, 20 March 1869, p. 17.

72   Financial statement, *AJHR* 1870 B-2, p. 12.

73   Morrell, *Provincial System*, pp. 273–75.

74   'To Lake Wakatipu in quick time', *Bruce Herald*, 16 July 1878, p. 5; 'Lake County', *Otago Witness*, 27 July 1878, p. 10; 'Opening of the Bluff and Kingston (Lake Wakatipu) Railway', *Southland Times*, 11 July 1878, p. 2; 'Opening of the Bluff and Kingston Railway', *Southland Times*, 12 July 1878, p. 3.

75   'Opening of the Bluff and Kingston Railway', *Southland Times*, 12 July 1878, p. 3.

76   The shed was demolished in 2014. Heritage New Zealand, 'Lost Heritage 2010–2015': www.heritage.org.nz/the-list/lost-heritage/heritage-lost-2010-to-2015

77   Paul Mahoney, *The Era of the Bush Tram in New Zealand* (Wellington: Transpress, 2004), pp. 14, 19, 74.

Chapter 18

1   Quoted in Helldorado Incorporated, *Helldorado Headstone* (Tombstone, AZ: Author, 2012), p. 6.

2   Tom Griffiths, *Beechworth: An Australian country town and its past* (Melbourne: Greenhouse Publications, 1987), p. 81.

3   Ibid., pp. 82–98.

4   Warwick Frost and Jennifer Laing, 'Fictional media and imagining escape to rural villages', *Tourism Geographies: An International Journal of Tourism Space, Place and Environment*, vol. 16, no. 2, 2014, 207–20.

5   Dydia De Lyser, '"Good, by God, we're going to Bodie!" Ghost towns and the American West', in Gary Hausladen, ed., *Western Places, American Myths: How we think about the West*, (Reno & Las Vegas, NV: University of Nevada Press, 2003), pp. 273–95; Warwick Frost and Jennifer Laing, 'Gender, subversion and ritual: Helldorado Days, Tombstone, Arizona', in *Rituals and Traditional Events in a Modern World*, eds. Warwick Frost and Jennifer Laing (London and New York: Routledge, 2014), pp. 206–20.

6   See, in particular, the following by Warwick Frost: 'A pile of rocks and a hole in the ground: Heritage tourism and interpretation of the gold rushes at the Mount Alexander diggings', in *Interpreting the Land Down Under: Australian heritage interpretation and tour guiding*, eds. Rosemary Black and Betty Weiler (Golden, CO: Fulcrum, 2003), pp. 204–18; 'Making an edgier interpretation of the gold rushes: Contrasting perspectives from Australia and New Zealand', *International Journal of Heritage Studies*, vol. 11, no. 3, 2005, 235–50; 'Visitor interpretation of the environmental impacts of the gold rushes at the Castlemaine Diggings National Heritage Park', in *Mining Heritage and Tourism: A global synthesis*, eds. Michael Conlin and Lee Jolliffe (London and New York: Routledge, 2011), pp. 97–107. See also Warwick Frost, Keir Reeves, Jennifer Laing and Fiona Wheeler, 'A golden connection: Exploring the challenges of developing interpretation strategies for a Chinese heritage precinct on the central Victorian goldfields', *Historic Environment*, vol. 24, no. 1, 2012, 35–50; Jennifer Laing, Fiona Wheeler, Keir Reeves and Warwick Frost, 'Assessing the experiential value of heritage assets: A case study of a Chinese heritage project, Bendigo, Australia', *Tourism Management*, vol. 40, 2014, 180–92.

7   Freeman Tilden, *Interpreting Our Heritage* (Chapel Hill, NC: University of North Carolina Press, 4th edn, 2007; first published 1957).

8   Bruce Craig, 'Introduction to the fourth edition', in ibid., pp. 6–8.

9   Tilden, *Interpreting Our Heritage*, p. 25.

10   Ibid., p. 33.

11   Ibid., p. 133.

12   Ibid., pp. 34–35.

13   See, for example, Gianna Moscardo, *Making Visitors Mindful: Principles for creating quality sustainable visitor experiences through effective communication* (Champaign, IL: Sagamore Publishing, 1999). For examples of its strategic application to specific cultural heritage institutions, see Michael Evans, 'Historical interpretation at Sovereign Hill', *Australian Historical Studies*, vol. 24, no 96, 1991; see also Frost et al., 'A golden connection'.

14   John Tunbridge and Gregory Ashworth, *Dissonant Heritage: The management of the past as a resource in conflict* (Chichester UK: J. Wiley, 1996); Frost, 'Making an edgier interpretation of the gold rushes'.

15   Contrast this interpretation with the themes developed for the Bendigo Chinese Heritage Precinct, as discussed in Frost et al., 'A golden connection'.

16   Ibid.

17   Otago Goldfields Heritage Trust, *New Zealand's Otago Goldfields Heritage Trail* (Cromwell, Author: c. 2000). Also worth noting is Primary Industry and Resources South Australia, *Discover South Australia's Mining Heritage Trails* (Adelaide, SA: Author, 2003). Focusing on nineteenth-century copper mining, this is an attractive production aimed at visitors.

18   A particularly good and detailed example of such a guide is Mount Alexander Diggings Committee, *Discovering the Mount Alexander Diggings* (Castlemaine, Victoria: Author, 1999.)

19   Frost, 'A pile of rocks and a hole in the ground'.

20   For a discussion of walking trails and heritage, see Kevin Markwell, Deborah Stevenson and David Rowe, 'Footsteps and memories: Interpreting an Australian urban landscape through thematic walking tours', *International Journal of Heritage Studies*, vol. 10, no. 5, 2004, 457–73; Dallen Timothy and Stephen Boyd, 'Heritage tourism in the 21st century: Valued traditions and new perspectives', *Journal of Heritage Tourism*, vol. 1, no. 1, 2006, 1–16.

21   Frost, 'Making an edgier interpretation of the gold rushes'; 'Visitor interpretation of the environmental impacts of the gold rushes at the Castlemaine Diggings National Heritage Park'.

22   Those in costume may be divided between *re-enactors*, who follow a script, and *dresser-ups*, who tend to wander and interact without a script. It can be argued that re-enactors are attracted to immersion within a character or persona, whereas dresser-ups are drawn to image and clothing. The distinction is a fascinating one that deserves more research. See Terry Wallace, 'Went the day well: Scripts, glamour and performance in war-weekends', *International Journal of Heritage Studies*, vol. 13, no. 3, 2007, 200–23; also Frost and Laing, 'Gender, subversion and ritual'.

23   Russell Belk and J.A. Costa, 'The mountain man myth: A contemporary consuming fantasy', *The Journal of Consumer Research*, vol. 25, no. 3, 1998, 218–40; Warwick Frost and Jennifer Laing, *Commemorative Events: Identity, memory, conflict* (London and New York: Routledge, 2013); Dallen J. Timothy and Stephen W. Boyd, *Heritage Tourism* (Harlow: Prentice Hall, 2003).

24   Dydia De Lyser, 'Authenticity on the ground: Engaging the past in a California ghost town', *Annals of the Association of American Geographers*, vol. 89, no. 4, 1999, 602–32; Alan Mayne, *Hill End: An historic Australian goldfields landscape* (Carlton: Melbourne University Press, 2003).

25   Evans, 'Historical interpretation at Sovereign Hill'; Frost, 'Making an edgier interpretation of the gold rushes'.

26   Ian Clark and Fred Cahir, 'Aboriginal people, gold and tourism: The benefits of inclusiveness for goldfields tourism in regional Victoria', *Tourism, Culture & Communication*, vol. 4, no. 3, 2003, 123–37.

27   David Goodman, *Gold seeking: Victoria and California in the 1850s* (Sydney: Allen & Unwin, 1994), p. x.

28   Ibid.; De Lyser, 'Authenticity on the ground'; E. Gable and R. Handler, 'Deep dirt: Messing up the past at Colonial Williamsburg', *Social Analysis*, vol. 34, 1993, 3–15.

29   One of the best representations of Sovereign Hill is its use in the carnivalesque feature film *The True Story of Eskimo Nell*, director Richard Franklin, Quest Films, 94 mins., 1975.

30   There is also Shantytown in New Zealand, though I have not engaged in fieldwork there. For a discussion of Shantytown, see Mark Balcar and Douglas Pearce, 'Heritage tourism on the West Coast of New Zealand', *Tourism Management*, vol. 17, no. 3, 1996, 203–12.

31   Tseen Khoo and Rodney Noonan, 'Going for gold: Creating a Chinese heritage festival in Nundle, New South Wales', *Continuum: Journal of Media & Cultural Studies*, vol. 25, no. 4, 2011, 491–502.

32   Geoff Hocking, *To the Diggings! A celebration of the 150th anniversary of the discovery of gold in Australia, 1851–2001* (Melbourne: Lothian Books, 2000), pp. 130–31. Hocking reproduces a contemporary watercolour of the meeting by Thomas Ham.

33   'Monster Meeting Project', Monster Meeting of Diggers 1851: www.monstermeeting.net

34   Tony Robinson, 'Eureka', *Tony Robinson Discovers Australia*, season 1, episode 4, aired 24 May 2011 (Burbank, CA: Knowledge Network). This documentary also makes good use of Sovereign Hill.

35   Frost and Laing, *Commemorative Events: Identity, memory, conflict*.

36   Wallace, 'Went the day well'.

37   Warwick Frost, 'Refighting the Eureka Stockade: Managing a dissonant battlefield', in *Battlefield Tourism: History, place and interpretation*, ed. Chris Ryan (Oxford: Elsevier, 2007), pp. 187–94.

Chapter 19

1   Lloyd W. Carpenter, 'Rich in myth, gold and narrative: Aspects of the Central Otago gold rush, 1862–2012', PhD thesis, University of Canterbury, Christchurch, 2013, p. 11.

2   Tony Perrett, 'Managing the Otago Goldfields Park', paper presented at the Industrial

Archaeology Seminar, Christchurch, 1983. Updated and published by the Department of Conservation, Wellington, 2010.

3   Cited in ibid., p. 5.

4   Ibid., pp. 5–6.

5   Ibid., p. 9.

6   Ibid.

7   Ian Smith, 'The development of historical archaeology in New Zealand 1921–1990', *The Australasian Journal of Historical Archaeology*, vol. 9, 1991, pp. 6–13; Neville Ritchie, 'An introduction to historical archaeology in New Zealand', *Australian Historical Archaeology*, vol. 9, 1991, pp. 3–5.

8   C.F.W. Mason, G.M. Higham and S.J.E Moore, 'Clutha archaeological survey', *University of Otago Anthropology Department Studies in Prehistoric Archaeology*, vol. 8, 1976; G.M. Mason, *The DG3 Dam: An assessment of its impact on prehistoric and historic remains* (Dunedin: Department of Anthropology, University of Otago, 1977).

9   Mary Newman, *Archaeological Survey along the Route of the Proposed Cromwell Gorge Highway* (Cromwell: New Zealand Historic Places Trust, 1977).

10   Neville Ritchie, 'The prehistoric role of the Cromwell Gorge, New Zealand', *New Zealand Journal of Archaeology*, vol. 4, 1982, pp. 21–43.

11   Neville Ritchie, 'Archaeology and history of the Chinese in southern New Zealand during the nineteenth century: A study of acculturation, adaptation, and change', PhD thesis, University of Otago, Dunedin, 1986.

12   Neville Ritchie, *Kawarau Valley Archaeological Survey Report* (Cromwell: New Zealand Historic Places Trust, 1983).

13   Neville Ritchie, '*Luggate–Upper Clutha Archaeological Survey* (Cromwell: New Zealand Historic Places Trust, Cromwell, 1980).

14   Neville Ritchie, 'The excavation of a nineteenth century Chinese mining settlement: Cromwell's Chinatown', *New Zealand Archaeological Association Newsletter*, vol. 23, no. 2, 1980, pp. 69–85; Neville Ritchie, 'Archaeological research on nineteenth century Chinese settlement in the Cromwell area', *The Courier: Bulletin of the Queenstown and District Historical Society*, no. 29, 1983.

15   A.P. Harrison, 'Lake Roxburgh archaeological survey'. Report prepared for the Department of Conservation Otago Conservancy, Dunedin, 1982.

16   Neville Ritchie, *Queensberry Archaeological Survey* (Cromwell: New Zealand Historic Places Trust, 1980).

17   Chris Jacomb and Sheridan Easedale, *Bendigo Survey Site Record* (Dunedin: New Zealand Archaeological Association, 1980).

18   Athol Anderson and Neville Ritchie, 'Pavements, pounamu and ti: Dart Bridge site in western Otago, New Zealand', *New Zealand Journal of Archaeology*, no. 8, 1986, pp. 115–41.

19   Neville Ritchie and A.P. Harrison, 'Clutha Valley archaeology 1980–81: An interim report', *New Zealand Archaeological Association Newsletter*, vol. 24, no. 2, 1981, pp. 97–105.

20   Ibid.

21   Neville Ritchie, 'The prehistoric role of the Cromwell Gorge, New Zealand', *New Zealand Journal of Archaeology*, vol. 4, 1982, pp. 21–43.

22   Neville Ritchie, 'Two sub-fossil faunal deposits uncovered near Cromwell, Central Otago', *New Zealand Archaeological Association Newsletter*, vol. 25, no. 2, 1982, pp. 86–102.

23   Ritchie, 'Archaeology and history of the Chinese in southern New Zealand during the nineteenth century'.

24   Neville Ritchie, 'Archaeological interpretation of alluvial gold tailing sites, Central Otago, New Zealand', *New Zealand Journal of Archaeology*, vol. 3, 1981, pp. 59–69.

25   Barry Fankhauser, 'The Maori use of ti (cabbage trees) for food', in *Nga Mahi Maori o te Wao Nui a Tane: Contributions to an international workshop on ethnobotany, Te Rehua Marae, Christchurch, New Zealand*, eds. W. Harris and P. Kappor (Wellington: Botany Division, Department of Scientific and Industrial Research, 1990), pp. 43–47.

26   Neville Ritchie, 'Bobs Cove–Twelve Mile Creek archaeological and historic sites survey'. Report prepared for the Lands and Survey Department, Dunedin, 1982.

27   Anderson and Ritchie, 'Pavements, pounamu and ti'; Ritchie, 'Archaeology and history of the Chinese in southern New Zealand during the nineteenth century'.

28   Simon Holdaway and Debbie Foster, *Lower Clutha Valley Archaeological Survey: A survey of prehistoric and historic sites in the Lower Clutha area, Central Otago* (Cromwell: New Zealand Historic Places Trust, 1983).

29   Neville Ritchie, *The Arrowtown Chinese Settlement: Report on the excavation and management recommendations* (Cromwell: New Zealand Historic Places Trust, 1984); Neville Ritchie, 'An interim report on the excavation of a small Chinese mining settlement and store at Arrowtown, Central Otago', *New Zealand Archaeological Association Newsletter*, vol. 27, no. 2, 1984, pp. 83–103.

30   Lyn Williams, *Report to the New Zealand Historic Places Trust on the Archaeological Investigation of Ackers Cottage, Stewart Island* (Wellington: New Zealand Historic Places Trust, 1983).

31   Neville Ritchie and Athol J. Anderson, 'Preliminary report on test excavations at a newly discovered moa-hunting site at Coal Creek, Central Otago', *New Zealand Archaeological Association Newsletter*, vol. 23, no. 3, 1984, pp. 174–80.

32   Neville Ritchie, *Alpine Archaeology 1: The first Hermitage site, Mt Cook. Excavation of the associated dumps* (Cromwell: New Zealand Historic Places Trust, 1985); Stuart H. Bedford, *Alpine Archaeology 2: The first Ball hut site, Tasman Valley, N.Z.* (Cromwell: New Zealand Historic Places Trust, 1985).

33   Stuart H. Bedford, *The History and Archaeology of the Halfway House Hotel Site, Cromwell Gorge, N.Z.* (Cromwell: New Zealand Historic Places Trust, 1986).

34   Neville Ritchie, *The Phoenix Quartz Mining Company's Dynamo Site: An excavation report* (Cromwell: New Zealand Historic Places Trust, 1985); Neville Ritchie, 'Excavation of the Phoenix Quartz Mining Co.'s dynamo site, Shotover River, Central Otago, N.Z.', *New Zealand Archaeological Association Newsletter*, vol. 28, no. 4, 1985, pp. 208–17.

35   Ritchie, 'Archaeology and history of the Chinese in southern New Zealand during the nineteenth century'.

36   Alexy Simmons, *The Old Cromwell Bridge: Historical background and structural description* (Cromwell: New Zealand Historic Places Trust with Clutha Valley Development, 1986).

37   Dimitri Anson, 'Typology and seriation of wax vesta tin matchboxes from Central Otago: A new method of dating historic sites in New Zealand', *New Zealand Journal of Archaeology*, vol. 5, 1983, pp. 115–38; Stuart H. Bedford, 'A simplified classification system for tin wax vesta matchboxes', *New Zealand Archaeological Association Newsletter*, vol. 28, no. 1, 1985, pp. 44–64.

38   Neville Ritchie, 'Analysis of the glass containers and bottles from Cromwell's Chinatown', *New Zealand Archaeological Association Newsletter*, vol. 26, no. 4, 1983, pp. 235–48; Neville Ritchie and Stuart H. Bedford, 'An analysis of the metal containers from Chinese sites in the Cromwell area, Central Otago, New Zealand', *New Zealand Journal of Archaeology*, vol. 7, 1983, pp. 95–116.

39   Stuart H Bedford, 'For beautifying and preserving the teeth and gums: Bone toothbrushes and ceramic toothpaste pots from historic sites in the Cromwell district', *New Zealand Archaeological Association Newsletter*, vol. 28, no. 3, 1985, pp. 172–82; Fiona R. Cameron, 'An analysis of buttons, clothing, hardware and textiles of the nineteenth century Chinese goldminers of Central Otago', BA Hons. diss., University of Otago, Dunedin, 1985; Deborah Foster, 'Clay pipes from the Cromwell area, Central Otago', *New Zealand Archaeological Association Newsletter*, vol. 26, no. 2, 1985, pp. 94–101; Andrew K.S. Piper, 'Nineteenth century Chinese goldminers of Central Otago: A study of the interplay between cultural conservatism and acculturation through an analysis of changing diet', BA Hons. diss., University of Otago, Dunedin, 1984; Neville Ritchie and A.P. Harrison, *An Archaeological Analysis of Opium Smoking and Associated Artefacts from Chinese Sites in Central Otago* (Cromwell: New Zealand Historic Places Trust, 1982); Neville Ritchie, 'The written word: Writing equipment from Chinese sites in Central Otago', *New Zealand Archaeological Association Newsletter*, vol. 29, no. 1, 1986, pp. 41–51; Neville Ritchie and R. McGovernWilson, 'A study of avifaunal remains from Chinese sites in Central Otago, New Zealand', *New Zealand Journal of Archaeology*, no. 8, 1986, pp. 61–71; Neville Ritchie and G.S. Park., 'Chinese coins down under: Their role on the New Zealand goldfields', *Australian Journal of Historical Archaeology*, vol. 5, 1988, pp. 41–48.

40   Neville Ritchie, 'The Clutha Valley Development Archaeological Programme', *New Zealand Archaeological Association Newsletter*, vol. 4, 1979, pp. 162–72; Neville Ritchie, *The Preservation*

of Goldfield Sites in Otago: Towards a N.Z.H.P.T. goldfield site preservation strategy (Wellington: Historic Places Trust, 1981); Neville Ritchie, *The Clutha Valley Archaeological Programme: An inhouse assessment* (Cromwell: Historic Places Trust, 1981); Neville Ritchie, *Reservoir Archaeology in New Zealand: Guidelines for mitigation and management* (Cromwell: Historic Places Trust, 1982); Neville Ritchie, *The Phoenix Quartz Mining Company's Skippers Creek Generating Plant (Established l885–86): A report on the remains with suggestions for their preservation, management and interpretation* (Cromwell: New Zealand Historic Places Trust, 1983); Neville Ritchie, 'Assessment, presentation and interpretation of Central Otago's industrial heritage', paper presented at an Industrial Archaeology in New Zealand seminar, Christchurch, 1983; and others.

41   Neville Ritchie, 'Archaeology: Clutha Valley development'. Illustrated colour brochure on the Clutha archaeological project, produced for the project's information centre for free public distribution, 8pp.

42   See Jill Hamel, *The Archaeology of Otago* (Wellington: Department of Conservation, 2001).

43   Peter G. Petchey, 'The archaeology of the New Zealand stamp mill', PhD thesis, University of Otago, Dunedin, 2014. Peter's reports from across Otago can be found in the Hocken Library archives (Dunedin). They cover Alexandra, Arrowtown, Bannockburn, Earnscleugh, Hyde, Kawarau Gorge, Macraes Flat, Otekaieke, Poolburn, Round Hill, Waikouaiti, Weston, Windsor and other Central Otago areas.

44   Charles Higham and Brian Vincent, *Gabriel's Gully: An archaeological survey* (Dunedin: Anthropology Department, University of Otago, 1980).

45   'Lawrence Chinese camp', Southern Pacific Archaeological Research (Anthropology Department, University of Otago): www.spar.co.nz/lawrencechinesecamp.html

46   Kevin L. Jones, *Ngā Tohuwhenua mai Te Rangi: A New Zealand archaeology in aerial photographs* (Wellington: Victoria University Press, 1994).

Chapter 20
1   Robert Hoskins, *Goldfield Balladeer* (Auckland: Collins, 1977).

Notes on Contributors

John Angus, who died shortly before publication of this book, was a historian by academic training, a social worker by craft and a policy advisor by inclination. He obtained a doctorate in history from Otago University in 1977. His thesis was a comprehensive account of politics in Otago and Southland from 1877 to 1893. John went on to write several histories of companies and local bodies, including a history of Vincent County Council and a brief history of European settlement in the Upper Clutha. John's career then took a different tack, which involved him as a social worker in Dunedin from 1977 to 1986, a social policy advisor to government in Wellington for 20 years, and New Zealand's Children's Commissioner from April 2009 to June 2011. John's interest in history, inherited from his mother Janet Cowan, did not end and was rekindled by his return to the south, where he lived at Lowburn near Cromwell until his death.

Joanna Boileau completed a PhD in history through the University of New England in Armidale, New South Wales, in 2014. Her thesis was a multidisciplinary study of the history of Chinese market gardening in Australia and New Zealand. Before embarking on her PhD, Joanna gained an MA Honours in archaeology and anthropology from the University of Auckland. She has worked in museums in New Zealand and Australia, including Auckland Museum, the Powerhouse Museum in Sydney and Tweed Shire Regional Museum in northern New South Wales. She has also worked at the Australian Heritage Commission and on community-based heritage studies for local government. She is currently working as a historian and heritage consultant in Auckland.

Julia Bradshaw is the director of Hokitika Museum, New Zealand. She has been working in museums for 20 years and has a special interest in research and interpretation. Julia has curated exhibitions on topics as varied as sawmilling, crime, dredges, whitebaiting and Chinese miners. She has published several local history books and a very popular biography of legendary cattle-man and tourist pioneer Davey Gunn titled *The Land of Doing Without* (Canterbury University Press, 2007). Her most recent project has been editing a new annotated and illustrated edition of the 1914 classic account of the West Coast gold rushes, *The Diggers' Story* (Canterbury University Press, 2014). Julia has been collecting stories about women on the New Zealand goldfields for more years than she cares to count and hopes to eventually publish this work.

André Brett was awarded his PhD at the University of Melbourne in 2014 where he is currently a research assistant involved in multiple projects on the history of Australia and of higher education. His first book, *Acknowledge No Frontier: The creation and demise of New Zealand's provinces 1853–76*, will be published by Otago University Press in 2016. André's close investigation of national and local politics reveals that the provinces failed to open hinterlands to economic development, which meant that New Zealand developed as a unitary state. His wider interests include the history of colonial Australia and New Zealand, particularly the intersections between public works, politics and the environment.

Tom Brooking specialises in New Zealand and comparative rural and environmental history, New Zealand political history and the historical links between New Zealand and Scotland. His research in this regard has focused on environmental transformation and the role of colonising peoples in that process, particularly farming and its economic, environmental and sociological impacts. Tom has published six sole-author books and numerous book chapters, essays and articles. His last major book, with Eric Pawson, was *Seeds of Empire: The environmental transformation of New Zealand* (I.B. Tauris, 2011). Tom also co-edited (with Jennie Coleman) *The Heather and the Fern: Scottish migration and New Zealand settlement* (University of Otago Press, 2003) and (with Eric Pawson) *Making a New Land: Environmental histories of New Zealand* (Otago University Press, 2013). His biography of Richard John Seddon, New Zealand's longest serving prime minister, was published by Penguin in 2014.

Lloyd Carpenter completed a BSc and a post-graduate diploma of secondary teaching in economics and mathematics in the 1980s, taught at Christ's College, then left for a career in sales and management in insurance and stationery manufacturing. He later became a Salvation Army officer and then returned to teaching (for seven years) at Aranui High School. In 2008/09, while on a secondary teacher's study award, he completed a BA Honours in English and history. In 2010, as the Sir Apirana Ngata Centennial Doctoral Scholar, he began his PhD focused on an examination of aspects of the Central Otago gold rush. As part of this work, Lloyd organised in August 2012 a University of Canterbury conference in Cromwell titled '150 Years of Riches: The Central Otago Gold Rush 1862–2012', an event which provided the impetus for this book. Lloyd lectures in Māori Studies and early New Zealand history at Lincoln University.

Daniel Davy is an assistant professor of history at Ave Maria University in Ave Maria, Florida, where he teaches courses on the British Empire, Victorian Britain and the American West. He recently completed his doctorate in history at the University of Otago under the supervision of Professor Angela McCarthy. His thesis, 'Lost tailings: Gold rush societies and cultures in colonial Otago, New Zealand, 1861–1911', was placed on the university's List of Exceptional PhD Theses in the Division of Humanities. Daniel is currently editing his thesis for publication as a book.

Fiona Farrell is the published author of novels, poetry, non-fiction and plays. Her first novel won the 1992 New Zealand Book Award. Since then, four titles have been shortlisted and nominated for the International Dublin IMPAC Award. Her poetry is widely anthologised, and her plays have been performed throughout New Zealand and abroad. Fiona has received numerous awards, including the Prime Minister's Award for Fiction in 2007. In 2012 she was awarded an ONZM for services to literature. Fiona is currently working on twin non-fictional and fictional accounts of the rebuilding of Christchurch following the 2010/2011 earthquakes.

Jeremy Finn is a professor of law at the University of Canterbury, where he has taught since 1978. He has a particular interest in the legal history of New Zealand and, more generally, of the settlement colonies of the former British Empire. He has written extensively in these fields. Jeremy is currently involved in a long-term research project into the development of the history of the New Zealand legal profession, a work that has generated several articles and book chapters. He is the author of *Educating for the Profession: Law at Canterbury 1873–1973* (Canterbury University Press, 2010) and is a co-author, with Peter Spiller and Richard Boast, of *A New Zealand Legal History* (Thomson Reuters: 2nd edn, 2001). Jeremy also researches and teaches in the fields of criminal law, criminal justice and contract law.

Lyndon Fraser is a research fellow in human history at the Canterbury Museum and te Amo Tuarua Toi Tangata/Associate Dean of Arts (Research and Postgraduate) at the University of Canterbury/Te Whare Wānanga o Waitaha. He recently co-edited with Angela McCarthy *Far From Home: The English in New Zealand* (Otago University Press, 2012) and was a historian for *One Land* (2010), an award-winning six-part television series that set three contemporary families in 1850s' New Zealand.

Warwick Frost is an associate professor at the School of Business, La Trobe University, Melbourne. Originally an economic historian, he has since extended his research to tourism and heritage, with a strong emphasis on the Pacific Rim goldfields. Warwick was the convenor of the meetings to establish Gold 150, which staged in 2001 the 150th anniversaries of the Victorian gold rushes. Like many of the authors in this current book, he has a personal connection to the gold rushes, with family lore placing his ancestors at Ballarat and Tarnagulla in the 1850s. They did not find their fortunes. His most recent book (with Jennifer Laing) is *Imagining the American West through Film and Travel* (Routledge, 2015).

Terry Hearn received his PhD from the University of Otago for a thesis on resource policy and resource-use conflict in nineteenth-century and early twentieth-century New Zealand. A particular focus of his doctoral work was Central Otago. Terry spent six years as the Historian of British Immigration in the Ministry of Culture and Heritage and was co-author, with Jock Phillips, of *Settlers: New Zealand immigrants from England, Scotland, and Ireland, 1840–1945* (Auckland University Press, 2008). He was also a contributor to *Environmental Histories of New Zealand* (2002) and to the revised edition of *Making a New Land: Environmental histories of New Zealand* (Otago University Press, 2013). Since 2001 Terry has worked as a consultant on claims lodged by Māori under the Treaty of Waitangi. During this time, he has contributed to most of the major regional inquiries, in particular Te Rohe Pōtae, focusing in particular on land issues and the social and economic experience of Māori. He retains a keen interest in the Otago gold rushes and is preparing a history based on letters written by those who participated.

Robert Hoskins is an associate professor of music at Massey University. He is the series editor of a number of musical projects and has published on Charles Thatcher, Robert Louis Stevenson, and eighteenth-century English music, including an edition of the 1777 score of *Polly*, sequel to *The Beggar's Opera*. His most recent book is *Douglas Lilburn: Memories of early years and other writings* (Steele Roberts, 2014).

Chris McConville is Senior Research Fellow Regional Studies at Federation University Australia, Ballarat. Chris was foundation lecturer for the public history programme at Monash University, Melbourne. He also taught in the post-graduate heritage and planning programmes at Footscray Institute of Technology (Victoria University) and was one of the first staff appointed to the new University of the Sunshine Coast in 1996. Chris has published widely in urban history, sports history and heritage studies. His most recent publications include two edited collections of papers, the first on horse sports, *A Global Racecourse: Work, culture and horse sports* (Australian Society for Sports History, 2008), and the second on migration titled *Hopeful Places: Migration and belonging in an unpredictable era* (Connor Court Publishing, 2015). Chris has also run a heritage consultancy business and worked as an adviser to an independent member of the Australian House of Representatives. He has a long track record in commercial, community and public radio, including a regular programme on Australia's racing network broadcaster. His current interests include the history of the fur trade in Otago and the growth of artisanal food industries in Australia and New Zealand.

Paul Macgregor is a historian who is the convenor of the Melbourne Chinese Studies Group and was the curator of Melbourne's Museum of Chinese Australian History from 1990 to 2005. He is the editor of *Histories of the Chinese in Australasia and the South Pacific* (Museum of Chinese Australian History, 1995) and joint editor of both *Chinese in Oceania* (2002) and *After the Rush: Regulation, participation and Chinese communities in Australia 1860–1940* (2004). He has organised four international conferences on the Chinese diaspora in Australasia and has curated numerous exhibitions on the history and material heritage of Chinese Australians. Paul is currently researching Chinese economic activity and trade in Australia as part of a wider investigation into the development of nineteenth-century political, business and trade partnerships between Europeans and Asians in Australasia, Southeast Asia, China, South Asia and the Indian Ocean.

Rosemary Grace Marryatt, née Rees, graduated with a BSc from Victoria University of Wellington and then worked as a biologist with Animal Research, New Zealand Forest Service and Australian Forestry and Timber Bureau, Canberra, in the early 1960s. She was a registered science teacher from 1969 to 1998 at Heretaunga College and Te Puke High School, during which time she was awarded a visiting teaching fellowship to Victoria University (1980) and a Woolf Fisher travelling fellowship (1987). She married John Marryatt in 1962 and now, in retirement, her roles as parent and grandparent keep her busy. A lay minister at Saint Luke's Church, Waikanae, a member of the church choir, a member of 'The Friends of the Waikanae River' and a volunteer on NIWA's community river-monitoring study, Rosemary is also a great granddaughter of William Gilbert Rees. Family history is her passion.

James Ng MBE, CNZM, DLitt, FNZMA is a retired family doctor and community historian of the Cantonese in New Zealand. He is the author of the four-volume *Windows on a Chinese Past* (progressively published between 1993 and 1999), for which he was made DLitt by his alma mater, Otago University. He is close to New Zealand Cantonese history and literature as chair of the Chinese Poll Tax Heritage Fund and is additionally chair of the Lawrence Chinese Camp Trust. He has long been involved in the southern Chinese Presbyterian Church and Chinese language school and is a recipient of the Queen's honours of MBE and CNZM. James is currently completing a book on the progress to eventual settlement by New Zealand Chinese, *From Sojourner to Settler.*

Sandra Quick's Otago University MA thesis focused on women and the liquor industry on the Central Otago goldfields. Her study was prompted by her falling in love with the landscape of Central Otago while doing research for the University of Canterbury Origins of New Zealand English project, and also by curiosity about the women in the liquor industry in a period often remembered for temperance women. Now living on another old goldfield, by the famous Watson Creek gold discovery in Greymouth, Sandra is head of Greymouth High School's English/languages department.

Andrew Reeves is a professorial fellow at Charles Darwin University and Deakin University, where he works on collaborative research and cultural projects. A historian by training, he worked for many years in Australian museums and more recently as a senior advisor to Senator Kim Carr, then minister for innovation, industry, science and research. He has published widely in the fields of labour and industrial history and material culture studies. Andrew is co-author, with Anne Stephen, of *Badges of Labour, Banner of Pride: Aspects of working class celebration* (HarperCollins, 1985), a pioneering study of the place of banners and celebration in the Australian labour movement. He wrote a history of the mine workers in Victoria's black coal industry, *Up from the Underworld: Coalminers and community in Wonthaggi, 1909–1968* (Monash University Publishing, 2011) and recently co-edited (with Andrew Dettmer) *Organise, Educate, Control: The AMWU in Australia, 1852–2012* (Monash University Publishing, 2013).

Keir Reeves is a professor of Australian history and director of the Collaborative Research Centre in Australian History. His current research concentrates on cultural heritage, regional development and history. Keir is currently involved in two major Australian Research Council projects that interrogate war and memory. In 2013 he was a visiting fellow (now life fellow) at Clare Hall, Cambridge, and a visiting researcher at the McDonald Institute for Archaeological Research, University of Cambridge, where he worked with the Cambridge Heritage Research Group in the Department of Archaeology and Anthropology. He is also a visiting researcher at Ghent University. Keir has furthermore been a Rydon and Bicentennial Senior Fellow at King's College London and at the School of Oriental and African Studies, University of London. Keir's publications include co-editing (contributing) *Places of Pain and Shame: Dealing with 'difficult heritage'* (Routledge, 2009) with Bill Logan, and *Deeper Leads: New approaches to Victorian goldfields history* with David Nichols (BHS Publishing, 2008). He also contributed to the Bruce Scates-led *Anzac Journeys: Walking the battlefields of the Second World War* (Cambridge University Press, 2013), which was shortlisted for the 2014 Australian Historical Association Ernest Scott Prize.

Neville Ritchie, a University of Otago Anthropology Department graduate, has been involved in archaeology since 1968. In 1977 he was appointed project archaeologist on the Clutha Valley Archaeological Project based in Cromwell, a position he held for 10 years until the project's completion in 1987. His work while he was in Cromwell formed the basis of his doctorate. Since then, he has been employed as regional archaeologist (Waikato) by the Department of Conservation in New Zealand. His specialist research interests include the archaeology and history of the overseas Chinese in New Zealand, mining and industrial archaeology and history associated with the Waikato campaign (1863/64) of the New Zealand Wars, and the archaeology and conservation of the sites associated with the Scott and Shackleton polar expeditions in Antarctica. Neville has published widely on these and many other subjects. He was president of the Australasian Society for Historical Archaeology from 2001 to 2006.

Index